**Reco**

# RECOGNITION ODYSSEYS

*Indigeneity, Race, and Federal Tribal Recognition Policy
in Three Louisiana Indian Communities*

## Brian Klopotek

Duke University Press

Durham and London

2011

© 2011 Duke University Press

All rights reserved.

Printed in the United States of America on acid-free paper ∞

Designed by Heather Hensley

Typeset in Monotype Dante by Keystone Typesetting, Inc.

Library of Congress Cataloging-in-Publication Data
appear on the last printed page of this book.

# Contents

## About the Series

Narrating Native Histories aims to foster a rethinking of the ethical, methodological, and conceptual frameworks within which we locate our work on Native histories and cultures. We seek to create a space for effective and ongoing conversations between North and South, Natives and non-Natives, academics and activists, throughout the Americas and the Pacific region. We are committed to complicating and transgressing the disciplinary and epistemological boundaries of established academic discourses on Native peoples.

This series encourages symmetrical, horizontal, collaborative, and auto-ethnographies; work that recognizes Native intellectuals, cultural interpreters, and alternative knowledge producers within broader academic and intellectual worlds; projects that decolonize the relationship between orality and textuality; narratives that productively work the tensions between the norms of Native cultures and the requirements for evidence in academic circles; and analyses that contribute to an understanding of Native peoples' relationships with nation-states, including histories of expropriation and exclusion as well as projects for autonomy and sovereignty.

An empathetic yet critical examination of how struggles for federal recognition, and the conflicts over the state policies associated with them, have affected three tribes in central Louisiana, Brian Klopotek's *Recognition Odysseys* is a most welcome addition to our series. By analyzing federal recognition policy as a particular project of national and racial power that reproduces colonial relations, Klopotek critically contributes to conversations around indigeneity and nationhood in the United States. He shows as well how the shining promises often attached to the achievement of federal recognition can sometimes ring hollow for the people involved. Finally, his historically and regionally grounded study of specific Native peoples and their experiences provides both empirical and theoretical depth to the criticisms leveled at the fields of cultural, ethnic, and American studies for tending to lump indigenous peoples into a broader category of racial minorities, without attending to the differences between race and indigeneity. Klopotek's ability to combine a critical and politically committed analytical perspective with a deep empathy for the Tunica-Biloxis, the Jena Band of Choctaws, and the Clifton-Choctaws who are at the heart of his story provides us with an important model for the kind of methodologies we wish to highlight and foster in our work.

# Acknowledgments

I wish to thank first and foremost the Indian people of Louisiana whose stories I discuss in this book. I feel an overwhelming debt of gratitude for the generosity of Tunica-Biloxi, Jena Choctaw, and Clifton-Choctaw tribal members in particular, but also the Choctaw-Apache, Apalachee, Houma, Caddo-Adai, and Coushatta tribal members who took the time to work with me in the early stages of this project. All the people I talked with are ethnohistorians in their own right, and I thank them for modeling tribal knowledge, strength, vision, and persistence for me. Special thanks are due to John Barbry, Brenda Lintinger, Cheryl Smith, and Theresa Clifton Sarpy, without whom this book would not have been possible. In addition, thank you to Aimee and Lydia Barbry, Donna and Michael Pierite, Jean-Luc Pierite, Elisabeth Pierite, Rose Pierite White, Anna Juneau, Marshall Sampson Sr., Inez Sampson, Earl Barbry Sr., Becky Wambsgans, Greg Lintinger, Emily Lintinger, Alfred Barbre, Steve Johnson, Debbie Johnson, Joe Barbry, Harold Pierite Sr., David Rivas Jr., David Rivas Sr., Robert Barbry, Dante White Owl, Daniel Barbry, Linda Bordelon, Mary Jackson Jones, Jerry Jackson, Christine Norris, Christy Murphy, Clyde Jackson, Barbara Chapman, Rusty Smith, Corine Tyler, Myrtlene Shackleford, Roy Tyler, Amos Tyler, Norris Tyler, Les Sarpy, Sabrina Webb, and Betty Clifton, who each contributed to this work in ways large and small. I would like to express my deep esteem for several people who have passed away since I began this research: Mary Jackson Jones, Jerry Jackson, Roy Tyler, and Norris Tyler were each helpful and influential on this project, and each beloved by their families and communities. I am sure that even the people who guided me the most would have written these stories differently, but I hope I have done them justice in this book. Any shortcomings are my own, however, and not theirs.

This project began as a dissertation at the University of Minnesota, where Brenda Child, David Wilkins, Jean O'Brien, Carol Miller, Riv-Ellen Prell, and Patricia Albers made up an exceptionally talented and intellectually generous dissertation committee. I am particularly grateful to Brenda Child for the advice, guidance, and support she has given since we both arrived at the University of Minnesota in 1996. I am grateful to Jay Gitlin for early guidance on this road in college. Thank you too to my incredible friends from the University of Minnesota, who have provided a stimulating intellectual community and bonds that just keep growing, especially Anne Martinez, Matt Basso, Angela Smith, Heidi Stark, Jill Doerfler, Tiya Miles, Hokulani Aikau, Matt Martinez, and an honorary Gopher, Joe Gone, among many others.

My colleagues, friends, and students at the University of Oregon and in Eugene have been fantastic in every respect, providing all manner of support, camaraderie, and intellectual spark, especially Donella Alston, Alison Ball, Natalie Ball, Tom Ball, Niva Bennett, Charise Cheney, Deana Dartt-Newton, Chris Finley, James Florendo, Lynn Fujiwara, Sangita Gopal, Michael Hames-Garcia, Dennis Galvan, Dan HoSang, Shari Huhndorf, Adria Imada, Lamia Karim, David Lewis, Enrique Lima, Ernesto Martinez, Norma Martinez, Michelle McKinley, Hector Miramontes, Dayo Mitchell, Steve Morozumi, Angie Morrill, Jeff Ostler, Priscilla Ovalle, the late Peggy Pascoe, Beth Piatote, the late Rob Proudfoot, Irmary Reyes-Santos, Katie Rodgers, Lynn Stephen, Rennard Strickland, Melissa Stuckey, Martin Summers, Thomas Swensen, Diane Teeman, Cynthia Tolentino, Tania Triana, and David Vazquez.

I would like to thank several people for reading drafts of this book, especially Shari Hundorf, John Barbry, and Tom Biolsi, in addition to the three anonymous readers at Duke University Press. Fred Kameny's thorough and thoughtful copy-edit of the final manuscript was invaluable. Thank you to Valerie Millholland at Duke University Press for bringing me through this process so helpfully. At various stages Brenda Lintinger, Jerry Jackson, Sabrina Webb, Chad Allen, Elizabeth Martinez, William Starna, and members of my dissertation committee have read and responded to drafts of chapters or the entire volume. They have each helped me sharpen my arguments considerably and prevented some embarrassing errors.

Thank you to those who invited me to present this work at their institutions in various forms, including Florencia Mallon and Ned Blackhawk at the University of Wisconsin, the American Indian Studies program at the University of Michigan, Evan Haefeli at Columbia University, Ross Frank and Denise Ferreira da Silva at the University of California, San Diego, Hoku Aikau and Noenoe Silva at the University of Hawaii (and mahalo to Kaipo for all the music and hospitality), and Brenda Child and the Institute for Advanced Study at the University of Minnesota.

I have been very fortunate to receive support for this project from many sources. Thank you to the University of Minnesota Graduate School for naming me (or simply recognizing me as) a "Disadvantaged Minority Fellow," to the MacArthur Interdisciplinary Program for International Peace and Cooperation, to the Department of American Studies at the University of Minnesota for various grants, to Ted Jojola and the Society for the Preservation of American Indian Culture for the Lynn Reyer Award in Tribal Community Development, to the American Philosophical Society Phillips Fund for Native American Ethnohistorical Research, to Rayna Green and the Smithsonian Institution for a Native American Visiting Student Award, to the School for Advanced Research in the Human Experience for the Katrin H. Lamon Fellowship, to the Michigan State University American Indian Studies Program for the American Indian Studies Predoctoral Fellowship, to the University of Oregon for various substantial grants, to Margaret Hallock and the Wayne Morse Center for Law and Politics at the University of Oregon Law School for a resident fellowship, to the Ford Foundation Diversity Fellowships for a Postdoctoral Fellowship, and to the University of California, Office of the President, for a President's Postdoctoral Fellowship at the University of California, Berkeley.

Thank you to the 2001–2 cohort at the SAR and to the SAR staff for an unforgettable experience. Steve and Carolyn Plog, Katie Stewart, Eduardo Kohn, David Nugent and family, and Dennis and Barbara Tedlock all contributed to an intellectually vital and personally fulfilling year that helped me organize and refine my thoughts on federal recognition.

My family has shaped this book in subtle and not-so-subtle ways. My mother, Kate Gable, nurtured the intellectual itch and thirst for justice that put me on this path. My big sister, Kelley Mosley, inspires me and keeps me grounded at the same time. My adopted dad, Wayne Klopotek, has always demonstrated the beauty of humility, humor, and congeniality. My biological father, Barry Wallihan, taught me the value of second chances. My long-lost cousin Melanie Morrison and her daughter Sierra have been treasures to me in Eugene (thank you, grandma). My little sisters, Chloe Klopotek and Anndi, Nikki, Lizzi, and Debbie Schutz, my goddaughter Alex Puls, my nieces Emily and Elizabeth Mosley, my nephews Leonard Shotridge and Saul Aranda, and my little buddies Diego and Mateo Martinez make me smile every time I think of them, and so deserve thanks for inspiration as well. Ah-hyeh-heh to all the turkeys in the Yazzie family and the turkeys in the Garcia family too. Thank you to Elizabeth Martinez, who helped me in the late stages of this book, and fills my heart to overflowing, giving me faith in what the world may bring. Finally, a giant thank-you and love without end to my sons, Gabriel and Isaiah Koiishe, who bring sunshine and happiness into my life every day. You are my greatest treasures! Yokoke and much love to all of you. I could not have done it without you, and would not have wanted to.

# Introduction

American Indian identity is formed, expressed, and policed in many subtle ways in a variety of contexts, but the federal government's tribal recognition decisions provide a uniquely explicit, public, and potent arena for the dramas of identity to be enacted. Current procedures require tribes petitioning for recognition to document their history, race, culture, and genealogy and submit the documents for semipublic review to the Office of Federal Acknowledgment (OFA) of the U.S. Bureau of Indian Affairs, making this tiny federal office the unelected arbiter of Indian identity in many ways.[1] Scathing reviews of OFA's efficacy have come from more than two dozen Congressional hearings, two investigations by the Government Accountability Office, various journalists, scholars, and tribes, and even the head of the Bureau of Indian Affairs. OFA wields enormous material and discursive power as it structures access to federal resources while drawing on and contributing to American racial thinking, making federal recognition policy an urgent site of scholarly inquiry.

This book examines the impact of federal recognition policy on three small Indian tribes within fifty miles of each other in central Louisiana that have petitioned for recognition through OFA. The Tunica-Biloxi Tribe (federally recognized in 1981), the Jena Band of Choctaw Indians (federally recognized in 1995), and the Clifton-Choctaws (currently petitioning for federal recognition) share a mix of similarities and differences in size, historical experiences, racial composition, cultural persistence, and various social health indicators that allows for revealing direct comparisons. Important

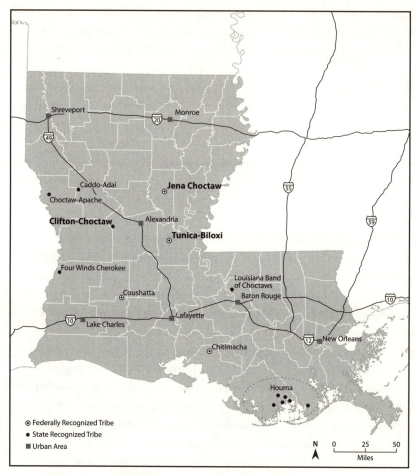

State and federally recognized tribes of Louisiana. The Houmas are currently divided into several closely related communities represented by distinct tribal governments. Map by Derek Miller.

new insights into the political and racial dimensions of Native American identities emerge from their stories, with significant implications for the study of race and indigeneity more broadly in the United States.

At its most basic level, federal recognition (also called, more formally, acknowledgment) establishes a political and legal relationship between a tribe and the United States that carries particular rights and responsibilities for both parties under federal law: it affirms the status of a tribe as an indigenous nation with inherent rights to self-government in its homeland, but it simultaneously validates the colonial authority of the United States over the nation. While the federal-tribal relationship has routinely been a means through which the United States has exerted control over tribes, the government-to-government relationship also affords tribes unique standing to protect their political, legal, and cultural rights.

Because formal federal recognition procedures were not established until 1978, most of the 560-plus federally recognized tribal governments in the United States never went through any formal evaluation of their status as tribes.[2] The United States government simply accepted their tribal status as obvious almost any time Congress, the president, a federal court, or the Bureau of Indian Affairs or its predecessors interacted with a tribe based on its status as an Indian nation through treaties, lawsuits, or policy enactments.[3] In the 1830s, for example, the United States did not ask for evidence that the Cherokees were an Indian tribe; that was an accepted fact. While federal recognition of many tribes was maintained as the status quo with little fanfare, the political status of other tribes became more and more nebulous through the nineteenth century, as their ability to militarily uphold their sovereignty slipped away, removal treaties rendered remaining Indians politically enfeebled, and Indians became increasingly dominated by local non-Indian peoples and governments, to the extent that the federal government ceased to deal with them as distinct tribal nations. Other tribes never entered into any formal relationship with the United States, having lost too much of their land and military strength through earlier colonial encounters to be of concern or value to the federal government, while still other nonfederal tribes had their federal status terminated at some point through governmental fiat or oversight. To lack status as a tribe within the meaning of federal law means to live without the limited protections and benefits available for tribes under that law—tribes must be federally recognized to exercise legal jurisdiction over their own land, be exempt from state taxes, or operate high-stakes gaming facilities, for example. But because federal recognition has been as much a means of domination and subjugation as a means of protection for tribal sovereignty, its appeal to tribes has ebbed and flowed with shifts in federal Indian policy and race relations in the United States more generally.[4]

Tribes seeking recognition since formal procedures were created in 1978 have been regularly funneled through OFA by Congress, the courts, and other offices in the executive branch that used to regularly decide independently to recognize tribes, making the office the bearer of a troubling amount of definitional authority. At first glance OFA's criteria for tribal recognition seem reasonable (see Appendix): they require that a group demonstrate "a reasonable likelihood" that its members descend from an Indian tribe or tribes, that surrounding populations have considered them Indians, and that they have been socially and politically cohesive and distinct. Racial, cultural, and political shifts since first contact—many of which have been a result of assimilationist pressures from Anglo-Americans—have made it at times less obvious to outsiders who counts as an Indian tribe or nation in the present day, and these contested definitions and interpretations have been at the core of the controversy over recognition policy. Scholars and tribal members have challenged both the criteria themselves and OFA's administration of them, identifying a series of significant problems: the criteria have been applied inconsistently, so that what qualifies as proof of tribal existence in one case often does not in the next; the level of proof required to meet individual criteria keeps going up, and OFA does not inform tribes of this until after the fact; certain staff members have been characterized as incompetent and unqualified; there is evidence of pre-decisional bias; OFA serves as prosecutor, defense, and judge; the criteria for recognition are much more stringent than the precedents on which they claim to be based; the staff is too secretive about its sources and findings; OFA expects unrecognized tribes to have the same form as recognized tribes; the regulations rely too heavily on non-Indian observations about petitioners, observations that are bound to rigid conceptions of "authenticity"; OFA will not accept oral history as evidence; the process favors petitioners without African ancestry; and petitions are reviewed at such a sluggish pace that decades pass before determinations are made on active petitions.[5]

On the other end of the spectrum are those who feel that OFA is incompetent because it recognizes too many tribes too quickly. Politicians in Connecticut, pandering to the white backlash against tribal sovereignty and casino gambling, have led this assault, hijacking scholarly criticisms of OFA and misconstruing them for their own use.[6] Senators Chris Dodd and Joe Lieberman have introduced legislation to place a moratorium on recognition decisions until problems with the process are solved, and allegedly even threatened to remove Secretary of the Interior Gale Norton from office if she did not reverse a recognition decision on the Schaghticoke tribe.[7] Attorney General Richard Blumenthal, an ardent leader of Connecticut's anti-tribal attacks, has testified before Congress on the matter and vowed to support the legal battles of Connecticut towns against tribal entities. These politicians have received a chilly reception from federally recognized tribes, since their posturing very transparently expresses anti-tribal and antigambling sentiments much more than any real concern with the fairness of the recognition process.[8]

Tribes have invested millions of dollars, decades of labor, and immeasurable emotional energy into their petitions for federal recognition, providing ample reason for close scholarly attention to the matter. This book builds upon established critiques of recognition policy, taking them as a starting point as it moves beyond policy study to explore the limits and opportunities of both recognition and nonrecognition in tribal life.[9] Though recognition has acquired a transformational aura, seemingly able to lift a tribe from poverty and cultural decay to wealth and revitalization through federal funding, casino development, new protections for tribal sovereignty, and federal affirmation of tribal identity, the cases of the three tribes examined here reveal that reality has been more complex. First, transformation and revitalization need to be understood more broadly as ongoing processes for federal and nonfederal tribes, so that the event of a federal recognition decision is placed in the context of a longer trajectory of change in tribal histories. Second, while transformation after recognition can be significant, it is largely gradual, occasionally compromising, and always incomplete. Both federal and nonfederal tribes are deeply affected by the other people and events that shape this world; recognition does not shield tribes from racism, colonialism, or other social forces, just as federal nonrecognition does not prevent tribes from participating in revitalization movements or developing their political and economic infrastructure. Moreover, recognition consistently undermines certain aspects of traditional tribal cultures, especially in the areas of government and the regulation of community boundaries, suggesting the need for careful attention to the negative aspects of federal recognition as well. Plainly delineating what recognition can and cannot do helps frame recognition status as one factor in tribal life, returning a degree of agency to both federal and nonfederal tribes that is absent in more deterministic narratives.

Beyond the immediate impact of a recognition decision, the tensions and contradictions of the federal recognition process provide opportunities to scrutinize the explicit production of race, nation, and power it entails. Recognition policy can usefully be thought of as a battle of competing racial projects, following the discussion by Omi and Winant of a racial project as an attempt to define the boundaries of racial identity for the purposes of structuring race relations and controlling the distribution of resources based on those racial definitions.[10] Federal Indian policy always influences the direction of social, political, and cultural transformation among Indians, and federal acknowledgment policy specifically has been particularly significant in influencing Indians in Louisiana because of the large number of nonfederal Indians and competing racial projects there, but Indian people have always challenged, shaped, and responded to the impositions of the federal government by asserting their own visions of tribal life and the federal-tribal relationship. At its heart, this research is a discussion of those tribal challenges to federal attempts to define and control the boundaries of Indian identity and the ways that context has shaped the lives of Louisiana Indians.

Omi and Winant theorize racial formation as an ongoing, multisited, multiscaled process of competition among various racial projects, reminding us to account for the entire array of racial projects, rather than just examining the primary conflict between these particular tribes and a government agency, or between Indians and whites in general. Federal recognition policy is representative of a particular kind of racial project, but it is far from being the only racial project affecting Louisiana tribes. Of particular importance to this book is that racial projects emanating from—or directed toward—other communities of color, other tribes, and other individuals matter deeply for Indians. Earlier work in the various fields of ethnic studies understandably tended to focus on the relationship of each group to whites, but recent work confirms that a similarly rich set of knowledge lies relatively untapped within other racial relationships.[11] For the three tribes in this book, discourses around blackness and whiteness shaped the boundaries of Indian identity in ways that have not previously been explored, leaving profound implications and opportunities for efforts at social justice and future academic research.

White supremacist ideology in particular has been a central racial project shaping relations among racial and ethnonational groups in the United States.[12] While popularly the terms "white supremacist" and "white supremacy" typically conjure up images of Klan robes and neo-Nazi skinheads, the terms as they are used in this book (and increasingly in the field of ethnic studies) refer primarily to the everyday ways of thinking and acting on an entrenched, often unspoken, unconscious, and reflexive set of beliefs about white racial superiority, beliefs carried even by people who do not consider themselves racist, including people of color.[13] It is an ideology that understands white people and their ancestors as morally, intellectually, politically, and spiritually superior to nonwhites, and therefore entitled to various forms of privilege, power, and property. It wields power even in the absence of explicit legal protections because it so often goes unnoticed, making social and political inequalities seem "natural."[14] The *ideology of white supremacy* is the set of thoughts, while *white supremacy* is the set of relations that the ideology creates as people *act* on these thoughts. The ideology and the practice are closely related and mutually constituted, so that a change in one can precipitate a change in the other. But the process of changing ideology—deeply cultural and layered as it is—and of changing practice—heavily premised on the social relations that the ideology constantly reproduces—has been a monumental challenge.[15] Thus making visible both whiteness and the ways it accumulates privileges and resources to whites has been a central project in ethnic studies over the last two decades, and it is a task that this book takes up as well.[16]

In Native American studies scholars have tended to focus on the political status of tribes as sovereign nations, external to the racial politics of the United States, which has tended to divert scholarly attention from racial theory in the field. Such an approach has been warranted time and again, since too many people understand Native Americans as simply racial minorities without any categorical distinction from other communities of color in the United States. Indigeneity distinguishes Native American historical experiences and grievances against the United States from those of other groups, and nationhood provides the basis for the ongoing government-to-government relationship with the United States.[17] The distinctive relationship between Indian nations and the United States is encoded in federal law in many ways, beginning with the Constitution and continuing through a range of legislation and federal court decisions that determine the extent of tribal governmental independence. The hundreds of ratified treaties, which can only be entered into by nations (not minorities) and only apply to the specific nations that participated in them (rather than to the *racial* group called Indians), provide perhaps the most easily accessible evidence of the distinction. Legally, politically, and morally, indigeneity and nationhood set Native Americans apart from other racialized minorities. Tribal sovereignty has been paramount in Native American studies because it protects Native peoples from dissolving into the political mass of the United States—a central concern of indigenous groups living under Anglo-American racism and colonialism.

In arguing for people to understand indigenous nations as distinct from racial minorities, however, we have too often ignored the racial components of Native American lives. While the racial relationship between Indians and whites has been explored often, attention to broader processes of racial formation and the position of Native peoples within constellations of race relations would help develop a framework for effectively incorporating racial theory into Native American studies, allowing for new insights even while maintaining the centrality of indigeneity and sovereignty. Native peoples have both a racial status and a political status in the United States; the many shared experiences of racial discrimination with other communities of color attest to the racial status of Indians, just as the many aspects of Indian experiences that are unique to indigenous groups justify a distinction.

As an example, in Louisiana, where during the Jim Crow era local whites and Washington officials alike tried to erase or downplay tribal rights by racializing Indians as "colored," Indians fought for access to education and economic opportunity in part by engaging in anti-black racism to distinguish themselves from blacks. There was a complicated tangle of racial projects and colonialism at work in this situation, and an investigation that does not attempt to comprehend each will fail to shed light on a problem that has created grief, shame, anger, and antagonism in each community. Likewise, federal recognition policy in the present day presses tribes to distance themselves from blacks—even pressing tribal members who do not have African ancestry to distance themselves from tribal members who do—in order to have their Indian racial and political identity validated. The racial and political are closely tied. Attention to the racial elements of these stories reveals how Indian anti-black racism undermines tribal well-being on many levels that would not be apparent otherwise. Since race has been integral to culture in the United States since its inception, every tribe has been deeply affected by the multiple racial projects of the nation in ways that have not been interrogated thoroughly, creating a gap that has only recently begun to be addressed in the field.[18] Native American studies will benefit immensely from the ongoing robust exploration of this component of tribal existence.

At the same time as Native American studies has avoided racial theory, the various allied fields of ethnic studies, American studies, and cultural studies have not demonstrated a solid understanding of the distinction between indigenous nations and racial minorities, and scholars in these fields often fail to highlight how the relationship between the colonizer and the indigenous is both central to and distinct from other racial projects. The routine failure to account for the distinction between race and indigeneity is the failure of these fields to provide an adequate framework for people contemplating indigenous issues or indeed racial formation in the United States more broadly. Such failure is not simply benign neglect; Haunani-Kay Trask has noted how ignoring the distinction between race and indigeneity in Hawai'i has sabotaged valid, distinct, and critical Native Hawaiian grievances.[19] Robert Warrior further notes that attempts to erase that distinction under the rubric of "inclusion" in ethnic studies similarly erase the unique value of the relationship of indigenous to colonizer as a "miner's canary" for the general political atmosphere in the United States, because tribal rights are linked to federal law and policy in distinct ways, making Indians deeply vulnerable to shifting political winds to an unusually direct extent.[20] Thus in addition to meriting study on its own terms, the relationship of indigenous to colonizer matters for every community, because it provides insight into the history, scope, scale, and function of related racial projects in the United States.

The experiences of the Tunica-Biloxis, the Jena Band of Choctaws, and the Clifton-Choctaws reveal that the relationship between federal recognition policy and American Indian racial and tribal identity is more complicated than at first appears. The ongoing discourse in Indian country about the boundaries of Indian identity is an important function of Indian and tribal self-regulation, and OFA is part of that process. As Mark Miller has noted elsewhere, criticism of acknowledgment regulations contains an apparent conundrum, in that the regulations largely reflect the views of members of recognized tribes who worked with and for the Bureau of Indian Affairs to help develop the criteria.[21] The predominantly Indian-run BIA today has begun to shed its historical image as the epitome of bureaucratic incompetence and white paternalism, but exerting colonial power remains part of the BIA's legacy and function too, whether intentionally or not, as OFA policy demonstrates. The existence of supposedly objective federal recognition procedures clouds the multiplicity of indigenous perspectives on the issue; indigenous people, whether federally recognized or not, hold a range of views so broad as to be oppositional at points, yet federal recognition policy gives the appearance of settled precision. Federal bureaucrats thus become colonially empowered voices in Indian identity debates. The conversation is not resolvable in the way that the federal government attempts to resolve it, because there are so many competing definitions and racial projects at play. This only makes it all the more urgent for OFA to establish liberal recognition procedures so that tribes are being evaluated in a way that does not simply cater to the most restrictive definitions of tribal status.

To move beyond the tightly bound definitions that official discourses of tribal existence imply, equal attention needs to be paid to unofficial discourses in which nonfederal tribes are embraced and supported as Indians by other tribes and other Indians, even if they are opposed and shunned by some too.[22] Variables such as genealogy, blood quantum, family histories, connection to place, size and cohesion of community, skin tone and other racially loaded features, political histories, and cultural markers factor into the calculus of tribal existence in varying degrees, depending on who is doing the calculating, in what context, and for what purpose. All tribes, recognized or not, are subject to multiple discourses, and federal tribes sometimes contend with much the same racial, political, and cultural challenges to their identity as nonfederal tribes do.[23] Once it is understood that every tribe is subject to multiple discourses and is multiply constructed, the subjective and deeply invested position of official federal discourse becomes more apparent. Tribes are composed of the same people with the same history before and after a recognition decision, and the continuities outweigh the changes that come with recognition. Transformation and revitalization efforts in place before an OFA decision proceed under different circumstances depending on the decision, but they proceed nonetheless. Recognition efforts have been but one segment of tribal persistence struggles that began long before the BIA existed and will continue long after a recognition decision is rendered for or against a tribe.

Recognition needs to be reframed in this manner so that we can better understand how OFA decisions matter and how they do not. Perhaps more important for tribal well-being is not the decisions themselves but how the tribes respond to those decisions and the racial, cultural, and political cues that come to them through the process. As it happens, there is both more and less at stake in OFA decisions than is apparent at first blush—more, because of the centrality of recognition to identity and wellness across the spectrum of Indian communities; and less, because the financial benefits of recognition are smaller and slower than typically imagined for most tribes. However, if tribes can work toward these goals with or without recognition, and if recognition does not bring with it the benefits that people have imagined, tribal attention might turn inward, focusing on means of promoting community-defined conceptions of wellness that do not rely upon and endorse federal authority, as an increasing number of nonfederal and federal tribal members have suggested.

To illuminate these issues of authority and entitlement, race and indigeneity, and official and unofficial discourses, this book examines how recognition policy and recognition itself have been a part of the revitalization and transformation of the Tunica-Biloxi Tribe, the Jena Band of Choctaws, and the Clifton-Choctaws. Taken together, their histories illustrate the varied impacts of the process on social and political structures, community cohesion, cultural revitalization projects, identity, and economic health in Indian communities.

After reviewing the legal and political development of federal recognition policy, the book moves into discussions of each tribe's history. The discussion of the Tunica-Biloxis is somewhat longer than the others both because of the tribe's long and pathbreaking struggle to achieve recognition, and because it has had over twenty-five years of experience with federal recognition. Similarly, the discussion of the Clifton-Choctaws is the shortest of the three because as yet the tribe has no recognition decision or post-decision years to discuss.

The Tunica-Biloxi discussion proceeds chronologically from the early years of contact with colonial groups, when the tribe's ancestors belonged to several tribes that eventually formed a community where the tribal reservation now exists. The predecessor tribes were all living in small enough groups to be overlooked during the removal era of the 1830s and 1840s. They posed little threat to American settlers by then and occupied a small amount of land, so relations with the federal government were never formalized through treaty agreements.[24] While this arrangement allowed the tribes to remain in their home area, it also meant that they lacked the status of nations in the eyes of the federal government. Being ignored by the federal government was a mixed blessing: the Tunicas and allied tribes were never removed or sent to boarding school, but neither were they afforded the meager benefits and protections that the federal government developed for Indian tribes over the years.

Ernest Downs, a scholar of Tunica history who helped the tribe to compile a petition for recognition in the 1970s, notes that the Tunicas "began to realize that Federal recognition was going to be absolutely necessary for them to be able to carry on . . . as early as 1917" because of a clash between state inheritance laws and tribal customs.[25] While there had been sporadic efforts before this time in response to white encroachment on their land and sovereignty, the chiefs of the tribe consistently sought federal recognition from the Bureau of Indian Affairs thereafter. The Tunica-Biloxis had compiled a formal petition for recognition by 1976, using earlier precedents for recognition within the BIA as a guideline, but the bureau waited until it had developed standardized procedures for tribes seeking recognition before reviewing the Tunica-Biloxis' case. The Tunica-Biloxi Tribe was the third tribe in the country recognized under the new procedures, the first in Louisiana.

Tunica-Biloxi tribal members have benefited culturally from recognition in identifiable ways. Tribal identity has always been fairly strong, though distinct markers of tribal culture had been fading since even before the death of the last Tunica speaker in the early 1950s, and a considerable number of tribal members had moved away from the reservation by the 1970s. They have steadily built up their community strength since recognition, though expectations for what recognition could accomplish were fairly low when they were recognized in 1981. Access to the small amounts of federal money and programs available for things like health care, housing, and construction of a tribal government building helped them to address a few of their most pressing needs. Perhaps more significantly, federal recognition helped the tribe to intervene in a lawsuit to win custody in 1985 of a collection of looted grave goods known as the Tunica Treasure, an event that has become an immense source of pride and a focal point of Tunica-Biloxi identity. In the repatriation of the grave goods, elements of historical trauma based in racism and colonialism become visible, and the redemption and healing that accompanied the repatriation of the grave goods parallel the impact of recognition on the Jena Choctaws.

As a federally recognized tribe, the Tunicas were able to open a casino in 1994, an event that has dramatically affected the tribe. The creation of jobs with decent pay in the area has helped tribal members move to the reservation, where they can renew and maintain important family and tribal relationships, and casino money now funds important cultural projects such as a summer camp, an annual powwow, and a new Cultural and Educational Resource Center. On the other hand, a few tribal members have expressed concern that the influx of nonlocal tribal members looking for jobs has the potential to dilute Tunica-Biloxi cultural identity. Effects on the centers and boundaries of tribal communities are among the perhaps unforeseen results of recognition on tribal identity and cultural persistence.

The Jena Choctaws did not have the same kind of activist chiefs as the Tunica-Biloxis, so their efforts to gain federal recognition as a tribe did not begin until much later. Some of the tribe testified before the Dawes Commission at the beginning of the twentieth century, and for several years in the 1930s a local white woman ran a school for Choctaw children using money secured from the Bureau of Indian Affairs, but that was the extent of Jena interactions with the federal government.

Education activism was a surprisingly consistent arena for the development of tribal political activism and racial identities in Louisiana during the

New Deal. Tribes in Louisiana had a variety of experiences, but in most instances Indians sought enrollment in white schools and refused to enroll in black schools. In such cases Indians endorsed white conceptions of both blacks and whites, undermining in unnoted ways both their racial position and their political position as indigenous nations. The Jena Band's brief interlude of federal services further illustrated the extent to which federal anti-black racism, not just southern Jim Crow laws, influenced tribal and racial identities in the South.

The Jena Choctaws were eventually integrated into white schools during the Second World War, and tribal activism virtually disappeared for several decades. Political activism resurged in the early 1970s, though, and in 1974 the Jena Band organized formally to seek government funds and services. The Jena Choctaws toyed with the idea of seeking federal recognition, but that seemed unattainable and even a little bit dangerous at the time. Some members of the older generation were leery of diving headlong into the federal relationship, knowing its coercive history, so recognition plans took a back seat to other projects. Further, Jena Choctaws did not feel that they needed recognition to validate their identity, which is often cited as a reason for seeking recognition; half the tribe still spoke Choctaw fluently at the time, so their identity as Choctaws was never in doubt.

By the 1980s tribal feelings about recognition began to shift, and efforts to complete a petition began in earnest. In the early 1990s the Jena Choctaws decided that the tribe would benefit from partnering with a gaming company that would provide it with the money needed to attain recognition and help it to develop a lucrative casino after recognition was granted. Partnerships of this sort have become fairly routine since the advent of tribal casinos, but the practice has brought with it a host of problems. White responses to tribal casinos are often deeply imbued with racial and colonial discourses, in which people and nations of color are either supposed to be subordinate to whites or forbidden to have any rights different from those of whites. Politicians in Louisiana often curry voters' favor by invoking intertwined conceptions of white supremacy and federal authority to oppose federal recognition of Indian tribes on the grounds that it facilitates tribal gaming. The basic question of tribal existence inherent in OFA procedures becomes a referendum on tribal gaming instead.

Still, with the help of money from gaming investors and the support of the Mississippi and Oklahoma Choctaws, the Jena Band received federal recognition in May 1995, after the tribal casino movement was under way nationally and in Louisiana. In contrast to the modest expectations of tribes in the 1980s, by the time of Jena Choctaw recognition, acknowledgment decisions had become so closely associated with casino development that anything short of instant wealth would be experienced as failure. At this writing, though, the tribe still has no gaming facility, and prospects for opening a class III casino in the near future appear slim.[26] The divergence between expectations and reality caused tumult and frustration in the tribe for years, but amid the chaos a sense of equanimity and resolve emerged, and projects designed to serve tribal needs have gone forward successfully in several arenas, even without the luxury of casino funds. The impediments that the tribe has faced are a reminder that recognition is only a small part of a broader racial and political relationship with the United States, and that the effects of recognition are more complex than they at first appear. Yet recognition supports tribal well-being to the extent that it helps to alleviate historical trauma, and the tribe has been persistent in pursuing its goals of political strength, cultural vitality, social cohesion, and economic growth, just as it was before the recognition decision. The extent to which tribal response shapes tribal futures is evident from the example of the Jena Choctaws.

Contemporary Clifton-Choctaw recognition efforts began with a chance meeting of tribal elders in a hospital in Alexandria in the 1970s, and the narrative in this book moves backward and forward from that point. Following the lead of other Louisiana tribes, the Clifton-Choctaw tribal government incorporated as a nonprofit and submitted a letter of intent to petition for federal recognition in 1978. Until 1970 the Clifton-Choctaws had been extremely isolated, attending only their own community school, which went to eighth grade, because they were not allowed in white schools in Rapides Parish and refused to attend black schools. The resulting low educational attainment rate, combined with an economic bust in the timber industry, forced many people to move away to find work in the 1960s. Facing the same economic, educational, medical, and cultural concerns as other nonfederal Indians, they hoped that organizing to attain services available for Indians could help their community stay together and thrive economically and culturally.

The Clifton-Choctaws are still not close to achieving federal recognition, more than thirty years after they initially organized. Their political and cultural histories are not as well documented as those of the Tunica-Biloxis and Jena Choctaws; they are clearly a distinct group with a persistent Indian identity, but their political forms have tended toward the informal and they have not retained the range of cultural markers that the federal process expects from Indian tribes. In that sense they pose a challenge to federal procedures largely based on producing evidence of the very traditions that they lack, and the federal procedures likewise pose a disturbing challenge to the Clifton-Choctaws' sense of self. Issues like those confronting the Clifton-Choctaws lead to questions about internal and external determinations of identity and indigenous status, about the place of multiple discourses in tribal senses of self, and about whether federal recognition is an emancipatory or decolonizing project at all.

Like the Tunica-Biloxi Tribe, a significant portion of the Clifton-Choctaw community has African ancestry, which has led some outsiders to classify the community as black or "Redbone" rather than Indian. While the BIA claims that blackness plays no role in determinations of tribal status, tribes with African ancestry face many obstacles that tribes without black ancestry do not face. Some members of each of the three tribes discussed here have responded to the racial projects underlying these obstacles by distancing themselves from blacks through anti-black rhetoric (even though two of the tribes do have a significant portion of tribal members with African ancestry), while other tribal members dismiss this rhetoric as racist and unfair. Examining the echoes of black-Indian relations in educational segregation that reverberate through recognition efforts provides insights into the interwoven nature of racism and colonialism that will help efforts to understand and undermine both.

With over three hundred groups now involved in the petitioning process and a rate of resolution of approximately two cases a year, OFA lacks adequate resources for completing its increasingly difficult caseload, much less assisting tribes with their petitions. Moreover, with significant gaming revenues at stake and tribes spending more than $10 million on petitions, a small tribal community such as the Clifton-Choctaws uninterested in gaming partnerships is severely outmatched in a contest with federal officials, so achieving recognition will be an uphill battle. Yet without recognition the Clifton-Choctaws have not withered but rather have proceeded to pursue community goals of educational attainment, economic development, and cultural revitalization through other available means. Certainly federal status would be welcomed, but their right to exist is not dependent upon it. Seen in this light, it is easier to understand Clifton-Choctaw recognition efforts as a component of broader goals, much as the recognition movement in general is a component of a broader revitalization campaign in Native America. As with other tribes, how the Clifton-Choctaws respond to federal policy matters deeply for their racial and political identity. That tribal life continues at Clifton outside the federal domain despite troubling racial and political cues from the federal government suggests that tribal goals can be—and indeed have consistently been—pursued with or without federal recognition, putting recognition in perspective of the *longue durée* without undermining its significance for tribal well-being.

One of the goals of my research has been to provide information about tribal life after involvement in the federal administrative acknowledgment process, whether a tribe attained recognition or not. Side-by-side examination of tribal experiences after each case has been reviewed reveals the potential benefits and hidden risks of recognition—the range of advantages, tensions, and problems that emerge in the economic, cultural, social health, and political realms. While this book discusses inherent problems with the Office of Federal Acknowledgment and suggests remedies, the more important lesson is that indigeneity persists independently of federal policy, and tribal identities have proven to be too variable for the federal legal structure to be capable of determining dependably.[27] Attempting to mold academic, legal, and popular Indian and American definitions of tribal identity into one unwieldy set of criteria, the BIA has assumed the task of creating an official line that clearly marks the boundaries of Indian identity, an impossibility given the diverse and complex identities of Indians around the country. The impact of attempting to do so nevertheless has been enormous.

*Methods and Methodology*

I am a nonfederal Choctaw with roots in Sabine Parish, Louisiana, so this project developed out of personal interest. In 1998 I began conducting exploratory interviews with leaders of seven tribes in Louisiana that either were or had been federally nonrecognized, and settled on these three because of their proximity and comparability. I am not a member of any of these communities, though my family history has flavored my research in many ways.

Formal interviews with tribal members provided the bulk of information about tribal perspectives on federal recognition and current tribal affairs, and the interviews were complemented by archival research and ethnographic fieldwork.[28] Most of the people whom I chose to interview formally were tribal leaders of one sort or another, and many had served in tribal government positions over the years.[29] Interviewing primarily tribal leaders gave me access to the internal workings of the petitioning process and the tribal government to some extent, so this might be called an intellectual history of the recognition movement.[30] Further work is needed to bring in the important voices of the many other tribal members who are not represented here, but the interviews provide a useful view that centers contemporary tribal perspectives, shifting the focus away from OFA and toward tribal experiences with federal recognition policy.

I have maintained a collaborative approach to research and writing whenever possible in order to present stories embodying some essential truths that make sense to tribal members. I have tried to center tribal members' understandings of the federal recognition process as they have expressed it to me in formal interviews and informal conversations. I sent copies of chapters regarding each tribe to members of each community for comments and suggestions, and I addressed tribal concerns where possible when they were expressed.[31] Though courtesy and ethics obviously come into play, collaboration also makes for better research, because it provides an added layer of expert review. That said, it is important to acknowledge the limits of this kind of work in representing the voices of others, because even someone who supports the project as a whole will not necessarily be interested in reviewing academically oriented manuscripts, not everyone had the opportunity to comment, and some tribal members would disagree with assertions that I make.[32]

The recentness of some of the events represented here is a reminder that these histories are neither finished nor complete, that this is a snapshot of tribal life in motion, and that some people and stories are more visible than others. The resolutions to the stories that I tell will prove inadequate in some respects, reinforcing the notion that the stories of the Tunica-Biloxis, the Jena Choctaws, and the Clifton-Choctaws belong to the people themselves and not to me or to the pages of this book. Christine Norris, the current chief of the Jena Choctaws, illustrated this point nicely when she said that the elders in her community were always wary of people who came in to ask them about their culture and history. "They always felt that the people would take advantage of them. They were there to gather information for books or whatever, but that it was always twisted. What came out in print was not what they really said. That's why they were very close-mouthed to non-Indians. Because they felt like, they just want to know what we do, how we live, and they're going to take that and try to use it and say they know Indian ways and culture." I ask the reader to keep in mind that these pages contain only my discussion of those parts of the people's lives that they have chosen to share with me or that are available in the historical record, rather than as the final word on what it means to be a Jena Choctaw, a Tunica-Biloxi, or a Clifton-Choctaw. The written medium sometimes creates the illusion that people and text are co-terminal, that a single, objective narrative exists and can be described, and I would rather remind the reader of this illusion here than insert myself into the stories recounted throughout the text.

Recognition policy forces us to confront race and identity in ways that are sometimes difficult to talk about, and doing so in a public forum will make some people uncomfortable.[33] Indeed, it makes me uncomfortable at times, but discomfort can be a useful tool that directs our attention to underlying problems. Troubling matters such as Indian anti-black racism in education and recognition activism appear in this book not as spectacle but as a means of moving us toward healing and decolonization. Anti-black racism is part of the legacy of white supremacy that all our families—across the racial spectrum—have inherited, and transformation in race relations and indigenous futures lies in taking responsibility for problems like it rather than burying them.

Similarly, many Indians around the country have been trying to cope with centuries of colonization, and federal and nonfederal Indians alike are sometimes self-conscious when trying to reconnect with aspects of aboriginal heritage lost in the colonial encounter. Because it is harder to maintain the economic and political structures that sustain tribal cultural cohesion without communal land and with fewer schools, tribal enterprises, or other institutional supports, nonfederal Indians have been particularly vulnerable to the forces of assimilation in the contemporary era. Federal recognition policy stokes anxiety, shame, anger, grief, and feelings of inadequacy over cultural loss when it is not understood for what it is: a particularly colonial racial project emanating from a particularly colonial source. Ngugi Wa Thiong'o describes a similar situation among postcolonial Africans, where, he assures his readers, "the present predicaments . . . are often not a matter of personal choice: they arise from an historical situation." It follows, as he suggests, that solving problems of this kind requires not simply personal transformation but a broader break from colonial ideologies and the people who espouse them.[34] When we recognize the historical and structural basis of these feelings, we can understand how they affect federal and nonfederal Indian tribes, and more confidently renew efforts to support and maintain indigenous identities.

## CHAPTER I

## The Origins of
## Federal Acknowledgment Policy

*Prelude*

The passage of the Indian Reorganization Act (IRA) in 1934 marked a substantial turn in federal Indian policy. Rejecting and condemning the antitribal policies practiced by previous administrations of the Office of Indian Affairs, as the BIA was formerly known, the newly installed administration of John Collier successfully lobbied Congress to legislate a new policy that supported Indian tribalism, as Collier saw it. The act professed to serve "all persons of Indian descent who are members of any recognized tribe now under federal jurisdiction, and all persons who are descendants of such members who were, on June 1, 1934, residing within the boundaries of any Indian reservation, and shall further include all other persons of one-half or more Indian blood."[1] The wording created a problem for bureaucrats in the Office of Indian Affairs, since they took it to mean they had to decide who was or should be under federal jurisdiction and just how to make that determination. Though such a distinction had existed previously in practice, as certain Indian groups had extensive relationships with the federal government while others were ignored, the IRA articulated the divide in fixed terms. Without a determination of recognition from the federal government, tribes would not be eligible to access the IRA's provisions.

According to this clause, however, members of federally nonrecognized tribes had the opportunity to receive benefits as Indians if they could prove they were half-Indian or more, a provision that offers an interesting prelude and parallel to the modern practice of determining tribal eligibility for federal services. Collier, who considered the issue of how exactly the office would make this determination "an administrative problem of some complexity," outlined procedures for the office to follow:

> The evidence upon which a determination of blood degree may be made divides naturally into five classes (1) tribal rolls . . . accepted [by us] as accurate . . . which record the percentage of Indian blood; (2) testimony of the applicant, supported by family records, . . . showing blood degree; (3) affidavits from persons who know the applicant['s] family background; (4) findings of a qualified physical anthropologist based on examination of the applicant; (5) testimony of the applicant and supporting witnesses, tending to show that the applicant has retained a considerable measure of Indian culture and habits of living. . . . burden of proof on applicant.
>
> Usually, however, investigation of the applicant's claim will be required. . . . Where the available evidence is insufficient to establish degree of blood, the Commissioner may appoint as a member of the [investigating] committee a competent physical anthropologist to examine the applicant.
>
> . . . In reviewing the findings of the investigator or investigators, the Commissioner of Indian Affairs will exercise administrative discretion in determining what comparative weight shall be given to the various kinds of evidence. Where the genealogical or biological data still leave doubt as to the applicant's claim, the commissioner will consider whether or not the attitude of the applicant and his manner of living tend to show the inheritance of Indian characteristics.[2]

Following these procedures, in 1936 Collier sent Carl Selzer, a professor of physical anthropology at Harvard, to investigate the applications of 209 Lumbees, then known as "Siouan Indians of Robeson County" by the Office of Indian Affairs, and make determinations regarding who among them displayed the appropriate physical characteristics to be considered one-half or more Indian in ancestry. While there were thousands more in the area who might have asked to be recognized as Indians, Selzer examined only those who had actually applied. After various tests and measurements of the hair, teeth, skin, blood, skull, and other physical features, Selzer decided that twenty-two of the applicants had the appropriate physical characteristics to qualify as at least half-Indian. Predictably, among those rejected were several full siblings of those who had been accepted.[3]

Similar tests to determine precise Indian ancestry were conducted in other Indian communities around the country, with similar results. Most notably, Albert Jenks and Aleš Hrdlička performed tests on residents of the White Earth Chippewa reservation in northern Minnesota in 1917 to determine who among them was "full-blooded." The results of their examinations not only invalidated tribal social categories and genealogical understandings but also contributed to precipitous land loss by declaring certain individuals mixed-blood and therefore "competent" to sell their allotments.[4] The reservation was reduced from its original 837,000 acres to less than 10 percent of that at present, in part because of the anthropologists' racial (re)classification of hundreds of members who had lost their land patents to con artists and timber barons. The impact on the White Earth band has been devastating.[5]

Racial anthropometry such as that practiced in these years has since been characterized as a product of the racialized and racist value systems of the eugenics movement, masquerading as impartial, objective science.[6] Within a single lifetime the absurdity of these "scientific" evaluations of Indians and biological measures of "race" has become evident. Yet the BIA's Office of Federal Acknowledgment, which is currently responsible for determining whether groups can be counted as Indian tribes, deploys many of the same misguided ideas about race and identity as Collier did in the 1930s. The same racial and colonial logic informs federal recognition policy, irrevocably damaging Indian communities now just as it did then. The BIA is still attempting to use academic assessments to draw a powerful, federally enforced line between tribal and nontribal people, but it will be instructive to remember earlier attempts to "have the illusion provided by expert opinion that all decisions, however complex, are fairly and logically made."[7]

## The Development of Federal Recognition Policy and the Federal Recognition Movement

The federal-tribal relationship has evolved through more than two centuries of treaties, legislation, policy, and case law,[8] but for present purposes the important point is that once the federal government acknowledges the existence of a tribe, tribal sovereignty is assumed, and a set of laws and policies governs the way the United States interacts with that tribe, though the federal government has historically failed to uphold most of its own rules that could be interpreted to protect tribal sovereignty.[9] Through the years the relationship between sovereign Indian nations and the sovereign United States government has been consistently revamped and redefined, but the basic characterization of the relationship as sovereign-to-sovereign remains the guiding principle from the tribal point of view.

From the point of view of the federal government, the relationship has been more ambiguous. While the sovereign-to-sovereign principle remains, the federal government has consistently whittled away the boundaries of indigenous tribal sovereignty in much the same way as it has carved away indigenous lands. Various doctrines, policies, and Congressional acts impede tribal sovereignty at all levels, which is how tribal sovereignty arrived at its current muddled state. Policy shifts and court decisions have persistently altered the contours of tribal sovereignty and thus the desirability of federal recognition for Indian people.

While federal Indian policy occupies many uneasy spaces between tribal sovereignty and plenary federal power, the significant issue to contemplate is the implication of semi-sovereign trust status for tribes trying to achieve recognition. Trust status, which implies that the federal government is entrusted with protecting the small nations within its borders, carries a contradictory assortment of implications. It simultaneously recognizes tribal sovereignty and asserts its lack; seeking federal recognition suggests tribal resistance as well as tribal acquiescence to federal authority. Recognition entitles Indian tribes to funding and social services and protects tribal political authority and trust land against state and local governmental intrusion, and each of these benefits help tribes to survive by making it feasible for people to live decent lives in their home communities, maintaining important relationships with other tribal members. Federally recognized tribes have limits, however, on how funding and land can be used and the extent of tribal authority, which diminishes the tribe's ability to make culturally appropriate decisions. They have less flexibility in determining community membership, and they must develop and administer formalized legal codes to ensure that they are meeting formal federal standards rather than using informal ideals to regulate community behavior.[10] Moreover, even a brief survey of federally recognized tribes reveals that trust status is hardly a panacea.

Unrecognized tribes, with none of the benefits of federal recognition, lead different struggles. They exist within the same colonial and racial order as recognized tribes, but they have little formal recourse for protection of their culture, values, or sovereignty aside from whatever internal authority they can exert. They have fewer resources available to fight social ills, and they have trouble maintaining organizations and securing and maintaining a land base. In most cases it matters little that the federal government does not limit unrecognized tribes in their exercise of power, since they have virtually none in the first place. It seems as though they can only gain by petitioning for recognition, but the negative effects of recognition on a tribe's internal sovereignty and cultural integrity, along with the inherent acquiescence to federal authority, are often forgotten in the effort to secure funding for health, social, and economic programs.

What might be called a recognition movement emerged from the wreckage of the termination and relocation era of the 1950s, when the federal government sought to erase tribalism and indigenous political status altogether.[11] Federal and nonfederal tribes alike responded to this era of repressive assimilationism and conformity by reasserting their sovereignty at the local and national levels.[12] Nonfederal tribes have continually sought to establish individual relationships with the United States government, even through the termination era, and occasionally regional efforts were made, but it was not until the 1960s that federally nonrecognized tribes began to consider themselves an interest group on a national level and to work together on shared issues of nonrecognition.[13] The American Indian Chicago Conference (AICC), a gathering of more than five hundred Indians that included at least twenty nonfederal Indians and produced the "Declaration of Indian Purpose" in 1961, was an important forum in several ways for developing a national recognition movement, just as it was for Indian activism across the country.[14] First, it provided moral support and some validation from other Indians and from anthropologists for the federally nonrecognized groups represented at the conference.[15] Second, it put nonfederal Indians in touch with each other and with federal Indians, and they were able to encourage one another and develop new ideas together. Chief Calvin McGhee, a longtime activist from the Poarch Band of Creeks of Alabama, then federally nonrecognized, stated that he had no idea there were "so many Indians in the same boat" before he attended the conference. Seeing recognition as a matter of broad historical circumstances rather than the shortcomings of an individual tribe was of immeasurable value.[16]

While it is fair to say that the AICC catalyzed a growing federal recognition movement, the movement actually began with various regional efforts that had been initiated by tribes in North Carolina, Virginia, New England, and elsewhere through the years. In Louisiana, the Tunicas took a leadership role in the 1920s, when Tunica subchief Eli Barbry attempted to form a coalition of tribes in an effort to secure federal assistance. The 1930s saw a flurry of activity in the state, with Houmas, Tunicas, Choctaws, and Coushattas repeatedly seeking federal assistance for Indians. "Recognition" was not the term used, but the goals and concepts were the same. What the AICC provided to the Indian people who had been working on these issues for several generations was a larger forum in which to network and strategize with other tribes, especially those who were similarly situated, and the movement continued to grow from there.[17]

By the time Vine Deloria Jr. published *Custer Died for Your Sins* in 1969, the nationwide recognition movement had grown considerably. Deloria mentioned the surprise appearance of the federally nonrecognized Tiguas (Ysleta del Sur Pueblo) at the convention of the National Congress of American Indians (NCAI) in 1966 near their land in El Paso as an eye-opening event. Their persistence for three hundred years in the middle of El Paso, with only occasional federal recognition, convinced attendees that tribes were not doomed to vanish, as termination rhetoric had begun to suggest to many of them. Heartened by the concept "that tribes were really entities that had no beginning or end, . . . the NCAI set its sights to contact as many groups as possible in the eastern portion of the United States," including the Tunicas.[18]

Deloria asserted that the Bureau of Indian Affairs had also begun "to push for recognition of bands which had always been eligible for federal services but which had been caught between reservations during frontier days."[19] Though he does not offer examples of the groups they had reached, the BIA extended recognition to seven tribes between 1962 and 1974, including the Coushatta tribe of southwestern Louisiana,[20] while Congress extended recognition to an eighth and restored one terminated tribe, confirming Deloria's notion that there was some attempt under way at the federal level to respond to requests for recognition that had been ongoing for a number of years.[21]

Tribes in the 1960s and 1970s sought recognition from the federal government through the "informal" administrative channels supposedly available to federally nonrecognized tribes (as opposed to Congressionally terminated tribes, who can only have their federal recognition restored through an act of Congress), but not all were able to achieve it. Since there was no formal process for tribes to follow until 1978, the decision over whether to recognize a tribe was generally at the discretion of key BIA personnel. The bureau had standards for evaluating whether to acknowledge that certain groups should be served by the federal government as Indian tribes, despite claims that no formal procedures were ever drawn up. These standards were somewhat similar to the criteria that would eventually become codified as the formal recognition procedures, since both were supposedly based on definitions of

Indian tribes sketched in the 1930s by Felix Cohen in his capacity as solicitor for the Department of the Interior, but there was not a significant consistency of practice in applying these criteria to petitioning tribes.[22]

Cohen noted that eligibility for federal services as an Indian tribe first became an issue when the Office of Indian Affairs attempted to determine who was eligible to organize under the Indian Reorganization Act (IRA) of 1934, which he had helped draft. The defining legislation for the "Indian New Deal" under the commissioner of Indian affairs John Collier, the IRA limited benefits to "recognized" tribes and individual Indians of half or more blood, as mentioned earlier. The executive branch decided that because of this phrasing, it needed a way to decide who was eligible for services or protections under acts passed by Congress. After Cohen determined that the political branches of the federal government (Congress and the executive branch, including the secretary of the interior) both had authority to acknowledge tribes, the Office of Indian Affairs in 1937 extended recognition to the Mole Lake Band of Chippewas of Wisconsin, a federally nonrecognized group at the time, so that it could organize under the IRA, setting a clear and unchallenged precedent allowing the BIA to recognize a tribe as long as Congress had not specifically terminated it.[23]

While the BIA had recognized a string of tribes from 1962 to 1974, it began reconsidering its authority to recognize tribes sometime after extending recognition to the Sault Ste. Marie Chippewa tribe in February 1974. By August of that year an attorney from the solicitor's office reconfirmed the authority of the BIA to extend recognition, but this did not resolve the matter of how and when this authority would be exercised.[24] The bureau still needed to establish consistent procedures for making recognition decisions.

The bureau used Cohen's determinations of federal practice as a guideline. Cohen noted that in cases where it was not immediately clear to the BIA whether a group qualified as an Indian tribe, an opinion as to its tribal status should be requested from the solicitor of the Department of the Interior. He further suggested that

> the considerations which, singly or jointly, have been particularly relied upon [by the solicitor and others in the bureau] in reaching the conclusion that a group constitutes a 'tribe' or 'band' have been:
>
> > That the group has had treaty relations with the United States
> > That the group has been denominated a tribe by act of Congress or Executive order.

That the group has been treated as having collective rights in tribal lands or funds, even though not expressly designated a tribe.

That the group has been treated as a tribe or band by other Indian tribes.

That the group has exercised political authority over its members, through a tribal council or other governmental forms.

Other factors considered, though not conclusive, are the existence of special appropriation items for the group and the social solidarity of the group.[25]

The extent to which the modern regulations are based on these understandings will become evident in the coming chapters, but for the time being I note that the guidelines are fairly specific in terms of which evidence had been used in the past to determine tribal existence, but still very unclear in terms of instructions for most of the tribes seeking recognition in the 1970s. Would meeting any one of the criteria suffice, or would a tribe have to meet several or all of them? What types and levels of evidence would the BIA accept? Who would decide, and how long would a decision take? Lack of clarity made it easy for the BIA to be evasive and hard for tribes to force the issue, hence the lack of "consistency of practice in giving 'federal recognition' " noted by the BIA in 1974.[26]

Even with the solicitor's opinion of 1974 and the precedent of previous unchallenged recognition of Indian tribes, the Department of the Interior still claimed at various times afterward that it had no unambiguous authority to recognize tribes.[27] Despite this inconsistency, there are indications that by early 1975 the BIA had begun to develop formalized procedures. The associate solicitor for Indian affairs, Reid Peyton Chambers, stated as much in a response to a request for help in restoring federal recognition for the Clatsop and recognizing the Lower Band of Chinook Indians. After suggesting that the groups follow established informal guidelines in preparing information in support of a bill for restoration and recognition, he wrote that "recognition standards are currently undergoing review within the Department."[28] This is the earliest indication available that the department was working on revising recognition procedures. By May the endeavor was fully under way. At that time Kent Frizzell, acting secretary of the interior, wrote to Senator Henry Jackson regarding the Snohomish tribe's petition for federal recognition, stating that "standards and procedures for determining requests such as the

Snohomish petition have never been established. Accordingly, this Office has undertaken a general legal study of the concept of recognition in order to aid in the development of such standards and procedures if possible." He added, optimistically, "it is intended that all pending requests for recognition will be dealt with following completion of this study within the next month or two."[29]

The new phase of research at the bureau was more concerned with the obligations of the federal government to federally nonrecognized tribes, and accelerated as a result of the *Passamaquoddy* decision of 11 February 1975.[30] The *Passamaquoddy* decision changed the playing field by saying that federal laws regarding Indian tribes applied to all tribes, whether the federal government had previously recognized the obligation or not. Thus the Passamaquoddy successfully argued that the cession of their land in 1794 to the state of Maine (then part of Massachusetts) should have been null and void, since it was carried out in contravention of the Indian Trade and Intercourse Acts that stated relationships with Indian tribes to be solely the province of the federal government. While the decision itself was simply a declaratory judgment that the Indian Trade and Intercourse Acts applied to the Passamaquoddy Tribe and that the acts established a trust relationship between the United States and the tribe, the decision did force the federal government to reassess its obligations to tribes that it had not served previously—any Indian tribe that existed in the United States had a trust relationship with the federal government, whether or not the government had historically acknowledged it.[31] The decision brought a wave of new petitions to the office, as tribes gained hope that they would finally be eligible for federal protections and services.

Shortly after the *Passamaquoddy* decision the American Indian Policy Review Commission (AIPRC) provided further impetus for the BIA to revisit federal recognition policy. In response to issues highlighted by the armed occupation of Wounded Knee by Indian activists in the spring of 1973, two Indian legal activists, Kirke Kickingbird and Vine Deloria Jr., urged Senator James Abourezk of South Dakota, a non-Indian raised on the Rosebud Sioux Reservation, to initiate a review of all aspects of federal Indian policy and make suggestions to Congress for reforming and revising them.[32] Composed of eleven "task forces," each dedicated to a separate area of Indian law, policy, or administration of services, the commission had ambitious goals. Task Force 10 of the commission was charged with assessing the needs of federally nonrecognized and terminated Indians around the country and developing a coherent and just policy that the federal government could follow in determining its responsibilities to these tribes.

Beginning work in August 1975, the staff of Task Force 10 was composed of several Indians from communities that did not receive federal services: Jo Jo Hunt (Lumbee), Robert Bojorcas (Klamath), George Tomer (Penobscot-Maliseet), and John Stevens (Passamaquoddy). The work of the task force was exceptional inasmuch as it provided a forum for discussing federal recognition issues by people who knew them best, as well as large amounts of data and testimony from numerous tribal members and expert tribal assistants across the United States.

Task Force 10's impact on the bureau's federal recognition policy is hard to gauge. At a minimum the task force pressed the issue for the bureau through sharp criticism and provided it with a solid needs assessment for nonrecognized tribes around the country. As indicated above, the bureau had been (very slowly) developing what it believed would be sufficient standards for review of tribal status based on the expanding number of groups petitioning for recognition, but Task Force 10's information forced the bureau to rethink what its recognition standards would look like and what its obligations would be toward those tribes not currently receiving services.[33]

In its own final report, however, Task Force 10 provided recommendations that could not realistically be used by the BIA. For instance, it never recommended that formalized criteria and procedures be instituted for tribes to follow in petitioning for recognition. Instead it recommended that all distinctions between federally recognized Indians and federally nonrecognized (including terminated) Indians be erased, since the *Passamaquoddy* decision clearly indicated that such distinctions had no basis in law. Task Force 10's definition of Indians to be served included all those descended from persons indigenous to the United States.[34] This definition reduced Indian identity solely to biological ancestry, though, which was not typically the way Indian people or Indian nations defined themselves or had been defined by others. Further, the BIA refused to open its service pool to just anyone calling himself or herself Indian without evidence, for to do so would be just as arbitrary and capricious as a decision not to recognize Indian tribes at all. The reality stated by Ted Jojola, that "no other people . . . have ever had to reestablish and reaffirm their identity as many times as the American Indian,"[35] remains frustratingly relevant because of the political status, rights to land, and other benefits tied to American Indian tribal status.

The final report of the AIPRC (as opposed to the earlier final report of Task Force 10), issued in May 1977, does eventually recommend the establishment of standards for use in determining whether a given group of Indians should be treated as a tribe under federal law.[36] Here the recommended standards were again too liberal, since they demanded that any group recognized as a tribe by any other tribe or state, county, or local municipal government should be automatically recognized as a tribe by the United States. The legitimate point being made was that "the BIA has no authority to refuse services to any member of the Indian population,"[37] and that if left to their own standards the federal bureaucrats would almost certainly be too stringent in defining Indians to be served. But it would be unwise to leave the government with absolutely no discretion in deciding whether to give political status and resources intended for Indians to any group claiming to be an Indian tribe that could persuade a completely uninformed city council to vouch for it. Moreover, there was no indication of what would happen if city and state governments disagreed about whether a group was a tribe. The task force's recommendations were not implementable in that regard.[38]

The task force pressed for resources to be provided to petitioning tribes to help them complete the research necessary to compile a defensible petition, and in this they were apparently successful. The AIPRC final report noted the obstacles that lack of education and funding created for a tribe that would have to perform an enormous amount of research to document its history for a recognition petition.[39] To this end petitioners were directed to apply to the Office of Native American Programs (later the Administration for Native Americans of the U.S. Department of Health, Education and Welfare) for funds to perform research in support of their petition, and many groups have used these funds almost exclusively to pay for their research.

Whatever its impact on the eventual policies adopted by the federal government, Task Force 10 further stimulated the recognition movement and provided people from tribes not currently receiving federal services with a degree of hope that at some level the federal government was looking into their situations. Task Force 10 tried to provide as much information as it could during site visits and hearings held around the country, and it gathered critical information and testimony that had not been gathered before. The hearings were important meeting grounds that helped make the recognition movement more cohesive, and helped to legitimate the concerns of the tribes involved. This was the first time the needs of federally nonrecognized Indians as a group had been studied in detail and by sympathetic people, and the final report helped situate their struggles within the broader struggles of Indians in the United States.

The AIPRC, combined with growing complications and disputes from the eastern land claims, litigation from the Stillaguamish tribe,[40] pressure from the NCAI, and increasing petitioning efforts of nonfederal tribes around the country, induced the bureau to establish uniform procedures for recognition, and the BIA squirmed as the stakes of recognition decisions rose.[41] By February 1976 the secretary of the interior was claiming that the DOI did not have the authority to recognize Indian tribes, and therefore decided to propose legislation that would explicitly grant the department that authority and "establish rather restricted standards or criteria to be applied in determining whether a Tribe should be recognized."[42] In July 1976 it was reported orally to an attorney for an influential organization called Small Tribes of Western Washington (STOWW) that yet another solicitor's opinion demonstrating secretarial authority to recognize tribes was being drafted.[43]

In June 1977, the month after the release of the AIPRC's final report, the BIA published draft acknowledgment regulations in the *Federal Register* that provided recourse only for tribes seeking to establish that they had already been and should continue to be federally recognized, despite the clear statement in the *Passamaquoddy* decision that the Indian Trade and Intercourse Acts, and thus the federal trust relationship, applied to all tribes, whether the federal government had previously recognized them or not.[44] The response from tribes, attorneys, and academics to the initial proposed regulations, in addition to the comments collected at public hearings held around the country, was "so overwhelming" that the BIA completely revised the regulations and published them again as a new set of "proposed regulations," inviting a second round of comments.[45]

On 5 September 1978, after a year of public comment and review, final procedures were set that attempted to allow more broadly for the acknowledgment of any group that could demonstrate its existence as an Indian tribe from historical times to the present following official criteria.[46] The BIA conceded that drawing a line between tribes and non-tribal Indian communities could be very difficult. There are numerous ways to define tribal existence, and many were discussed over the course of developing the new procedures, but the bureau finally settled on what it believed would be the best criteria for determining whether a group could demonstrate having maintained political and social solidarity as an Indian people throughout its history. The BIA clarified that this process was designed to recognize Indian polities, and that "failure to be acknowledged pursuant to these regulations does not deny that the group involved is Indian. It means these groups do not have the characteristics necessary for the Secretary to acknowledge them as existing as an Indian tribe and entitled to rights and services as such."[47]

The statement that race and polity are not equivalent is an accurate one, but one must challenge nonetheless the viability of the statement that "the failure to be acknowledged . . . does not deny that the group involved is Indian." The racial and colonial authority of the federal government creates a particularly powerful racial project that determines for many purposes whether a group can in fact be accepted as Indian or avail itself of benefits and protections intended for indigenous peoples. While federal status remains one of many discourses on Indian identity, it is still an incredibly powerful one because of the material, political, and legal benefits tied to it and the definitional authority that it carries. Its discursive and legal effect is to "deny that the group involved is Indian" in many contexts, whether intended or not.

### The Racial and Tribal Politics of Federal Recognition

The national recognition movement must be understood as a part of—and a product of—the political and creative surge in Indian arts, literature, cultural production, tribalism, historical writing, and activism known as the Indian renaissance that began in the early 1960s and has lasted to the present day. The Indian renaissance has its roots in a variety of sources, including the continued activism of tribal leaders in response to termination policies, the American Indian Chicago Conference, the formation of organizations such as the National Indian Youth Council, the broader social and political movements of the 1960s, and the educational achievement of a growing number of Indians. The term "Indian renaissance" denotes the renewed vigor in American Indian tribal identities, political efforts, and artistic production in the face of decades of repression from all quarters.[48] This renewal did not honor the boundary between federal and nonfederal Indians. For federally nonrecognized Indians, one of the most significant ways to participate in the Indian renaissance was to assert their strength of identity, reinforce tribalism, and pursue political justice on behalf of their tribe by working for federal recognition. Not all unrecognized tribes pursued this strategy, but a good number became convinced that recognition was the linchpin to tribal persistence and renewal of political strength.

The movement for recognition has consistently alarmed a fair number of leaders from tribes with long-standing relationships to the federal government. Responding to the placement of Lumbees in certain Indian preference positions, Roger Jourdain, the longtime tribal chairman of the Red Lake Chippewas, complained in 1975 that "as it now stands because of certain legislation, any group of people who want to call themselves Indians can be Indian and derive benefits which should go to land based, federally recognized Indians."[49] Jourdain's assertion was by no means unique. The theme had been sounded by numerous other leaders of recognized tribes before Jourdain's statement, and has been reiterated since. In fact, leaders of recognized tribes founded the National Tribal Chairmen's Association in 1971 at least partially in response to the threat to their sovereignty that they perceived from federally nonrecognized tribes and urban Indian coalitions, which they believed were attempting to "water down the definition of an Indian."[50]

Task Force 10 of the AIPRC was ultimately not very influential in the federal arena precisely because of these sentiments. A key incident at the NCAI convention in Portland, Oregon, in 1975 demonstrates the reception that the task force was given in certain quarters. A poignant memorandum from George Tomer, Task Force 10 specialist, to Ernest Stevens, AIPRC director, details the degrading experiences that the members of nonfederal tribes endured there.

> Prior to the actual decision of the Task Force to attend the NCAI Convention as a member of a discussion panel on "Federal Recognition," the task force members and specialist had carefully considered the following:
>
> 1. The possible constructive ramifications of attending a National Congress of American Indians initially designed to serve the interests of all American Indians;
> 2. The possible destructive—and endangering—aspects of any position paper written by NCAI in face of the harsh realities of modern-day practices and pseudo-ideologies of the body politic in "Indian Country";
> 3. The grim possibilities of being "shouted off the podium" by merely being associated with a task force investigating the subject area of "terminated and nonfederally recognized" Indians; and most importantly;
> 4. The vague feeling that something would happen in Portland, Oregon which could negatively affect Task Force #10 directly or indirectly, either immediately or in the intermediate future.

Indeed it would have been my extreme pleasure to say "Yes, there were 'constructive ramifications' while attending NCAI . . . Yes, there was an attempt to 'shout us off the podium,' but our friends came to rescue us from the bad-guys . . ."; Only, this world we live in is hardly a soap-box melodrama.

To paraphrase Mr. Allen Sockabasin, Tribal Governor of the Indian Township Passamaquoddys:

I've been to a lot of National Indian meetings, but I've never felt so out-of-place and so goddam frustrated . . .

We participated in the workshop immediately after the spokesmen for United Southeastern Tribes, Inc. had spent about one-half hour of work-shop time in the room assigned for the workshop in an obvious attack on Commissioner Dial and Jo Jo Hunt, Task Force #10 chairwoman. The experience prior to the workshop was very demeaning and put us on the defensive. Ms. Hunt attempted to respond to some of the accusations but she had even not heard all of them. She was the only Commission em-ployee to speak in defense of Lumbee people, Commissioner Dial and her-self. This left little doubt in anyone's mind the kind of support we have.[51]

Later in that same meeting the NCAI passed a resolution opposing federal recognition of the Lumbees and the disbursement of funds to "organizations that are not Federally recognized Indian Tribes."[52]

Yet the NCAI president, Mel Tonasket, noted the NCAI's support in 1976 for the Passamaquoddy tribe, then federally nonrecognized, stating that "our stand must not exclude consideration of the valid but nonfederally recog-nized Tribes and groups," and in fact the NCAI had previously recognized the Lumbees, and would recognize them again in later years.[53] Rather, the NCAI only opposed "wholesale and indiscriminate recognition of every group claiming to be Indian."[54] While there is goodwill from some federal tribal leaders, skepticism and antagonism exist alongside it. Indian leaders have said that they do not support services for federally nonrecognized Indians, and have then proceeded to say that there are a number of federally nonrecog-nized Indians deserving of federal recognition and services. If there are legiti-mate nonfederal tribes, those tribes ought to be receiving full federal services immediately, but the multiple conflicts over Indian identity produce a com-mon default position that a person is probably not a real Indian until the federal government confirms that he or she belongs to a tribe. Such a position carries an inherent willingness to ignore the needs of nonfederal tribes for the sake of expedience and a misguided faith in federal decision making on this single issue. The stigma of federal nonrecognition is difficult to erase; some tribal groups are not universally considered Indians even after they are federally recognized.[55]

The Tulalip Tribe of Washington has been a key opponent of petitioning tribes in the Pacific Northwest, beginning with the Stillaguamish Tribe in the 1970s, and it continues to oppose recognition of more Puget Sound tribes to the present day. In 1976, after opposing recognition of the Stillaguamish, the Tulalips grudgingly accepted the Stillaguamish into the inner circle of recognized tribes. The Tulalips' service manager, Francis J. Sheldon, issued a statement to the effect that they accepted the federal designation of the group as an Indian tribe. In the same letter, however, he argued that the Tulalips still believed "that if a group of people have left their culture, disappeared into the general society, and only now are resurfacing because there is money around, then the question of 'recognition' becomes destructive of Indian culture, identity and continued existence as an Indian tribe . . . Everyone wants to be Indian now, but when the blood line is watered down so much, and there is apparently no effort being made to check out whether the claims of individual Indians are actually valid as to being a member of any tribe, what do you expect us to do who have maintained our identity, in the best way we know how?" While Sheldon later states his affection and respect for the tribal leader Esther Ross, his indictment of what he describes as opportunistic Indian descendants still stands. He groups the Snoqualmie, Samish, and Snohomish in this class as well.[56]

Twenty-five years later the Tulalip tribal government pursued a similar tack. Speaking on the Duwamish petition for federal recognition, Herman Williams Jr., chairman of the board of directors for the Tulalip Tribe, argued that only the Indians who moved to the reservation at the time of the treaty signings in the 1850s deserved to have a continued relationship with the federal government. Williams asserted that the Tulalips "ceded our land and moved to reservations, went through the hardships, sifted bugs out of our flour and endured the disease. We were Indian when it wasn't popular to be Indian, while other people got to assimilate into the community."[57]

The problem with this line of reasoning is that it bases Indian identity not on culture or even ancestry, but on suffering at the hands of the federal government. It makes unsubstantiated claims that the descendants of Indians who chose not to move to reservations, who may or may not have assimilated at all with surrounding populations, and who may have stayed away from reservations because they were more traditional in the first place, have less of a right to call themselves Indian than reservation Indians do. It also assumes that there was no suffering among non-reservation Indians, but reviews of statistics by the AIPRC show that federally nonrecognized Indians fell behind their federally recognized cousins according to many socioeconomic indicators. It is particularly frustrating when people like the former Mississippi Choctaw chief Philip Martin and the Eastern Cherokee chief Jonathon Taylor assert that they have the right to call themselves Indian because of the suffering they endured as Indians, while people such as the Lumbee, who have been living under the same American racial and colonial system, have not.[58] Without undermining the feelings of those seeking to protect their tribe's integrity, accusations that only federal, reservation Indians suffered from racism or colonialism cannot be maintained under close examination.[59]

Federal recognition involves continuing discussions of Indian nationalism, racial and cultural inclusion and exclusion, access to federal resources, and the right to assert tribal sovereignty. People involved in the debate are multiply positioned, and no simple line separates them into two opposing camps. The NCAI has described its own position, and therefore the position of much of the leadership of federally recognized tribes, as one of "selective recognition moderatism."[60] That means that as an organization it will support tribes it considers legitimate and grant them full membership in the NCAI. Indeed, the NCAI and many recognized tribes have supported recognition efforts of a number of petitioners over the years. They acknowledge that communities involved in the recognition movement have always been diverse in their composition. These communities range from tribes predominated by full-bloods with near universal language retention to mixed-blood tribes with faded cultural distinctiveness to "descendant organizations" of unrelated people connected only recently by real or imagined ties to a common ancestral tribe. A significant number of Indians from recognized tribes consistently link the recognition movement to descendant organizations and Indian hobbyists rather than legitimate tribes, no matter how peripheral these groups have typically been to the recognition movement, creating an ongoing struggle for nonfederal tribes.

The NCAI has noted that opponents of further federal recognition share four common concerns. First, they are concerned that federal funds for Indians might be funneled away from people who are "completely" Indian to people who are "not very" Indian, if they are Indian at all. This is an important distinction. Tulalip opposition to recognizing many petitioners falls under this category. Second, they are concerned that petitioners are predominantly of some other race. If a group is "predominantly" white, black, or Latino, some argue, it should probably not be considered Indian. Such thinking relies heavily on racial logic rather than traditional conceptions of belonging based in kinship and affinity or even on the political (not racial) boundaries of a nation that provide the basis for the federal-tribal relationship.

Third, opponents believe that most petitioners have lost their cultural traditions and their language, and when that happens, there is nothing left that makes them Indian. While these losses are attributable to historical circumstances of white racism and colonialism, that does not make up for the fact that the petitioners are not culturally Indian in the present in a way that is satisfying to some people in other tribes.

Finally, opponents of further recognition are concerned that recognizing groups not perceived as racially and culturally Indian at first glance to most people will diminish the strength of arguments for tribal sovereignty in the public eye. They argue that this central legal concept protecting Indian tribes is too precious to risk having it become an issue of public debate because of the "questionable" Indian background of newly recognized tribes. Their recognition will "lead to greater opposition to tribal sovereignty in general, and would result in support for legislation to abrogate treaties and dissolve present tribal governments."[61] Pragmatic and astute as this argument may be in its assessment of white racial and colonial logic, it reinforces that same logic, doing the work of white supremacy by preemptively requesting that the federal government continue to ignore struggling indigenous groups.

Still, efforts to paint leaders of federally recognized tribes as "pawns of the federal establishment who refuse to share abundant federal resources"[62] are misleading. Tribal leaders have an obligation to protect the well-being of their tribes, and they sometimes see tribes with lower blood quanta, few distinct cultural markers, and rumors that their dark skin results primarily from African ancestry as impostors who have no right to claim a shared indigenous or racial experience, much less the meager benefits and protections that tribes have sacrificed so much to achieve and retain. On the surface, it thus seems unimpeachable for a tribal leader to contend with such groups for limited resources.

But definitions of Indianness vary by tribe, by region, and by individual, and they shift over time and according to context. In this sense conceptions of tribal survival and Indian identity can be thought of as parallel to the racial formation process—race and federal recognition are part of the calculus of tribal and individual identity, but family connections, cultural considerations, and place of residence have been at times far stronger than race in determining belonging, and multiple agendas are always in play.[63]

Making racial and colonial projects visible is an important part of the process of strengthening relations between federal and nonfederal tribes. A view that recognizes the federal government as a historical state entity that promotes its own interests rather than a neutral and natural institution makes it easier to argue that there does not need to be a federal monitor of tribal identity. Moreover, the failure of the United States to recognize an indigenous nation does not mean that it ceases to exist. Indian identity is negotiated, shifting, and mutable, as are all social identities, and the state does not have any inherent right to play the arbiter in deciding the boundaries of any ethnic group or indigenous nation. In the short term, however, indigenous nations and the federal government alike have distinct interests to protect in deciding who should participate in their relationship. The intensity with which the present boundaries of Indian identity are patrolled would be significantly curtailed and tolerance conversely increased if access to resources and federal protections were not at issue.

Ray Fogelson comments insightfully on this issue, stating that "in long-term perspective, the current federal recognition process may come to be seen less as a needed gate-keeping mechanism and more as a belated exercise of hegemonic power to divide and conquer Indian people, as well as a major influence on the commodification and arbitration of Indian authenticity."[64] In the interim, however, tribes want and need to be acknowledged as tribes, and the government needs a mechanism to recognize the existence of those who can document their tribal status. There needs to be some method of ensuring that legitimate tribes have access to federal services and protections while at the same time keeping non-Indian groups from obtaining federal recognition as Indian tribes, even if that leaves in the lurch groups that cannot document their status. The more difficult questions are what kinds and levels of evidence will count and whose definition of an Indian tribe should be the standard, and these are questions that have bedeviled the recognition issue from the beginning.[65]

There are probably petitioners currently in the process who should not qualify for federal recognition as tribes, but most completed petitions reveal stories of indigenous survival in the face of overwhelming odds. The typical petitioner—meaning a serious petitioner who moves beyond merely submitting a letter of intent to petition—is a group of related people of Indian descent who have stuck together as best they can, and who are continuing their efforts to stay together by petitioning for federal recognition. That nontribal groups have submitted letters of intent to petition is beyond doubt, but there is no chance that any such group will ever be recognized as a tribe under federal law.[66]

It is hard to miss the racial and cultural determinism in popular definitions of tribal existence that are based solely on high blood quanta and retention of aboriginal culture. As James Clifford notes, writing about the Mashpee Wampanoag land claim case of 1976 that turned into a referendum on the tribe's existence, "A community, unlike a body, can lose a central 'organ' and not die. All the critical elements of identity are in specific conditions replaceable: language, land, blood, leadership, religion. Recognized, viable tribes exist in which any one or even most of these elements are missing, replaced, or largely transformed."[67] Reliance on high blood quanta and aboriginal cultural retention fails to account for tribal persistence through other means. While it is true that these are each clear evidence of tribal persistence, they cannot be the only measures by which tribes are evaluated for federal recognition. Vine Deloria Jr., a longtime activist on behalf of nonrecognized tribes, suggests that "a traditional Indian community more closely resembles what we find in Robeson County [North Carolina] among the Lumbees—large extended families who exert social and political control over family members, and who see their family as part of an extended people."[68] What constitutes tribal existence is the persistence of an extended family network, with all the informal social controls that it entails, revolving around a core of indigenous ancestry and a persistent social identity as an Indian group. The majority of groups in the recognition movement, including most of those who have been denied recognition by OFA, have met those criteria from the beginning, but their opponents have focused on deviances from a normative image of Indian tribes—typically defined by western, reservation-based federal tribes.[69]

Consistent opposition and suspicion from the federal government and some federally recognized Indians has been demoralizing for federally nonrecognized Indians, so much so that if recognition were not a terribly important matter and if they were not entirely confident of their tribal status, many tribes would have given up their efforts to that end long ago. Federally nonrecognized Indians have to endure the community-wide psychological distress of being treated as "snotty-nosed step kids," as the former Choctaw-Apache tribal chairman Tommy Bolton put it. Unrecognized tribes face being attacked at national Indian meetings, being told that "real" Indians need federal services more than they do and that their tribe ceased to exist years ago (or never existed in the first place). Overcoming these constant challenges to maintain pride in a tribal identity requires endless determination and self-assurance. Before recognition Skip Hayward, chair of the Mashantucket Pequots, summarized his indignation at the label "unrecognized": "I resent the implication," he said, "that I am a second-class Indian."[70] The constant assault on the identities of federally nonrecognized Indians needs to be understood as a serious threat to community well-being, considering the observation by Joseph Gone, a Gros Ventre cultural psychologist,that identity is central to the mental health of American Indian communities.[71]

The social, political, cultural, and economic consequences of federal non-recognition have been important as well. The AIPRC summarized the status of nonfederal tribes in 1976: "The results of nonrecognition upon Indian communities and individuals has been devastating, and highly similar to termination: the continued erosion of tribal lands, or the complete loss thereof; the deterioration of cohesive, effective tribal governments and social organizations; the elimination of special federal services, through the continued denial of such services which the Indian communities in general appear to desperately need."[72]

Federally nonrecognized Indians are poorer and less well educated than their federally recognized counterparts, with less access to health care. Their tribal organizations consistently lapse, with little economic or political support for their existence and therefore limited ability to support their constituencies in meaningful ways. Skip Hayward perceived how this erosive process was harming the Mashantucket Pequots in 1975, when the Pequots were just another bunch of broke Indians. "Is this how you finally try to put an end to us," he asked, "by denying us services that would allow us to return to our reservation and survive as an Indian community?"[73]

In the struggle for indigenous survival and well-being, tribes seeking federal recognition are engaging in an inherently anticolonial and antiracist act. They hope that recognition will promote economic development, give them access to better education and health care, make the tribal unit a resource for its members, gain a land base, end speculation about their tribal legitimacy, and ultimately help the people survive as a tribe. Recognition can help tribes achieve these goals, but—without implying that people should be nonchalant about the continuing injustice of nonrecognition for legitimate tribes—research in Louisiana reveals that even with recognition, these goals may not be achieved as fully or as quickly as advocates hope they will.

For tribes that do not achieve recognition for one reason or another, these goals are still attainable if approached in different ways, so long as it is remembered that these goals, rather than federal recognition, are the ultimate objective. Tribes do not currently need the approval of the federal government to continue to survive as tribes. The benefits of federal recognition are numerous, and the federal government is wrong to withhold these benefits from so many unrecognized tribes, but all the unrecognized tribes have survived until now without them. By putting resources into other projects, the so-called unrecognized tribes can survive long into the future. N. Scott Momaday articulates this thinking in *House Made of Dawn*. Speaking of the Jemez Pueblo, he writes, "They have assumed the names and gestures of their enemies, but have held on to their own secret souls; and in this there is a resistance and an overcoming, a long outwaiting."[74]

The "long outwaiting" is the will to endure that Indians have been exercising since Europeans arrived in this hemisphere, long before the BIA existed.

## CHAPTER 2

## The Tunica-Biloxi Tribe's Early
## Recognition Efforts

The Tunica tribe first asked the United States government for protection based on its status as a sovereign Indian nation in 1826, and it requested federal services and protections with increasing regularity for the next 155 years before finally being granted federal recognition in 1981.[1] Federal officials had assumed and perhaps hoped that the tribe would fade into obscurity with continued neglect, but the remarkably persistent Tunicas eventually prevailed at an opportune moment. Their tenacity in pursuit of recognition makes their story among the most compelling in the federal recognition movement.[2]

Nonrecognition proved to be an ongoing burden on the tribe, and failure to protect the Tunicas from white land grabbers had been particularly detrimental to tribal well-being. It borders on the absurd to speak of the United States government as a potentially protective entity for Indian tribes in the mid-nineteenth century, a time when it was actively mandating the removal of all Indians from their lands in the South. But the moral argument that the government should have been protecting Tunica land is buttressed by its legal obligations under the Indian Trade and Intercourse Acts and the Louisiana Purchase Treaty, both of which should have protected Tunica land. Tribal dispossession is a common enough story of injustice for Indian tribes, made only slightly unusual in this case by its having happened without federal directives.[3] In that light, the Tunicas' experiences instructively point us not to federal policy but to the ideology in which that policy had its roots—the underlying script that guided efforts at the federal and local levels. The same script allowed the federal government to ignore the tribe throughout the nineteenth century, knowing that the machinery of colonialism and racism would be effectively implemented by local forces.

At least six historic tribes contribute to the modern Tunica-Biloxi Tribe of Louisiana, informally referred to as the Tunicas. The tribes followed the trend in colonial Louisiana that saw various small, formerly distinguishable peoples, or petites nations, blend with each other by the late eighteenth century. Interaction was so close that by 1775 it became "difficult for the European administrators to distinguish them one from another."[4] While the membership of the modern tribe is primarily Tunica and Biloxi, members of the Choctaw, Ofo, Pascagoula, and Avoyelle tribes became permanently affiliated with these ancestral tribes by the late eighteenth century.

It is likely that de Soto's expedition encountered the historic Tunica tribe in 1541 at the town of Quizquiz, but the earliest indisputable encounter between Europeans and Tunicas occurred in 1694, when the Tunicas were living near present-day Vicksburg, Mississippi, at the confluence of the Yazoo and Mississippi rivers.[5] From that time the Tunicas maintained a close alliance with the French and the Spanish, and fought at their side against the Natchez, Chickasaws, and English over the next hundred years. During this time the Tunicas also strengthened their connections with the Ofos and the Biloxis, who joined them in nearly all their military expeditions. They also began developing ties with the Avoyelles tribe; the Avoyelles' homelands were on the Avoyelles Prairie in central Louisiana, where a large segment of these allied tribes established their current home by 1786.[6] Shortly after 1800 a group of Biloxis and Pascagoulas, who may have been associated with the Avoyelles Prairie group earlier, established a community at a place now known as Indian Creek, thirty miles to the west. This community eventually incorporated a number of Choctaws, and maintained close enough ties with the Avoyelles Prairie settlement that its descendants are unambiguously identified as Tunica-Biloxi tribal members today.

The purchase of the Louisiana Territory by the United States government in 1803 initiated the problem of nonrecognition for the Tunicas, since the United States was the first government they had encountered which would not recognize their aboriginal sovereignty. Instead the government catered to white colonists, failing to uphold protectionist language in the Indian Trade and Intercourse Acts and the Louisiana Purchase Treaty that would have preserved Tunica land and sovereignty.[7] In an article published in 1980, an attorney for the Tunica-Biloxi Tribe, Donald Juneau, analyzed the documentary record of several attempts by white intruders to defraud and dispossess the tribe.[8] The first involved a colonist named Celestin Moreau, who claimed a tract of land at Bayou Rouge Prairie (near present-day Goudeau, Louisiana) occupied by one of the two Tunica villages in existence at the time. The Tunicas secured the aid of a lawyer, George Gorten, to protest the claim and protect their village. On 7 September 1826 Gorten wrote to the registrar of lands, the receiver of public moneys, and the state land office, protesting the pending grant of Tunica land to Moreau and others. In a well-informed argument Gorten opined, "I consider it a misfortune of the Indians that their claims have not been known to the government. It is the duty of the government to inquire into their rights. There are Indian agents appointed for that purpose, and I do not think the Indians should forfeit anything by neglect. It is different with a nation or a tribe and an individual—the one has right that the other has not. The Indians govern themselves and the title to their lands is vested in them as a nation. . . . Whereas an individual holds his title from the government and depends upon the government for the protection of his rights, the Indians were conscious of their good title and of their power as a nation to hold their lands."[9] In a brutal decision against the tribe, the Tunicas' claim was denied based on the assertion that "the spirit and intentions of the law does not exclude them as Indians, but it certainly does as savages . . . Mr. Bordelon says they have not been reclaimed from their savage mode of life. We are, therefore, bound to say that their applications must be dismissed."[10] Thus the Tunicas lost title to the land surrounding their village at Bayou Rouge Prairie, about thirty miles southeast of the current Marksville settlement.

At the main Tunica village near Marksville, the colonist François Bordelon attempted to act out the same script as Moreau had used in Bayou Rouge Prairie. He claimed to have settled a tract of land within the borders of the town of Marksville and submitted his claim to the proper authorities to have his title confirmed. His claim included the Tunica village, apparently unbeknown to the land office in Opelousas. Bordelon had his title confirmed without mention of the Tunicas, but his claim became the center of a lawsuit between his successor in title and the Tunica tribe.[11]

The conflict that precipitated the lawsuit over Tunica land rights in the Marksville village had been brewing for some time. In an event clearly preserved in tribal oral history but not in the documentary record, the Tunica chief Melacon was shot and killed in a dispute with Bordelon's successor in title, Celestin Moreau Jr., over the boundaries of the Tunica tract. Earl Barbry Sr., the current tribal chairman, recounted the incident: "The non-Indian land owner [Celestin Moreau Jr.] had his crew of slaves building fence, moving the fence over to the property line. Or so he claimed. He was moving it over onto the tribe's land. Every year he would have his crew come in and build a new fence, but every year he would move it onto tribal land, encroachment on their land. And the chief at that time [Melacon] went there and saw what was being done, and he proceeded to pull the fence posts out that the slaves were driving in. And the non-Indian that was there walked up to the chief and shot him with a rifle. He killed him. And, sad thing about it, there was no justice whatsoever. Nothing was done to the guy."

Moreau was never tried for the murder of Melacon, and in the following year he sued to evict the tribe from "his" land.[12] While the Tunicas' legal case was strong, they opted to settle out of court, leaving them with approximately 130 acres of land. Their land remained untaxed as an unofficial Indian reservation from that time, a reservation that the federal government had no part in creating or maintaining.[13] The United States declined to protect the tribe's larger Spanish land grants, but considering the Indian removal policy of the era, not being under federal protection may have helped the Tunicas to stay on their land.

If the tribe had not settled the suit out of court in 1848, it is possible that the tribe would have been taken under federal jurisdiction at that time. According to Donald Juneau, the tribe appeared to have the upper hand in the lawsuit. Had the Tunicas won and been granted the square league demanded in their counterclaim, Juneau believes that the federal government would have begun oversight of Tunica affairs based on the contention of the Tunicas' attorney, Ralph Cushman, that the United States was obligated to uphold its treaty obligations.[14] If later developments in Tunica history are any guide, it seems more likely that the federal government would have declined that responsibility, assured by a general belief in a "natural progression" toward assimilation and extinction that the prevailing racial and colonial ideology consistently produced, even without federal attention. The federal government is more easily identifiable as an agent of racial and colonial oppression, but the underlying ideology of white supremacy was shared widely by whites and produced similar behavior and policies even without direct federal supervision.[15]

The tribe's lack of federal recognition produced mixed results again in 1896, when Fulgence Chiqui attacked his fellow tribal member Ernest Pierite in a drunken rage. The tribe could not control Chiqui's continued acts of violence through its own means, so tribal leaders pressed charges in state court in an effort to have Chiqui imprisoned. Chiqui's attorney argued that since the crime had been committed between Indians "within the reservation allotted to [the Tunica-Biloxi Tribe], by the United States Government," the state had no jurisdiction. The judge accepted the argument and dismissed the case.[16]

The state appealed the decision to the Louisiana Supreme Court. One of the justices wrote to the secretary of the interior for information on the Tunica relationship with the federal government and was told that the Interior Department "does not have any knowledge of any land in Louisiana set apart for the Tunica or any other Indians for an Indian Reservation . . . The Federal government does not have jurisdiction over any Indians in Louisiana."[17] The Louisiana Supreme Court sent the case back to Avoyelles upon learning this information, but the local authorities did not pursue the case, and Fulgence Chiqui was killed mysteriously before the case went any further.[18] If the tribe had been federally recognized at this time it could have had Chiqui prosecuted under the Major Crimes Act of 1885, which listed assault with intent to kill as one of the crimes committed in Indian country prosecutable in federal courts.[19] While the Major Crimes Act has generally been scorned as an intrusion on tribal sovereignty, it might have served the Tunica-Biloxi Tribe well in this instance.

The intention of the Major Crimes Act was to take from tribes the power to adjudicate crimes committed on Indian lands. American politicians disapproved of tribal laws that did not match their own sense of justice, so they unilaterally extended federal jurisdiction over all Indian lands when any of a list of seven crimes was committed. Whether tribes punished murderers with death or ostracism from the tribe, or justified a murder as a witch killing, federal officials could not or would not give credence to the effectiveness and virtue of tribal laws. For federally nonrecognized Indians there should have been no need to extend federal jurisdiction, since they had no officially acknowledged sovereignty that would limit local authority over them, but the case of Fulgence Chiqui suggests otherwise. According to some tribal members, Fulgence Chiqui was killed by his sister, Arsene Chiqui, in an act of tribal justice, exactly the type of self-governing deed that the Major Crimes Act was intended to prevent.[20] His mangled body was found on the railroad tracks near the reservation a couple of years after the original case had been remanded by the Supreme Court. Fulgence Chiqui's murder was never resolved, and some say he was killed not by his sister but by trainmen who left him on the tracks after beating him.[21] In 1915 Arsene Chiqui was killed by the same train that killed her brother, inviting quiet speculation about connections with her brother's death and adding to the long list of hardships that befell the Tunicas.

Arsene Chiqui's death led directly to the beginning of the twentieth-century effort for federal recognition of the Tunica-Biloxi Tribe, when her son Sesostrie Youchigant tried to sue the railroad for wrongful death of his mother.[22] The local court ruled against him, and the Louisiana Supreme Court affirmed the local decision in 1920 based on inheritance laws intended to uphold white political authority and property rights. The Supreme Court ruled that since his parents were married only by tribal custom, and since the tribe was not federally recognized as a sovereign political entity, the tribe had to operate under the civil code of the State of Louisiana. The marriage of Youchigant's parents under tribal custom was therefore never officially sanctioned or recorded, according to the court. Thus Youchigant was illegitimate and under Louisiana law not a legal heir to either of his parents, so he could not sue for his mother's wrongful death.

Inheritance laws were clearly tied to white supremacist racial projects, in that they were intended to prevent property from passing from white hands to nonwhite hands through illegal interracial unions, and to funnel property to whites by undermining the rights of nonwhites, who were much less likely to have their marriages recognized by the state for various reasons. The upshot is that although it seems that the laws were predominantly aimed at taking property from blacks in Louisiana, they were actually designed with whiteness at their center, so they worked in a broad range of situations in which whites and nonwhites vied for property.[23] Just as they prevented children of white fathers and "octoroon" mothers in New Orleans from inheriting a father's estate, the laws were used against the Houmas in south Louisiana to evict them from their land when oil companies wanted to tap the massive Gulf Coast oil deposits beneath them, and against Youchigant to prevent him from suing a white company for wrongful death of his mother.[24] Moreover, they negated the political authority of tribes, extending white jurisdiction into any realm of tribal life deemed necessary to sustain white power. His failure to obtain redress prompted Youchigant—who had been the tribal chief since 1911—to believe that the tribe would need to harness the power of federal recognition to protect itself from local manifestations of white supremacy such as this that continued to badger them.[25]

Youchigant and his successor chiefs, Ernest Pierite and Eli Barbry, thus began a constant and resolute effort to acquire federal protection of the tribe's sovereignty, appealing to federal officials, lawyers, and anthropologists for aid. As a result of their efforts, Representative J. B. Aswell inquired into their situation at the Office of Indian Affairs in December 1925, trying to clarify the Tunicas' very confusing status as an unrecognized tribe that somehow had a reservation.[26] The commissioner of Indian affairs, Charles Burke, responded, stating that the only Indians in Louisiana under federal jurisdiction were the "Chettimanchi Band," who had been recognized in 1916,[27] and cited John Sibley's report on the Tunicas from 1806, a secondhand sketch that federal officials continually claimed was their only information on the tribe. It read as follows: "Tunicas: These people formerly lived on the Bayou Tunica, above point Coupee, on the Mississippi, East side; live now at Avoyelles; do not, at present, exceed twenty-five men. Their native language is peculiar to themselves, but speak Mobilian; are employed occasionally by the inhabitants as boatmen, etc; in amity with all other people, and gradually diminishing in numbers."[28]

These last words, "in amity with all other people, and gradually diminishing in numbers," seemed invariably to signify to the federal government that no further action was necessary, since the tribe made no trouble for its neighbors and appeared to whites to be on the verge of disappearing.[29] The racial and colonial projects of white supremacy were being accomplished without federal intervention, they seemed to think. Federal officials did not anticipate a succession of activist chiefs who would protect their tribe and pursue recognition of their sovereignty with such vigor.

### Activist Chiefs and the Office of Indian Affairs under the New Deal

The Tunicas generated a flurry of activity through their activist chiefs from the mid-1920s to the late 1930s in their efforts to be recognized. Sesostrie Youchigant retired as chief in 1921, though he lived much longer and influenced tribal politics long after his retirement. The tribe elected Ernest Pierite as chief in 1921 and Eli Barbry, Youchigant's half-brother, as subchief.[30] Barbry succeeded Pierite as chief in 1932, but even before that time Barbry was the more politically active of the two. He initially wrote to the Department of the Interior in 1922 inquiring into the status of Tunica lands, possibly in an attempt to secure title or gain federal services.[31] In 1924, believing that strength in numbers might help attract attention, Barbry formed a coalition of Louisiana Indians that included some ancestors of the modern Jena Band of

Choctaws, possibly an ancestor of the Clifton Choctaws, and some Choctaws and Biloxi-Choctaws from the Indian Creek settlement near Woodworth.[32] Borrowing language from the United States Constitution, the coalition was forged "for the purpose of forming a more perfect union of people of our race, to promote our welfare and to secure for ourselves and our descendants educational and religious training, to the end of our becoming better citizens." Eli Barbry, then subchief of the Tunica tribe, was named chief of this coalition, and authorized by the signatories "to bring about a union of our Tribes with the Tunica Tribe."[33] Similar coalitions were attempted with the Coushatta and Chitimacha tribes but did not succeed.[34] Tunica tribal members—Chief Ernest Pierite in particular—might have viewed Barbry's installment as chief of this coalition as a grab for power,[35] but the coalition was also a continuation of his desire and that of his brother Sesostrie Youchigant to bring federal status as an Indian tribe and perhaps some form of aid to his people. On the need for federal recognition there was no disagreement.

Undaunted by earlier disappointments in their recognition efforts, the Tunicas continued to enlist outside support. Friends of the Tunicas called on the Office of Indian Affairs repeatedly to restore Tunica lands and offer aid to the tribe. In fact Indians and their allies across Louisiana made a significant number of inquiries to the OIA, their efforts corresponding not only to increasingly difficult economic times but also to a rapidly developing American interest in Indian affairs that began in the early 1920s and continued through the 1930s.[36]

The federal government met such inquiries with the same rebuffs, typified by a response in 1932 from the Department of the Interior to the Louisiana Superintendent of Education, T. H. Harris. Secretary of the Interior Ray Lyman Wilbur rejected Superintendent Harris's appeal for funding for the education of Louisiana Indians, stating, "we do not believe that for the Federal Government to assume responsibility for the Indians of Louisiana today would be any kindness to those Indians."[37] Wilbur based his harsh assessment partly on the blunt fact that Indians already receiving aid and education from the federal government at that time were generally not in enviable circumstances, and partly on a callous notion that Louisiana Indians deserved no special aid, despite Harris's statement that the educational needs of Louisiana Indians were not being met. "A main objective in the work of the Federal Government for the Indian," Wilbur contended, "is to bring him to the point where he can stand on his own feet in whatever community his lot happens to lie. Admitting the unfavorable conditions to which my attention is invited, I would question whether the Indian is any worse off than thousands of negroes and poor whites in the same environment. Without Federal aid the Indians in Louisiana exist free of the handicaps of wardship; to impose wardship upon them would be to turn the clock backward."[38]

Wilbur's response reveals the sensibilities of federal officials of the time. Though this was a transitional moment in federal Indian policy, as the public became aware of and reacted against hardships endured by Indians under the federal bureaucracy, federal policy was not intended to protect sovereignty in the long run. Rather, the primary motivation of Indian policy was still to prepare Indians for assimilation into American society through the erasure of tribal cultures and polities. Embedded within that policy was the idea that Indian cultures represented a lower, weaker stage than western European cultures in the evolution of human societies. Replacing tribal cultures with a white culture that valued "civility," capitalism, and discipline, it was thought, would allow Indians to be self-supporting within the American society being imposed upon them. Of course, as is now widely understood, the assimilation program failed to account for how white racism works actively to keep nonwhites subjugated in a racial hierarchy, making any attempt at assimilation permanently incomplete, just as it failed to account for the strength and value of Indian tribalism. But Wilbur thought that assimilation had been achieved and that granting federal recognition to Louisiana Indians would "turn the clock backwards"—both in an evolutionary sense (in that the Indians would be encouraged to return to an infantile stage of social and cultural development) and in the policy sense (in that erasure of tribal sovereignty and assimilation of Indians into the American working class was the goal of federal Indian policy in the first place). Complete assimilation would solve several problems for whites and for the United States, since it would remove impediments to federal title and moral authority, in addition to relieving a portion of federal expenses. Wilbur's statement illustrates the racial and colonial logic that prevented many small tribes from being recognized, and provides an eerie precursor to the rhetoric of the termination era.[39]

In some areas the BIA would pay money to school districts for the education of Indian students who lived on untaxable federal trust land, since local property taxes usually provided the bulk of school funding.[40] Since the Chitimacha tribe had the only federal reservation in Louisiana at that time, the BIA did not feel compelled to provide funding for Indian children elsewhere in the state.[41] The Tunicas, however, were caught in a paradox. They could not receive federal recognition or aid because they had no federal reservation, and their reservation could not be put in trust because they were not federally recognized.[42] As a result, the federal government demurred on Harris's request for support for Louisiana Indians.

The 1930s were indeed hard years for people across America, and the Depression hit poor people of color the hardest, particularly in the South.[43] For the Tunica tribe the small reservation could no longer support their growing population, and tribal members began leaving in large numbers in search of work. The Biloxi community at Indian Creek had largely dispersed, and the reservation population in Marksville was cut in half. The most common destination for émigrés at the time was eastern Texas, where the forestry jobs that supported a number of tribal members had moved. A couple of tribal members ended up farther north, in the Chicago area, where they worked as migrant farm laborers with Mexican-American families into which they married.[44]

One of the remedies the tribe was considering to alleviate poverty was to try again to regain title to the land lost at Bayou Rouge, which they could sell to generate money for the struggling families who remained at the Marksville reservation on the Coulee des Grues. Correspondence in 1933 and 1934 between William Morrow, an attorney from Marksville, U.S. Senator John Overton (who was originally from Marksville), and the commissioner of Indian affairs John Collier reveals that the Bayou Rouge land claim generated considerable confusion. Morrow took up the Tunica cause with the federal government at the suggestion of Sesostrie Youchigant, whom he cited as the chief of the tribe. He proposed to both Collier and Senator Overton that the federal government might buy back the nebulous 240-acre land grant at five to ten dollars per acre to raise money for improving the Marksville reservation.[45]

By the mid-1930s John Collier had supposedly brought new respect for tribalism to the administration of Indian affairs, but his compassion did not extend to the Tunica-Biloxi Tribe. In a reply to Morrow's request for Tunica recognition lifted straight out of Commissioner Charles Burke's response to a similar query in 1925, Collier repeated the assertion in the Sibley report that the Tunicas were declining in number and "in amity" with their neighbors, and again stated that the federal government had no jurisdiction over the Tunicas.[46] He also repeated Burke's assertion that the Tunicas had missed their chance to file for title to their land, citing Congressional acts that allowed all French and Spanish land grantees—including Indian tribes—to maintain their grants after the Louisiana Purchase by filing claims in district court in Missouri before 1849.[47] Tunica land, however, had already been confirmed under those acts to François Bordelon in Marksville and a group of French settlers on the Bayou Rouge Prairie tract, but that was unknown to Collier, Senator Overton, or Morrow at the time. Overton requested that Morrow find and identify the Bayou Rouge Prairie land grant so that a transaction might be made, but Morrow was apparently never able to track it down.[48]

Federal officials were consistently reluctant to take responsibility for Louisiana Indians for several reasons. First, they were already under tight budget constraints, so then, as today, they did not want to assume any more responsibilities than they already had. Every little outlay for a new tribe, even if only a small grant for a schoolhouse, would result in more requests for aid of other kinds and obligate the bureau to the tribe perpetually. Second, the officials were often skeptical of the identities of Louisiana Indians. They were more willing to provide funds for groups that had not mixed much with other races at that time, such as the Jena Choctaws and the Coushattas, and hesitant to accept responsibility for groups that were rumored to have intermarried to any degree with blacks or to a significant degree with whites, such as the Houmas and the Tunica-Biloxis. A. C. Hector, superintendent of the Choctaw agency in Philadelphia, Mississippi, expressed the idea bluntly: "As you have probably heard," he wrote to the BIA education director, W. Carson Ryan, in 1934, "there are many other so-called Indians in Louisiana particularly in Terrebone [sic] Parish, such people being of various racial mixtures. I believe the State of Louisiana should more properly handle such mixed races."[49] Hector defined Indianness by racial purity. People of mixed race, according to his thinking and the thinking of others in the bureau, were common American citizens if they were not already members of federal tribes, especially when they had black ancestry. White Americans typically followed the rule of hypo-descent, or the "one-drop rule," which meant that known African ancestry in any amount automatically classified a person, a family, and even a community as black, making them unentitled to benefits as an Indian tribe. Hector's letter and the phrase "various racial mixtures" implied that African ancestry in a tribe in even a small degree meant no responsibility by the Office of Indian Affairs to the group as a whole. At any rate, the bureau's mission had long been to put Indians on the road to assimilation, and as far as Hector was concerned, that was an accomplished fact for the Houmas and the Tunica-Biloxis. Surely Collier's pro-tribal, sympathetic visions of Indian policy were sinking in by this time, but even he denied responsibility for Louisiana Indians in the beginning. As evidenced by the phrasing of the Indian Reorganization Act that entitled individual Indians of half or more "blood" to benefits, Collier also defined Indian identity by racial purity—though tribalism was central to his conception of Indian policy reform, he had difficulty conceiving of it separately from racial considerations. Further, there was a lingering sentiment among agency personnel that whenever feasible federal responsibility should be denied, and as many Indians as possible should be removed from federal jurisdiction.

Third, the size of Louisiana Indian communities made it easier to ignore them. Federal officials repeatedly referred to Indians in the state as scattered little groups or as remnants of Indian tribes. The smaller and more isolated the group, the harder for the BIA to provide cost-efficient services to them, and the less troubling it would be to withhold federal support. Such small groups, bureau officials argued, could surely be accommodated by local schools and state programs, though that rarely happened.

Bureau officials and John Collier shifted their stance as Louisiana Indians and their allies continued to educate the bureau about the circumstances of Louisiana Indians, and subtle changes became apparent in federal responses to requests for aid. By 1935 the Choctaw agency superintendent A. C. Hector was no longer bemoaning requests for educational funding for Louisiana Indians or accusing them of being racially suspect. He confidently assured John Collier that allocation requests for schools for the Jena Choctaws, the Chitimachas, and the Coushattas were all worthy of funding.[50] A year later he urgently requested even more money for these students, whose present funding was "barely adequate" in his opinion, and he repeated the request in 1937.[51] The bureau authorized increases each year, apparently eager to use the fourfold increase in its budget since Collier's tenure had begun.[52]

Because of continuing social and political connections with other Indians, the Tunica-Biloxis probably knew that other tribes in the state were receiving federal funds, and were encouraged that they might find federal support for themselves. John Barbry, a Tunica-Biloxi historian, suggests that anthropologists such as Robert Neitzel, Frances Dormon, Frank Speck, and Mary Haas also encouraged the Tunicas to seek federal assistance and pointed them in the direction of the appropriate authorities in Washington.[53] Evidence of tribal efforts can be found in inquiries by Senator Overton and Representative A. Leonard Allen to the Office of Indian Affairs asking whether the tribe might be eligible to organize under the Indian Reorganization Act.

The first glimmer of hope for the Tunicas came when the assistant commissioner of Indian affairs William Zimmerman suggested in June 1938, "there is a possibility of extending the benefits of the Indian Reorganization Act to these Indians if individuals within the group can furnish satisfactory proof of being one-half or more Indian." He noted, however, that "individuals, not the groups as a whole, would benefit."[54] While recognition as indigenous individuals would likely have been welcome, tribal recognition was much more important. If the tribe had been recognized, Arsene Chiqui's marriage would have been recognized as valid, and Sesostrie Youchigant would have had standing to sue the railroad for wrongful death. If the Tunicas had simply been receiving services as individual Indians, the state would still not have recognized the marriage, because the marriage would not have been sanctioned by a recognized political body. Culturally, legally, and politically, indigenous nation status was vital to tribal well-being.

Undeterred by the pessimistic federal response, tribal leaders began raising money from tribal members to make a trip to Washington, where they would make their case to the Office of Indian Affairs. By September they had raised enough money to send a delegation including Eli Barbry, his son Sam Barbry, Horace Pierite, and Clarence Jackson to Washington in a model-T Ford.[55] Once there the delegation had a meeting with the assistant to the commissioner Fred Daiker, D'Arcy McNickle, and a Mr. LaRouche, and they explained the tribe's history in detail, from the lost Spanish land grants to the murder of Melacon to the settlement that left them with 130 acres of swamps and gullies with a few acres of tillable soil. They noted that a number of their kin—including Clarence Jackson himself—had moved to Texas but would be happy to return if there were opportunities to make a living in Marksville. To this end they hoped that the bureau would assist them in purchasing new land or returning lands lost to them in amounts sufficient for supporting all tribal members. Since Zimmerman had suggested in his letter to Senator Overton and Representative Allen that land might be taken into trust for those of half or more Indian blood, these expectations seemed reasonable. Further, noting that the Tunicas were not allowed to enroll in white schools and would not attend "colored" schools, the delegation hoped that the government might make some provision in that area. They were told that the bureau would look into matters, but that they should not harbor any expectations of support.[56]

The Office of Federal Acknowledgment's anthropological report, based on field research in 1979, suggests that community members felt the delegation's failure to comprehend bureaucratic procedures, such as writing ahead and setting appointments with the appropriate officials, prevented them from achieving their goals during their visit.[57] A copy of the Indian Reorganization Act found in the papers of Eli Barbry, who could not read, reveals that the group may have had some idea before leaving for Washington of the benefits to which the Tunicas were entitled.[58] Clearly there is some merit to the idea that more bureaucratic and political sophistication might have opened more doors for the group in Washington, but they never let their lack of literacy interfere with their phenomenal effort and their confidence that their tribe had the right to federal recognition.

## The Underhill Report

While the delegation to Washington did not achieve its immediate goals, it did persuade the bureau to send an investigator to survey the Tunica community in the following month. The anthropologist Ruth Underhill, who was associate director of Indian education, was dispatched to Louisiana to evaluate the status of the Marksville Indian community as well as the Houmas. Unfortunately Underhill's report was riddled with historical, linguistic, and ethnological inaccuracies, and she approached the tribe with a palpable skepticism. Underhill only stayed with the group for five days, and her level of understanding reflected this. She failed to appreciate the deep connection of the people and their culture to place and did not challenge the oppressive local conditions from which the people sought relief. Moreover, she envisioned the Tunicas' problems as predominantly racial, when in fact they emerged from both their racial status and their status as an indigenous nation in a colonial society. To the tribe's detriment, Underhill's initial impressions represented the official version of Tunica history and culture in the Office of Indian Affairs, and in her report she would contribute to the ongoing racial and colonial oppression of the tribe in various ways.

To begin with, Underhill claimed that the Tunicas were "obviously much mixed with other Indians, negroes, and whites. The people of Marksville class them socially as negroes and allude to them as Redbones, or negroes with Indian ancestry."[59] It is true that they had mixed much with other Indians, some whites, and a few blacks by 1938,[60] but this characterization of them as a group with an ambiguous identity leaves the impression that they were not a legitimate Indian tribe, and therefore not worthy of any assistance from the Office of Indian Affairs. This is the impression that Underhill's report made on the director of Indian education Willard W. Beatty, who, based on her report, described the Tunica-Biloxi Tribe as a "group also believed to be largely Indian, tho not quite so free of negro admixture as the Houma."[61] Underhill apparently took the social classification of the group by local non-Indians at face value, failing to grasp how locals deployed the term "Redbone" as a weapon that kept Indians subordinated to whites rather than as an accurate genealogical descriptor.

Accusations that the Tunicas were black undermined their claims to indigenous status and thus their claims to land and sovereignty. The racial epithet "Redbone," the origin of which is the subject of various inconclusive theories, implied that the person so called was racially impure, something like a mongrel.[62] Even though the term implies some degree of Indian ancestry, the significant connotation is that the people called Redbones are "really" black, meaning that they cannot "really" be classified as Indians. Marksville whites knew this when they referred to the Tunicas as Redbones, and Underhill should have known this too. Using the term was a means of disempowering Tunicas by erasing their indigenous legal and political status and highlighting their racial status. Black or "colored" people did not have a collective right to the land or sovereignty under United States law. Indian tribes did.

Underhill also claimed that the tribe's "chief purpose in inquiring about land claims was to inquire if they could sell the 127 acres they occupy" because they were "desirous of leaving Marksville where their children are excluded from school and where they are treated as negroes."[63] Again, Underhill's lack of understanding comes through. The Tunicas were undoubtedly inquiring about securing title to the land that they occupied and adjacent land lost to Moreau in the 1840s, but it is much more likely that the land they wanted to sell was the land lost at Bayou Rouge Prairie and the so-called Bosra claim, which they had expressed interest in selling during their recent trip to Washington so that they could make improvements on the land in Marksville.[64] Among tribal members only Joseph Pierite Sr.'s three children were school-aged at the time. Underhill said that Pierite was planning to send his children to Texas to live with his sister and attend white schools, but he never did, despite Underhill's advice that he should. There was apparently a dispute divided along Barbry and Pierite family lines, with the Pierites in favor of maintaining the land and tribal traditions instead of selling the land and moving to Texas for the sake of educational opportunities.[65] Since Pierite was in a faction opposed to moving the tribe to Texas, the statement's accuracy is debatable. Some of the group did want to leave Marksville for Houston or elsewhere in East Texas, but to say that the group was "desirous of leaving Marksville" ignored the misgivings that the tribe had over what must have been a glum proposition for them. One of the chief purposes of the initial visit to Washington a month earlier had been to find some funding or have land confirmed to the tribe so that the Texas émigrés could move back to Marksville, so Underhill is clearly missing or ignoring some of the tribe's sentiments.

"All the young people," Underhill wrote, "are anxious to move to Houston, Texas, where they will be free of racial discrimination and feel they will have a better chance. Unless they can be content with their present very meagre scale of living, this seems the best plan, for Marksville is a small town with limited opportunities for work and with very strong color prejudice. Before moving they wish information as to their rights to sell the land or possible money aid."[66] This statement is more accurate, since it mentions some of the forces at work on the tribe, and specifies that the young people were the ones most interested in leaving. Certainly they would have felt most keenly the lack of opportunity available to them in Marksville, since they had no real options there aside from tending to a few acres of land on a reservation that could not possibly support the entire tribe. Typical wanderlust and the romance of adventure among most young people must have been augmented by the dismal existence of an Indian in Marksville in the 1930s. Many tribal members did leave, but a core population refused to do so, and that is the best evidence of the sentiments left out of Underhill's report.

The Tunica-Biloxis relied on their land for subsistence, but what Underhill failed to understand was their deep attachment to the land in other ways.[67] The graves of their ancestors lay there, and these were central to the annual fête du blé (green corn ceremony) and community identity more broadly. The Trou' Poupone, a ritual diving pool said to be where the Avoyelles people emerged from underground, lay there in the Coulee des Grues. Nearby were the Marksville Mounds, where archaeologists dug up graves with impunity in the early 1930s against the wishes of the tribe, and the resulting state park allowed visitors to walk over the gravesites, again over the objections of the tribe.[68] Ongoing racism and colonialism constantly pressed at a strong Tunica connection to place, and by 1938 they had been fighting for over 150 years to keep their land.[69] Their traditions existed only with their own people, and that small patch of land that still belonged to them was central to their collective sense of self. With fewer than fifty tribal members at the time, they saw their traditions acutely endangered. If the Tunicas had left their land in 1938, their political connection to that land, to each other, and to the United States government would have been irrevocably changed. If Underhill saw any of the agony that must surely have gripped the Tunicas as they faced the possibility of leaving their land, she did not report it.

Underhill's report reflects her skeptical approach to the tribe. She offered no hope that the federal government would recognize the tribe or offer any tribal services. Whether her report was based strictly on her assessment of the tribe or on an order to err on the side of nonrecognition mandated before her investigation began is not clear. It is likely some combination of the two, since it would have been odd for the bureau to expend resources on the trip if it had *no* intention of offering aid regardless of the tribe's status. In any case no real aid was ever offered to the tribe. Instead of finding a way to help the Tunica-Biloxis stay in their traditional homes and facilitate a return of tribal members from Texas, Underhill encouraged them to move to Houston and essentially give up their tribal status, their aboriginal sovereignty, and their cultural ties to each other and their homeland. She placed little value on Tunica-Biloxi tribalism, partly because she did not believe the Tunica-Biloxis to be much of a tribe in the first place, and partly because she valued education and material comfort over what she viewed as quasi-tribal persistence. Her report reflected a belief that Indians as such were on a steady road to extinction, and that the best course of action for the Indian office and "friends of the Indian" was to help them assimilate into American society as painlessly as possible. Fortunately, Tunicas envisioned a different future for their people.

Anthropology at the time of Underhill's report was still heavily focused on "salvage anthropology," which relied on interviews with the oldest people in a tribe to find out what life was like when Indians presumably had less contact with whites, while ignoring contemporary racial and political issues that the tribes faced. While the products of salvage work could be valuable to tribes such as the Tunicas as they prepared their federal recognition petitions in the late twentieth century or tried to revive tribal languages, it had major ideological shortcomings that were central to the problems with Underhill's report: salvage anthropology constructed Indian cultural forms of the past as more "authentic" than cultural forms of the present, a logic that made cultural assimilation a justification for political assimilation. Underhill and other anthropologists were trying to grasp Indian cultures of the late nineteenth century through the memories of living informants, believing that modern Indian tribes were being too heavily influenced to be considered discrete cultures any longer. Her report suggests that she saw the Tunica-Biloxis as nearly assimilated, uneducated remnants of tribes in need of a final push toward Americanization, and saw no need for the federal government to help them hold on to their besieged tribal culture. Contrary to the suggestion that they emigrate, however, staying in their homeland and maintaining tribal sovereignty was the most important investment they could have made in their future, not only for its eventual material and political value but for its spiritual and emotional value as well.

Whatever the cause of Underhill's decisions, the effect was that the Tunica-Biloxis still had no federal recognition or federal assistance of any kind. It must be said that not all anthropologists were from the same mold as Underhill. As noted earlier, Mary Haas, Robert Neitzel, Caroline Dormon, John Swanton, and Frank Speck were friends and advocates of Louisiana tribes.[70] They understood, respected, and helped tribal members as fellow human beings rather than merely as objects of study,[71] according to John Barbry, who also cites them as indispensable in the Tunica-Biloxi recognition efforts, since their work helped document the strength of the community in the first half of the twentieth century.

Underhill's report probably grew out of—and ultimately contributed to—a renewed sentiment in the Office of Indian Affairs that the federal government should stay out of Indian affairs in Louisiana. Willard Beatty expressed concern in 1939 about the extent of OIA involvement there. In discussing whether to offer educational funds for the Houmas, he did not openly question their identity as an Indian tribe. Rather, he noted that though the federal government had initially granted funds for the education of the Coushattas, it now seemed to be on the hook for various other kinds of aid to the Coushatta tribe as well. "I don't doubt [that the Coushattas need other kinds of aid], but it certainly means that if we are going ahead with this program [of educational funds for the Houmas], expenses will far exceed those of mere education. I suggest a conference for the exploration of our obligation to the Louisiana Indians."[72] No doubt Beatty meant a conference to determine how best to exclude Louisiana Indians permanently from the federal domain.

Within two weeks Fred Daiker would confirm the outcome of that conference in a patronizing letter to the Tunica subchief Horace Pierite:

Here and there throughout the United States there are people who have Indian blood and who can trace their ancestry back to Indian tribes. However, it is not always possible for the Federal Government to help these people because their tribes were never taken under the protection of the United States Government. Such remnants of tribes can be found in various southern states and along the Atlantic Coast, all the way to the State of Maine. Nobody doubts that their descendants are Indian, but it is not possible to spend money in their behalf. When Congress appropriates money for Indian use, that money must be spent in accordance with recognized laws. The Commissioner of Indian Affairs is guided by those laws, and he is not free to follow his own judgment and use the money in behalf of any Indian who happens to appeal to him for help.[73]

Underhill's assessment of the tribe's composition clearly held sway in a bureau already disinclined to spend money in Louisiana.

Although Underhill's report was couched in academic terms and used a passive voice that made it sound objective, it largely reflected the racial and colonial thinking of the era, as might be expected. It provides an early example of how a misleading academic evaluation could be combined with political expediency to make an unjust federal recognition decision, and it is a reminder that current academic assessments in the recognition process are probably affected by similar kinds of racial and colonial thinking, though these are more difficult to see without the benefit of historical distance. When these assessments are combined with politically expedient decisions at the federal level, the result is significant harm to indigenous communities.

Eli Barbry appealed to the BIA twice more over the next year and a half after the tribe received the rejection letter from Daiker, still insisting that his tribe had a right to federal services and protections. Zimmerman rejected his overtures, and Barbry never corresponded with the bureau thereafter.[74] Perhaps he felt it was inappropriate to burden federal resources during wartime, or perhaps he finally gave up on the federal government. In either case members of the tribe eased him out of office in 1947 because they tired of his efforts to move the tribe to Texas. They replaced him with Horace Pierite Sr., who favored keeping the tribe in place while seeking aid and federal recognition of its sovereignty.[75]

## CHAPTER 3

# Tunica Activism from the Termination Era to the Self-Determination Era

Horace Pierite quickly renewed tribal efforts for recognition and federal assistance upon his election as chief, contacting officials at the Chitimacha School and the Choctaw Agency in Philadelphia, Mississippi, in 1948 and 1949. After a visit from Chief Horace Pierite and his nephew, Subchief Joe Pierite Sr., the Choctaw agency superintendent, A. H. McMullen, conceded that Tunica-Biloxis "have within their veins more Indian blood than many of the now recognized Indians that our government now has jurisdiction over," but his letter stating that opinion to the commissioner of Indian affairs, William Zimmerman, had no effect, coming as it did at the beginning of the termination era.[1]

Still, the visit with McMullen was not in vain. Horace and Joe Pierite had approached the Marksville school board before their visit with McMullen, in an unsuccessful attempt to obtain the admission of tribal children into white Marksville schools. According to Rose Pierite White, after McMullen heard their story he wrote to, and later met with, the Avoyelles Parish school board, imploring them to allow Tunica children into white schools.[2] How he negotiated his proposition is unclear, but Tunica children—at least those without African ancestry—began attending white schools in 1948. Tunica-Biloxi enrollment in white schools did not so much signal an end to racism against tribal members as a growing shift in discourse and ideology around the Indian past and future in white society, but educational integration marked one of the first significant victories of the twentieth century. It meant that the tribe finally began to reap the benefits of its activism after years of efforts that bore little fruit.

A few years later, in 1951, another local attorney wrote on the Tunicas' behalf to Senator Russell B. Long, arguing that "if they are not under the jurisdiction of Interior they should be brought thereunder even tho it takes an Act of Congress."[3] Senator Long had requested federal recognition for the tribe a year earlier, but no action was taken by the Office of Indian Affairs.[4] The mood in Washington at the time was decidedly anti-tribal, and the termination era provided no reason for federally nonrecognized tribes to believe that requests for recognition or assistance would be met with approval. The Tunica-Biloxi federal recognition campaign seemingly went on hiatus during this time, but tribal leadership continued to work for the tribe in other ways.

In 1955 Chief Horace Pierite Sr. died and was succeeded by his subchief, Joe Pierite Sr., without an election.[5] The tribal recognition petition and the OFA evaluation of tribal history indicate that this period marked a gap in political and diplomatic efforts, but only because some types of efforts were overlooked. Chief Joseph Pierite continued politicking on a local level, if not the federal level. He encouraged tribal members to participate in local activities and educated people as much as possible about his tribe's history. In this spirit he designated his daughter Rose as tribal princess for the celebration of Marksville's sesquicentennial in 1959.[6] She was eighteen or nineteen years old at the time, and the first tribal member to graduate from an Avoyelles Parish high school.[7] Her father believed that this made her ideal as a goodwill ambassador for the tribe and as an assistant in his recognition efforts. In Rose, Chief Joe (as he was called) had a person who had not only the ability to read and research the many documents establishing the details of tribal history for their recognition case but also an unshakable commitment to justice for the tribe that could not be duplicated by the various friends who had helped the tribe over the years.

Of course the chief was the primary tribal ambassador, but he often made his family a part of his politicking. In 1961 he and his three daughters appeared on a television show in Alexandria, Louisiana, dressed in "Indian" regalia. Appearing with them was the amateur archaeologist Michel Smith, who had recently conducted the first archaeological dig on the reservation.[8] Rose Pierite White referred to the program as a "preview" show, intended to give exposure to local organizations and their causes. They were trying to achieve state recognition as an Indian tribe at the time, and her father considered an appearance on the show part of an effort to generate public support for their cause.[9]

According to his longtime friend, the anthropologist Pete Gregory, Chief Joe always knew that the tribe had indigenous sovereignty and acted that way. For him it was just a matter of convincing the federal government of that fact. Chief Joe told a story that Gregory believed conveyed his firm belief in the tribe's sovereignty. "Once, the chief had a message to send to the sun," Pierite said. "So the chief gave the message to the eagle, who flew to the place in the sky where the sun lived. The sun was so pleased that she plucked a feather from the eagle's tail, and kissed it, leaving a scorched spot. She gave the feather back to the eagle to take home to the Tunica people, and told us to wear it always." With that feather the sun sent an assurance that the tribe would persist. "We have a promise from the sun. As long as there is the sun, there will be Indian people. As long as there are Indian people, we will have the medicine."[10] Gregory suggests that "the medicine" ought to be understood as power, akin to sovereignty in that it implied strength, well-being, and healing.

Always sure of his tribe's sovereignty, Pierite began testing the federal waters again by 1965. He enlisted the support of Representative Speedy O. Long in this endeavor to renew the tribe's crusade for federal recognition. Long wrote to Secretary of the Interior Stewart Udall in 1965, asking him to send the commissioner of Indian affairs Graham Holmes to Marksville to "meet with Chief Joe Pierite of the Tunica Indians and discuss the various possibilities of securing federal financing and to assist the Tunica Indians in any way possible."[11] Holmes expressed the continued favor that termination policy had within the bureau at that late date. "Current policy in Indian Affairs," he stated, "is to promote the social and economic development of Indian tribal groups under our jurisdiction so that, as rapidly as possible, they may become independent of their special relationships with the Federal Government."[12] While once again nothing came of this effort, it indicates the patience and determination of the Tunica-Biloxi Tribe's leadership. The members of the tribe understood themselves as a sovereign entity (even if that particular term never crossed their lips), and therefore they continued to seek acknowledgment of that fact from the outside world.

Chief Joe Pierite finally made a contact that would lead somewhere in 1967, when he communicated with Vine Deloria Jr., then executive director of the National Congress of American Indians. Because of the NCAI's central position in Indian politics at the time, to have Deloria's ear was deeply meaningful for the tribe. Deloria was one of the most outspoken intellectuals in American Indian law, policy, and philosophy throughout his career, and at the time the Tunicas contacted him, he was just emerging onto the national political landscape.

Chief Pierite contacted Deloria at the suggestion of state and federal officials as he continued his search for avenues to federal recognition, and Deloria thought that the tribal history aptly illustrated the injustice of non-recognition and the tenacity of tribes persisting outside the federal domain. Deloria laid out his philosophical commitment to federally nonrecognized communities in his seminal manifesto *Custer Died for Your Sins*, naming the Tunicas specifically in the final chapter.[13] The tribe gained a national audience aware of its status and its validation by an important figure in Indian politics. Through this contact the Tunicas became members of the NCAI for a number of years and came into contact with the national Indian leadership. More importantly, Deloria and the NCAI vouched for the tribe at the national level and consistently supported its recognition efforts.[14]

Deloria advised the Tunicas on matters related to federal recognition, advocated for them, and introduced them to people and organizations that could help. As a result of these connections they became involved with the Coalition of Eastern Native Americans (CENA), a short-lived entity formed in December 1972 that organized unrecognized tribes all over the South and East, lobbied on their behalf, and provided technical assistance to help them achieve recognition and funding at various levels, as well as pressuring the federal government to maintain Indian policies that applied equally to Indians in the East, the West, and urban centers.[15] Rose Pierite White attended the organizational conference as a tribal delegate and became a CENA board member for the next three years.

Attending with White were several other Louisiana Indians, among them Sarah Peralta, a woman of Apache heritage who in 1969 founded an Indian political activist group and aid society called the Indian Angels.[16] Modeling themselves after other urban Indian organizations such as the American Indian Movement (AIM) and Indians of All Tribes, Peralta and the Indian Angels, like the better-known urban Indian activist groups that they imitated, expertly manipulated the media for political ends. Operating out of the state capital in Baton Rouge, they spun images of beaded, moccasin-wearing, pseudo-radical minorities that resonated with public sympathies of the day. Chief Pierite must have appreciated the tack, considering that he had a habit of appearing in a headdress at public events, and that he had started a "trading post" and mini-museum on the reservation in 1968 as an educational and public relations effort.[17] His son, Joe Pierite Jr., carried on his tradition of making public relations and education an important mission of tribal leadership.[18] The Indian Angels and the Tunicas each appreciated the importance of a broader public political campaign that would support their goals by generating public sympathy.[19]

Although some state Indians—the Coushatta tribe in particular—did not esteem the group very highly, the Indian Angels inspired state Indians to assert their identities more strongly. Their meetings were always intertribal, and they tried at least to incorporate all the state's Indian communities into their efforts. They encouraged a spirit of activism and cooperation among Louisiana Indians through meetings, powwows, newsletters, and educational efforts. If nothing else, they forced the tribes to speak to the press and the press to pay attention to the tribes in ways that they had not done previously. The Indian Angels remained active in state Indian politics into the early 1980s, when the death of Sarah Peralta essentially ended its viability. The group's effectiveness had begun to wane long before that time, however, as various tribally based coalitions and governmental offices supplanted its high media profile.

The governor's Office of Indian Affairs (LOIA), created by Governor Edwin Edwards in 1972 as part of a campaign promise to support people of color, tussled with the Indian Angels for domination of state Indian politics in the early 1970s.[20] For various reasons the state Indian affairs official Ernest Sickey did not see eye to eye with the Indian Angels. Sickey and many members of the culturally conservative Coushatta tribe did not approve of what they viewed as gaudy public demonstrations by "questionable" urban Indians who claimed to represent Indian opinion in the state. The Coushattas preferred to gain access to power by having their own leaders approach the appropriate authorities and discuss policies for their own tribe, government to government. The Indian Angels, on the other hand, balked at the Coushatta tribe's apparent willingness to work with white authorities in the established power structure, and read their disapproval of radical activism and public demonstrations as a lack of outward pride in their Indian ancestry.[21]

The Tunica-Biloxi Tribe did work with the Indian Angels, but it began to move more toward groups that were tribally focused, such as the LOIA and CENA, and a newly formed group, the Inter-Tribal Council of Louisiana. Whereas the Indian Angels' basic unit of membership was the individual Indian person, intertribal alliances established the tribe as the basic membership unit, reflecting an investment in political strategies based in powerful government-to-government relationships. Intertribal alliances provided opportunities for tribal leaders to communicate about the problems they were facing and the means they were employing to overcome them, acknowledging the commonalities between tribes but at the same time promoting the singular sovereignty vested in each tribe as a political entity as the most effective way to achieve power. The Tunicas supported each kind of organization and appreciated the high profile that groups such as the Indian Angels gave to Indian issues in general, but their vision and needs more consistently meshed with the tribally based organizations.

The chairman of CENA, a Lumbee named W. J. Strickland, visited the tribe on a number of occasions in late 1973 in an effort to help it organize for recognition. On one occasion both he and Vine Deloria Jr. visited with the group while an ABC News crew documented the visit for a series of segments "dealing with the contributions of minorities to our society."[22] Strickland and Deloria likely steered the tribe away from the Indian Angels to some extent too. Strickland told the tribe during one meeting, "The demonstration route does not solve anything."[23] Deloria was not as subdued in his assessment of public political confrontations: "We can handle things much more peaceably and much more efficiently by working behind the scenes, by having the documents and by going step by step, than . . . than we can with a whole bunch of shouting and screaming. [Tribal claims] can be handled in a much better and much easier way, in a way that you have the white people in this community and in the neighboring area supporting you and not against you."[24] The Tunicas had been trying for years to cultivate relationships with local, state, and federal officials and had had some success, although recognition had not yet been attained. Deloria and Strickland reinforced the validity of their methods, and with the added voice of Ernest Sickey probably made the Tunicas wary of continuing to work with the Indian Angels. Federal recognition continued to be the Tunicas' primary goal, so the Indian Angels became essentially irrelevant to their plans. Based on the advice of a new generation of Indian leaders, they set aside their frustrations with the past inability of politicians to achieve anything substantial for them.

## State Recognition

Ernest Sickey's main concern, and therefore the main concern of the Louisiana Office of Indian Affairs, was organizing tribes to help them attain recognition, with the long-term goal of developing tribal economies so that

Indians could make a living in their home communities. The LOIA had helped organize the Coushattas and assisted their recognition efforts with the BIA under David Garrison, a non-Indian who had limited familiarity with Indian people and who had been appointed commissioner of Indian affairs for Louisiana in 1972. He consulted with the Coushattas immediately after his appointment, and based on their advice he made organization and recognition of the Coushattas one of his first goals. He obtained legal assistance to have the tribe incorporated under Louisiana law, making it eligible to receive funding, and then helped the tribe file for recognition with the BIA.[25] The tribe elected Ernest Sickey chairman under the new charter, and Garrison quickly made Sickey his vice-commissioner.[26] Sickey became the driving force behind the commission even before he was appointed director of the Office of Indian Affairs.

The successes of Sickey and the Office of Indian Affairs were measured. Sickey held an appointed position as director of the LOIA and controlled a very limited state budget of about $18,000, most of which paid his own salary. He arranged for technical assistance for tribes and held meetings among the tribal leadership. He administered all the Indian funding from the Comprehensive Employment Training Act (CETA),[27] totaling $500,000, which paid salaries to tribal members around the state to do work for their tribes. With the assistance of CENA and the precedent set by his own tribe, he helped the Tunicas incorporate in 1974 and backed state legislation to recognize the tribe a year later.[28]

Louisiana Indians enthusiastically supported the Louisiana Office of Indian Affairs and the Governor's Commission on Indian Affairs in their conception, but by 1976 the usefulness of state efforts for tribes began to be questioned. Helen Gindrat, chairperson of the Houma Tribe, contended that "when it was established, it sounded terrific. . . . But it seems like along the way that a million and one things happened." The commission, while trying to help the tribes, became a sort of burden as well. Gindrat testified that communication was poor, the technical assistance often confusing, and the meetings hard to travel to, and that the leaders had to pay for their food and travel out of their own pockets. They went for two years at one point without convening the board of directors for the Commission on Indian Affairs, which had only been in existence for four years. There were no funds to facilitate programs, there was no direction, and confusion ran rampant.[29] It seems that only when Sickey personally involved himself in a tribe's efforts was the state able to have any effect. Sickey resigned from the Office of Indian Affairs in

1975 to devote more time to his duties as chairman of the tribal council for the recently federally recognized Coushattas, and with little political weight and extremely limited funding, the role of the office has dwindled further since that time.

Perhaps the most important outside organization to help the Tunica-Biloxi Tribe achieve recognition was the Institute for the Development of Indian Law. Vine Deloria Jr. and Kirke Kickingbird founded the Institute in 1973 in an effort to research treaties and federal Indian policies, educate tribes about their rights, and guide tribes in their dealings with the federal government. As part of that effort they wanted to bring to national attention instances when the federal government had neglected not only its own Indian policies but its constitutional obligations under treaties. The Tunica-Biloxi Tribe was "an outstanding example" of this neglect because of its documented status as a distinct Indian tribe with a continued existence and a history of suffering repeatedly for the federal government's failure to protect its rights as an Indian tribe.[30]

After a series of community meetings, many of them held at a livestock auction house called the Cow Palace near where the Tunica-Biloxi casino now stands, the Tunicas incorporated as a nonprofit organization in October 1974 and elected a governing body similar to that of a federal tribal council's or nonprofit organization's board of directors, following the advice of the Institute for the Development of Indian Law, CENA, and the LOIA. They elected four council members, from whom the council then named Joe Pierite Jr. as the first tribal chairman; his sister, Rose Pierite White, as the first tribal secretary; Horace Pierite Jr., whose father had been chief before Joe Pierite Sr., as vice-chairman; and Sam Barbry Sr., the son of Eli Barbry, who was married to Horace Pierite Jr.'s sister, as the sole councilman. By 1978 another councilman was added, with two more added since. As in many small tribes, tribal government is a family affair, with members of the tribal council closely related to one another and their predecessors. Chief Joe Pierite Sr., who was old and frail by the time the council was organized, approved of the change in governmental form since his son and daughter, Joe Jr. and Rose, had more or less assumed most of his duties by that time anyway.

The tribe incorporated to become eligible to apply for and administer grants and to make it easier to achieve recognition from the State of Louisiana and eventually the federal government. Formal reorganization affected how the Tunica tribe ran its internal affairs less than it affected other tribes; electing leaders was nothing new, since the tribe had been electing chiefs and subchiefs since time out of mind. The chairman took on the responsibilities that the chief had had formerly, the biggest difference being that he had a formalized council working with him and had to seek reelection at regular intervals. According to the tribe's petition for recognition, the new arrangement, with a chairman and council, merely "institutionalized the role family heads had traditionally played in the tribe."[31] Chairman Pierite described the power structure of the tribe as very decentralized: "We don't actually like to think that we control anyone," he said, "but we'd like to think in a way of that we're working for them because they thought enough to . . . make us their leader; and at any time that we have any discussion on different matters, we bring it to the floor and let the body know just exactly what's going on because so many tribes have took it on their own—their council have taken it on their own—just go ahead and do for the people and later on it wasn't what the people expect. So, I feel certain, as the chairman, in working with the council, if we get into trouble, let's all get in trouble at the same time. And we have rules and regulations within our bylaws that we can work by and work with. And this always was within a tribe discussion."[32] Traditional leadership styles—where groups of family leaders made decisions and enlisted one from among them to represent those decisions to outsiders—remained strong within the tribe even after the reorganization of the government.

Ernest Sickey, through his role as director of the Louisiana Office of Indian Affairs, helped the newly reorganized Tunica-Biloxi Tribe write a recognition bill and guide it through the state legislature in 1975. State recognition was moderately useful for the tribe, in that it provided a small degree of validation and made it eligible for a number of federal Indian programs not housed within the Bureau of Indian Affairs, which had in place restrictions on the service population that other agencies did not. The Tunica-Biloxis became eligible for and eventually received a grant from HUD to build a community center in which they held community meetings. Avoyelles Parish received Title IV Indian Education funds for Tunica children totaling $8,500 through the Department of Health, Education and Welfare before recognition, though that money did not go directly to the tribe.[33] The tribe participated occasionally in Indian Manpower programs under CETA, but again, it was eligible for those even before recognition because of how the laws were written at that time. State recognition remains a critical component of tribal well-being for many tribes in the petitioning process, because states have the flexibility to recognize tribes that are not perfectly documented, allowing something like a probationary or intermediate form of recognition.

Old home of Joseph Pierite Sr. on the Tunica-Biloxi reservation, 2004. Recognition brought a few new houses to the reservation. Photo by the author.

Still, the Tunica-Biloxi Tribe's primary needs were not being met. Most tribal members went without health care. Tunica homes on the reservation were small and dangerously dilapidated, often without running water. The Tunicas did not own enough land to support tribal members, because the federal government had not upheld their rights to their original land base, which eventually prompted many tribal members to look elsewhere for work. Modest educational funds went to the parish instead of the tribe, and since the tribe was terribly educated to begin with because of past segregation, it needed extra funds specifically appropriated to help make up lost ground. Economic opportunities were minimal, so tribal members struggled to make a living in their home community.

The tribe was sustaining cultural damage as a result of nonrecognition, as well. The local mound complex had not only been excavated but made into a state park that allowed visitors to stroll over gravesites, even though the tribe asked the park managers to keep visitors off the mounds.[34] The state put in a dam project along the Coulee des Grues that eroded some of the tribe's already small plot of land and drained a ritual diving pool.[35] A local treasure hunter looted the graves of an eighteenth-century Tunica village and was trying to sell the artifacts to the highest bidder.[36] Federal recognition could not solve all these problems outright, but the Tunica-Biloxis hoped that it could endow them with rights that they could invoke to protect themselves as a tribe. The political status associated with state recognition did not approximate the benefits of federal recognition as a sovereign tribe in the 1970s.

Ernest Downs, a researcher from the Institute for the Development of Indian Law, worked closely with the tribe over four years to help compile a solid petition for federal recognition. Downs's research was crucial to the tribe's recognition case. The tribe had been trying for years to win federal services through predominantly political channels. The perennial stumbling block was that they had never had a thorough, accurate documentation of their history. The only information that Washington had was John Sibley's paragraph-long report from 1806 and Ruth Underhill's report from 1938. Sibley's report hardly gave reason to recognize the tribe, and Underhill's was laden with inaccuracies and barely touched the historical records. Without substantial paper documentation and written arguments to validate its claims, the tribe lacked the trump card needed to attain recognition.

Since tribal members were denied education for so long and were therefore almost entirely illiterate until after the Second World War, they had no way of doing their own research. Rose Pierite White, as the first Tunica high school graduate from the Marksville community in 1960, was able to do important work for the tribe, especially during the time she spent at the Smithsonian's archives in the American Indian Cultural Resources Training Program in 1974, but partnership with the Institute for the Development of Indian Law cannot be underestimated. An exchange between the tribal council chairman Joe Pierite Jr., Ernest Downs, and the AIPRC Task Force on Terminated and Nonfederally Recognized Indians demonstrates the significance of combined efforts from tribal members and their educated assistant from a highly competent Indian legal research organization. Pierite had never attended school and could not read but was encouraged by his father to take up the crusade for tribal recognition. When the AIPRC panel asked Downs whether the informal Tunica reservation was from a Spanish land grant, Downs replied with a statement revealing his understanding of the subtleties of Indian law. "I wouldn't call it a Spanish land grant, because the land is Indian land. It was in their hunting territory. They own it now as they owned other land prior to de Soto . . . I think Joe [Pierite Jr.] has something to add to this."

Pierite commented, "We still recognize it as a Spanish grant, I mean, as far as when we come in to talk to people. We always bring that in because it's tax-free land. It's never been taxed. And it must be something to it, because the town of Marksville many years ago—I'll say as far back as twenty years ago—they've been trying to incorporate further than where the reservation is. But the reservation is run sort of like this [demonstrates with hands], and then the incorporation comes this far. And they could go . . . another mile or two to incorporate the town, which would enlarge the town more than it is now. Because of the land that we own, they won't come past the reservation. So [there] must be something to that." Pierite went to a blackboard to draw an explanatory map, and Downs continued the conversation about the Spanish land grants: "It's certainly true that there is a Spanish grant to that land, but the Tunicas' title does not rely on the Spanish government."

Pierite completed the map of the reservation boundary with the town along the Coulee des Grues and continued to make his point: "[Downs] mentioned something about the Coulee des Grues was running something along this line here. I'm not too much a good artist at drawing, but giving you an idea that the incorporation and the town comes no further than this [the boundary of the reservation]. This is where the line stops [any further] incorporation. Something . . . there's got to be something to this, because if this wasn't Indian land, they would have by now, after so many years, would have brought that incorporation out. Now, they have tried, but then they can't go beyond Indian property. It's got to be something to that. Chuck might could add something to it."

With the issues clear to him, Downs blithely added, "That's all correct." The confused panel asked for interpretation. Downs explained: "One of the things that demonstrates the fact that the Tunica title to the 130 acres is clear and legally acceptable is the fact that the town of Marksville has never extended its own corporate limits into the Tunica village. It always maintained the Tunica village line as its own boundaries."[37]

This exchange demonstrates the overwhelming disadvantages that people with little formal education must surmount to successfully make their case for recognition. Outside legal help was an absolute necessity for the Tunicas because of the handicap placed on the tribe by illiteracy and being denied access to education. Joe Pierite Jr. could not express the Tunica case to members of the AIPRC panel in terms that were clear to them and legally sustainable, but he did have a thorough enough understanding of his tribe's history to point out instances where their existence as a distinct tribal entity was confirmed by local practices. He needed to collaborate with the representative of the Institute for the Development of Indian Law to effectively convey that knowledge, though, and make a case for federal recognition. Participation in the broader Indian movement and national Indian organizations allowed this small tribe to effectively challenge the federal government's long neglect of its sovereignty.

Of course tribal involvement with other Indian organizations was pivotal to Tunica-Biloxi recognition efforts, but the efforts always began with Tunica-Biloxi initiative. Ernest Downs, Sarah Peralta, W. J. Strickland, and Vine Deloria Jr. were only part of the picture. Tribal leadership by Joe Pierite Sr., Rose Pierite White, Joe Pierite Jr., Earl Barbry Sr., and others before them was always at the center of the movement for Tunica-Biloxi sovereignty. Even when they sought the advice, technical assistance, and advocacy of outsiders, it was the tribal leaders' own knowledge and ambition that lay at the heart of the drive for recognition. At the same time, willpower was never enough. The national Indian movement that flourished in the early 1970s and a few key members of that movement finally provided the opportunities that made Tunica-Biloxi recognition possible.

Reflecting on that history in 1976, Joe Pierite Jr. talked about the attorneys the tribe had hired and the people who had helped them over the years:

> Most of the time we had to chip in and get the money. And there was times that the lawyer would charge so much and we could come up with the amount he wanted, and he'd do just so much of the work. And then that was the end of the line as far as continuing with us.[38] It's been through history, those are the kinds of things that we have been doing. . . . When the Institute [for the Development of Indian Law] start working with us, it's been more effective. And Rose [Pierite] has done a lot of research and supplying some of these things, materials. . . . And those are the kinds of people that we really appreciate that could do something for us. And then, they'll say, well now here we've gotten through this great wall, there's no more, no further I can do for you, nothing else . . . Not only to the Tunicas. I would think that all tribes had the same problem when they come to this wall and there was nothing anybody could do. It left a sad thing for them going back home to forget it. And maybe two or three years later, someone else would come through and say I could do this for you. They would trust them, and see just how much they could do for them. Some of them was very successful in getting things done. Some of them wasn't. But, however, we had to ride those ups and downs ourselves.[39]

Fighting for recognition had been a long, sometimes lonely journey. Supporters and detractors came and went, but a steadfast vision of Tunica tribalism at the center motivated successive generations toward the same goal.

*The Final Phase of Tunica Federal Recognition Activism*

Developments outside the Tunica realm in the mid-1970s made it increasingly likely that the Tunicas would be recognized soon. The Task Force 10 report on terminated and federally nonrecognized Indians brought the issues faced by federally nonrecognized tribes into clearer focus. It recommended that the distinctions between federally nonrecognized tribes and federally recognized tribes be erased immediately, but the BIA demurred at the thought of letting any group claiming to be a tribe have federal services. The bureau conceded that legitimate tribes not currently served had a right to be federally recognized, though, so it worked on developing a formal procedure that would allow tribes a well-defined means of demonstrating their tribal status and petitioning for federal recognition. The BIA had already been developing the procedures by the time the task force report was released, based not only on the information collected by the task force but also on the results of the *Passamaquoddy* case in Maine and growing pressure from Indian organizations and federally nonrecognized groups across the country.

The Tunica-Biloxis had been anticipating federal recognition for years. They continued to gather information and submit it to Washington without a clear timeline for a decision, but they were disappointed repeatedly. Without formal procedures it was unclear what kinds and levels of evidence would suffice, when decisions would be made, and who would make them. When Joe Pierite Jr. told a newspaper reporter in 1976 that he expected recognition during the bicentennial year, the BIA still did not know if it was even authorized to recognize tribes where no previous treaty or federal relationship existed.[40] Though the BIA had enough information to extend recognition to the tribe by 1976, it wanted to wait until new procedures were in place before it recognized any more tribes, and it wanted to wait until the AIPRC had concluded its reports and recommendations before making new procedures. The bureau wanted the Tunicas in particular to wait, because it wanted to push through the tribe's application early to prove that the procedures could work.[41]

The Tunica-Biloxis continued to garner support for their petition from politicians in Louisiana,[42] but strong support from state politicians became scarcer in the wake of the *Passamaquoddy* decision because states feared being named in similar lawsuits. In the mid-1970s state support for pro-tribal legislation remained politically fashionable in some areas, since it usually involved very little real sacrifice on the part of the state and could even bring an influx of federal money to non-Indian constituencies surrounding Indian populations. Once state resources were at stake, though, states began to withdraw their initial support for federal recognition of Indian tribes within their borders. States have played a central role in defending colonialism (and thus white supremacist ideology) in land claims suits, since they have so often defended thefts of indigenous lands by white settlers.

In Louisiana, Attorney General William Guste began backpedaling even before the Tunicas submitted their petition in 1978 under the new federal regulations. Guste's primary concern was that federal recognition would give Louisiana tribes standing to sue for land claims under the Indian Trade and Intercourse Acts—a standing he believed they would not have as federally nonrecognized tribes. Guste was "deeply concerned" with the potential for a number of land claim suits in Louisiana, so he kept close tabs on the recognition process. He cautioned the Department of the Interior, as if it were unaware, that recognition "would not be simply honorary but could very well represent the foundation for very serious, complicated and far-reaching land claims against Louisiana and / or private landowners." While he alleged that the state was "certainly not trying to deny recognition to any groups which have a legitimate right to such recognition," he urged the department to handle recognition "with great care and attention because of the rather grave consequences in the area of Indian land claims which this kind of federal recognition seems to involve."[43] Earlier in 1978 Guste had urged the state legislature to repeal or amend any legislation designating any Louisiana Indian groups as tribes because of the same concerns.[44]

While Guste claimed that he was not opposed to recognizing legitimate groups, the tone of his statements implies otherwise. He exhorted the Department of the Interior and the Louisiana legislature to err on the side of the states, and not to give tribes the benefit of the doubt. As attorney general he sought to protect his state just as any attorney would protect a client—winning, rather than justice, was the goal. The possibility that the Tunicas and other Louisiana tribes had valid rights to lands taken illegally did not deter him. In fact, knowledge that the Tunicas would have a viable claim motivated him in the first place. He issued preemptive strikes to prevent recognition so that the culpability of the state might never come to light.

Guste likely justified his actions based on a growing, misguided attitude in the state that certain recently incorporated groups were inauthentic opportunists trying to cash in on an Indian identity. Controversy over the "new" tribes made for fertile soil in which Guste could plant seeds of doubt about even well-established tribes such as the Tunicas.[45] He knew that if tribes were held to no longer exist, the State of Louisiana would be protected from having to answer for wrongs committed against tribes in the past. Guste's conduct is reminiscent of that of numerous other state officials across the country, before and after his time, who protected white and American power and property from indigenous claims.

Luckily for the Tunicas, Guste's efforts did not prevent thoughtful consideration of their petition in Washington. The tribe obviously invested a great deal of energy and resources in the petition and pinned many hopes on its success. Future funding to address problems plaguing the tribe, such as poor health care, low educational attainment, housing problems, and various other social issues associated with rural Indian poverty remained a major impetus for the tribe to seek recognition, but there was more at stake. Legal standing as a tribe changes the way courts approach a group, and as Guste anticipated, the tribe had been waiting until it attained recognition to pursue a land claim for over seventeen thousand acres. The estimated value of the land in 1981 ranged from $48 million to $150 million. It would be extremely helpful, the tribe and its attorneys believed, to have status as a federally recognized Indian tribe to remove any questions regarding the tribe's standing under the Indian Trade and Intercourse Acts.[46] The Mashpee tribe of Massachusetts had been denied standing to sue as an Indian tribe by a federal court in 1978 because it was not federally recognized at the time, and the Tunicas did not want their land claim to be dismissed in the same manner.[47]

In addition to the land claim, the tribe was waiting until it achieved federal status before intervening in another case in which the rights to a collection of pilfered tribal grave goods known as the Tunica Treasure were at stake.[48] Without federal recognition the Tunicas' standing as heirs and custodians of the goods could be questioned (maybe successfully, maybe not), but with recognition the tribe's standing would be established and unquestionable as far as the court was concerned. Thus although the trial for custody of the goods began in 1974, the Tunicas did not intervene until shortly after recognition in 1981. The Tunicas were just as much a tribe the day before federal recognition as they were the day after, but without federal determination of their status as a tribe, they were much more vulnerable in the case.

Earl Barbry Sr. became tribal chairman in 1978, after the petition for recognition developed under the previous administration had been submitted to the Bureau of Indian Affairs.[49] Just as all the previous tribal leaders had taken up the battle for recognition of the tribe's sovereignty, so did Barbry. Every year the tribe had to wait and each time the BIA denied that the Tunica-Biloxis existed as an Indian tribe, it fostered an increasing contempt by each new leader for bureau officials. By 1979, after 150 years of effort, continued federal nonrecognition bordered on the absurd.

Barbry saw the formalized recognition procedures as even more absurd than the previous hoops that the tribe had been forced to jump through in trying for recognition. "I guess there was a reason for it, but to us, it seemed rather ridiculous. You know, we knew we existed as a tribe. We knew who we were. And it's kind of frustrating that Indians are the only ones that have to prove who they are, where they came from, have to be assigned a number like an animal. I suppose that number's like a brand. It's rather insulting, as far as I'm concerned. In our tribe's case, I find it even more insulting when the Spanish, French, and British governments recognized our tribe—were allies of the Tunica-Biloxi—for years. And there's documentation to that effect: letters written by those governments acknowledging that the tribe existed as a nation and should be treated as such, with respect. Yet the United States government didn't see fit to recognize us—recognize our existence—until the 1980s."

Even with a petition that seemed rock solid, the bureau was unsatisfied. That OFA has to verify the details is understandable, but "verification" has been taken to inordinate levels because of the threat that states and sometimes other tribes feel tribal recognition poses to them.

The Office of Federal Acknowledgment acquiesced to pressure to extend the research period and place as many obstacles as possible on the road to recognition. "A lot of states have a lot invested in what we're going to do," conceded John "Bud" Shapard, who was in charge of the federal acknowledgment office at the time. Shapard helped to draft the original regulations and procedures and admitted that the process was deliberately protracted. "What we're trying to do is keep it on the table. We're talking about telling the states that some of their citizens are quasi-sovereign and [will] deal with the United States government rather than the state government. Now that's going to upset some states."[50]

There is a fine line between erring on the side of caution and trying to avoid recognizing tribes. OFA has crossed the line consistently, and Shapard's quote demonstrates one of several conflicts of interest inherent to the process. OFA knew the Tunica-Biloxis deserved recognition, but it continued to make them wait because it wanted to use them as a test case in the new process they had created. OFA took longer than necessary because it wanted to give the State of Louisiana the opportunity to produce any relevant information (presumably against the Tunica-Biloxis' case, since the two parties are competing entities in OFA regulations).[51] If justice delayed is justice denied, then the BIA's failure to immediately recognize the Tunica-Biloxis as early as 1976, when their petition was initially prepared, constituted a breach of ethics that would be unfortunately repeated on an ever grander scale while the Federal Acknowledgment Project (as it was initially called) continued. The federal government—particularly the Bureau of Indian Affairs—is charged through the Indian Trade and Intercourse Acts, the Snyder Act, and several Supreme Court decisions with a trust responsibility to protect the interests of Indian nations within its borders, and yet when the interests of the tribes conflict with the interests of the states or the federal government, that responsibility is too easily revised to accommodate decisions unfavorable to tribes. The plenary power concept so central to federal Indian law is of course premised on the priority of non-Indian rights over Indian rights, and the pattern of giving primacy to the needs of non-indigenous people over indigenous nations is evident in the recognition process as well. It is evident in the lack of attention to nonfederal tribes, in the practice of giving states a say in whether tribes are acknowledged, and in making nonfederal tribes bear the burden of nonrecognition even in cases where an initial assessment suggests that a tribe is legitimate.

For the Tunicas it took three years from the date they submitted their petition to OFA under the new regulations to the date they received federal recognition, which would be miraculously fast by today's standards. Nonetheless, the Tunicas had provided substantial historical documentation to the BIA as early as 1976 and had been requesting recognition for many years before that, so even three years seemed excessive at the time. The BIA kept asking for more and more documentation. Earl Barbry remembers that the bureau wanted "tons" of information: "It took years to compile everything that was asked. Once that was sent forward, we had to come back and provide additional information. We had to spend months and months in gathering information about each individual tribal member and how they were connected to this tribe." Barbry's statement reveals that like many other tribes forced to spend years without federal recognition, the Tunica-Biloxis found the need to provide genealogical documentation for the petition daunting, even though the tribe was very small in 1978. It had seemed that documenting the existence of a community and its historical leadership was the keystone of the recognition regulations, and that a community could decide for itself who was a member simply by stating so in its petition. One way of establishing membership according to the regulations, in fact, is to simply present "affidavits of recognition by tribal elders, leaders, or the tribal governing body, as being an Indian descendant of the tribe and a member of the petitioning entity."[52] And some of the early tribal rolls were based on lists of tribal members that were compiled from memory by tribal leaders and submitted to federal officials at several times during the twentieth century.

The genealogical issue highlights the impact of racial logic on tribal approaches to community membership and recognition. The federal government wanted paper documentation of births, marriages, and deaths, so that it could verify which individuals belonged to the tribe, whose political existence as a unit had been clearly established in the original petition. Once the existence of the polity is established, it should be entirely the prerogative of the polity to determine membership, but the need for extensive and redundant documentation of tribal membership compelled the Tunicas to use racially informed standards for regulating community boundaries—standards that more closely matched policy guidelines and racial logic used by OFA in evaluating the tribe's petition, as well as the racial logic of federal policy. At the time the petition was submitted, tribal members with African American ancestry were still excluded, as were those of less than one-quarter Tunica-Biloxi ancestry. While the tribe lowered the blood quantum requirement after recognition, and Earl Barbry followed through on a promise to Herman Pierite to end the exclusion of black tribal members,[53] Anglo racial expectations tied to recognition of indigeneity shaped the boundaries of tribal membership and created lingering memories of exclusion and betrayal within the tribe. Traditional membership regulation, which had formerly been adaptable enough to allow for influxes of people from other nations, gave way to less flexibility in decision making because of the need for recognition. Once federal recognition was attained, tribal leadership felt safe in removing restrictions on tribal membership based on African American ancestry and lowering the blood quantum threshold of Tunica-Biloxi ancestry to one-sixty-fourth, but even then federal recognition exerted its own pressures on community boundaries, as described in more detail below.

With so much clear evidence of community history in the original petition, Rose Pierite White also remembers constant puzzling requests for more genealogical information and other seemingly extraneous details. The tribe did not realize exactly what a professional genealogist would be looking for, and the OFA genealogical report speaks contemptuously of the problems that the tribe had in compiling genealogical charts for every tribal member. Rose Pierite White recalls that she and her brother, Joe Pierite Jr., and a handful of other core tribal members had fortunately been steeped in tribal history and social networks while growing up, so they could at least begin to formulate responses to the continued inquiries. Still, the process seemed to plod along tediously. If OFA had offered anything more than minimal guidance, the genealogy would have been completed much sooner, and perhaps the final evaluation could have been made sooner.

In addition to prolonging cases purposely with waiting periods, extensions, and response periods that typically last several years if not decades, OFA completes research slowly. While it is true, as Shapard argues, that "most people don't appreciate the time it takes to do historical and anthropological research," this claim is hardly sustainable considering that the majority of the historical research had already been completed by the Tunica-Biloxis before they submitted the petition and that the OFA anthropologist in the case only spent five days in Marksville. Even the genealogical reports should not have taken long with a tribe of two hundred members.

Shapard declared, "We've got to assure ourselves that their work is adequately done and not slanted. We simply want to verify what they've done, and see if there's any other data available."[54] OFA ambled through the process from September 1978, when the tribe submitted the very first petition under the new regulations, until September 1981, when the bureau finally officially acknowledged that the Tunica-Biloxis existed as an Indian tribe. It would be longer still before any benefits would arrive. Three years may not have seemed very long compared to the 175 years that the tribe had already waited, or even compared to the wait of twenty-plus years that other tribes would endure later in the process, but it was another three years unnecessarily wasted primarily because of bureaucratic regulations. The one great advantage of the ad hoc system that had been in place previously was that the secretary of Indian affairs could make a recognition decision much more quickly and easily and do the dirty work of compiling detailed genealogies after recognition. The Bureau of Indian Affairs started the entire recognition program on the wrong foot by taking so long to recognize a tribe that should have been an easy evaluation. At the time that the bureau established recognition procedures, it called the entire undertaking the Federal Acknowledgment Project (FAP), which suggests a different conception of the undertaking. It intended for the FAP to have a finite existence, since it expected to review just over a hundred petitions and be done with the "project." With the applicant pool fairly limited, the Federal Acknowledgment Project could have resolved all the foreseeable cases much more quickly if its administrators had not decided to purposely prolong the decision-making process. Further, the FAP had just seven staff members, and at the rate at which it began could not have completed a hundred petitions within even fifty years. Instead of a "project" an "office" had been created, with no end in sight. Had the bureau viewed recognition with the same urgency that tribes felt about recognition, with an understanding that nonrecognition could be irreversibly detrimental to tribes, it would have assigned a massive research staff to complete the process as quickly as possible. Taking three years to handle a case as straightforward as that of the Tunica-Biloxis set a precedent that led directly to the quagmire in which OFA now sits.

## CHAPTER 4

# Treasures

## Tunica-Biloxis in the Federal Recognition Era

The Tunicas had been struggling to attain recognition since the theft of their land in 1826 by Celestin Moreau and the United States government, but like many tribes in the 1970s they wondered what recognition might entail. They had a pretty clear idea that they would be granted some funds and become eligible for certain programs, but they were never really sure how they would have to work with the federal government or what kinds of rights their recognition restored or limited. Throughout the AIPRC hearings on federal recognition in 1976, tribal representatives from Louisiana and around the country expressed the same perplexity. Ernest Downs, representing the Tunica-Biloxis, Clyde Jackson, representing the Jena Choctaws, and Helen Gindrat, representing the Houmas, each indicated personal and tribal confusion. Downs requested clarification from the AIPRC panel: "I think it might be appropriate today if you could explain to these people, Madam Chairwoman, what recognition might mean," Downs said. "Most of the people in this room only know what lack of recognition has meant to them. And it's meant that they can't go to the court; it's meant that they've lost all of their land; and it's meant that their tribal government continually had been told that they had no jurisdiction over their own people."[1]

When Chief Joseph Pierite Sr. and his predecessors were working toward recognition, they viewed it as an inherent and basic right, a status that had to be established to protect the tribe on many fronts. Without it their existence was constantly threatened.

Leaders from Melacon down to Earl Barbry fought to protect their land, their integrity, and their livelihood in many ways, and working for federal recognition simply enhanced all those goals.

Chief Joseph Pierite, for example, had four goals for his tribe. First, he wanted to win the right to vote for his people, which he did. Second, he wanted to win the right of Tunica children to be educated alongside whites, which he managed to do for non–African American Tunicas, without the federal funds he had thought would be necessary. Third, he wanted to have the Tunica-Biloxi land surveyed and officially placed in the ownership of the tribe, which only happened after recognition, but he also wanted all of the old Tunica-Biloxi land returned, which still has not happened.[2] Fourth, Downs said a week after the chief's death, "he wanted to be recognized, and he used the term recognized, and he knew that it meant recognized by the local community when we would go and talk to them—recognized by people across the country. . . . He wanted the Federal Government to admit that the people on that land were Indian people, that they were carrying on Indian ways."[3] Chief Joe expressed the sentiment clearly in his declaration to the NCAI convention in 1969: "It is the desire of the Tunica Tribe that they receive federal recognition since a backing of this type would give some form of dignity to their people. With every passing year, more of their land is taken, their religion repressed, and their culture ridiculed."[4] For Chief Pierite his efforts were a matter of justice, of forcing the outside world to give the tribe its due, and recognition was a part of that. Nonrecognition, even without considering all the legal, political, cultural, and economic problems that accompanied it, had been an assault on the tribe's psychological well-being.

For Chairman Joe Pierite Jr. and his successor, Earl Barbry, the motivations for seeking federal recognition were similar to Chief Pierite's, though they shared a second, more pragmatic view of federal recognition: they saw it as a stepping stone toward providing small services to the tribe. Barbry wanted to aid the needy elderly in particular. "When we were growing up on the reservation, in the 'young folks' days," Barbry said wryly, "the hardship was there, and there was still some discrimination practices here, but nothing compared to what our ancestors went through. In fact, they were not allowed to go to any of the schools—denied education. They'd get turned away. There was just nothing here. Just a constant attack on the tribe. Always the fear of losing what little they had, which, besides their culture and their children, the most important thing that they had was the land, and that was constantly taken away from the tribe." Barbry wanted to ensure that the ones who had suffered the most, fought the longest, and had the least to show for it would be taken care of immediately, and he hoped that federal recognition would allow him to accomplish that goal. He wanted to make sure that the elders would not have to continue the same old struggles, that the land would be secured and tribal identity acknowledged.

The Tunica-Biloxis' efforts for recognition were consistently based in a desire for economic development that they hoped would eventually lead to independence. John Barbry noted the irony: "A lot of the tribes that get recognized, they're trying to become self-sufficient. I know it's sort of a paradox that you get recognized and you get on the federal tit, but you're trying to get some sort of funding where you can develop your own tribal business and become less dependent. It's sort of a vicious cycle." To achieve tribal sovereignty, he later added, "it's one step forward and two steps back. You have to enter into this relationship with the federal government that takes away some sovereignty, but hopefully, as you learn the ropes, you start flexing, trying to get back some of the sovereignty you've given up." If federal recognition is conceived of not as entering a federal program but as establishing a degree of economic stability and political independence from the surrounding local governments, the irony of sovereignty within the federal-tribal relationship disappears.

*Recognition*

Despite the years of hard work, collaborative research, and waiting that went into the petition for federal recognition, the arrival of federal recognition in late September 1981 was anticlimactic for the Tunica-Biloxis. For most of the tribe there was no special feeling of excitement, no celebration on that day.[5] The members of the tribe never doubted that they could pass the formal review of their culture and history, and the bureau had issued a "proposed finding" in favor of federal acknowledgment some nine and a half months earlier. Like a victim receiving past-due restitution from a thief, the Tunica-Biloxi Tribe was unmoved by the final act of recognition. It was an important act of justice, to be sure, but somehow not a cause for celebration. Many of the tribal members more peripheral to the daily operations of the tribe at the time do not remember anyone in their family talking about it much. At that time recognition did not carry with it the same transformational aura that it has today. Joe Pierite Jr.'s family seems to be the only group that reported a strong sense of elation, a pride at finally having achieved federal recognition that lifted Pierite's spirits and helped him to put the poverty and struggles of his past behind him, according to his daughter-in-law. The rest of the tribal leaders, including even Rose Pierite White, the former chairman's sister, say that they viewed recognition as a qualifying step toward certain benefits and protections more than a triumphant accomplishment in its own right.

Earl Barbry, with perfect hindsight, understands that recognition does not bring with it an immediate reversal of fortune. "Actually, it gives you an opportunity, but it's something that you have to work real hard and try to make things happen. These programs don't just happen. You have to work at it. You have to look at other sources besides that to really develop your tribe and your reservation . . . It's up to us to keep moving forward and provide for ourselves." Examining the changes that actually did occur immediately after recognition offers a sense of the unexciting nature of the event. John Barbry remembers that though he did not really understand the significance of recognition as a teenager at the time, he started to see a few buildings and houses pop up on the reservation that had not been there the last time he visited, without really comprehending their links to federal recognition and tribal standing. Tribal land was taken into federal trust, but no new land was added to the reservation at that time and the reservation had existed for as long as anyone could remember by then, so there was no change in appearance or use of the land.

Looking back, he understands that recognition had a relatively small impact because the Tunica-Biloxis were such a small tribe. BIA funding is based primarily on population, and with a tribe of only two hundred members in 1981, federal money could only support a bare minimum of expenditures. The kind of clinic that a tribe with a health budget of $100,000 could build, for example, would be quite different from the kind of clinic that a tribe with a health budget of $10 million could build. Even if the budgets were proportionately equal, economies of scale would mean that larger tribes would be able to obtain more services than smaller tribes for their members. Before the casino era, small tribes were thus at a disadvantage since they generally operated strictly on federal dollars. Certain funding inequities for small tribes have been redressed by the federal government over the years, and now small tribes have a potential advantage in that they can raise the same amount of money from a casino as a larger tribe (since casino revenue is independent of federal funding and varies dramatically based on proximity to population centers), but the money does not have to be spread nearly as thin. The difference between the services that a tribe of two hundred can provide with $10 million a year from a casino and the services that a tribe of twenty thousand can provide with the same amount is enormous. Likewise, the federal funding of small and large tribes in the early 1980s proved quite disparate.

The Tunica-Biloxis did not begin reaping the material benefits of federal recognition until 1982, when Indian Health Services sent just enough money for the tribe to set up a medical program. Their grant in the following year allowed them to begin delivering medical services. About the same time the tribe began receiving new money from the Department of Housing and Urban Development, the federal agency charged with providing housing to needy reservation residents, among other responsibilities. The tribe built eleven homes for elderly members on the reservation, and some tribal members were hired by the local non-Indian contractor who built the houses for the tribe. HUD money also enabled the tribe to develop some of the infrastructure on the reservation, paying for running water, a sewage system, and paved roads. By the late 1980s the Tunica-Biloxis added three modest new government buildings. These surely were positive accomplishments addressing some of the most pressing needs of the local tribal members, but it would be an overstatement to say that these were monumental changes.

New funds provided jobs for a handful of tribal members and health benefits for the 65 percent of members whose employers provided no health care, as long as they were living in the "service area" designated by the BIA.[6] For residents of the reservation, it meant that they no longer had to ignore medical problems as they had done in the past.[7] The reservation was still not a place of opportunity, but the tangible and intangible benefits of recognition made it a more stable place for the tribal members who had never left Marksville. For them tribal life did improve somewhat, and that was a start on the road to bigger things.

When the tribe's status was institutionalized and funded, tribal service and governance became more manageable, since there were more benefits now than in the past, when maintaining the tribe had been a liability in many ways. The tribe could take care of its local members more easily because of the new resources available, even if the resources were limited. Those resources allowed the core of tribal members that remained in Avoyelles and Rapides Parish to raise their standard of living a bit, stemming the trend of employment-related emigration that had taken hold in previous decades.

Earl Barbry expressed frustration that he was unable to provide for members outside the "service area" designated by the federal government in these years. Unless tribal members lived in Avoyelles or the adjacent Rapides Parish, they could not participate in the medical program. Further, they could not use federal funds to build or repair houses off the reservation, no matter how desperate their need. It seemed unjust that so many tribal members could not benefit from the federal recognition for which all their ancestors had fought.

The incentives of recognition were not enough to lure many tribal members back to the area initially, because the economic opportunities in Marksville were too few. So for the most part, people stayed where they had been before recognition, returning to Marksville for important events such as funerals or occasionally the revived fête du blé. People who had lived in Marksville all along and those who had returned by the late 1990s mostly repeated the same refrain: "There was nothing to come back to." Visits were common enough, but with few exceptions people could not fathom moving to Marksville, where tribal incomes hovered at around 50 to 60 percent of the already low income for the rest of the parish, even after recognition.[8]

Their neighbors in Mississippi, the Mississippi Band of Choctaws, had begun to use recognition to their advantage to an unheard-of extent in the 1980s. Using tax incentives and funds made available under the Job Training Partnership Act, they were able to create an industrial sector on their reservation that virtually erased unemployment on the reservation and made them one of the largest employers in Mississippi. With five thousand tribal members, however, they could offer a large, cheap workforce to partner corporations that the Tunica-Biloxis and other small tribes could not duplicate.

Surprisingly, the Tunica-Biloxis gained as much access to scholarship funds from their status as a state-recognized tribe as from their status as a federal tribe. The State of Louisiana, flush with oil revenue during the fuel crisis of the late 1970s and early 1980s, set up a scholarship fund in 1979 for all state-recognized Louisiana Indians. Until the bottom fell out of the oil market in 1983, about thirty Louisiana Indian students a year were granted an average of $1,000 toward higher education expenses.[9] Federal recognition had never been a requirement for certain federal educational funds, and the tribe had begun to take advantage of those funds even before recognition. An internal tribal emphasis on the importance of education—based partly on earlier struggles for federal educational assistance and integration into Avoyelles Parish schools—had improved the tribe's educational attainments by then as well.[10] Yet federal status offered surprisingly few new opportunities for educational support for most tribal members.

Recognition did not turn out to be the catalyst it was hoped to be in the land claims suit either. Though the tribe knew that recognition would solidify its standing in court, other snags delayed the process. In the opinion of the tribe and its attorneys, they have "an ironclad case" against the United States for allowing land to be taken from them, but the federal government has set the terms of the case in such a way that it would pit the tribe against its neighbors, which the tribe refuses to accept. According to Earl Barbry,

> The federal government wants the state to pick up half the settlement, whether it be a million dollars or a hundred million, they would want the state to pick up at least half of it, and the federal government would match it. [For that to happen] we would probably have to file something against the state of Louisiana, and that would be . . . It would have a devastating effect, in particular on our local community, with our neighbors, individual landowners. Because once that suit is filed, that puts a cloud on the title of everybody's property. It could be difficult to get insurance. They couldn't mortgage their property to build homes or get financing for anything. And we don't feel that the state is at fault for the tribe losing the land. It's the United States government that had a responsibility to the tribe and chose not to do anything about it. So we haven't filed anything against the state or the individual land owners. These people are our neighbors, friends, and in many cases, some tribal members own property within that claim area.

The members of the tribe are unwilling to sink the local economy into chaos, but the federal government, in a political maneuver, demands that they make public enemies of themselves before the government will hear the suit.[11]

### The Tunica Treasure and the Repatriation of Sovereignty

One of the finest accomplishments for the tribe after recognition came on 18 March 1985, when the 20th Judicial District Court of the State of Louisiana awarded to the tribe custody of the looted collection of grave goods from an eighteenth-century Tunica village. The seeds for the case were planted in 1967, when a local treasure hunter, Leonard Charrier, took his metal detector to the Trudeau plantation near Angola, Louisiana, where he judged, based on archival maps, that a village had been located. The metal detector indicated that there would be a fine haul underground, and over the next three years, with the permission of the plantation groundskeeper but not its owners, he unearthed an amazing array of grave goods which he stored in his home in Bunkie, Louisiana. The collection, called the Tunica Treasure, consisted mostly of items of European manufacture, such as earthenware, stoneware, glass bottles, iron and copper kettles, various iron tools, a number of guns, some decorative items, and about 200,000 glass beads. Items of native manufacture included pottery of various types, shell ornaments, catlinite pipes, and bits of basketry and clothing. Of course there were also numerous skeletons: Charrier dug up over 150 graves, though he left most of the human remains at the gravesites. The material collection had significant monetary value on the antiques market, but it had a greater value as an archaeological documentation of the extensive economic and political interactions between the French and the Tunicas in the mid-eighteenth century.[12] For the Tunica-Biloxi Tribe, yet unaware of Charrier's enterprise, assigning a dollar value or even an academic value to the collection would be problematic.

Charrier asked an archaeologist in Marksville, Robert "Stu" Neitzel, to view the collection in his home, hoping that Neitzel would offer an appraisal. Neitzel was flabbergasted by the collection but could offer no appraisal to Charrier. Instead he contacted his friend and colleague, Stephen Williams, then director of the Peabody Museum at Harvard, to tell him about the extraordinary situation and see if the Peabody could acquire the collection. Williams showed Neitzel's letter to Jeffrey Brain, who was working on the Peabody's Lower Mississippi Survey, and the Peabody team began to pursue the endeavor heavily. During an exploratory trip for the museum in May 1970 the Peabody offered Charrier $8,000 for the collection. Charrier scoffed, demanding $40,000. The Peabody, concerned that Charrier might sell the collection off bit by bit, destroying its archaeological value even further than his amateur digging had done, worked out an agreement with Charrier to bring the entire collection to the Peabody Museum so that it could then raise enough money to purchase it. Their primary motive was to study, conserve, photograph, and catalogue the collection in case Charrier did eventually divide it up for sale.[13] What they did not know at the time was that Charrier had never received permission from the plantation owners to dig on their land, so he could never prove ownership of the Tunica Treasure and therefore could not legally sell it.[14]

In 1974, fed up with the process of trying to confirm ownership and sell the collection to the Peabody, Charrier filed suit to gain clear title to the collection. He sued the owners of the Trudeau plantation, but the State of Louisiana intervened as a third party soon after at the urging of the newly formed Louisiana Archaeological Survey and Antiquities Commission (LASAC). The state attorney general, William Guste, claimed that "there are no lawful heirs to the Tunica Indians who originally buried the artifacts and that, under state law, the succession of persons who die without heirs or which are not claimed by those having a right to them, belong to the state."[15] His outrageous argument that there were no legal heirs to the Tunica Indians would become the basis of later litigation, but he further asserted that the goods were part of the public history of the state and therefore belonged properly to the people of the state and not to any individual. The state was making tenuous arguments, but it hoped that a victory would set a precedent that would prevent looters from benefiting from despoiling important archaeological sites in the future.[16]

Charrier and the plantation owners, with the assistance of their lawyers and in the presence of a few archaeologists, worked out an agreement that would split ownership of the treasure, with two-thirds to the plantation owners and one-third to Charrier. As part of the deal the state would have the opportunity to purchase the Tunica Treasure, with the proceeds divided according the terms of the agreement. A few days later the state backed out of the agreement, because it did not want to reward looting of significant archaeological sites. Eventually the state bought the Trudeau plantation as well as the landowners' claim to a portion of the collection so that it would have a stronger position in court proceedings to determine ownership. Jeffrey Brain remained concerned too about the "threat" that the Tunica descendants might join the case, claiming that they were the proper owners of the treasure.[17]

Sentiments among the tribe about archaeological excavations were not as fixed and certain as some would like to claim today or as the tribe presented them in the media. While Eli Barbry had confronted archaeologists at gunpoint for working at the nearby Marksville mounds in the 1930s, Chief Horace Pierite, along with Chief Joe Pierite and his brother Percy, worked with archaeologists conducting digs on the reservation in the 1960s. Though Joe Pierite Sr. took special care with the remains and reburied them, presumably with a small ceremony, he encouraged and actively participated in the excavations as a means of strengthening the tribe's ties to its past.[18] According to Jeffrey Brain, Pierite even encouraged Leonard Charrier to conduct a dig on the reservation in the spring of 1971, though Pierite demanded that the tribe be allowed to keep the artifacts, which he probably placed in the small museum and trading post that he established on the reservation.[19] Other tribal members, including Earl Barbry, forced Charrier to stop digging under threat of police arrest.[20] It is not clear whether the Tunica chiefs Horace

Pierite and Joe Pierite would have supported these excavations were it not for the context of nonrecognition—a context that made archaeological proof of the tribe's long presence in the area and its cultural and historical distinctiveness potentially valuable enough to the tribe's future to warrant taking new positions on archaeological excavations—but the issue does demonstrate a diversity of beliefs, values, and strategies of Tunica-Biloxi tribal members regarding archaeological endeavors.

Despite the range of opinions within the tribe over whether archaeological excavation was ever appropriate, tribal members agreed without hesitation that Charrier had absolutely no right to the grave goods of their ancestors, and his actions were universally considered insulting to Tunica people. In Calvin Trillin's sympathetic portrayal of Charrier in the *New Yorker*, his assertion that the tribe was interested in the treasure as "a potential source of employment" and "as a possible bargaining chip in negotiating a settlement" of its land claims came just a few days after the tribe received word of a final determination for federal recognition in July 1981, and only added to tribal members' anger and mortification over the matter.[21] It must have seemed a particularly belittling gibe to tribal members (despite Trillin's attempts at impartiality elsewhere in the article), but they would soon intervene in the lawsuit and demonstrate that their commitment was based on their desire for justice rather than the feeble economic rationale that Trillin had suggested.

Fred Benton Jr., a member of the Louisiana Archaeological Survey and Antiquities Commission who was appointed special assistant to the attorney general to litigate this case, had been trying to persuade the Tunica-Biloxis to intervene on the side of the state since 1979, but during that time the tribe felt overextended with the land claim suit and the recognition petition in process.[22] Unlike in the land claims case and the recognition process, in which the federal government had assumed the tribe and the state to be competing and diametrically opposed, the state eventually sought partnership with the tribe to protect what it saw as their mutual interests. After being federally recognized on 25 September 1981, the tribe immediately entered the fray in the treasure case, as Benton had hoped. Joining the tribe's private attorney, the Native American Rights Fund helped to represent the tribe, viewing the case as an opportunity to set an important precedent in Indian law.

Three and a half years later, in March 1985, Judge Lenton Sartain of Louisiana Circuit Court ruled against Charrier and granted ownership of the Tunica Treasure to the Tunica tribe. Charrier had been arguing that the tribe had abandoned the property and therefore its rights in 1764, when it left the site. The judge ruled that burial goods—and these were clearly burial goods—could not be considered "abandoned property."[23] In 1986 the Louisiana First Circuit Court of Appeals affirmed Sartain's decision: "While the relinquishment of immediate possession may have been proved, an objective viewing of the circumstances and intent of the relinquishment does not result in a finding of abandonment. . . . The relinquishment of possession [of burial goods] normally serves some spiritual, moral, or religious purpose of the descendant / owner, but it is not intended as a means of relinquishing ownership to a stranger."[24] In other words, items buried with the dead and the bodies of the dead themselves were not abandoned in the same sense that a broken pot thrown on a junk heap is abandoned. Charrier appealed the decision to the Louisiana Supreme Court, but the court declined to hear the case.

One of the foundations of Charrier's initial appeal of the lower court decision was the assertion that the Tunica-Biloxis were not the legal descendants of the Tunica Indians who inhabited the Trudeau site, an assertion that had no merit in the court because the federal government had already certified the history of the Tunica-Biloxis through federal recognition.[25] The tribe might have succeeded in winning the rights to the grave goods had it not been federally recognized, but being federally recognized beforehand removed the possibility that the tribe could be denied standing as the proper descendants of the people who had buried the items in the first place. The tribe had lost cases in state court earlier for lack of federal recognition.[26] Because its status as a tribe was finally recognized by the federal government, it won possession of an important part of its heritage and set a vital though unheralded precedent for the Native American Graves Protection and Repatriation Act (NAGPRA) of 1990. The ruling and the ensuing legislation affirmed the right of Native American people to the grave goods taken from them and displayed at countless museums across the country.

The Tunica Treasure was not immediately returned to the tribe at the time of the ruling. It had been stored in the Old U.S. Mint, a state-run museum in New Orleans, since the Peabody Museum shipped it there in 1981 as a result of a court request, and it stayed there until the tribe could prepare adequate facilities in which to store and preserve the items. The tribe raised nearly $2 million to invest in an archaeological conservation lab once its leaders saw the deteriorating condition of the items, and it trained two tribal members in techniques of artifact conservation. Ever careful to show respect for tribal ancestors, the tribe built a museum housed entirely within a newly constructed mound, symbolically reburying the material goods while at the same time preserving the knowledge that they documented. The few human remains associated with the collection were buried together in the ground beneath the floor of the museum mound.[27] Unfortunately the museum was demolished in 2003 because of continuing difficulties with keeping moisture from the wet central Louisiana soil from seeping through the walls and damaging the collections, but the new Cultural and Educational Resource Center that replaced it promises to maintain the sense of respect and integrity that inspired the museum mound.

The Tunica Treasure has become an anchor for tribal identity since it was repatriated. Tribal members rank its return with federal recognition and the opening of the casino in 1994 as among the most important achievements for the tribe in recent memory. The repatriation affirmed the tribe's sovereignty and newfound power in a way that none of the other humdrum changes after recognition could do. For the first time in years the tribe had the power to demand and receive respect for its sovereignty and its traditions. This surely must have delivered an empowering, refreshing sense of justice, and indicated that a degree of sovereignty had been repatriated along with the grave goods. Being able to honor and defend its ancestors, its eldest elders, was invigorating and satisfying after such a long history of marginalization and oppression.

Likewise, the material goods became a touchstone for the tribe's heritage in a time when tribal members worried that they were becoming further removed from a distinctive tribal culture in their daily lives. The last fluent native language speaker had died in the early 1950s, though in the 1980s, when the treasure was returned, a handful of people still remembered a few words or phrases of the tribal languages passed down to them from parents or grandparents. Many in the tribe—especially those without Latino ancestry— were becoming phenotypically less and less "Indian"-looking, though certain common physical traits remained. Tribal religious traditions had been reduced to stories remembered by only a few. When younger Tunica-Biloxis thought about themselves and their identity, they may have had a hard time explaining what made them distinct. They knew they were Indian, but what did that mean? By the 1980s most members of the tribe dressed the same as their non-Indian neighbors, ate the same foods, worked in similar jobs, spoke the same languages, and listened to the same music. What made them different was their history; their polity, indigeneity, race, and cultural heritage are all legitimated through reference to that history. Certainly there were other differences, but they are differences that are easier for an elder or an academic to identify than for a Tunica-Biloxi ninth-grader to understand. Many of the older tribal members knew their history well, but the new collection of items made that history more tangible to those who were not as familiar with the Tunica past. The treasure and the struggle to gain custody of it makes Tunica history easier to incorporate into a sense of collective identity. It is a physical reassurance of the tribe's history and continued sovereign existence.

The Tunica Treasure is not the only source of identity for the tribe, but it bonds the tribe to its past, promoting a stronger sense of tribal identity in the present and future. For tribes whose cultural distinctiveness has faded on many fronts, material goods often play an important role in articulating tribal identities. Traditional crafts such as split-cane baskets, for example, are much easier to grasp as a symbol of tribal continuity, literally and figuratively, than messy cultural interpretations of "postindian survivance," to borrow one of Gerald Vizenor's poetic and academically useful—but generally inaccessible—terms.[28] Tribal members do not visit the collection all that often, and kids can become a bit bored by it from overexposure, but the knowledge that it is there is meaningful and compelling. The Tunica Treasure acts in much the same way as a split-cane basket, giving tribal members something solid to wrap their minds around, a cultural mnemonic device that reinforces the more elusive aspects of a continuing and distinctive tribal identity.

## CHAPTER 5

## Tribal Enterprise and Tribal Life

The Tunica-Biloxi Tribe began developing a casino in 1991, which has since created significant benefits and presented new challenges to tribal cohesion, culture, and identity. Like many federally recognized tribes the Tunica-Biloxis took advantage of a series of court decisions and the Indian Gaming Regulatory Act (IGRA) of 1988, which together establish, delimit, and regulate the rights of federally recognized tribes to operate certain gaming facilities depending on the laws of the states within which their reservation lies.[1] From the time they began planning, it took three years for the Tunica-Biloxis and their partners to work through the red tape and complete the physical construction needed to open the Grand Casino Avoyelles. The tribe bought out the last year of a seven-year management contract with Grand Casinos in 2000 to become the sole owner and operator, renaming the facility the Paragon Casino Resort. The business has been an enormous financial success for the tribe and Avoyelles Parish since it opened in 1994.

While most non-Indians support tribal gaming rights, many people outside the Native American world fail to realize that tribal casinos are not individually oriented capitalist enterprises in the same sense that Donald Trump's casinos are, and this misunderstanding has led to constant legal, political, and public relations problems for tribes.[2] Gaming tribes have developed casinos with the hope of helping themselves to thrive socially and culturally, not just economically, and the Indian Gaming Regulatory Act takes measures to assure that tribal casinos function similarly to a state lottery, with tribal programs funded first, before per capita payments are made.[3] Adequate funding has been a dream deferred for tribal governments across the country, because it has been so hard to develop reservation economies. The majority of tribes funnel their casino profits into programs that have been unfunded or underfunded for years. Though a few hypervisible examples of tribes with annual per capita payments reaching six figures skew the public's perception, three-quarters of all gaming tribes do not even have per capita payments for tribal members.[4] As Jessica Cattelino has argued, money is not solely exchangeable for material goods, so even when tribes have sizable per capita payments, they have often directed significant resources toward political and cultural efforts that protect tribal members, tribal political status, and tribal cultures according to tribal values.[5] Gaming profits pay for new schools and educational programs. They construct hospitals and homes for the elderly. They fund language revitalization programs, powwows, and museums. They build new roads and adequate sewer systems. They create emergency relief funds and new businesses to diversify the tribal economy. They pay for attorneys and lobbyists to protect tribal sovereignty. These are all things that tribes struggle to do without a tax base or consistent sources of revenue.

States have consistently tried to tax reservation-based casinos, failing to realize, as the Tunica-Biloxi tribal council member Brenda Lintinger has noted, that casino profits are taxed at a rate of 100 percent already, with the revenue going to the tribal government rather than the state government. For the state of Louisiana to demand a portion of the Tunica-Biloxi Tribe's gaming revenue would be like Arizona taxing California's lottery or—more aptly, given that tribes are nations under federal law—taxing Mexico's oil because it shares a border with the United States. Moreover, even if they are not directly taxed, tribal casinos still generate tax revenue for states through pay for employees, vendors, and other partners who are not tribal members. Like other forms of individual income earned by tribal members on reservations, per capita distributions of gaming revenue are taxed by the federal government, but these too are off-limits to state tax agencies as a result of federal protections of tribal sovereignty.

Since the state of Louisiana legalized gambling in 1991, the operation of casinos in general was not a significant source of friction when the Tunica-Biloxi Tribe began negotiations to open a casino. Of more concern was the ability of the state to tax the casino operations to the same extent as they could tax riverboat casinos and the innumerable video poker machines in bars, restaurants, and truck stops around the state. Legally the state is not

Brenda Lintinger, 2004. Photo by the author.

supposed to be able to tax business conducted by the tribe on the reservation. However, states have wrangled various "donations" out of tribes at the negotiation table, because the Indian Gaming Regulatory Act requires that tribes negotiate gaming agreements (compacts) that are acceptable to the states in which their reservations are located. In Connecticut gaming tribes "donate" a significant portion of their slot revenues in return for a monopoly on casino gaming in the state, but Louisiana does not have that kind of leverage since there is legalized gaming elsewhere in the state.[6] The state of Louisiana has considered resorting to other measures, such as setting up toll roads on the highways leading to the casinos or taxing the food and beverages served in the casinos, but these efforts have never succeeded.[7]

The state's primary tool in leveraging payments is to threaten not to sign the required gaming compacts until the state's demands are met. The IGRA as written required that states and tribes negotiate "in good faith" to reach a reasonable agreement, but the U.S. Supreme Court struck down this provision as inconsistent with constitutional protections of state sovereignty.[8] Cattelino notes that the Seminole tribe later won a case asserting that it had a right to sovereign immunity, which would seem to allow tribes to operate class III casinos without a state compact, but to date the federal government has not implemented procedures for tribes with no state compact to follow.[9] Federal law thus gives states leverage that conflicts with the sovereignty of federally recognized tribes, because states can in effect block the rights of tribes to open casinos if the tribes refuse to pay a portion of their profits to the state. In that sense the law authorizes not only state taxation of tribal revenues earned on the reservation (in the form of "payments in lieu of taxes") but also state frustration of the tribal rights that lay at the heart of the *Cabazon* decision.[10] The impasse gives states a coercive advantage over tribes in that respect, marking it as one more aspect of colonial power exerted over tribes.[11]

The Tunicas, like other tribes, have consistently recognized the impact that development of their casino has had on local communities, so they have been willing to contribute enough of their revenue to the local tax base to offset the increased costs of service to the reservation, but state politicians have not always been willing to recognize their sovereignty in return. Earl Barbry, frustrated that the state would stake a claim to the Tunica-Biloxi Tribe's revenues after years of participating in their dispossession and segregation, remarked during compact renegotiations in 1998 that "as long as we had nothing, nobody gave a damn." Crystallizing the hypocrisy of the state's position, Governor Mike Foster scoffed at the suggestion that historical context mattered, saying, "I'm not into the past."[12] Rather than an escape from previous colonial relations or complete independence from state control, federal recognition gives tribes a new and better position from which to negotiate, but these constant colonial impositions on tribal sovereignty reflect the inherent conflicts that newly recognized tribes must learn to navigate upon entering the intergovernmental federal-state-tribal matrix.[13]

Economic development is a linchpin to the success of many tribal endeavors, and tribes have tried repeatedly to develop economies that would let them be self-sustaining. Stories abound of reservation enterprises that have failed for lack of expertise or sound advice, poor location, or inadequate access to capital, and the Tunica-Biloxi Tribe contributes the story of a pecan-shelling factory that began with modest hopes but met its demise fairly quickly, never becoming the building block for future development that it was hoped to be.[14] Gaming offered a rare and compelling opportunity for many tribes—particularly small tribes—to develop strong, independent economies, and the Tunicas took advantage.

The tribe's Paragon Casino Resort, complete with a hotel, entertainment hall, movie theaters, a four-story atrium with live alligators, several attached

The new atrium at the Paragon, with a simulated bayou and architecture designed to evoke the French Quarter. Photo by the author.

restaurants, an RV park, cabins, a convention center, and a golf course, has been very successful since it opened in 1994, now grossing over $100 million a year.[15] Using profits from the casino, the tribe has purchased several profitable fast-food franchises.[16] Tribal investments in the stock market have generally been lucrative, and the tribe has ventured into casino management and consulting for other tribes as well, with mixed results. Economic prosperity has funded a broad array of tribal services that were unavailable or underfunded before the casino started. Even when the global and national economies have sputtered, Tunica economic development efforts have maintained a steady profitability.

In addition to material benefits, economic development on the reservation offers surprising cultural benefits for the tribe. Development efforts provide

Tunica-Biloxi people with jobs on the reservation. Being able to live in the tribal homeland, deeply rooted as it is in people's sense of the tribe, allows Tunicas to experience the tribe as an enduring political and governmental entity in daily life. The tribe will provide a job to any tribal member or tribal spouse, in positions ranging from entry level to management, based on experience and education. The jobs have made the reservation a place of opportunity for tribal members, keeping many from leaving and drawing back into the community many families who left because of a lack of economic opportunity. These jobs have also kept Tunica-Biloxis connected to one another. Where there were once only three occupied houses remaining on the reservation, by 2004 there were so many trailer homes and applications for housing from tribal members moving back to the reservation that there was a waiting list for permits. Further, development has been so extensive that it has created all-Indian and predominantly Indian workplaces. The dozens of tribal members working in tribal government or government services can interact almost exclusively with other tribal members, since they do not have to leave the reservation to find work. Such constant proximity promotes cultural retention and growth, tribal cohesion, and a stronger sense of identity.[17]

As an example, Elisabeth Pierite had lived her whole life in New Orleans, but she moved back to Marksville with her parents, Michael and Donna Pierite, as a teenager when their home was destroyed after Hurricane Katrina. Her parents had been quite extensively involved with tribal life before returning to Marksville; Michael's father was Joe Pierite Jr., and Michael and Donna had participated in tribal organization and cultural education efforts since the 1970s. Elisabeth grew up in a household in which her Tunica-Biloxi identity was always central to her sense of self, but after graduating from high school in 2007 she began working for the tribal housing authority, a job that put her in an office where she both worked with and served other tribal members and their families exclusively every day. As a result, she began to feel connected to other tribal members in a way that she had not realized she was missing when she lived in New Orleans.

Michael Pierite offers another example of the cultural impact of tribal employment. He had been employed in public works for St. Tammany Parish just outside New Orleans when Katrina hit in 2005. While he had no interest in the gaming industry as a career, and most of the entry-level jobs for which he would be qualified paid near the minimum wage, when a position as a manager of environmental quality for the casino resort became available he leaped at the opportunity. The position made use of his experience in public works and gave him responsibility for taking care of wildlife in the lavish new hotel atrium, where live alligators, turtles, and fish populated a simulated bayou. He and his family, including his son Jean-Luc, who left a career in video game development in California to join his family in Marksville in 2007, now conduct shows in the atrium on weekends that include Tunica-Biloxi stories and songs about alligators, a deeply meaningful animal for the tribe culturally. The Pierites have been consistently involved in tribal cultural education for many years; the shows are a natural extension of their previous educational work involving Tunica songs, storytelling, and traditions. Working with alligators and doing educational outreach together as a family enhances their sense of belonging to a distinct community. The tribe provides opportunities for emotional and spiritual healing that have been lacking for so many Katrina evacuees, and culturally relevant jobs and opportunities such as theirs are only available because of economic development on the reservation.

Similarly, adequate economic development allows tribal communities to keep a critical mass of people of different ages that is necessary to keep traditions alive.[18] This is especially important for smaller tribes such as the Tunica-Biloxis. While precise figures are not available for the pre-recognition or pre-casino years, there are currently over three hundred tribal members living in the Marksville area, more than at any time in the twentieth century. A larger reservation population can support cultural events more consistently, and provides enough members to keep alive many traditions, rather than only the most dearly held traditions that a community gives up last. Many tribal members are needed to support sizable public events such as the powwow, and the smaller fête du blé will be more likely to continue if it has a broader base of participants that comes more easily with a larger reservation population.

The tribe now has money from its casino and from the government to fund cultural projects such as the Cultural Education and Resource Center, summer language and culture programs for youths, and an annual powwow. The tribe has even paid for tribal members living out of state to come back to Marksville for the powwow on occasion. The tribal newspaper, while it has been unfunded since 2008, was helpful during its ten years of operation in connecting the tribal members—especially those living out of state who could not attend regular community meetings—to their government, to one another, and to events and concerns around Indian country.[19] Language camps and newspapers may not be how tribal cultures and cohesiveness were maintained in the past, but for a small tribe whose language has been largely dormant for half a century, with families widely dispersed across the map and isolated from tribal traditions at times, invigorating tribal culture and consciousness may best be accomplished through concerted, centralized efforts such as these.[20]

The tribe as a government entity was never a resource before as it is now, according to Donna Pierite. The tribe helps keep families together through social services, domestic violence intervention, and substance abuse counseling. Where previously tribal members turned to their families for help, now there is a tribal structure to turn to. Part of that shift began with recognition, but in the casino era there is assistance at every turn, and not just monetary benefits. When a young tribal member was fighting cancer, for example, not only was the tribe able to cover medical expenses through the Indian Health Service (IHS), but the director of social services, Marshall Pierite, was able to assist with practical details that eased the burden on the young man and his family through a time of intense anguish.[21] The tribe also helps families to care for children with disabilities.[22] When Hurricanes Katrina and Rita displaced dozens of tribal members, the tribe provided a wide range of assistance that helped tribal members come through the disasters in a better position than their non-tribal counterparts.[23] The tribe has federal funding and tribal revenue to provide an organizational infrastructure that supports tribal members during even the most difficult personal trials. Tribal membership has become more valuable on a strictly economic level and more meaningful on a personal level as tribal members have come to rely on the tribal government in more situations, and thus the tribal entity has become increasingly vital in tribal members' daily lives.

Because of the casino the tribe's role in the broader community has completely changed as well. Once a community in grim decline, Marksville has seen its economy and population grow since the casino opened. The tribe has contributed millions of dollars in wages to the economy through direct employment at the casino, tribal restaurants, and construction projects, in addition to all the taxes taken out of those paychecks and money from the development of peripheral, nontribal businesses. Of their several thousand employees, fewer than 2 percent are tribal members. While the wages are not terribly high for entry-level workers, the casino offers a decent benefits package and opportunities for advancement not available in many other industries in the parish. The casino brought in executives from elsewhere in the country as well—people making upper-middle-class incomes who could contribute immediately to the local economy, until many were replaced by local people moving up the ladder of the casino. Further, the newly available jobs have created a housing shortage in the area, boosting the building industries. During Hurricanes Katrina and Rita in 2005 the tribe proved to be a valuable asset to the state as a whole, volunteering its hotel and casino to serve as a Red Cross evacuation center, housing and feeding thousands of evacuees, and spending many thousands of its own dollars and employee hours to provide every conceivable service to evacuees. Add that to direct payments to the Avoyelles Parish government because of the gaming compacts, and the tribe has become an economic force in a place where racism and colonialism had previously diverted economic resources away from them.[24]

This success has caused minor resentment in the non-Indian community, but people have at least accepted if not welcomed the tribe's new role, because the Paragon provides economic prosperity and entertainment that would not otherwise be available in Marksville.[25] That said, the tribe remains guarded about public enthusiasm for its new enterprises. David Rivas Jr., a tribal council member who moved to Marksville after growing up around Washington and later working as a police detective in Houston, easily recalls the humility of the tribe's past. He frequently reminds himself and his children to remember the sacrifices of their ancestors and the strength they needed to endure hard times before the recent turnaround. Most of their ancestors never lived to see the times of plenty. "Six years ago," he said in an interview in March 2000, "we didn't even have paved roads. Six years ago, we had gravel. Before that, it was nothing but a mudpit." He cites a tribal leader who is constantly asked what he thinks of the tribe's new prosperity, to which he usually replies, " 'It's wonderful. I really enjoy, you know, what's been happening with the tribe. But not more than ten years ago, if I was on Main Street in Marksville, and somebody had poured gasoline on me and lit a match, you couldn't pay anybody to spit on me to put out the fire.' " There have always been people in the surrounding community who have supported the tribe and those who have attacked the tribe, as the Tunica-Biloxi people remain keenly aware. The tribe maintains good relations with the surrounding community for pragmatic reasons, but the memory of historic relationships has never faded.

Extensive economic development has led some tribal members to express concerns about changes that the casino has brought to the tribe. The influx of tribal members from outside the area seeking jobs at the casino and housing on the reservation concerns a few of the people who have been active for their whole lives in maintaining tribal culture. Some have suggested that some of the people moving back are disconnected from the identity, history, and culture of the Tunica-Biloxi Tribe and only interested in the financial benefits of tribal membership. While the general sentiment is that the tribe will benefit immensely from having members reconnect with the tribe and extended families reunite, apprehension dwells in some quarters that the less tribally oriented returnees will dilute the core identity of the tribe. Rather than a permanent division, reintegration is an issue that the tribe encounters as it finally begins to counteract decades of tribal dispersion in the twentieth century. Tribal members who left Marksville in the 1930s continued to return regularly, ensuring for the most part that their children and grandchildren would remain connected to their relatives, their tribe, and their homeland. Most of the emigrants maintained an enduring hope for the future of the tribe, despite having moved away for economic opportunity, and initial tensions between longtime residents and recent returnees has begun to fade as new bonds and alliances have formed.

Still, a few people have returned for money alone. The number of returnees for whom money or the prospect of money was a major consideration, though, is larger. That is a different orientation from that of the Marksville group—the families who insisted on staying in their homeland despite the hardships—and alters the identity of the Marksville community. As an example of the shift, the formality of dress on the reservation has risen with the new business climate, from blue jeans to business casual and even business formal in some offices, particularly at the casino. That causes resentment for some of the people who feel that traditional Tunica-Biloxi life did not involve corporate ladder climbing, ostentatious clothes, or other signs of consumerism. Of course some people claim that the Tunicas were "traditional capitalists," since they had been known for trading and accumulating goods even in the seventeenth and eighteenth centuries, as indicated by the wealth of materials in the Tunica Treasure. It should be said that there was income stratification among tribal members before the casino, but the casino seems to highlight a class division that did not exist as strongly previously. The casino administration jobs are white-collar, while tribal members were almost entirely in blue-collar positions or the service industry in years past.

The careers of tribal members before the casino depended to a great degree on their generation. Most tribal members born in the 1950s or earlier had jobs that were clearly blue-collar—butchers, welders, truckers, farmers, and the like. The next generation began to see some class mobility, with a few college graduates, small businessmen, and people in civil service jobs with good pay moving into the middle and lower middle classes. But the casino made a set of tribal members into corporate executives. These individuals may not be earning much more than blue-collar tribal members, but their class position has shifted toward the white-collar realm, and that threatens tribal unity in the view of those with more of a working-class identity. The connotations of boss and worker inherent in the split between white collar and blue collar make stratification harder to bear, because it is laid on top of existing family and tribal relationships, which can include love as well as resentment, cooperation as well as rivalry.

Many tribal members took pay cuts and sacrificed significantly to be able to return to Marksville and work for the tribe. David Rivas Jr. took a 40 percent pay cut from his job as a detective in the Houston police department to work for the tribe. John Barbry left a job as an archivist for the National Museum of the American Indian to work in the casino's marketing department. Each had a rewarding career, but the draw of working for the tribe and living in Marksville proved more important. Brenda Lintinger says of the many tribal members who moved to Marksville to work for the tribe, "They could get a *job* anywhere; it's the *tribe* that brings them back here."

Even the tribal members who have white-collar positions are concerned about the way money is changing the tribe, though. Steve Johnson, a phenotypically white tribal member who ran a successful home appliance store in Shreveport, Louisiana, before working for the tribe, says that he moved back in 1994 for purely financial reasons. He is grateful nonetheless for the opportunity to live among his tribal relatives. He thinks that some of the kids are too spoiled in the casino era, though he jokingly admits that maybe that was a problem for his own kids even before the casino. On the other hand, he sees a cultural reawakening under way, within the tribe and within himself, that he did not anticipate. He reported in 2000 that his perspective changed significantly while he was involved in tribal affairs as the director of economic development and vice-chairman of the tribal council. As the tribe has come back together with recent economic development, people like Johnson have developed a new consciousness of themselves as tribal members, as belonging to a tribal community.

Some tribal members remain concerned with the younger generation's perception of themselves as privileged. They are identifying more and more with the consumer-oriented culture of the United States and the privileges of the middle class. Donna Pierite expressed similar frustrations with what she saw as the arrogance of young tribal members. As director of summer culture programs for Tunica-Biloxi youth, she saw teenagers being pampered by money and convenience, which she felt mocked their past. When some kids in her program made fun of an old man collecting cans while they were on a field trip in Alexandria in the late 1990s, the incident demonstrated to her how spoiled they had become. She told them that they were not so far removed from that kind of life and the kinds of prejudice they were dishing out. She made them recycle their cans to remind them of that fact—unlike elsewhere in the country, recycling was (and still is) a rarity in rural Louisiana. While other tribal members might attribute their impetuousness to the general state of youth in America, and she is not sure how effective the lesson was, to her the episode reinforces an urgent message that needs to be conveyed to Tunica youth about what it means to be Tunica.

Despite the presence of more cash in Tunica hands, there remain a number of tribal members who have moved back and are not now in high-paying jobs and may never be. These are the tribal members working as cashiers at the casino who have not been moved up yet for one reason or another—for lack of experience, lack of education, or lack of ambition. In 1999 tribal members received from $200 to $1,000 a month in per capita payments, with a couple of special bonus distributions in the course of the year. Five years later the per capita payments were averaged to $1,500 per month. Add that to a seven-dollar-an-hour job at the casino or RV park, and these tribal members are just breaking $30,000 a year if they work full-time. That kind of income lifts people out of poverty but does not tend to incline them toward arrogance.

Tribal members work through these issues of access to power in occasionally volatile open tribal council meetings.[26] Since the casino opened and so many people have moved back, the meetings have been well attended, sometimes drawing upwards of eighty people. The meetings are in some ways a stale exhibition of *Robert's Rules of Order*, Indian style, beginning with a prayer and followed by a reading of the minutes from the previous council meeting and reports from various committees. Revenue reports are often the most important topic, since many more people feel the effects of tribal income fluctuations than of, say, decisions by the tribal housing authority, and access to revenue seems more mystifying. When people have felt that they were being blocked from access to the tribe's prosperity because they were not part of a privileged insider network, tempers have flared. One council member,

Marshall Sampson, suggests that most of the time tempers have risen when people have not had access to all the information about how decisions have been made, so he generally welcomes questions: it keeps the governing process more open and helps tribal members feel connected with their government. These are standard issues for open governments around the world, and tribal governments are no exception, but a governmental meeting for a small tribe differs significantly from small-town politics in general in that everyone is related and permanently bound to the polity, and this flavors every discussion. Tunica-Biloxi tribal members acknowledge that their council meetings could be volatile even before the casino opened, but for several years after the casino opened there were more people at each meeting representing more diverse family interests and a lot of new money and power was at stake, so there was a new level of contestation in the meetings. There are still disagreements over issues, but Sampson suggests that the days of volatility have passed as people have become better informed about tribal government processes and taken part in them.

### Tribal Enrollment, Gaming, and Recognition

As with many gaming tribes around the country, tribal enrollment has become an issue among the Tunica-Biloxis with the success of their business enterprises—an issue made particularly interesting in this case by its parallels to the federal tribal recognition process. The tables have turned somewhat, as tribal governments make decisions about who ought to be recognized as a member of the tribe. Issues that should not matter, such as the financial and political ramifications of recognizing an individual as a tribal member, have perhaps started to affect decisions that would ideally be entirely social and cultural.[27] Further, tribal governments have become suspicious that anyone trying to enroll at this late date is only doing so for the money, just as many United States politicians are concerned that tribes petitioning for recognition are motivated solely by money.

Without delving into details of specific cases, several problems that the Tunica-Biloxi Tribe is trying to unravel merit discussion. Any discussion of membership must begin with the understanding that it is the absolute right of the tribe to decide who is eligible for tribal citizenship. Self-definition is a matter of legal and cultural sovereignty. The tribe has a deeply held sense of self, so it is understandable that the tribe should be reluctant to add people to the membership roll who lack both continued mutual relations with the tribe and ancestors who have maintained continued identification with the tribe.

Among other tribes the issue of disenrolling tribal members for political and financial reasons, though clearly related to the issue of new enrollments, is somewhat distinct from it. In the Tunica-Biloxi Tribe no one has been disenrolled who had previously been enrolled. The question is when, whether, and how descendants of more distant tribal ancestors might (re)establish tribal membership now that the possibility of financial and potential social gain has complicated the equation.

Cases are not always easy to resolve, especially when there is a degree of mutual relationship between a family and the tribe. One of the problems has been that some members of a family line may have maintained close ties to the tribe, while the majority of that line maintained no connection whatsoever. In order for the individuals who have maintained close relations to be enrolled, the entire line of ancestors they claim would have to be added to earlier tribal rolls. Under formalized and bureaucratized rules of descent based in blood quantum alone, anyone descended from those ancestors would also become eligible to be a tribal member. This means that instead of recognizing a couple of people who have strong ties to the tribe, the council could be enrolling dozens, some of whom have no connection in any other way to the modern tribal community.

The council may take political considerations into account in deciding enrollment cases too, at least thinking about how newly enrolled families might work for or against them in the polls, and bluntly asking themselves whether they like the families. It could be said that these influences have always played a role in delineating tribal communities, but federal recognition has changed the process by drawing strict boundaries around community membership and descendancy. In the past biological descendancy was neither an automatic assurance of permanent tribal belonging nor an absolute requirement. A person who was considered a borderline community member in the days before federal recognition could live on the border of the community, literally or figuratively. Belonging to a community that is not bureaucratically regulated is not an all-or-nothing proposition, as it has become in some ways for modern, bureaucratically monitored American Indian tribes.

Related to political and personal considerations, financial considerations are entering the picture, and that is a new impact of gaming money. Not that the tribe would ever enroll anyone who had no connection to it, and not that it would deny enrollment to anyone solely for financial reasons, but finances have become an issue for consideration. Some of the people seeking enrollment in the tribe for themselves or their children are not financial opportunists and have not been portrayed that way, but there is an understandable wariness on the part of the tribe in instances where it is not patently obvious that a person should be enrolled. Indeed, the emergence of several groups claiming a connection to Avoyel ancestors around Marksville since 2000 raises the ire of some Tunica-Biloxi leaders, since these groups had no public social existence as Indians before the casino became successful. Several of these groups have gone so far as to submit letters of intent to petition for federal recognition.[28]

The role of financial considerations in tribal enrollment decisions is secondary at best, but let us consider a hypothetical situation. If a tribe of eight hundred enrolls a hundred new members from a given family line, per capita payments will have to be cut more than 10 percent; thus an annual per capita payment of $10,000 would be cut to about $8,900 for each tribal member. Before the casino opened, expanding the tribal rolls would have meant an increased federal budget, and therefore a larger membership would not amount to political suicide as it would now, according to one tribal member. In fact, the tribe did expand its tribal rolls significantly after recognition, cutting the blood quantum requirement from one-fourth to one-sixty-fourth and scuttling old tribal rules that excluded people with African ancestry: these changes increased the tribal population from two hundred at the time of recognition to five hundred after recognition to eight hundred in the 1990s and about a thousand in 2010. Of course there were several reasons for lowering the blood quantum. The tribe would have gradually extinguished itself if it kept the one-quarter Tunica-Biloxi blood requirement, but tribal members also simply felt that their relatives who were less than a quarter Indian had a right to be enrolled as tribal members. Though not the key reason for expanding the rolls, the small increase in federal funds that the change brought to the tribe certainly made the proposition more attractive. If adding a hundred people descended from a resident Indian of the nineteenth-century Tunica village brought money to the tribe, the change would be more likely to be made. If doing so cost the tribal members 10 to 15 percent of their per capita payments, the council would feel pressure to disapprove for political and financial reasons.[29]

Tribal membership has always been a complex mix of blood relationship and political and social ties between families, and it is perhaps an overly convenient argument to say that casino money is corrupting some imagined pure tribal culture, but the integrity of tribal boundaries would not be such an issue were it not for the tribal relationship with the United States government. One of the consistently troubling aspects of federal recognition has been the recurrence of federal demands regarding the tracking of blood quantum and descent. Before the days of federal oversight tribes had the ability to determine their membership for themselves. Descent from other groups did not usually diminish tribal citizenship and was not tracked over time, as has been well documented elsewhere.[30] Borderline cases now include people who would have been considered community members (and therefore tribal members) in days past, but notions of "tribe" under federal law and in general parlance have become formal, externally regulated, and based on genetic descent from a supposedly pure original set of ancestors. Such an understanding of the existence of Indian nations rests on outdated anthropological constructions of cultures and tribes as strictly bounded, racially coherent entities. To assume that the Tunica-Biloxi Tribe has existed as a bounded set of people since time began, which is a central assumption of establishing a base roll of "full-blood" tribal ancestors, is absurd, especially considering the very well known history of tribal conglomeration. The way tribal descent is figured now follows federal rules of fractionalized blood descent, which have been internalized and naturalized as though they were the means by which the Tunica tribe always bounded itself. Yet no tribe counted membership in racial fractions before the arrival of racial thinking under white supremacy. Even in the 1970s, just before recognition, nontribal spouses of Tunica-Biloxi tribal members were allowed to vote in tribal elections, revealing that the tribe's conception of itself as a unit diverged sharply from federal definitions. Federal policy demands a limited, permanently identifiable, rigidly regulated service unit based strictly on genetic inheritance for recognized tribes, contrary to many tribal traditions. Ideas about tribal community membership around the country have shifted dramatically because of the tribal relationship to the federal government.

Ironically, the growth of tribally based resources tied to federal recognition, including per capita payments for economic enterprise revenues, also changes the ways tribes bound themselves. The Tunica-Biloxi council closed its tribal rolls in 1995, shortly after the casino opened, because of concerns that those trying to enroll at that point were only doing so for money. The tribe largely agreed with the council's decision to close the rolls, both for financial reasons and out of a sense that it would be unfair to compel those who had been enrolled all along to share the rewards of tribal membership in the present with those who had not cared enough to share the burden of tribal membership in the past. Angela Gonzales has noted in the context of disenrollments following gaming development, "Where once tribes were organized and governed through systems of kinship, clan, and community, they have since become increasingly governed by market relations and exclusionary formal rules regulating membership and political participation."[31] Among the Tunicas these rules have crept into the way people think of the tribal body. A few people have been able to go before the council to resolve enrollment problems, but barring some unforeseen change, official definitions of community membership will remain tightly patrolled in ways that are more closely connected to bureaucratic discourses and attendant racial projects than they were previously. Not that the tribe would benefit from opening the rolls to anyone who claimed tribal descent, but federal recognition and economic development do put new kinds of pressure on tribes to follow formalized regulations that change how people think about a tribal community.

Aside from enrollment conflicts, the casino has created other challenges for the Tunica-Biloxi Tribe, but these challenges have brought about growth and learning. One challenge has been negotiating the tribal council's role in business developments. The council oversees the affairs of the casino and other tribal economic enterprises. They are essentially the business managers for the tribe. While there is a separate economic development office, it is also closely managed by the council and has had some of its duties stripped in what was called a streamlining effort by some and political revenge by others. The council does not run the daily affairs of the casino, but it is closely involved in the larger decisions. It worked with an outside casino management company before buying out its contract in 2000, so it had accumulated six years of guided experience in the gaming industry before beginning to work independently. Now, in addition to building on its own experience (one member of the tribal council holds a master's degree in business administration), the council has hired competent personnel who know the business well, but a layer of complexity is added when a governing body runs multimillion-dollar operations and makes multimillion-dollar deals for the tribe. Not only is polity laid atop the family structure, but business is laid atop them both.

Inexperience and lack of business education are a problem for many tribes, all the more so for almost any tribe seeking federal recognition. Risk is inherent in business, so there will be occasional failures, especially in the early years of development. Expectations from the tribal members are always going to be high, and any mistake by tribal leaders will be closely scrutinized. More than that, for tribes entering the process now, the outside press will follow their every move, since Indian gaming stories make good copy. The Tunica-Biloxis have come through the industry learning process well, all things considered—their businesses are profitable, and they have made some wise decisions along with others that were unwise in retrospect, some that were popular and others less so.

A few misconceived elements of the casino management venture undertaken in 2001 should give other tribes entering the recognition process reason to pause and consider how their political structures might change after recognition. In the business world, which has become the focus of the tribal council, management is expected to make decisions on behalf of shareholders—in this case that would be the tribal members—and only later report back to them about the results. In the tribal context, though, if it turns out that the people did not agree with a decision, the council takes criticism for having been secretive and having acted against the group's wishes. The Tunica-Biloxis' traditional leadership style, with the whole group making decisions and the leaders representing those decisions to outsiders, remained strong within the tribe even after reorganization of the government in 1974, but that system has been shifting lately toward an Anglo-American model in which leadership is elected to make decisions on behalf of the electorate. The tribe still maintains a largely open political process, with accessible monthly council meetings and informal systems of regulation, but there is an imperfect fit between traditional decision making and modern business and political demands.[32]

Another important question for tribes entering casino development is whether the tribal council is the appropriate body to handle business decisions for the tribe, even when its members have appropriate business training. Clearly the council needs to have decision-making authority in tribal investments, but for elected political officials to make decisions for the tribe presents conflicts of interest. On one level it is politically and personally in the council's best interest to make sure that tribal businesses operate at maximum profit. On another level, though, hiring decisions made by elected officials are always political, and the best person for the job does not necessarily get the job. People have had their career ladders toppled and even their lives threatened for politically opposing certain individuals within the tribe. Tunica-Biloxi politics can be occasionally brutal, and not surprisingly, some people claim that it shares the nepotism and kowtowing inherent to most governments. Casinos can exacerbate nepotism by tying extra resources and powers to the tribal council. These new issues have arisen side by side with economic development opportunities after federal recognition, and they have had unanticipated effects on tribal political processes and on power relations between the tribe and the tribal government.

Similarly, federal recognition and economic development affect the balance of power between men and women. The Tunica-Biloxis possess a strong bias toward male leadership, with the council comprised predominantly—sometimes exclusively—of men. One woman currently serves on the council. Other women have served before her and are active in political affairs, but women are in many ways diverted from positions of power, a problem that is all the more troubling with the increasing significance of access to tribal political power. Most of the tribe would not feel that women's political activities are actively suppressed, but tribal leadership is primarily viewed as a masculine domain.

This view is part of a fairly recent tribal tradition. Women were not even allowed to speak at the political gatherings of men in the 1940s, although women had important roles in informal political processes even then. The tribal elder Anna Mae Juneau recalled, "When I was a little girl, I remember the old ones then—Joseph Pierite Sr. (my father), Uncle Horace Pierite, and Eli Barbry—the three of them would sit under a tree and talk about the tribe. While they discussed tribal business, the women would make the coffee and food. We were not allowed to get into the talk."[33] This tradition may be a reflection more of southern white masculine prerogative than of aboriginal leadership patterns. The named chiefs of the tribe in the historical record seem always to have been male, but the lawsuit between the tribe and Celestin Moreau Jr. in the 1840s named only Tunica women as the defendants.[34] After the murder of Chief Melacon in 1841, oral history suggests that his infant son was named chief and hidden away so he would not be killed. But in the interim no chief is named. Instead Mme. Valentine, an old woman, seems to be the acknowledged tribal leader, at least in the lawsuit. The five women listed in addition to Mme. Valentine must have seemed to be the proper people for Celestin Moreau Jr. to name as defendants. It was these women who had "taken possession of" land he claimed as his own, and "cut down and destroyed . . . the wood and timber of said land."[35] It is possible that they were named defendants because women were the ones in charge of gathering wood, but it is more likely that these women were the acknowledged leadership of the tribe at that time, even if that was primarily because of an absence of male leaders of the appropriate age.[36] None of them are named in successions of chiefs in any historical rendering, but the large gap in leadership between the time of Melacon's murder and the ascension of his infant son, Zenon La Joie, lends support to the idea that Mme. Valentine and the other women were tribal leaders at the time.[37]

Michelene Pesantubbee's research suggests that women often participated in political affairs among the Tunica tribe specifically and Southeastern Indians in general when Europeans first arrived, but that continuing patriarchal influences later rendered their participation nearly invisible. She notes, for example, that twenty Tunica men and women participated in a calumet ceremony with Bienville in 1722, and that power among the Choctaws and other nearby tribes in Louisiana in the eighteenth century could be transferred from men to women if male heirs were unavailable.[38] The reluctance of Europeans to deal with women in leadership positions, she notes, contributed significantly if not exclusively to the decline in political participation of Native American women.

The coalition of Louisiana Indians formed by Eli Barbry with the Biloxis and Choctaws from central Louisiana in 1924 suggests that at least among the Biloxi-Choctaw community near Woodworth in the 1920s, women could participate in political affairs. The first on a list of otherwise male names appended to the document in approval of the coalition is that of Aber Dosey, followed by an "X" surrounded by the phrase "her mark."[39] This and other clues to the participation of women in Tunica and Biloxi political affairs suggest that the present situation, in which women occasionally take leadership roles in a predominantly masculine domain, has cultural roots predating the early- and mid-twentieth-century tradition of shutting out women from the political process.

Other women since 1924 have been prominent tribal members, and women are honored and valued within the tribe. But oral tradition indicates that there was a period beginning in the 1930s at the latest and ending with the election of Rose Pierite White as secretary of the tribal council in 1974 when women were excluded from formal political affairs almost entirely. Rose Pierite White's educational achievements and her political activism, developed under the guidance of her father, Chief Joe Pierite Sr., helped pave the way for other women to participate in the new tribal government. Yet a history of excluding women ripples through the current tribal political structure, which continues to be male-dominated. While several women since Rose Pierite White have been elected to the council and many lead or participate in important tribal committees, a glass ceiling seems to limit women's political power. Women's authority is often subordinated to men's even though women are active in the political process, which reflects some level of tribal tradition mixed with influences from the surrounding southern society. Gender inequity in the tribal sociopolitical structure is more visible and carries more significance when men wield so much more power as members of the tribal council.

Federal recognition and casino development highlight tribal government stresses that may not have been as visible before recognition, and the shift toward centralized power that accompanies federal recognition introduces new challenges for tribes. This is hardly a reason for members of any group to wring their hands over gaming or halt their petition for federal recognition, but laying governmental and business processes on top of a previously informal and small-scale structure is a radical change that tribes seeking federal recognition need to take into account.

*Money and Culture*

Whatever troubles have arisen in connection with casino and tribal economic development, they are offset by a number of benefits. As with many gaming tribes, the Tunica-Biloxis have thought of the casino as an engine of re-distributive justice—something that contributes to a just result after poverty and dispossession characterized the experience of being indigenous for so many years—and therefore an affirmation of an enduring tribal identity. Moreover, as casino revenue strengthens the tribe's political and economic power, it can also strengthen the tribe's ability to protect and incubate its cultural projects. Although there has been a persistent concern that casino funds will lead to a materialism that is antithetical to tribal culture, the tribe has committed significant financial resources from the casino to cultural endeavors. Even people who have no desire to work in the casino or other tribal businesses support the casino and the tribe's other economic development projects. There are many ways of participating in the tribe's prosperity, and more culturally oriented tribal members have appreciated the well-funded tribal powwow and cultural programs, just as those who are more politically or economically oriented value the cultural work done by others. The Tunica-Biloxi case confirms that the presence of money and economic opportunity does not automatically lead to the decline of cultural practices, and indeed some cultures in North America and around the world have been their most vibrant and innovative in times of relative plenty, when they have had the freedom to focus on pursuits other than subsistence.[40]

The Tunica-Biloxi powwow, for example, has become an important cultural event for the tribe since John Barbry initiated it in 1996, despite some lingering resistance because of its roots outside Tunica-Biloxi culture. While even groups with very little money can produce powwows, by 1996 Tunica-Biloxi economic development funds and corporate sponsors could pay for significant prizes that drew talented dancers and drummers from around the country. With more dancers and drums come more craft and food vendors, more visitors, and higher gate receipts, and the Tunica-Biloxi powwow has become a sizable event. Since the powwow is intended to be a cultural event for the tribe and an educational event for the surrounding community, the powwow committee brings in various other performers to expose people to a variety of customs and art forms, from traditional to contemporary. A troupe of Aztec dancers, a Nipmuc indigenous woodwind player and craftsman named Hawk, the Cherokee legend keeper Jackalene Crow, and the Tunica-Biloxi Singers and Legendkeepers provide access to traditional sounds and stories from various indigenous North American cultures. Native performers such as Ulali, Joanne Shenandoah, Walela, and Irene Bedard have performed at the powwow. Barbry believes that some people grow tired of hearing powwow music after a while, so he invites other performers as a way of keeping people's interest throughout the weekend. More than that, he wants all members of the audience to find something they can connect with, be it crafts, powwow music and dancing, or harmonizing Indian women.

Critics of the powwow have suggested that the tribe should not participate in it because it is too heavily based in Plains Indian traditions, which makes it undermine a unique Tunica-Biloxi tribal cultural identity. Barbry responds to critics, "Maybe we didn't have something called a powwow, but we lived among other tribes here . . . and all these people got together and they played stickball, they danced, they probably sang and told stories, and you know, they didn't call it a powwow, but that's what it was. It was different tribes, different cultures, getting together, sharing what they know, sharing food, and having a good time together, and that's basically what a powwow is." While the powwow is still a new event for the tribe, it has quickly become solidly tied into tribal tradition. In some sense it has replaced the fête du blé, the green corn ceremony, as a tribal homecoming event and public outreach event. Revived as a public event in the 1980s after fifty years of dormancy, the fête du blé became a sort of community-wide festival, but it had been fading by the mid-1990s as it blended into the Marksville Fourth of July celebration.[41] The tribe brought in outside dancers to do exhibitions because the Tunicas at

Jean-Luc Pierite and Donna Pierite telling traditional Tunica stories at the powwow, 2008. Photo by the author.

John Barbry at the Tunica powwow, 2008. Photo by the author.

the time did not know any tribal dances. When the casino opened in 1994 most people who came home spent their time there instead of at the fête du blé, and since then the ceremony has become private once more.

Disappointed that the fête du blé as a venue for public cultural celebration had faded in significance, John Barbry wanted to do something that would help tribal members connect with their indigenous identity in meaningful ways and host other Indians at the same time. Barbry had just moved to Marksville after a stint as the archivist for the National Museum of the American Indian, where he worked with a number of people living their tribal cultures and participating in powwow culture in a way that made him yearn for something similar. He decided that an annual powwow would provide an avenue for tribal members to participate in a cultural forum that would connect them with other Indians and at the same time provide opportunities to think about what made them unique as Tunica-Biloxis.

Participation from fellow tribal members was weak in the early years. Not many had been exposed to powwow culture, so they were unsure of how to act or participate in the event. Since then more people have grown comfortable with the setting and figured out ways to become involved. Seeing other Indians preserve old traditions and combine them with new elements encourages Tunicas to do the same. Some tribal members, such as Abe Reiszner, had been active on the powwow circuit before,[42] but they were a definite minority. Since the Tunica-Biloxi powwow began, several tribal members have put together their own regalia, and others work on crafts for sale at the powwow. Barbry himself has taken up gourd dancing.[43] Lee Lopez Sr. and his son, Lee Lopez Jr., both dance the men's "traditional" style. The Lopezes also created a tribal flag, an eagle staff fitted with a banner of symbolic color imagery specific to the Tunica-Biloxi, in 1998.[44] The family of Michael and Donna Pierite has been working on developing signature Tunica patterns for men's and women's traditional dance outfits based on old photographs and reconfiguring traditional elements in new forms.

While pine-needle baskets are not historically traditional to the Tunica-Biloxi, one tribal elder, Lula Cryer, taught herself to make them in the early 1900s and taught her daughters and a number of other tribal members to make them.[45] Tunicas traditionally made cane baskets, but the decline of river cane because of overharvesting and habitat loss in the early twentieth century made that a difficult tradition to continue, leading Anna Mae Juneau and her family to use tar vine and honeysuckle vine in its place.[46] Now several Tunica-Biloxi women sell pine-needle baskets at the powwow, highlighting the Tunica-Biloxis' traditions along with their relationships to other Indians, much like the powwow itself.

Similarly, Robert Barbry created a new art form that evokes tradition in a contemporary item. Understanding that gourds and gourd-based craftwork resonate with popular and tribal ideas about "the traditional," he thought for a while about how he could transform a kind of plantain-shaped gourd that grew near his home in Lake Charles, Louisiana, into an item that he could sell at the powwow. He decided to paint the gourds with abstract designs in vivid colors and shellac them. The painted gourds share a shiny vibrancy with Latin American papier-mâché art, but they are unique to this Tunica-Biloxi artist. The result represents the same fusion of cultural inspirations that Barbry's brother John imagined when he initiated the tribal powwow. The powwow has become an avenue for Tunica-Biloxi tribal members to express commitment to their tribal heritage and ensure its rich cultural future.

John Barbry contends that the powwow is especially crucial to the Tunica-Biloxis because three centuries of racism and colonialism forced the loss of so many of their traditions. The tribe was so assimilated by the time of recognition, Barbry asserts, that the vast majority had no idea what their traditional culture was. A small core of people kept that distinctive culture alive. By the 1970s that core was the smallest it had ever been, but the tribal council recognized the need to nurture that core and maintain the little things that make the Tunica-Biloxis a distinct community. Barbry clarifies: "I'm not saying we should move into thatched huts. I'm just saying we should know where we come from and why we're different."[47] The powwow helps foster a sense of cultural, historical, and political distinction.

The powwow provides a homecoming event for the tribe too. By the early 1990s a trip to Marksville might have been awkward for people who only had distant relatives there, since their family had been in Texas or Illinois for three generations. They could go back and look at the museum for half an hour, walk around the reservation for another hour, but then what? The powwow gives people a reason to come home together at the same time. With the economic development of the reservation, people are more likely to have close family living in town again whom they can visit. If not, they can spend time at the tribal casino, hotel, and entertainment complex after the powwow is over. The powwow provides an opportunity for tribal members to reconnect with their heritage.

John Barbry takes advantage of the public relations value of the powwow for the tribe, incorporating other educational events into the powwow weekend. He invites elementary school classes to educational demonstrations on the Wednesday and Thursday before the powwow, and several hundred students have come to the reservation each time. He makes education central to the powwow and asks the master of ceremonies to focus on educating the audience about the various dancing styles, regalia, and musical traditions throughout the weekend. Barbry understands, as have other tribal leaders since the time of Chief Joe Pierite, that winning the allegiance of local non-Indians promotes the welfare of the tribe. Coming from a not-too-distant past when Indian children could not enroll in white schools and townspeople consistently suppressed corporate and individual tribal rights, it could be considered a grand gesture for the tribe to reach out to local non-Indians. But the tribe understands that good local relationships protect it from unnecessary battles. Powwowing is politicking, making the powwow part of a strong Tunica-Biloxi tradition that dates to the French colonial era.

The Tunica-Biloxis passed the twenty-fifth anniversary of federal recognition in 2006. As one of the first tribes to maneuver through the BIA's new federal recognition procedures, they were leaders for other tribes in the region. The Jena Choctaws would follow them through the process by 1995, and several other groups are lined up behind them. Other groups study the Tunica-Biloxis' successes and failures as they try to emulate their eventual achievements. Recognized before the advent of casinos, the Tunica-Biloxis faced obstacles different from those confronting petitioners today, although their land claim against the state provoked opposition similar to that which casinos bring now. Members of the tribe are grateful that the state's governor supported their recognition petition, and that they were able to gather enough political support and documentary evidence to endure the tedious recognition process. While it seemed that little had changed immediately after recognition, victory in the Tunica Treasure case signaled that the tribe's political and legal status mattered immensely. Since then the casino resort has lifted the tribe out of poverty—significantly altering its experience of indigeneity and race—and powered developments that have allowed tribal culture and political status to recover and grow in new ways in Marksville.

Recognition has not come without problems. The tribe has had to rigidly enforce tribal boundaries to meet federal recognition policy demands. Formalized structures have created new stresses on previously informal relationships. Economic development has intensified—if not created—class stratification on the reservation, and positions of power have become fiercely contested. Other tribes will have to contend with many of the same problems that are inherent in maintaining a relationship with the federal government upon recognition. Bitter political disputes, nepotism, and sexism may have been present in tribes before recognition, but they are clearly exacerbated in newly recognized tribes.

## The Tribal Future

Because the Tunicas went for so long without recognition, because they were so important to the development of recognition policy, and because recognition has been so important to the tribe, it can be hard not to center federal recognition in narratives of tribal life. Without diminishing the significance of federal recognition for the Tunicas, an examination of the broad relationships between the tribe and the United States reveals that even after recognition the relationship remained fundamentally colonial. Not only is the tribe subject to the plenary power doctrine that permanently subordinates it to the will of the United States government (as evidenced by the intrusion of state authority into tribal gaming and economic development),[48] but local and nongovernmental racial discourses persist with or without recognition. Not that the focus on recognition has been misguided, but the challenges to tribal well-being are broader, at the ideological level rather than the policy level.

Evidence of persistent and emergent racial stereotypes confirms that an ideology of white supremacy continues to inform race relations at many levels in Louisiana. Donna Pierite, who is not enrolled in the tribe but has tribal ancestry and a last name that is immediately coded as Tunica by people in Marksville, was subjected to employment discrimination that provides a useful example. After Hurricane Katrina the state superintendent of education directed all evacuated teachers to report to local schools in evacuation centers to help shoulder the extra workload of teaching children relocated to those areas. Following this directive, Pierite applied for a job at Marksville High School, hoping that her twenty years of experience teaching French and Spanish in New Orleans and her postgraduate education would make her a valuable addition to the school's faculty. When she applied, however, she was brusquely rejected. "They said, 'Why don't you go find a job at the casino?' Okay? That's what they said." Pierite called the tribal chairman Earl Barbry Sr., who intervened on her behalf, and she was hired shortly thereafter. That Barbry was able to persuade school officials to give Pierite a fair chance indicates that the tribe has achieved a degree of authority locally and that the tribe and the town have come a long way from the days when Indian children were not even allowed to enroll in white schools; still, that he had to intervene at all shows that anti-Indianism is alive and well in Marksville.

Though Pierite says that her principal was very accommodating after she began working, her initial experience reveals the impact of what Katherine Spilde has termed "rich Indian racism."[49] The false stereotype of wealthy Indians with unlimited resources is "embraced despite overwhelming evidence to the contrary."[50] The Tunica-Biloxi Tribe has a successful casino resort and other economic development efforts, but tribal per capita payments are only enough to supplement but not replace a salary or wages. That Pierite applied for a job likely meant that she needed one. Yet the stereotype of rich Indians is accompanied by a related line of thinking suggesting that Indians (especially from gaming tribes) do not deserve—and ought not seek—jobs or support outside the tribe. This practice is doubly destructive, since it is used to justify the exclusion of people who according to statistics are already lagging economically. In this case the person who rejected Donna's application knew that the Pierite family had likely lost its home and that Donna had at least temporarily lost her job after Katrina, but still believed that Donna should not have applied for a job at Marksville High School.

While this might seem like a new kind of anti-Indian racism, it shares a familial resemblance with earlier, pre-casino and pre-recognition kinds of anti-Indian racism. It assumes the same kinds of character flaws in Indians, and more importantly, the same kinds of character strengths in whites. The old ideas—that Indians are always looking for handouts while whites seek evaluation on their merits, that Indians are incompetent while whites are competent, that Indians receive government money they do not deserve while whites have to earn their money through work—take their place alongside the new: that Indians are wealthy and advantaged because of casinos while whites are disadvantaged by racial preference programs and ought to have their jobs protected, and that Indians should be content to work in casinos while whites can have diverse career aspirations. The common thread is the ideology of white supremacy rather than the status of Indians.

Much of the behavior that we think of as damaging to Indians—the kinds of racism and colonialism that challenge individual and tribal well-being on many levels—persist even after recognition and even after successful economic development. Federal recognition is one component of a broader process of racial formation, and it affects the way a tribe operates and is seen by the outside world because of its economic and political status, among other factors. The Tunica-Biloxis' achievements since recognition represent what most petitioners would think of as ideal: political empowerment (in particular at the local and state levels), economic development, the return of tribal members to the homeland, a revitalized and innovative tribal culture, and an affirmation of tribal history. But these advances have still been achieved in a broader cultural context of white supremacist racial formation. The experiences of the tribe and tribal members after recognition confirm that while recognition has come to be regarded as transformational, it would more usefully be thought of as a tool that helps tribes to pursue their own agendas more effectively. It changes the status of the tribe under United States law and moves the United States toward a more just position of respect for the sovereignty of one of the original nations of this land, but the persistence of racial and colonial ideology means that recognition is only a starting point.

Because of this, whether a tribe is federal or nonfederal it cannot focus on legal thinking alone. As Vine Deloria Jr. suggested several decades ago, the greatest struggle for Indians continues to be in the ideological realm, because most of the challenges to Indians can be traced there.[51] Respect for tribal sovereignty on a legal level is absolutely central to undermining white supremacist ideology, because colonial political and legal structures inform and are informed by that ideology. Hence, if a colonial practice such as the exercise of federal plenary power is weakened, so is the ideology that produced the concept of plenary power in the first place—the ideology of white supremacy. Still, ideology runs deeper and wider than the politico-legal structure; it is mutually constituted with multiple practices of racial and colonial domination. It lies not just in the relationship of federal governent, state government, and tribe but in the relationships between judges and defendants, teachers and students, the media industry and its subjects, employers and job seekers. The ideology informs and is informed by not just governmental relationships but also incarceration rates, levels of educational attainment, portrayals in the media, and the socioeconomic status of whites, indigenous communities, and communities of color alike. In that sense tribes need to pay close attention to—and combat—ideologies external to the tribe that continue to affect tribal well-being at the global, national, local, and personal levels, even after federal recognition. Tribes formed ideologies that helped guide them before the recognition process existed and must continue to do so afterward, carefully considering the impact of external ideologies and practices on their internal identities, values, and practices.

## CHAPTER 6

## Jena Choctaws under Jim Crow and
## outside the Federal Purview

With around 250 tribal members in 2010, the Jena Band of Choctaws were a small extended family with a dwindling number of
Choctaw language speakers and a relatively high average blood
quantum. Among unrecognized tribes they were unusual in the
extent to which they had maintained aboriginal language, culture,
and blood quantums—so unusual that even the largely conservative Mississippi Band of Choctaws supported their petition and
offered to accept qualifying Jena tribal members onto their own
tribal rolls if recognition fell through. And yet, in their efforts
to achieve recognition and in their interactions with other tribes
the Jena Band encountered many of the same obstacles as other,
more acculturated unrecognized groups, revealing that unreasonable challenges beset even indisputably Indian groups in the recognition process—challenges that are blamed on the supposed shortcomings of more culturally and racially mixed groups in other
cases. Jena Choctaws had significant interactions with the federal
government, notably receiving federal Indian educational funding
for an Indian school for their children for several years in the
mid-1930s. The Jena Choctaws' educational choices and circumstances during the New Deal reveal how Indians have been affected
by and participated in broader racial formation processes in previously unexamined ways, and provide a long-term view of federal
inconsistency in recognition policy.

The origins of the Choctaw community near Jena, Louisiana,
remain cloaked in the shadows of time. Choctaws had been living

in northern and central Louisiana since at least the eighteenth century, and by the beginning of the nineteenth century the area had become a favorite hunting territory for many Choctaws. Numerous reports from about 1730, after the decimation of the Natchez by the French and the Tunica, to well into the nineteenth century report the presence of bands of Choctaws throughout the land west of their Mississippi homeland.[1] By the time John Sibley took his post as Indian agent for the newly purchased Louisiana Territory in 1806, numerous bands of Choctaws made more or less permanent homes in Louisiana, while others simply came to hunt and make war.[2]

In Sibley's first report in 1807 is a suggestion of a nascent community near Jena, but no solid ties to the modern community. Sibley notes a Choctaw settlement of about fifty people on Lake Catahoula, near Jena, led by a chief named Biachubby, but despite the likelihood of some connection there is no available evidence in documents or oral traditions linking Biachubby or the other Choctaws in Sibley's reports to the Jena Band.[3] Research conducted by the tribe, Marilyn Watt, Sharon Brown, and the Office of Federal Acknowledgment suggests that current tribal members descend largely from Choctaws who lived in Scott and Newton counties in Mississippi as late as the Civil War. It is possible that the families who moved into the area in the 1870s were linked in some way to earlier settlements at Lake Catahoula or Trout Creek, where they eventually settled, or that they passed nearby during an aborted removal effort and settled there at a later date, but there is no evidence currently available that would confirm such a claim.[4]

By 1870 some of the modern-day group's ancestors were being identified in the census in neighboring Grant Parish, and by 1880 many of the ancestors had begun their long association with a family of wealthy white landowners and merchants in the area, the Whatleys.[5] In 1886 the anthropologist Albert Gatschet collected some Choctaw vocabularies from ancestors of the Jena Band for the Bureau of Ethnology. Interviews that he conducted seem to suggest that most, though not all, of the Jena Band's ancestors came from Mississippi just after the Civil War, having passed through the area several times when journeying back and forth from Mississippi to Indian Territory.[6] Census records in 1880 give conflicting information, with the self-reported birthplace of most of the community listed as Louisiana.[7] The records of the Dawes Commission seem to confirm that most of the Jena Choctaw ancestors had come from Mississippi after the Civil War, and that they probably told people seeking information about their birthplace whatever answer they imagined would best protect their interests.[8]

At the turn of the century the Dawes Commission set about identifying Choctaws eligible for enrollment in the Choctaw Nation, beginning the final federal attempt to remove Choctaws to the Indian Territories.[9] Oral history maintains that Jena Choctaw ancestors walked from Jena to Muskogee in the Indian Territories to enroll and receive allotments in 1902. When the opportunity arose for them to go to Oklahoma and receive land allotments under the Dawes Act, the possibility of owning land, living near other Choctaws again, and escaping their present lives must have enticed them, since traveling to Oklahoma to apply for land, whether by foot or by train, would have meant an enormous expenditure of resources and energy for impoverished Indians in 1902.

After giving their testimony most of the Jena Band's ancestors were identified by the commission as full-blood Choctaws who had never removed to Indian Territories and were eligible for enrollment.[10] For unknown reasons the majority of Jena Choctaws who testified before the Dawes Commission, though approved for enrollment, failed to occupy their allotments or enroll. Oral tradition suggests that they did not have the means to return to Oklahoma after they received word back in Louisiana nine months later that they were approved. It is also possible that they had begun to hear about the unfavorable circumstances of other recent Choctaw immigrants and the threats of the Snakes, a traditional element of Creeks, Choctaws, Seminoles, Cherokees, and Chickasaws in the Indian Territories who opposed allotment, sometimes violently.[11] One Jena Choctaw did move to Oklahoma and enrolled in the Oklahoma Choctaw Nation at that time, and several others moved to Oklahoma at a later date but were not enrolled.[12]

The group's interaction with the Dawes Commission is significant, because one way a tribe petitioning for recognition can establish tribal existence is to have the federal government deal with it as a tribe. If this can be demonstrated, then the tribe only has to prove tribal existence from that point forward in its petition. Interacting with the federal government as a tribe "proves" tribal existence at all points prior to that interaction, according to OFA regulations. In this case, however, the Dawes Commission only dealt with the Jena ancestors as individuals eligible to enroll in the Choctaw Nation of Oklahoma, rather than as a distinct political entity.[13] For this reason OFA asserted that the federal government treated the Jena Choctaws as part of the Mississippi Band of Choctaws rather than as a separate tribal entity for the purposes of the Dawes Commission. However, the tribe did use the Dawes Commission records to establish some of its ancestral history, including its likely origins in Mississippi and increasingly exclusive use of the Choctaw language.

Declining English-language proficiency demonstrated how insular the Jena Choctaws were—some of the older group members who had likely come from Mississippi in the 1870s spoke English, while their Louisiana-born children and grandchildren could not.[14] The entire population of Choctaws in the Jena Band hovered between thirty and forty from 1880 to the early 1900s, and consisted of only five households in 1910.[15] When the population dipped into the teens in 1914 or 1915, after the removal of two households to Oklahoma, the community nearly disintegrated. It survived because the Lewis family, which consisted of fourteen Choctaws from a nearby parish, joined the group shortly thereafter and stabilized the population, allowing more marriages between Choctaws for that generation and continued insularity.[16]

The Jena Choctaws made their living in the early twentieth century by performing wage labor, selling baskets, taking in laundry, tanning hides, and sharecropping land that is remembered to have belonged to them at some point.[17] Watt analyzed account ledgers of the Whatley family store from 1906 to 1935, noting that Jena Choctaw accounts in the early years are recorded in the ledgers using a person's first name followed by the designation "Indian." Thus Will Jackson was recorded as "Will Indian," providing a record of the thorough social distinction of the group from surrounding populations.[18]

After prices for cotton, the overwhelmingly predominant cash crop of the South, dropped dramatically in the mid-1930s, tenant farming became unviable as a means of support.[19] As a result the Jena Choctaws entered into wage labor where it was available, working in the timber industry or moving to towns where jobs were slightly more plentiful. Those who remained in the rural areas moved in and out of little shacks on various plantations as the availability of employment changed. The local white power structure narrowly circumscribed their choices through the first half of the twentieth century, as local whites overtly and directly prevented Choctaw economic and educational mobility. A Jena Choctaw elder recalled how local whites enforced the boundaries of white privilege in the 1930s and denigrated tribal members: "They said to me, 'Indians don't need land. You don't need to buy land.' They would not loan me the money. Then they said, 'Indians don't need education—they got work!' "[20]

The collective anger, humiliation, and resentment that develop from interactions such as these last beyond the lifetime of the people who experience them. Memories of such experiences reinforce tribal identity to this day.

Contemporary Jena Choctaws experience racism as well, though not in the same form or to the same degree as their ancestors, who faced a totalizing, institutionalized racism in every aspect of their interaction with non-Indians. But the racism that tribal members experience today combines with the racism experienced then to form a collective memory, a pool of experience that reinforces tribal identity and the Jena Choctaws' sense of their right to be federally recognized as an Indian tribe.[21] These experiences can be productively understood as forms of historic trauma that federal recognition addresses in profound ways.

## Education of Indians under Segregation

The racial status of the Jena Choctaws as nonwhites kept them locked economically and socially to the bottom rungs of the surrounding white supremacist society. They were not allowed to enroll in white schools, and they were barred from access to a variety of other economic opportunities. In the 1920s the Jena Choctaw chief Bill Lewis was the first to actively pursue for his people formal education along Anglo lines. He likely saw it as a way to open new opportunities for Choctaws, concerned about the limits that illiteracy and declining English-language proficiency placed on them. In 1929 he approached the LaSalle Parish superintendent, E. E. Richardson, about providing education for Choctaw children. Richardson hired the assistant principal of the Jena high school, Jay Pipes, to teach twenty-four lessons to Choctaw children at a local church, using money from the newly established literacy campaign in Louisiana.[22] Typically state literacy funds were designated for the education of illiterate adults, but parish officials saw use of the funds for children as a reasonable solution to the problem of where to place the ten school-aged Choctaw children in a system designed for segregation in black and white. After the initial twenty-four lessons, however, those in charge of the white church where the classes were taught decided not to allow them to be held there anymore, leaving the Jena Choctaws without educational opportunities for the next several years.[23]

There was an effort under way to acquire federal funds for other Louisiana Indians in 1931. Responding to an inquiry from U.S. Representative René Louis DeRouen, the Office of Indian Affairs sent Special Commissioner Roy Nash to investigate the status of Indians in Louisiana. Nash's report began with a survey of the Coushatta tribe in DeRouen's district in southwest Louisiana, concluding that they should not receive aid, because aid would "brand as paupers one of the few groups of Indians who, unaided, have won full citizenship and equality."[24] The Coushattas, he noted, had a separate elementary school in their community but attended high school with whites in Elton, where "far from discriminating against them, the schools of Elton regard the Indians as favorites because of their athletic prowess."[25] Moreover, he said, the Coushattas were no poorer than their white and "colored" neighbors, and their situation compared favorably with that of the state's three thousand Houma Indians, "whose plight is infinitely more pathetic."[26] Local whites had barred the Houmas from attending white schools because some of the tribe had African ancestry, and the Houmas, like every other Indian group in the state, would not attend black schools. Nash thought that the Terrebonne Parish school board seemed amenable to opening a school strictly for Houmas in the following year, a contrivance that prompted him to comment, "One can only pity a state where three sets of public schools are required to educate American citizens."[27]

Nash concluded from his brief visit with the Coushattas and Houmas that the Indian communities of Louisiana were too scattered to make it feasible for the federal government to provide school facilities for them. He was aware that there were "a few Tunica Indians about Marksville," and listed some other parishes with Indian populations, but he was entirely unaware of the Choctaw community at Jena or any other group north of Cajun country. More importantly, he never suggested the possibility of federal contracts with Louisiana school districts to pay for separate Indian education, closing a door for the Jena Choctaws even if he was never aware of their presence. The assistant to the commissioner of Indian affairs, Fred Daiker, accepted Nash's conclusions in August 1931: "No action is recommended," he stated, "altho[ugh] the Indians are poor, etc. Apparently except to inform ourselves and others who may inquire, there is nothing to do on this report."[28]

The state superintendent of education T. H. Harris, who had met with Nash in 1931, inquired further about the possibility of funding schools for Louisiana Indians in February 1932. He was rebuffed by the secretary of the interior Ray Lyman Wilbur, an avowed assimilationist who argued that bringing Louisiana Indians into federal programs would run counter to the bureau's goal of eventually forcing Indians to survive in American society without federal protections or support.[29] But communication between the State Department of Education and the Office of Indian Affairs would continue throughout the decade with more success for tribes in later years.

Mattie Penick, a white schoolteacher who had been forced to resign her position under Louisiana law after she married, was likely behind Harris's inquiries in 1932.[30] She became interested in educating Jena Choctaw children, she said, after seeing two of them that summer, "look[ing] mournfully at the white people in the swimming pool."[31] She learned that they spoke no English and were not allowed to enroll in white schools, and according to a newspaper article in 1938, "she thought suddenly she could help them and help herself by going back to teaching—there were no bars against a married woman teaching Indians."[32] She contacted Senator Huey Long to find out whether the Jena Choctaws might be eligible for a government-funded day school. Long in turn contacted the Indian affairs commissioner C. J. Rhoads, who replied that only groups with a previous relationship with the federal government were eligible for such schools, not "scattered groups of Indians who have never been under the jurisdiction of the federal government" such as the Jena Choctaws.[33] Their status as nonfederal Indians meant that not only did they suffer the effects of segregation because they were Indians, but they were doubly excluded, denied educational opportunities available to other Indians because they were not federally recognized in 1932.

While efforts for federal intervention failed that year, Penick found other resources to provide education to the Jena Choctaws. She persuaded a local lumber company to pay for supplies to build a one-room schoolhouse for the Jena Choctaws and enlisted Superintendent Richardson in her cause. Penick and Richardson found money still available from the state literacy campaign to pay for supplies and a salary for Penick, whose marital status was over-looked in this special circumstance so she could teach the Choctaw children.[34]

Students from five to eighteen were enrolled in the school the first year, and all worked with the same reading materials. A representative of the state Department of Education who visited the school in 1933 suggested that "only two or three knew any of the English language" when they began in the fall, but that they had now completed a primer and were all working on first-grade English reading materials.[35] Unfortunately the literacy program funds upon which the school relied for this anemic curriculum derived from the state malt tax, which evaporated after the end of Prohibition in 1933.[36] With its principal source of support gone, the school had to close, and Penick and Richardson resumed requests for support from the federal government.

Richardson's initial efforts for federal funding were as unsuccessful as those of Penick and Superintendent Harris. In May 1932 Richardson wrote to U.S. Senator John Overton requesting federal educational funds for the Jena Choctaws: "There are about fifteen full-blood Choctaw Indian children in this Parish growing up almost totally illiterate. They will not, and should not, attend our negro schools, and they are too far behind in their studies (most of them cannot even read) to attend the white schools, embarrassment alone preventing . . . Anything you might get done for these Indians will be highly valued by the citizens of the Parish."[37]

Setting aside for a moment the question of federal support for the Jena Choctaws, the superintendent's letter is instructive in that it assumes blacks and Indians to be categorically distinct. Indians in Louisiana, while not treated as the equals of whites, were far enough from being black that the white superintendent was willing to advocate for funds to be disbursed on their behalf and suggested that it would be inappropriate for them to attend black schools. Opinions such as his were supported by recent legal precedents in the state that distinguished between blacks and Indians, even going so far as to prevent intermarriage between blacks and Indians, but not between whites and Indians.[38] It is also likely that the popularity of "the Indian cause" in the United States in the 1920s and 1930s had reached a few liberal-minded people in the area, stimulating some movement in the positioning of racial barriers. In Jim Crow Louisiana of the 1930s even full-blooded, non-English-speaking Indians were becoming nearly "white" enough to attend white schools. The Jena Choctaw case for integration was certainly aided by their refusal to attend black schools, since attendance at black schools would have confirmed their inferior racial status, and by their own lack of black ancestry, which would have automatically designated them as black for most purposes. Indians began attending white schools in Jena by the end of the Second World War, long before most whites in LaSalle Parish would educate their children alongside black children in the area, indicating again the prevalence of a graded distinction between the social, economic, and political position of the races. In fact, in areas only a slight distance from large Indian populations, individual Indian children were often allowed to enroll in white schools, as was one Jena Choctaw student who was half-white.[39]

While the Choctaws themselves clearly remember being barred from white school in Jena at this time and other documentary evidence supports their memory, the superintendent's letter implies that they stayed away from white schools by choice—that it was only their embarrassment over lack of adequate preparation and English-language proficiency that kept them away from white schools.[40] Richardson lied about the school board's willingness to enroll Choctaw students in white schools. That Richardson expended any effort on behalf of the Choctaws indicates that there was some interest in obtaining educational facilities for the Choctaws, but this interest stemmed from a belief that a white education might make the Choctaws less of a "liability in the community," as Richardson's successor would characterize them, rather than a belief in racial equality between Choctaws and whites.[41] Richardson's closing statement that "anything you might get done for these Indians will be highly valued by the citizens of the Parish" suggests that he and the white citizens of LaSalle Parish considered the Choctaws a bewildering public burden, since they did not neatly fit into the system of racial oppression that provided facilities for only two races.[42] Richardson hoped that federal funds could be used to "uplift" a people described by local whites as lacking in moral character, since local whites would not approve of expenditures on behalf of such a project.[43] Parish officials and newspapers displayed similar enthusiasm for rudimentary education for blacks under segregation.[44] Richardson probably concealed local discrimination against the Choctaws to make the request for separate school funding more palatable to federal officials. By appearing to have made every effort to induce the Choctaws to attend available local schools, he could give the impression that the Choctaws' own reticence—rather than the segregated school system—was to blame for the lack of opportunity available to them. Thus the parish could preserve white privilege under segregation and at the same time relieve itself of the obligation to pay for the education of Indian citizens, whose racial classification muddled the established system.

It seems likely that opinions in the parish and on the school board were mixed regarding integration of Choctaw students. While some members of the school board might have allowed Choctaw children into the white school, there was a stronger contingent at the time opposed to integration. Since schools in LaSalle Parish finally integrated Indian students by 1945, some sentiment in favor of Choctaw integration must have been present before that time, though even as late as 1940 the school board expressed opposition to Choctaw integration.[45]

Because of the continued segregation of Choctaw students from white students, efforts to find federal funding were under way even before the school closed in 1933. Funding for the school was discussed at a meeting in Baton Rouge in March 1933 between officials from BIA and from the Louisiana education department, including T. H. Harris, who had inquired about federal Indian educational funding a year earlier. Samuel H. Thompson, supervisor of Indian education in charge of public school relations for the Office of Indian Affairs, misidentified the Choctaw school run by Penick as "the Cherokee Indian School" in his report on this meeting, and seemed skeptical that the school would merit federal Indian funds. Since the Louisiana Department of Education had no firsthand information on the school, the assistant state supervisor of elementary education, Helene Sliffe, was sent to investigate its status and report back to the department. While Sliffe's report on the school's activities glowed, no funding was forthcoming at that time.[46]

In 1933 Charles J. Rhoads was commissioner of Indian affairs and W. Carson Ryan was director of Indian education for the Office of Indian Affairs, and they had been slowly trying to reformulate federal Indian education policy to meet the recommendations of the Meriam Report (1928), which Ryan had helped to research and write. The report revealed the heartbreaking conditions that Indian children endured in federal boarding schools, forcing the Indian Bureau to reconsider not only the way it ran those institutions but its entire conception of Indian education. Before that time federal education for Indians was unabashedly assimilationist in design. Universally spartan conditions in boarding schools resulted from federal stinginess toward Indian programs and a policy of using constant student labor to support the schools and quasi-military drilling to instill discipline and industry in Indian children. Ryan, appointed by Rhoads in 1930, was an advocate of progressive education who believed that a school should be cherished by the community it served and that its curriculum should reflect the needs of the community. Boarding schools, which removed children from their homes at a tender age, forced them into a brutal daily regimen of work and discipline, and taught white history and values while banishing tribal languages and cultural practices, clearly did not fit this mold. Ryan began trying to close federal boarding schools, opting where feasible to enroll children in community day schools that would keep the children in their homes.[47]

While he was only able to close or convert ten boarding schools during his term, Ryan eventually hoped to replace all boarding schools with community day schools or enter into contracts with states for the education of Indian children in local public schools.[48] Ryan's efforts to channel Indians into public schools contradicted his desire to use curricula that reflected Indian interests, since public schools almost universally taught a curriculum that villainized Indians in American history (where it mentioned Indians at all). Further, as the Office of Indian Affairs would discover over the next decade, many of the surrounding white communities were hostile to Indians, and most were more interested in the money that came with Indian students than in educating the students themselves.[49] But Ryan's advocacy for the public school education of Indians was important to Louisiana Indians, because it meant that there was opportunity, at least, for some form of federal support for their education.

The policy shift away from boarding schools had contradictory effects for the Jena Choctaws. Brenda Child has documented how some Indian families viewed boarding schools as a resource to be used in hard times to prevent greater hardships. The grinding poverty of the Depression in the 1930s, the death of parents, the lack of other educational opportunities, the desire to be educated with other Indians, and racial hostility at predominantly white public schools all led some Indian families to send their children to boarding schools despite an acute awareness of the difficulties the children would face there.[50] Neither the documentary record nor oral histories suggest that the Jena Choctaws were informed of the possibility of attending a boarding school. Whether because of federal efforts to decrease boarding school enrollment or to decrease the federal service population overall, the effect was to eliminate a potential choice for the Jena Choctaws.[51] Boarding school enrollments were actually increasing in the 1930s, despite the closure of a number of boarding schools. Combined with the repeated refusals from the Office of Indian Affairs to requests for services for other Louisiana Indians, it seems likely that their status as nonfederal Indians precluded their attendance at boarding schools, even though as individuals of one-half or more Indian ancestry, they should have qualified under the Indian Reorganization Act if nothing else.[52] By 1940, after the Penick School had ceased to receive federal funds, Mattie Penick asked a Jena Choctaw parent whether she would approve of sending her children seventy miles away to Natchitoches to be educated at the state normal college there. The parent quickly assented, indicating that some of the group might have been open to this possibility in the early 1930s as well.[53]

Tsianina Lomawaima's observation that experiences at Chilocco Indian School and other boarding schools like it could foster pan-Indian and even tribal identity in students applies only partially to the Jena Choctaws of this generation.[54] Choctaw identity among this group was thorough and unshakable, so boarding school could only have weakened their identification with their community. What a school like Chilocco might have provided is a pool of eligible Indian, even Choctaw, marriage partners for the Jena Choctaws of this generation. Jena Choctaw marriage patterns shifted markedly in the 1940s, from Choctaw-Choctaw to Choctaw-white, because of the scarcity of eligible local Choctaw marriage partners.[55] Boarding school would have brought the Jena Choctaws out of relative isolation from other Choctaws.

Moreover, it would have provided them with a broader network of Choctaw and non-Choctaw Indian acquaintances to turn to as adults, and this network could have helped them to think about federal recognition and political assertion earlier than they did.

On the other hand, federal nonrecognition allowed the Jena Choctaws to avoid the more easily identifiable physical, emotional, and cultural assault typically associated with education in a federal boarding school. When coupled with other internal and external mechanisms identified by Watt as contributing to their enclavement, it is likely that ineligibility for boarding school enrollment left the Jena Choctaws more socially and culturally intact than they might have been had they been federally recognized.[56] That Jena Choctaw youths spoke little or no English in 1932 supports this hypothesis. Jena Choctaw children would likely have lost much of their Choctaw language if they had been placed in boarding schools long-term, since the faculty and administrations of federal boarding schools were slow to respond to the Office of Indian Education's new support for tribal cultures and Indian history courses in the 1930s.[57] Jena Choctaws kept their culture and language but had to sacrifice the broader economic opportunities that education might have brought them, even in a federal boarding school. Still, the assimilative impact of the colonial apparatus that accompanied federal recognition at the time should not be overlooked when considering its impact in the present day.

The federal government's preferred solution to the problem of where to place Choctaw students was for the LaSalle Parish schools to accept Jena Choctaw students without any reimbursements for their tuition, since the Jena Choctaws had no nontaxable land. Because of this, the government argued, they had the same status as other citizens of the state, so responsibility for their education rightly fell on local authorities. While local schools would not provide a curriculum that honored Choctaw culture and history, arguments about the values and culture reflected in the curriculum were moot for the Jena Choctaws in the 1930s. Looking back from the twenty-first century, they would presumably have chosen a bilingual education that reflected Choctaw history and culture, but at the time they simply sought a form of education that might help them move out from under the thumb of the Whatleys and other whites in the area. Having no familiarity with federal Indian education, they had no experiences on which they could draw to voice the kinds of criticisms that Ryan and others involved in the progressive education movement might have had. They could learn Choctaw culture and values at home. What they felt they needed most desperately was to learn to read and write in English. A federally funded Indian community day school represented the best opportunity for them given their circumstances.

The Penick Indian School, as it came to be called, had closed for the 1933–34 school year, but the Johnson-O'Malley Act, passed by Congress in 1934, provided new opportunities for federal funding. The act allowed the Office of Indian Affairs to contract with state governments to provide their public school districts with funds to educate local Indian students. Ryan had been contemplating such an arrangement in Louisiana when he sent a delegate to meet with Louisiana education officials in 1933. But the passage of the Johnson-O'Malley Act removed funding obstacles that had impeded federal assistance previously, and coupled with further pleas and more accurate information from Louisiana state officials and tribal advocates received by the Office of Indian Affairs, it provided the impetus to overcome earlier suggestions that nothing could be done for Jena Choctaws or Louisiana's other Indian tribes.[58]

There were plans to reopen the Penick Indian School in the fall of 1934 after an official with the Louisiana Department of Education, M. S. Robertson, interceded and persuaded Carson Ryan to fund the school.[59] A. C. Hector, superintendent of the Choctaw Indian Agency in Mississippi, was not pleased with the arrangement agreed to by Ryan. Hector suggested that rather than receive funds for a school, they "be offered an opportunity to remove to some of our Mississippi schools, otherwise, I do not believe I would be justified in recommending much in the way of assistance for such a small group who have for years been separated from any other Indians."[60] He later commented that "if we start taking care of other little groups in the State I am afraid the Department will be called on to keep it up indefinitely."[61]

At the time the bureau and Hector had never had any direct contact with the Jena Band, and Hector in particular wanted to make sure they were not mixed with blacks, as some of the other Indians in the state were rumored to be.[62] Hector's attitude indicates the reception that tribes with African ancestry received, but he believed, based on the reports of those in contact with the Jena Band, that they were a distinct group of nearly full-blooded Choctaws since he proposed that they might be moved to Mississippi to take advantage of resources available to other Choctaws there. Since he eventually became an enthusiastic supporter of education for the Jena Choctaws and the Office of Indian Affairs funded them separately from the Mississippi Choctaws, the Office of Indian Affairs acknowledged that they were a distinct group.[63] That federal funds for the Jena Choctaws were eventually cut off while the Mississippi Choctaw funds were not provides further evidence that the BIA did not consider the Jena Band a satellite of the Mississippi Band of Choctaws, which would later be a point of contention in the tribe's OFA petition.

The Office of Indian Affairs indicated that funding would be forthcoming for the school in 1934–35, but it is not clear whether this funding was ever disbursed.[64] The Penick Indian School began receiving federal funds for Indian students by 1935, and they were renewed every year until 1938. Funds provided for facilities, materials, the teacher's salary, transportation, and free lunch for the students.

Academic curriculum at the Penick Indian School seemed to consist largely of lessons in reading and writing in English, though progress in this area received mixed reviews from federal officials. There does not seem to be any evidence that Penick had been informed about the federal Indian school curriculum or new recommendations for Indian education, but she followed the federal pattern of making the students responsible for a large part of the upkeep of the tiny school, using it as a "model living environment." Students not only constructed some of the school's furniture but also cooked lunch for the other students and chopped wood for the stove.[65] Penick devoted a considerable amount of class time to crafts, such as baskets and beadwork items, and what might be called practical skills, such as sewing and wood-working. Students in later years recalled that they spent more time making crafts than doing schoolwork.

The school was closed in 1938 when the BIA deemed it a waste of money because of low attendance and the minimal accomplishments of the pupils under Penick's guidance.[66] Willard W. Beatty, director of Indian education by that time, visited the school that year, and it was at his suggestion that funding was cut off. He endorsed A. C. Hector's earlier suggestion that the group be moved to Mississippi to attend school there, and said that the several Jena families with whom he had talked about the matter were "entirely willing to make the move."[67] But L. W. Page, Hector's successor as super-intendent of the Choctaw Indian Agency in Mississippi, responded with clear frustration to the suggestion that the Jena Choctaws be given housing in Mississippi: "To date we have taken no action looking toward the transfer of these families for the reason that we have not, as stated in my former communication, sufficient homes to accommodate Indians already living in the Mississippi area who have made application for places."[68] He had hoped, he noted, accommodations could be made with the Jena public schools for educating the Choctaw children, but failing that he saw it as no great misfortune if the Jena Choctaws went without any schooling at all that year. A replacement teacher could have been found if the federal government had wanted to maintain recognition of the Jena Choctaws, but decisions were being made at the federal level that would prevent any further educational funding for the tribe.

In 1940 Robertson continued his earlier efforts to secure federal funding for the education of the Jena Choctaws, who had been without a school for a year and a half. He identified two new teachers for the Penick School and hoped that the federal government would pay their salaries. The new superintendent of the Choctaw Indian Agency, Harvey K. Meyer, recommended that funding be renewed, but he was rebuffed by Paul Fickinger, associate director of education for the BIA: "We have given considerable study to this entire matter and . . . we had a conference about the whole Louisiana group. With the possible exception of the Chittimanchi and Coushatta Indians it is the general feeling that there is little responsibility accruing to the Federal government for these groups. . . . It seems to us that our responsibility in the matter lies more in the line of insisting that the state assume its obligation for the education of these children, than for us to step in and finance such a program. These groups of people are to all intents and purposes in the same status as whites, negroes, and other groups in Louisiana, and the justification for paying tuition for them does not exist. After all, they own no land which is outside of tax paying status."[69] Marilyn Watt notes that Jena Choctaws were not "in the same status as white, negroes, and other groups in Louisiana," in that whites and blacks "at least . . . had schools to attend."[70] Thus after a brief interlude of federal acknowledgment, the Jena Band was again left with no resources for education. While the Choctaws' anti-black racism contributed to their own lack of school options, they also seemed to sense that their unique political, racial, and cultural status as Choctaws would be lost if they gave an inch on white efforts to classify them as "colored."

A solicitor's opinion by Felix Cohen from 1937 suggests that the Office of Indian Affairs knew it had the power to extend the benefits of the Indian Reorganization Act to any group that it chose to designate as a tribe, despite wording in the act that some interpreted as authorizing benefits only for previously recognized tribes. Indeed, the office allowed the previously "unrecognized" Sokaogon (Mole Lake) Chippewas of Wisconsin to organize under the IRA on the basis of the solicitor's opinion.[71] In Louisiana, however, the Office of Indian Affairs never attempted to organize even the Chitimachas and Coushattas, who had land held in federal trust, making it even less likely that it would consider doing so for the Jena Choctaws. Most likely for budget-ary reasons, the Office of Indian Affairs withheld information that would have provided important resources to help the Jena Choctaws and other Louisiana tribes address some of their more urgent needs.

When the bureau disavowed its responsibility to the Jena Choctaws in 1940, the Choctaw Agency superintendent Harvey Meyer protested. He had recently met with Superintendent Russell of the LaSalle Parish schools, who informed him that he had no intention whatsoever of providing a separate school for the Choctaws, and that they would not be allowed into white schools. The parish was too poor to begin with, Russell argued, and he saw no way to "overcome local prejudice" and persuade the school board to spend money on Indians at any rate. The $16 per pupil that the state had already allocated to the parish for the education of Choctaw children based solely on their status as "educable" citizens of the state had already been granted to the white and black school budgets. Superintendent Russell justi-fied his position, stating that "local merchants claim the Choctaws of the community steal smaller articles from the stores and that it is generally believed the Indians are a liability in the community and that schooling would not benefit them. . . . Doubt was expressed about any interest being shown in school work except on account of the lunch being provided."[72]

Meyer concluded from his visit that "if the Choctaw pupils at Jena are to have any school training, it must be provided from the payment of tuition from Federal funds."[73] Knowing that his decision meant depriving the Choc-taws of even an elementary education, Fickinger held firmly to the commit-tee decision that the federal government had no obligation to educate them, since they had no nontaxable land.[74] Perhaps his conscience was assuaged by his own sarcastic, chastising assertion that "it is difficult for us to believe that such a sentiment [prejudice against Indians] can actually exist and receive public support in the great commonwealth of Louisiana."[75]

There is some merit in the bureau's insistence that the state must take responsibility for educating its Indian citizens, but it was a feeble sort of logic that left the Jena Choctaws with no education, allowing local whites to continue diverting resources from them and their children. Local school boards might have allowed Indians into black schools if they would go, but the Choctaws themselves strictly maintained boundaries between themselves and blacks in an effort to maintain their distinct identity and to benefit from the privileges of being on the white side of the color line. There was never any censure of this sentiment among the bureau's files, and no suggestion that Choctaw enrollment in black schools was even an option.[76]

Indians have often had an ambiguous status in the racial caste system of the United States, somewhere apart from both blacks and whites, which is why Jena Choctaws were segregated for so many years and then integrated into white schools before blacks. That the Jena Choctaws also maintained strict self-segregation from blacks helped them to integrate with whites sooner; where there was any hint of African ancestry, whites were more reluctant to accept Indians into their schools because they were classified as black, not Indian. Jena Choctaws began marrying out extensively in the 1950s because of the lack of unrelated potential Choctaw spouses in the area and the increasing acceptance of Choctaws by local whites that accompanied integration, but they only married whites. Marriage of Indians with blacks was in fact made illegal under state law in 1920.[77]

Jena Choctaws maintained a strong prejudice against blacks in these years as a result of their own precarious racial situation. Like other Indian groups in Louisiana and the South whose children were refused entry into white schools, the Jena Choctaws pursued separate schools for Indian children.[78] Tribes were thus complicit in segregating and subjugating blacks in the South, even if at some level they were simply seeking respect and opportunity for themselves. But while their actions may have offered some emotional reward and helped them to avoid some of the indignities that whites in Louisiana heaped on African Americans, they also meant that Choctaws were participating in and benefiting from the oppression of African Americans, even if to a far lesser degree than their white neighbors did. Their prejudice against blacks cost them in some ways, because for many years it meant that they went without education while blacks had their own schools, terribly funded as they were.

Choctaw racism against blacks is fading and shifting as the racial hierarchy continues to evolve in Louisiana. Overt racism has been replaced, as Jena Choctaws politically support and receive support from local black community leaders in recognition of their commonalities as peoples of color in a racist nation. Prejudices now are more subtle and publicly disavowed by Jena Choctaws, remaining as a scar and a legacy of more brutally racist days for Choctaws and African Americans alike. To understand this history we have to see that the racial system was structured in such a way as to encourage antiblack racism among Indians (and thus support for the white supremacist system that produced it), in part because maintaining a distinction from blacks was vital to maintaining the Indians' unique indigenous status. While they never articulated it this way at the time, the moral, political, and legal position that southern tribes aimed for depended on maintaining a racial status distinct from blacks in the eyes of whites so that their own indigenous political and racial claims could stand. Without recognizing white supremacy as the center of the racist experiences that they shared with blacks and the colonialism that dispossessed them of their land, it would be easy to disconnect their own fate from that of blacks. A model that frames racism and colonialism as two products of the same root ideology reveals how Indians' anti-black racism undermined tribal well-being, because it bolstered the ideological foundation of their own oppression. White supremacy twisted the Choctaws' longing for racial respect and opportunity into something oppressive and even self-defeating.

Similarly, Jena Choctaw educational history reveals the ubiquity of white supremacist ideology in shaping both federal and local racial projects directed toward Indians. Though not operated by the federal government, the Penick School followed many of the same impulses as federal schools, evidence of a common racial and colonial ideology behind each. Penick drew on this ideology as a child, when she "often said to herself, 'When I grow up I'd like to go to Alaska and teach the Eskimos.' "[79] She knew the script from an early age; the racial, cultural, and national superiority of whites was assumed and enacted. The predominantly racial narrative of segregation and the predominantly colonial narrative of assimiliationist education for indigenous people collided in Jena. The white supremacist foundation of the Penick School is clear from not just the exclusion of Choctaws from white schools but the colonial impulse to "uplift" them, make them culturally white, and even display them through a series of visits from busloads of "Little Indian Clubs" around the state that Penick had formed.[80] It seems paradoxical to suggest that the education that the Jena Choctaws sought should not have been sought or offered, but the ways their education was intertwined with local and national racial and colonial ideologies must be understood as part of this history. Despite the desire of Jena Choctaws to have access to the opportunities that education would provide, the racial and colonial components are difficult to miss in comments made in 1938 by the Louisiana education official M. S. Robertson. Though he was one of the most effective advocates for Jena Choctaw education, he nonetheless told a reporter, "They are probably living on as low a scale as people ever get to. Shiftless, lazy, without direction or intention. They are interbred, too, I think. They seem to have forgotten all their ancestors ever knew."[81] That efforts were made to provide education for the Jena Choctaws should never lead to an assumption that racial discrimination against them had ended. Educational plans for Indians were thoroughly soaked in white supremacy, whether in federally operated or locally run schools.

## Implications for the Federal Recognition Petition

Federal funding of an Indian school for the Jena Band constituted federal treatment of the group as an Indian tribe, but since the funds were administered through the State of Louisiana Department of Education and officials occasionally denied responsibility for Louisiana Indians for various reasons, the Office of Federal Acknowledgment declined to consider the funding as unambiguous federal recognition. The OFA report claims that the Jena Choctaws were not treated as a tribal entity, just one example of the office's inconsistency.[82] There were admittedly vacillations and inconsistencies in statements of federal policy regarding Louisiana Indians and the Jena Choctaws in particular, but it is striking that even though the BIA decided to fund a school for the Jena Choctaws after corresponding extensively about their status, noted that they were not considered part of the Mississippi Choctaws, and supplied them with educational funds for an Indian school through a contract with the Louisiana Department of Education, OFA would not consider these actions unambiguous federal recognition.

That recognition was sporadically disavowed by certain officials during and after their several years of funding does not erase the fact of recognition. OFA, however, argues that statements of officials denying federal responsibility to Louisiana Indians in general override the simultaneous acts of recognition.[83] The particular example cited in OFA's historical report in support of a claim that the Office of Indian Affairs did not recognize the Jena Choctaws was a letter from William Zimmerman in response to a request for aid for the Houma Indians in Lafourche and Terrebonne Parishes. In the letter Zimmerman wrote that aside from the Chitimachas, the federal government recognized no responsibility to Louisiana Indians. He lied outright, stating that federal policy prevented him from disbursing funds to nonrecognized Indians such as the Houmas. Clearly this was a ruse, since both the Jena Band of Choctaws and the Coushattas were receiving federal funding at the time. It is most likely that Zimmerman used this smokescreen to prevent funding of the Houmas, whose Indian identity had been derided by federal officials on more than one occasion because of their mixed black, white, and Indian ancestry. OFA, however, interpreted the document as an unambiguous statement of policy, despite clear contradictions of its assertions in the very same BIA file in which it is found.

OFA also claimed that payments were granted to educate individual Indians of one-quarter or more Indian blood, not separate tribes, even though all the appropriations of federal funds for Louisiana Indians were divided tribally among the Jena Choctaws, the Chitimachas, and the Coushattas. Individual names and blood quanta are never listed in the documents, which only report the number of children enrolled from each of the tribes and the school district which was contracted to provide their education.[84] OFA interpreted the existence of a contract with the state to fund local school districts for separate schools for Indian education as meaning that the Office of Indian Affairs never dealt with the Jena Choctaws directly as a tribe, even though such contracting was the preferred procedure for providing education to students of recognized tribes in other states under the Johnson-O'Malley Act. Though OFA eventually concluded in favor of recognition for the tribe, unpredictable decisions about tribal histories such as this reinforce the impression that OFA seeks reasons to disqualify petitions rather than looking at the big picture in determinations of tribal existence.[85] The former Jena Choctaw tribal chairman Clyde Jackson comments, "I tell you, the BIA, if you got a weak point, they going to drive on that weak point!" OFA argues that it must be exacting to ensure that its decisions are completely defensible, but such a stance is designed more to protect the jobs of individual bureaucrats than the interests of recognized or unrecognized tribes, and it produces biased decisions regarding the histories of petitioners.

## CHAPTER 7

## Jena Choctaw Tribal Persistence from the
## Second World War to Recognition

The Second World War marked the beginning of a time of increasing integration for the Jena Choctaws in several arenas. Soon after the men had served in white units in the military, the children were integrated into white schools, marriages between Choctaws and whites became more common than those between two Choctaws, and tribal members began moving out of sharecropping on rural farms and into towns for employment. The integration was slow, and it involved the younger generations more extensively than the older generations, who would occasionally resist change.[1] But integration affected the educational attainment, economic status, occupations, marriage patterns, Choctaw- and English-language use, and religious inclinations of the Jena Choctaws, making for a thoroughly acculturative era. Despite cultural shifts, however, Jena Choctaws tenaciously maintained their identity and culture in other ways, and the community continued to be organized according to age, gender, and family relationships.

Although uncertainty surrounds the precise date when Choctaws became integrated into white schools as well as the reasons for integration, several factors likely contributed to it.[2] Choctaw leaders had of course requested access to white schools previously, and federal officials had intervened on their behalf to that end, so local school officials knew that Choctaws wanted to attend white schools and would not attend black schools. Military participation has been cited by several tribal members as the major force behind integration. When a number of Choctaw young men enlisted to

fight in the Second World War, they brought to the tribe a degree of validation in the eyes of local whites.[3] At the same time, the Jena newspaper ran
articles from national news wires about Indians from other tribes participating enthusiastically in the war, focusing attention on Choctaw participation
in the local context.[4] And surely the fact that Indians were fighting in white
units would not have escaped the attention of segregationists.

While military service stands out in Choctaw narratives of integration,
other factors contributed as well. In particular, a compulsory education
movement toward the end of the war provided a powerful impetus for
including Choctaw children in white schools. Editorials in the local paper
argued that supporting literacy for people of all races and classes was a
patriotic duty that would make citizens better prepared to serve in every
arena.[5] An editorial in May 1944 noted with a sense of ironic justice that the
educated sons and daughters of privilege were the ones fighting the war,
while the several thousand locals they had neglected or conspired to exclude
from educational opportunity were safe at home, having been classified as 4F
by the Selective Service—"physically, mentally, or morally unfit for service."
"Thus do our chickens come home to roost," one editor lamented. "We have
not compelled, by means of a real compulsory law, all the chidren [sic] in our
state, both white and colored, to attend our schools. In some parishes we
have even thought we were being clever in not compelling all children to go
to school, thinking, thereby, to gain better education facilities for our own
chidren, who, of course, were kept in school [receiving state educational
funds based on the number of 'educable' children in the parish, rather than on
actual enrollments]. And now those whom we allowed to live among us
without learning the fundamentals of reading, writing, and arithmetic are at
home safe and sound or in the cities making war wages in industry, while
those who have become literate are in the war, fighting to save not only us,
but also the great company of illiterates."[6] The movement succeeded, and
Louisiana passed a new compulsory attendance law in October 1944.[7] Ironically, Choctaw men were among the literate, some of them having had
several years of education despite years of white opposition to their integration into white schools.

Compulsory attendance for the Jena Choctaws could have meant enrollment in black schools against their will, but such was not the case. In addition
to their service in white units in the segregated military, their enrollment in
white schools may have been aided by Jay Pipes, who was elected to the
school board in January 1945 representing the district where most of the tribe

lived.[8] Pipes had taught the original literacy classes for the Choctaws in 1929, and most of the tribe lived on land belonging to his in-laws, the Whatleys. His wife, Mary "Pick" Pipes, suggested in an interview in 2004 that he had been in favor of Choctaw integration throughout his career. One Jena Choctaw told Marilyn Watt that the decision to enroll tribal children in white schools seemed abrupt,[9] indicating that the decision was made by whites at a time when Choctaws and federal officials were not actively lobbying for integration. This story lends support to the possibility that the election of Pipes, combined with a new zeal for the enforcement of compulsory education, contributed to Choctaw enrollment in white schools in the years after tribal efforts had declined and federal intervention had failed. Whatever the cause, the result was that by 1965 the tribe finally had its first high school graduates.[10]

During the 1950s and much of the 1960s the tribe still maintained a traditional leadership form, in which the eldest man in the community was the informal leader, mediator, and spokesperson for the community, wielding little authority beyond the power of persuasion and esteem. This system held sway until 1968, when the tribe adopted a more fully communal method of decision making, since there was no clear successor after the death of a respected leader.[11]

In the late 1960s, Clyde Jackson says, no one really knew that the community existed outside the town of Jena, and that was one reason why the Jena Choctaws began to organize themselves and seek recognition. They wanted to be recognized in the broader meaning of the word—to be identified as a tribe of Indians surviving in rural Louisiana. They were frustrated by living in a society that refused to acknowledge Indian existence: "white" and "colored" were the only boxes they could check on racial identification forms. While the federal government had recognized the Jena Choctaws briefly in the 1930s and local people knew who they were, it was not until they organized as a corporation in 1974 and received state recognition from Louisiana later that year that they again began to receive recognition outside LaSalle Parish.

The Jena Choctaws reorganized at the urging of Ernest Sickey, the Coushatta tribal leader who had recently been appointed director of the state Office of Indian Affairs. Sickey and the office eventually had a hand in incorporating many of the state's tribes as a precursor to state recognition, since tribes could not receive and conduct grants for themselves until they had incorporated. The Jena Band was one of the first state tribes that Sickey contacted, since his Choctaw grandmother, as it turned out, had originally come from that community, which he used to visit in his youth. This move-ment in Louisiana paralleled the recognition and revitalization movement among Indians across the country, and the steps taken by the Louisiana tribes were the same ones taken by many federally nonrecognized groups. Leaders from one tribe would talk with leaders from another tribe and offer advice about how to accomplish certain goals for their people, and then they would incorporate and begin competing for funding. Clyde Jackson, who was tribal chairman from about 1975 to 1984, says that the Jena Choctaws organized and incorporated because they realized it would help them gain access to certain services that they needed but were not receiving.

Jerry Jackson, the first elected tribal chairman, remembers that Sickey helped organize the first tribal meeting.[12] Sickey brought Jackson a copy of the Coushatta tribe's recent incorporation document for him to use as a model, allowing him to write the Jena articles of incorporation in one night and drive to Baton Rouge to file the document the next day. The State of Louisiana extended recognition shortly thereafter.[13] "That's all there was to it," he says, noting that it had no immediate impact on the tribe. "It's only later, as things started to move forward and there was some benefits out there, some money flowing, and they started seeing something" that they began to think recognition was important.

Mary Jackson Jones, a tribal elder who passed away in 2005, said that state recognition brought with it no significant changes or special feeling, nothing like what she and others felt after achieving federal recognition, but others have noted that all the coming together for meetings and all the research they began doing did have at least a little bit of a bonding effect. Despite what must have been at least a small degree of excitement over the celebration of "Indian Day" in Jena after state recognition, the event was never mentioned during interviews with tribal members.[14] In their first year of reorganization the Jena Choctaws had only a vague notion that they might pursue federal recognition too, but since there were no set regulations at the time, Jerry Jackson says they "didn't have a clue" how they would go about accomplishing that goal. "When you're outside looking in, you don't know how all this takes place, and it takes years to learn all this," he said.

State recognition and formal organization with *Robert's Rules of Order* did not transform the tribe overnight. "Back in the seventies," Jackson recalls, "you could have a fist fight real quick. But as time went on, everything got in more order, and people started to respect our leadership more than they had before. It was kind of a loose-type deal back in those days." There were several reasons for that tension and disorder. First, there had long been conflict between the two main Jena families, the Lewises and the Jacksons. That conflict continued to surface in this new arena, but it held new significance because now it was disrupting official tribal government duties that were expected by government entities and funding sources to be carried out with a certain level of decorum.

Second, after years of informal traditional leadership, there was now an entirely new way of operating and interacting for this extended family. Though they were a band or tribe of Indians, they were also an extended family of fewer than 150 people at the time, and they now had to run their family like a bureaucratic office or forgo the benefits of state and federal recognition. The most distant relationship between two council members was between first cousins. But circumstances being what they were, the Jena Choctaws decided to force themselves into a mold similar to that of tribal governments developed by the BIA and nonprofit corporations so that they could pursue funding and eventually federal recognition. The council did not replace every other structure in the family, but the structure and format of the formalized tribal government were new and foreign, and the inevitable wrinkles between the formalized structure and the informal family ties needed to be ironed out, a common problem in smaller tribes.

Third, the new council was composed almost entirely of people in their twenties, and a couple of the council members were women, which also broke with tradition. The positions of power that the young people on the council held, largely due to their education, extended only as far as the tribal government at that time, though. Elders still held authoritative positions informally. But dealings with outsiders on behalf of the tribe and many of the decision-making responsibilities were left primarily in the hands of the tribal members in their twenties who had been able to achieve high school educations. According to Marilyn Watt, certain duties that had formerly been the responsibility of the eldest man had been passed on to the council and especially the chairperson, including finding financial assistance or transportation for tribal members in need, organizing the annual cemetery maintenance, or serving as an informal tribal truancy officer.[15]

The appearance of women on the council, which, Mary Jones modestly notes, contradicted the informal tradition of designating the older men in the community the political decision makers, seems to have been fairly well received by the tribe because of changes taking place immediately before reorganization. Leadership uncertainties at that time meant that an elderly woman became an important leader and arbiter in community affairs. As in many other Indian communities in which men are the nominal leaders, a statement that men alone ran tribal affairs at any point must be taken with several grains of salt. Women did have some power in community decision making, even if the men did not usually allow them to participate in formal political meetings, which would help to explain the seemingly easy and thorough transition to the election of women to political positions.[16]

Moreover, it is likely that the designation of men to represent the tribe to outsiders was, as with the Tunica-Biloxi Tribe, rooted more in Anglo gender norms than tribal traditions, and Michelene Pesantubbee's research on Choctaw women's history tends to confirm this.[17] Cheryl Smith and Christine Norris, who have both served as tribal chairwomen and council members at various times, argue that women have always played a significant organizational role through events such as weddings and funerals, a role that has gone unacknowledged because it is not the kind of leadership that is obvious to the outside world, though it is clear within the community and within families. Moreover, Smith suggests that it was her mother, Mary Jackson Jones, who began urging young people to organize for recognition in the 1960s.

Using an election method in 1974 that had the tribe electing a council and the council selecting a chairperson from among themselves, the young council appointed Jerry Jackson as its leader. Jackson had attended college for two years, so they reasoned that he was the best equipped to serve the tribe on external matters. That there was no woman appointed to the position until 1998 indicates that there was a glass ceiling for women in tribal leadership, but the council has been fairly balanced in terms of gender representation throughout its existence. Serving on the tribal council since the 1970s provided opportunity and incentive for both Cheryl Smith, the first woman to be chairperson or chief of the tribe, and Christine Norris, the former tribal chief, to gain experience in politics and business affairs that equipped them well for their positions. The success of Smith and Norris quietly removed any perception of a glass ceiling in the tribe, even if gender inequities persist in other ways. As Norris suggests, a woman needs to work much harder than a man to have her leadership potential recognized because of deeply ingrained ideas about gender, but women and men have worked together for the tribal government since the first day of organization.

Jerry Jackson recalls that organizing for recognition was a political declaration much more than a quest for funding:

Cheryl Smith in her office, 2008. Photo by the author.

Christine Norris in Marksville, 2008. Photo by the author.

We didn't dream about becoming a [federal] tribe until 1974, and, see, that was way before gaming or anything else. It was not about money, because there was no money. It was something like $2,000 a head for your budget—146 people, you ain't going nowhere . . . It was just the issue that we knew the group was different . . . And nobody really knew what a tribe was supposed to be. See, they didn't know they were a tribe. Really, it's kind of crazy, but we had to educate them that you are a tribe, but that doesn't mean you do anything different than you've already done. When we wrote our bylaws and constitution, it actually was how things were done anyway. We just put it in writing. So it was no big change, but to get them to understand that here it is on written paper, what we are, what we do, what we want to do. So that took a long time, because you had a bunch of uneducated people there, and they thought it was just getting a pot of money and that was it. I guess [we spent] a long time educating the group.

Although the Jena Band of Choctaws knew beyond doubt that they were Choctaws, they had to learn to think of themselves as a tribe. The term as Jackson uses it does not refer to the social entity, the extended family network that Mary Jackson Jones would call "my people." Rather, "tribe" refers to a latent political entity. The community began a dramatic transformation in its self-conception from being a handful of Choctaw families to being a sovereign nation. Their metamorphosis implies that no group of Indians is a tribe unless and until its members construct themselves politically as a tribe in response to interaction with some other governmental body. Several of the other petitioners in Louisiana and many more across the South were not organized as tribes previously, but as communities of extended family. This lack of formal political structure should be considered normal for nonfederal tribes. Southeastern tribes in colonial times went through the same processes, moving from loose confederations of culturally similar autonomous villages to "tribes" or nations in response to European and Anglo-American encroachment.[18] Nonfederal tribes may mirror federal tribes in social organization, racial identity, and cultural distinctiveness, but communities lacking a relationship with the federal government must fuse a political structure onto the social entity to become a federally recognized tribe. The Jena Choctaws understood themselves as a distinct people and regulated themselves internally in various ways, but they had to learn that being a cohesive Indian community made them a distinct political entity based on indigeneity in North America. When they organized for recognition, they activated what had previously been a latent political status. They moved from family to polity.

## Navigating Tribal Reorganization

A year and a half after reorganization, turmoil hit the young tribal council. A political row with his cousins led to a special election which saw Jerry Jackson replaced as chairman by his first cousin, Clyde Jackson, whom he had tried to remove from the council earlier. Jerry Jackson's leadership style was much different than his cousin's. Jerry Jackson was aggressive, tenacious, and independent, and he felt that his primary role was to secure federal recognition for the tribe, which would lead to important financial and legal opportunities that could support the tribe. He was fiercely protective of the tribe's interests and had little tolerance for any person who interfered with his plans for the tribe, whether that person was a Jena Choctaw or a non-Indian politician. Clyde Jackson was slower to act, more concerned with the cultural aspects of tribal life, and more responsive to the concerns of others, especially tribal elders.

The contrasting approaches might be usefully framed in the old southeastern Indian dichotomy between red and white, though for metaphorical purposes only, since the Jena Choctaws are not explicitly acting on these principles. Jerry Jackson would be a red chief, or war chief, someone called upon to lead the willing into a fight. Clyde Jackson would be a white chief, or peace chief, who relied upon his ability to maintain tribal equilibrium and acted only when the community had reached a consensus. Each approach has advantages and disadvantages. Jerry Jackson twice lost his position as tribal chairman because he was too aggressive, forcing his vision on a sometimes unwilling tribe. On the other hand, he produced plentiful funding and eventually led the way to federal recognition—he did not not accomplish this single-handedly by any means, but he moved the tribe quickly toward that goal. Clyde Jackson was not as overbearing as Jerry Jackson, so tribal members felt they had a stronger voice in tribal affairs, but neither did he accomplish as much as quickly as Jerry Jackson. Clyde Jackson always deferred to the elderly, who because of birth patterns were much more numerous in the 1970s than in 2010, when only a few tribal members were over the age of sixty. Because of this approach, Clyde Jackson would not emphasize the federal recognition agenda until many of the elders had died. The elders, he said in an interview in 2000, were apprehensive about what a federal relationship might entail: "We started striving toward federal recognition, but back then we had so many problems with the federal government, that the elderlies down here didn't want the federal government involved . . . So when the word federal recognition come around, that was the first thing that hit their mind is they going to put us on a reservation, they going to lock us in, they going to put gates around, and we can't do nothing. So they didn't want federal recognition . . . we could have probably had our recognition fifteen, twenty years ago. But back then, I let the elderlies kind of control and dictate what they wanted to do . . . They just wanted to be recognized as a group of Indian people that lived in Louisiana, lived in Jena."

Through travel and meetings, Clyde Jackson learned more about the opportunities federal recognition might bring, but he believed older tribal members were still too concerned about the negative consequences to move forward. Jerry Jackson contended that if there were elders concerned about being detained on a reservation, they must have been a small minority. As he recalled, in his childhood his family would travel to Oklahoma to visit relatives who had removed and were receiving federal benefits. They wondered why these family members were receiving federal benefits, minimal as they were, while their cousins from Jena could not receive any. Further inquiries revealed that the Oklahoma cousins had married Oklahoma Choctaws and were receiving federal benefits because of that ancestry, and that their Jena Choctaw ancestry did not entitle them to any benefits. So many if not most Jena Choctaws knew that they would not be imprisoned on a reservation after federal recognition, though there was still a degree of confusion and suspicion over what kind of compromises recognition might entail. Jerry Jackson criticized his cousin for not educating the elderly tribal members on the matter, but that was Clyde Jackson's leadership style: wait for consensus. Clyde Jackson did not move as fast or as furiously as Jerry Jackson, but people knew what he was doing and did not feel overpowered by him.

When Clyde Jackson took over as chairman in 1975 the tribe had many of the same goals as every other Indian group in the country: to improve their housing, employment, education, transportation, and medical care; to obtain resources to assist elderly people living in poverty; and to establish cultural and language retention programs.[19] The tribe pursued its goals through various programs available to state-recognized tribes. They mainly participated in programs sponsored by the state Inter-Tribal Council, such as the CETA (Comprehensive Employment Training Act) program, now known as JTPA (Job Training Partnership Act), and they received some funds from the Department of Housing and Urban Development to purchase two acres of land and build a tribal office.[20] They supported their office with grants from the Administration for Native Americans, the Inter-Tribal Council, and other funding agencies.[21] In short, they were maneuvering themselves into what has been called the "grant economy" so common to Indian tribes, where all their funds were dependent on piecemeal grants and government programs that kept them afloat—though just barely—in an endless cycle of complicated applications for tiny disbursements. In a tribe without a single college graduate and only a handful of high school graduates, that was a hard road to travel. The Jena Choctaws realized that the best long-term solution for their problems would be to develop some kind of tribal enterprises that would afford them a degree of self-sufficiency, but at the time they had no viable opportunities to establish the kinds of businesses that could lift a community out of poverty.[22] This is just one of many indications that before the opening of casinos tribal leadership thought of economic development in terms of what it could do to help the tribe survive as a community and maintain its cultural traditions. Despite common misperceptions and assumptions about tribal motivations for economic development, tribal leadership around the country has consistently thought of it in terms of community centers, jobs, cultural programs, hospitals, and schools.[23]

Clyde Jackson testified before the AIPRC Task Force 10 in 1976 about how his tribe viewed federal recognition: "We haven't faced anything that required federal recognition as of yet," he said, indicating that many federal programs were open to any Indian group that applied because of the way many of the Great Society program rules were written.[24] Federal funding rules have been revised since then to make sure that money intended for Indians in most instances goes only to federal Indians. There are notable exceptions, but the money available to federally recognized tribes is much greater than that available to state-recognized tribes. Of course, Jackson also remarked in 1976 that his tribe was so busy with the few programs it was trying to establish that it did not even want any more information on other programs available to nonfederal tribes.

So at the time Clyde Jackson was unconcerned with obtaining federal recognition: "I've learned that along down the line, you've got to know what you're doing before you jump in. And that's the way of our tribal council. Like the federal recognition, we have talked about that within the tribal level, do we need recognition. We say, well, we'll just hold off and see what comes up. Now, we could go all the way without federal recognition with the programs that's available, but then on the other hand, like the health services, now, we had a problem there in our health services. And we may have to have federal recognition where we will get this type health service. . . . I've seen some of the stuff that they have done, but also seen some of the problems they created too as being federally recognized."[25]

A large part of the tribe's and Clyde Jackson's own hesitance was due to lack of information. The Jena Choctaws had heard stories both good and bad but did not have enough reliable information to know whether they wanted federal recognition. Jackson later stated that recognition would have been acceptable if the tribe could have received the services it wanted without having the BIA dictate policy: "And I believe that the federal government should in some way, somehow, help Indian people . . . assist them in every way possible, even without being federally recognized. I could even say that Indian tribes shouldn't even be federally recognized. Indian tribes are Indian tribes. It's just that."[26] Jackson expressed some resentment at that time and again in 2000 about the constant need to prove he was an Indian. He is seven-eighths Choctaw by blood quantum and speaks the language fluently, but he was still not officially Indian until the whole tribe was federally recognized: "Nobody else in the country, in America, had to prove who they are in order for them to say, 'Yeah, that's what you are.' Why did I have to prove that I'm an Indian? Nobody else had to prove who they are, but we had to. We had to prove who we were before anybody would recognize who we are. And that used to kind of irritate me, you know, and I couldn't understand, well why do I have to prove who I am? I know who I am! But nobody else had to do that."

By 1979 the Jena Band had lost some of its hesitance on the recognition issue and decided to begin work on a petition. Clyde Jackson claims he was able to do so at this time because a group of elderly people who opposed recognition had died. It is also likely that after five years of state recognition and competing for Indian funds, the tribe finally began to understand the nature of federal recognition a little better. As Jackson said, "You've got to know what you're doing before you jump in." They submitted a letter of intent to petition for federal recognition to the Bureau of Indian Affairs on 1 February 1979, the forty-fifth group to petition under regulations created a year earlier.

From that time until they finally achieved federal recognition in May 1995, the majority of the tribal government's time and money was spent trying to secure federal recognition. Certainly the tribe maintained other programs, but a petition takes up so much of a tribe's resources that it is easy for other projects to fall by the wayside. The research conducted in support of a petition is worthwhile in its own right, since it significantly bolsters the community's interest in tribal history, culture, and identity. But if given the choice the Jena Choctaws would likely have chosen the benefits of immediate recognition over the benefits of doing research and politicking for sixteen years.[27]

A petition for recognition has three major components. First, a tribe must compile a detailed genealogy, using every available record, to prove that it is descended from people identified as Indians in the historical record. As Clyde Jackson comments, "that has to be established before you could even walk through the front door." The tribe applied for grants and paid genealogists to do research for them. Doing genealogy for unrecognized groups is notoriously difficult. Census takers have often identified Indian people as white, black, or mulatto, so the census and other official records kept by whites have proved to be of marginal use to many petitioners.[28]

Second, the tribe must compile its history, showing that it has stayed together as an Indian community throughout the time covered by available records. While doing this has proved challenging because it has been in the interest of whites, who have typically been the record keepers, to erase the presence of Indian tribes, in some cases there are easily accessible records identifying Indian ancestors in the historical records, as was true of the Jena Choctaws, who were identified in the special "Indian Schedules" of the censuses of 1900 and 1910. The Jena Choctaws were also able to use the records of the Dawes Commission to uncover some of their family histories and the continuity of their community from 1870 onward, and even the local newspaper consistently noted their Choctaw identity.[29]

Cheryl Smith repeatedly lamented that the tribe had not begun recording oral histories until it started putting the petition together. So many elders died before any oral histories were recorded that large amounts of tribal knowledge had been lost. Smith's comments suggest that the process of gathering documentation for the petition changed the relationship of the tribe to its own history. Many tribal members had rarely reflected upon the value of the unique, fleeting histories known only to their elders, but constructing a Jena Choctaw historical narrative for the petition made them yearn for more information about the experiences of their ancestors.

In their original petition the Jena Choctaws theorized that their ancestors were descended from some of the bands of Choctaws who had been in Louisiana since the Spanish colonial period, but they could make no definitive link to known members of those groups. Later, in a second petition, they abandoned those theories and went on only what they could prove in the historical record, because OFA, taking a positivist approach, claims that it will not accept theories without conclusive evidence.[30] The office asserts that there can be no leaps of faith in the genealogical or historical record.

Still, the Jena Band could find nothing about its ancestors before 1870. It was "total darkness," according to Jerry Jackson. The tribe finally resolved the matter by securing a letter from the Mississippi Band of Choctaws' tribal council stating that they accepted the Jena Choctaws as having been members of their tribe before 1870, which conveniently resolved that issue. The Mississippi Band's support carried significant weight with the Office of Federal Acknowledgment because the band is so strict about its own tribal enrollment. Jerry Jackson recalls: "That Mississippi Choctaw endorsement, that was the one. That was the link that was missing. With that, that was our recognition. The [endorsement of] other tribes here in Louisiana, that was just icing on the cake. When the Mississippi Choctaws said that they agreed that we were once part of their tribe, that was it. We've met all the criteria. We had the community, we had the language, the interactions, all that kind of thing. Any sociologist could put it together after that point. But, it was that history, the unwritten history that we couldn't find anywhere."

Their biggest potential stumbling block in the historical report was proving that the Jena Choctaws were an entity distinct from the Mississippi Band of Choctaws, since the federal government kept stating that the Jena Choctaws were eligible to be members of the Mississippi Band, although the two groups had been living separately since at least 1870. The Mississippi Band offered to let the Jena Choctaws join their tribe and have one seat on the seventeen-member council if recognition fell through, but for a number of reasons the Jena tribal leaders wanted to maintain their independence.

The third component of a petition is the anthropological report, which documents present community relations, culture, and social and political structures, among other things. The Jena Choctaws fulfilled this component fairly easily, since they had retained their language and until the postwar years married almost exclusively within the group; each of those facts is considered excellent evidence of social and political cohesion. The members of the tribe had to offer further evidence that they maintained a community after 1959, which they did by providing evidence that they did annual graveyard cleanings as a tribe, attended each other's family events, visited constantly, and discussed matters of concern to the tribe.[31]

All through the 1980s and early 1990s the tribe maintained a focus on the recognition petition while at the same time trying to provide services for tribal members. They developed a tribal constitution. They used what resources were available to provide school supplies and free haircuts for children, reward students for good grades, instill a strong sense of identity and culture in the children, and help families in emergencies. They maintained a list of state and parish resources available to help when the tribe could not, thus shifting the burden to other agencies without taxing their own limited resources. For example, when a tribal member was trying to leave an abusive spouse, members of the tribal leadership called several agencies to find counseling, emergency support, and shelter for her because they could not provide it themselves. They continued to use this system after recognition with the addition of new tribally owned vans that could transport people to service agencies, since their own resources were still very limited.

Cheryl Smith, chief of the tribe from 1998 to 2002 and tribal secretary during most of the petitioning process, described the journey toward recognition as a "process of fits and starts." The process seemed to be progressing well in the early 1980s, when Clyde Jackson was working with a local anthropologist and genealogists to compile a petition, which they submitted in 1985. That same year Clyde Jackson resigned as tribal chairman and took a position with the State of Louisiana as the executive director of the Governor's Commission on Indian Affairs. George Allen won the next election, but the tribe forced him out of office the following year. Some considered his removal "an underhanded coup" while others considered it "a welcome effort to clean house and make the tribe respectable."[32] Either way the council appointed Jerry Jackson to replace him, but kept Allen working for a year as a grant administrator to close out certain federal grants and apply for new ones.

Shortly after Jerry Jackson took office, the tribe received the "Obvious Deficiencies" report that OFA gives petitioners after an initial review of their petition. After examining the petition closely for the first time, Jackson found so many holes that he felt the tribe would never be recognized based on the information it contained. He called OFA to ask that the petition be disregarded while a new one was prepared. They hired a new group of experts to fit the puzzle pieces together better.

There was never any debate about whether the Jena Choctaws were Choctaw Indians; that much was clear phenotypically, historically, and culturally, but that is not sufficient for attaining federal recognition. What was needed was to establish to the satisfaction of OFA that the Jena Choctaws had been a tribe since historical times under the meaning of federal law, and that was more difficult. The tribe hired Bud Shapard, who had recently retired as head of OFA and—in true Washington style—started doing consulting work.[33] With his thorough knowledge of the intricacies of the recognition regulations, they began putting together a new petition that would speak to the specific concerns of OFA.

Jerry Jackson went to Washington sometime in the late 1980s to meet with OFA staff and discuss the petition. "I was trying to get a handle on how long was this going to take," Jackson said in an interview in 2000, "and they said, 'Well, it looks like maybe uhhh, sixteen to eighteen years we'll get around to you.' They're underfunded, understaffed, blah blah blah. So I said, 'Well, this is not going to work.'" He decided that the tribe needed to be recognized sooner than that, and in consultation with the council he began efforts to have a bill introduced in the U.S. Congress to recognize the Jena Band, circumventing the tediously slow OFA process. He was able to meet with U.S. Senator Bennett Johnston, a powerful Democrat from Louisiana, who in three successive Congresses introduced a bill to recognize the Jena Band, for which he sought support by testifying about the moving story of the Jena Choctaw ancestors' walk to Oklahoma in search of land allotments. The bill was passed by the Senate the first two times and by both houses of Congress the third time, before being subjected to a pocket veto by President George H. W. Bush, acting at the request of OFA officials.[34] Jackson noted:

> We were kind of down about that, but at the same time, that was helping our case over at Acknowledgment, because we were clearly putting pressure on the BIA to do something in several ways. Senator Johnston was on the appropriations committee, [so] the BIA had to come before him for money, so he kept spurring them on, "Well why not, why not [recognize] this group here?"
>
> And we had another problem at the time, because gambling was starting to happen. So there was tribes that were getting into gambling here in Louisiana that didn't want us to be recognized, because it became an economic thing then. But they had already given me a letter of support, and they wasn't going to take it back. So we were able to just squeeze through the tunnel there. And then, also, the governor's office had given a letter of support . . . but I had to meet with the attorney general and sign a paper that we would not have a historic land claim against the State of Louisiana. That's all they were concerned about . . . But our documents had clearly showed that we had come from Mississippi, so I agreed, we

didn't have a land claim, so we signed the document. We got a letter of support from the governor, which went a long ways for federal recognition. So you're like playing on three different, four different fields at the same time, pushing toward the end result. A tribe cannot just say, "Okay, we meet the criteria," and sit back. You have to put political pressure both in Washington and through the state or you're not going to move in the system. Just meeting the criteria is not enough.

Jackson talked about other political maneuvering that was necessary to force movement on their acknowledgment case. Senator Don Nickles of Oklahoma held up the bill for a year because Hollis Roberts, chief of the Oklahoma Choctaws, asked him to do so. So Jackson flew up to Oklahoma and asked Roberts why he opposed the effort. He gave Jackson the "same old song and dance, you know, we don't want the BIA funding to be divided more than it is." Jackson told Roberts, "At 146 members, we are not going to be a big drain on the BIA." He said they could put a list of the tribe's 146 members in the bill to make sure that they did not change their membership criteria after recognition to allow 200,000 people to enroll. Roberts acquiesced and the bill finally moved past Senator Nickles, but the delay had cost the tribe a year.

But the biggest political impediment for the tribe in trying to attain recognition was the predominantly Anglo-American backlash against gaming. A sizable group of people opposed their recognition as a tribe because they did not want gaming expanded in Louisiana, so what should have been an ethnohistorical decision became a political referendum on gaming and white political authority. But Jackson contends that gaming is really the only means of giving his tribe any political power or prosperity. BIA funding is based on the number of members that a tribe has, so he believed that the Jena Choctaws could never secure adequate BIA funding for the cultural and social programs they needed to recover from generations of life under racism and colonialism, and that without economic power they could never have the political power to adequately protect tribal sovereignty. While some of the other tribal leaders disagreed, Jackson believed that gaming was the only viable prospect for the tribe.

The tribe was approached by a gaming corporation in 1991 and negotiated a deal under which the corporation would give the tribe the money it needed to do the research and lobbying required to achieve recognition, and in return the corporation would receive a casino management contract after recognition. Many federally nonrecognized tribes have taken this route, which provides excellent funding for petition research and politicking but has also brought significant opposition.[35] For the Jena Choctaws, money from the contract meant that the tribe could fly Jackson to Oklahoma to talk with Hollis Roberts and pay for a lobbying firm in Washington, in addition to being able to buy school supplies. The bills in Congress eventually failed, but the political pressure did influence OFA somewhat. Jerry Jackson remarked in 2000, "I was looking at what the tribe had to offer. What did it have to offer? It had the right to gamble, that's what it had. That's what attracted everything, that's what opened up the doors for the money to start coming in. And that's what ultimately got us recognized. They can say it's the grants, they can say it's our history, they can say it's all that, but I guarantee you, if we hadn't been able to put pressure on the BIA from several different angles, we would still be waiting for that petition, because they could care less."

Cheryl Smith agreed. There was a point, she said, when the Jena Choctaws thought, "Well, okay, we just fill out this form, fill in the blanks, and submit a petition," and they would be recognized. They even knew there was a waiting list. They had no idea it would take so much more than that. Politics is of major importance in the petitioning process, she said. Tribes have to worry about who is in Congress, the president's office, and the governor's office, who will support them and who will fight them.[36] The Jena Choctaws were fortunate to have some of the more important politicians such as Bennett Johnston on their side, actively supporting their recognition.

While OFA claims the recognition process is divorced from politics and is merely a matter of presenting facts for evaluation, this claim is belied by Jerry Jackson's and Cheryl Smith's testimony and by decisions in a few recent cases in New England. Politicians in Connecticut are doing everything they can to prevent any more tribes from being recognized there because of gaming and land claims, thus denying the legitimacy of the Paugussets, Schaghticokes, and Pauckatuck / Eastern Pequots, even though the government of Connecticut itself has maintained reservations for these tribes since colonial times. The actions of the state have led to reversals of positive determinations at OFA for both the Schaghticokes and the Pauckatuck / Eastern Pequots.[37] Moreover, under the administration of George W. Bush, the proportion of petitions for recognition decided favorably dropped from roughly half to two out of fifteen.[38] Political pressure weighs heavily in this process, which is supposed to be about evaluating objectively whether a community exists as an Indian tribe, and with the advent of gaming the influence of politics has grown exponentially.

## CHAPTER 8

## Jena Choctaw Recognition

Mary Jackson Jones remembered the day's events vividly because of a dream she had in the early morning. "I believe in dreams," she began:

> Some dreams that just hit you so real. That night, I dreamed. I don't know what it was, but we had good news. It was me, my daughter here [Cheryl Smith] and her husband [Rusty Smith]. We all just shouted, jump up and down and laughing! I don't know what it was. I don't know what is doing that. Then I woke up and I said why am I dreaming this? What is going to happen to me, Cheryl, and Rusty? . . .
>
> Cheryl come from work that morning, and she got to work ahead of time, and the chief [Jerry Jackson] was still there. And Cheryl come here and she called. She said, "Mama? You up?" And I said, "I been up! I been up since four o'clock this morning! I can't sleep!" She said, "Mama, I got good news!" And I said, "Did we get federal recognized?" She said, "Mama!" I said, "Cheryl, me and you and Rusty, I have never hear we laugh like we did! I knew something happened at four o'clock this morning." And that note come here at four o'clock that morning. So I don't know, but that was just [pause]. That's how I know. That's how happy we was.
>
> And [Cheryl] said, "I'm coming to get you, Mama. They going to call here, and I want you to be here." So she came and got me to the office. I didn't know, but yet I already know. It's hard to believe things like that, but it's real. That day, I could never

forget that day, that morning! I dreamed that night, we were just laughing, jump up and down, just . . . That's how it was. . . . That feeling stayed with me. It's still with me now. Something done told me that some good news is coming.

Finally, in May 1995, after all the fits and starts, the tribe achieved federal recognition. Mary Jackson Jones's contagious, spiritually tinged, heartwarming joy in recalling the day five years after the fact attests to the emotional weight that tribal members attached to the decision. Cheryl Smith felt the same way. "Sometimes I can remember that night so well," she said. "When it came on the news that the Jena Choctaws had received recognition, it was like, I don't know, I was in a dream or something! Because I never, never thought—with the headaches that we had been through and up and down and just turned around—that we would ever get it. It was just something that was too monumental for us few little people here to ever get."

The small but jovial ceremony of official acknowledgment attended by a handful of Jena Choctaws in Washington added to the overwhelming momentousness of the event. The tribe enlarged the two official acknowledgment letters to poster size and had them framed and hung on the wall in the chief's office. Mary Jackson Jones, who never thought she would live to see recognition, recalled that "the first few months after recognition, to me it was wonderful. It make us, all of 'em, glad. We don't know what we was happy for, but we was glad." Most of the other people involved reported the same kind of feeling, that it lifted up the spirit of the community. People felt good about themselves and their futures. They became local celebrities that day. Friends, neighbors, and well-wishers congratulated them at the grocery store and on the street. The whole experience gave the Jena Choctaws a feeling that after years of closed doors and holes in their pockets, they had something to look forward to, that things were looking up for them, that they mattered—a monumental accomplishment for any group of Indian people. Even the usually businesslike Jerry Jackson had a twinkle in his eye as he remembered calling every member of the tribe from the phone at the tribal center as soon as he received word of recognition.

While individual tribal members and leaders sought federal recognition for a variety of reasons, a sense of justice was a central motivation. The local press focused on the likely financial benefits, describing recognition as "lucrative," but the feelings of elation that followed recognition ran much deeper, particularly for the leaders who had spent more than twenty years working

Mary Jackson Jones in the old tribal office, 1999. The enlarged
notice of federal acknowledgment is on the wall behind her.
Photo by the author.

together to achieve it.[1] Recognition was psychologically transformational,
counteracting the historical trauma of nonrecognition and other injustices
embedded in the group's collective identity.[2] Even the possibility of economic
success was couched in terms of redistributive justice, as compensation for
years of racialized poverty. In much the same way as repatriation of the
Tunica Treasure marked the return of sovereignty to the Tunica-Biloxi Tribe,
the day of recognition marked the first time the modern Jena Choctaws had
felt appropriately empowered and recognized for who they were in a broader
sense. Justice had begun to be served, and recognition of their sovereignty,
their peoplehood, was an enormous step toward redressing years of oppression and degradation under white supremacy. Victory in a recognition case
reaches back through the generations.

Likewise, many tribal members were excited about the effect that recognition would have on coming generations. Some of the elders said, "Recognition is not for me; it is for my grandchildren." They felt satisfied knowing that their descendants, no matter how many generations they might marry out, would always be able to prove their heritage. Even if there were no other benefits, at least recognition would make that part of their heritage stronger. Though she shunned definitions of Choctaw identity based strictly in blood quantum, Mary Jackson Jones also hoped that recognition would bring the younger generations in contact with more Indians from other communities, making it more likely that they would marry other Indians, reversing the outmarriage trend of the last half-century.[3]

The specter of declining blood quanta gives some tribal leaders pause. The older generations still have high blood quanta, with a significant number being half-Choctaw or more by blood. Their racial status played a crucial part in their eventual recognition, since it provided evidence of their cohesion. Yet those who represent the future of the tribe, their grandchildren, might appear as phenotypically mixed or non-Indian as some of the groups whose recognition they currently oppose. Blood quantum requirements have already dropped from one-quarter to one-thirty-second since recognition, and the tribe may eventually drop the requirement to descendancy in any degree from the Jena Choctaw ancestors on the 1880, 1900, and 1910 censuses. Though most of the tribe voted in support of this move, apprehension remains that too much racial mixing with whites may be used against the Jena Band to suggest a lack of tribal cohesion or a diluted Choctaw identity in the years ahead, and the tribe has insisted on keeping the floor on tribal enrollment at one-thirty-second.

At this point it is impossible to gauge whether or how recognition will affect the outmarriage rate, but even with declining blood quanta the tribal descendants will be able to continue to define themselves as a tribe because of federal recognition. A nonfederal tribe would face stronger challenges to its identity than a federal tribe if most of the tribal members averaged one-thirty-second degree of Indian blood. With cultural programs, various kinds of support, and bureaucratic entrenchment attached to membership in a federal tribe, the Jena Choctaws are no longer at significant risk for fading into local memory if strictly phenotypical and racial markers of Indian identity become less obvious. Though recognition policy relies on racial definitions in many ways, once recognition is attained, political status as a tribal nation ironically makes racial definitions of tribal identity less pertinent to tribal persistence.

At the town of Jena's version of a county fair, the annual "Howdy Neighbor" festival, the Jena Band of Choctaws held a place of honor in 1995. The tribe sponsored the musical entertainment for that year, gave vouchers to tribal members to spend on food at the booths, and hired a Coushatta dance troupe to perform; in return the town gave each tribal member a pass to sit in the front row at the main show. The event and the tribe's role in it were gratifying for the tribe and the town, providing good public relations for each and adding to the feeling of importance for the tribe that came with recognition.

In a similar vein, the tribe held a banquet after recognition to thank and honor the tribal members and local people who had helped make recognition possible. Among the local people receiving a medallion for their service was Mary "Pick" Pipes, one of the daughters of the Whatley family and the widow of Jay Pipes, who had taught the literacy classes for the Jena Choctaws in 1929. In her mid-nineties at the time of recognition, Pipes had testified about the presence and characteristics of the Choctaw community near her family's home. A significant portion of her testimony centered on how Choctaws used to go out drinking and stumble back loudly to the Whatley farm late at night, reinforcing stereotypes about them even as she helped to distinguish the Choctaws from surrounding people. Cheryl Smith felt bittersweet about Pipes's testimony on the Jena Choctaws' behalf, since the Whatleys were a significant part of the racial power structure that made them into sharecroppers, but the tribe included her in the ceremony because doing so was politic.

Yet another enduring legacy of racism is that the tribe must bear a greater responsibility for maintaining good relations with surrounding peoples and government entities. The position of honor for the Jena Choctaws at the Howdy Neighbor festival after recognition represented on one level a genuine enthusiasm on the part of non-Indian town leaders for an important local event, federal recognition of the tribe. There is a sincerely warm sentiment that exists on the surface. But on another level the Jena Choctaws carry a significantly heavier burden in diplomacy. Even with supportive leadership in the town of Jena, the ever-lurking potential for white reprisal against tribal sovereignty makes it far more important for the Jena Choctaws to appease the local whites than vice versa. State and local politicians have a much greater ability to interfere with tribal decisions than the other way round.

As an example of how this racial and colonial imbalance works in everyday life, one day while driving to the tribal center with me, Cheryl Smith found that private citizens had blocked off the road entirely a half-mile before the tribal center—with no permit—to complete a project on private property.

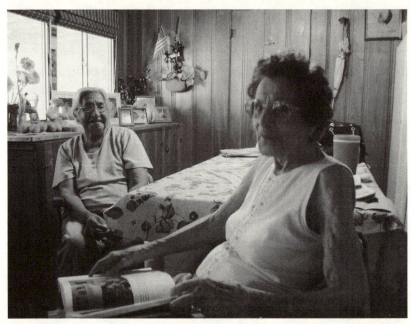

Mary Jackson Jones and Mary "Pick" Pipes at the Pipes home, 2004. Photo by the author.

This meant that she had to make a five-minute detour on a bumpy back road to make it to the tribal center each of the several times she came and went that day. Not that this was a great hardship—it was inconsiderate of the neighbor to block off both lanes of traffic unnecessarily, but Smith was not terribly put out by the detour. Yet because the neighbors were white and she was chief of the tribe at the time, she did not even have the option of asking them to be more considerate of people using the road, much less call the local authorities to complain.

Local race relations contribute to race relations on a grander scale, and public image is crucial to the Jena Choctaws' ability to function with minimal encumbrance, particularly as they try to set up a casino. The Jena Choctaws want to be good neighbors, and it is both economically and politically smart to keep good diplomatic relations, but there is an unspoken imbalance. The actions of any Jena Choctaw become representative of the entire tribe in the eyes of whites, an impediment that whites do not share. Mutually constituted with this racial imbalance, the colonial imbalance between the indigenous polity and local polities (such as the state and parish governments) means that local polities have not had to concede significant jurisdictional authority to the Jena Choctaws or let them pursue projects that they ought to be entitled to pursue as a sovereign nation. The tribe has the potential to become a vital economic force in the area, which could shift the political terrain, but for now the onus is on the Jena Choctaws to shoulder the bulk of the diplomatic load.

## Disappointment and Division, Unity and Persistence after Recognition

Mary Jackson Jones commented that some members of the tribe misunderstood the nature of recognition. "We went to Washington, got that paper, and come back. This younger generation, they think you went to Washington, when you get federal recognized, go to Washington, get some money, bring it back, and give them money. That's just the way they feel. But it don't work that way." Federal recognition leads to eligibility to participate in specific programs rather than immediate, no-strings-attached subsidies.

The tribal members and even the leadership could be forgiven for their confusion, however. By the time the Jena Band was recognized the Tunica casino had been open for about a year and the Coushatta casino for five months, and each casino was earning millions of dollars a month in gross revenue, according to the local newspaper.[4] Moreover, the state had recently legalized gaming in a variety of forms: a land-based casino in New Orleans, fifteen riverboat casinos around the state, video poker at virtually every truck stop, restaurant, and bar from Slidell to Shreveport; the industry seemed to be taking off full throttle.[5] Consequently the Jena Choctaws understandably became convinced that they would make millions immediately after recognition. Jerry Jackson says he fed these high expectations to encourage enthusiasm for the recognition project, but he was caught off guard by how slowly everything moved after recognition. No one could have predicted most of the difficulties that would significantly delay the Jena Choctaws' entry into the gaming industry.

Cheryl Smith recalls the gap between expectations and reality: "The tribe just thought money was going to fall out of the sky that night we got recognition. It didn't happen like that. Even after recognition, there was a whole year with not a penny coming in. I mean you have to apply for all these things . . . I think that was the biggest disappointment was everybody had waited on this so long and then there's nothing. The first year, nothing. It's like [the tribal members would say,] 'You mean nothing?' I think they were expecting to go to college totally free. They were expecting new houses to be built. They were expecting the government to give us land. They were expecting to be able to go to a hospital anywhere and do anything they want. I think our expectations were total complete help immediately. It was a letdown for the whole tribe."

One year after recognition Jerry Jackson agreed: "I expected more. I thought the Bureau of Indian Affairs would be down here. But you're on your own. You're in competition with other tribes for a slice of the financial pie . . . Not one thing has changed since getting federal recognition. Most benefits are tied to land, which tribal members do not have."[6] After an enormous amount of work for recognition, the Jena Choctaws found that they were still not eligible for many federal programs. As a newly recognized tribe they had to wade through the complexities of funding and grant eligibility at first. Then they had to wait for the applications to be processed and approved, and no assistance from the BIA was forthcoming in the meantime.

The AIPRC Final Report in 1977 recommended creating an agency independent of the BIA to make recognition decisions, immediately supply recently recognized tribes with funding, and then direct their transition into regular federal programs for Indian tribes.[7] Jena Choctaw experiences suggest that at the very least, the latter two policies ought to be considered by the secretary of the interior. A recognition transition protocol carried out by a team of experienced federal personnel remains an important, unmet need of recently recognized tribes.

The one benefit that the Jena Choctaws did begin receiving within a year was a health care grant, but even that was much lower than they had expected. With that they hired one staff person, Christine Norris, to run their health care program. They soon received other funds to hire office staff, and they began setting themselves up structurally to start receiving federal funds and apply for more grants. Norris recalled that one of the biggest changes was a shift toward running the tribal government "like a business," meaning that everything was much more structured than in the days before recognition. The tribe had to become more formal and meticulous, counting beans and shuffling papers to meet the demands of the federal bureaucracy and granting institutions.

For most tribal members day-to-day life had not changed even a decade after recognition. Most are living the same lives now as they did before recognition. But Cheryl Smith contends that being new to federal recognition meant that tribal members were still excited about the little changes taking place. Norris agrees. As she explained in 2000, "This is the first time these people have ever gotten anything. I was in one of the meetings up in

Nashville just last week and we were talking about the differences in people, and I said, 'But our tribe is so thankful for anything we've got.' Some tribes were saying, 'Well, our people are so spoiled, they've had so much.' And I said, 'Well, we're so new and we've had nothing, that these people here are just glad for anything.'" Everyone in the service area can now go to the doctor and acquire medicine for free, whereas in the past most people only went to the doctor if they were dying. A few tribal members have even been able to move into tribally provided houses or to take advantage of the Housing Improvement Program. There were at least ten tribal members working in the tribal office by 2000, a number that has increased to fourteen since then. "It's just such a different world for [us]," Norris says.

Jerry Jackson clarifies: "Probably ninety percent of our members don't need help at all. They're working," he says, implying that they are stable and providing for their families adequately. "There's a few that do [need help]. For whatever reason—their fault, not their fault—they need assistance. A lot of times the others get mad, because most of the things we administer for the housing is based on their income. So we help the lower [income] more than the upper [income]." Similarly, if a tribal member has a problem with substance abuse, the tribe can provide help. If the power goes out for a few days at a time—as it sometimes does in rural areas—the tribe has a generator to run the lights and air conditioner at the tribal center, which has cots and other accommodations for up to 250 people in the gym. For the most part, the tribe provides a safety net rather than a free ride.

Along these lines, the tribe has been "aggressively pursuing education as the key to a successful tribal future," according to Christine Norris. Whether in liberal arts or professional, vocational and technical, or K-12 education, the tribe assists its members enthusiastically, because doing so promotes individual and tribal self-sufficiency. Christy Murphy, the tribe's education director for several years, coordinated tutoring services for K-12 students twice a week, which are funded by Title VII programs available to both federal tribes and nonfederal tribes and organizations. Typically eight to ten of the approximately sixty school-aged students in the tribe participate regularly, most of them in elementary grades,

For post-secondary education the tribe offers modest tuition assistance of up to $1,200 a semester for full-time students and $600 a semester for part-time students. Participation in the tuition program has increased from three students shortly after federal recognition to more than ten in 2004. The tribe had its first college graduate in 2000, its first student received a graduate degree in 2008, and the proportion of students graduating at every level of education continues to rise every year. The investment in education for tribal members is returning immediate dividends.

Like other programs, the education program is always available but only used in time of need. It is designed to assist tribal members in maintaining or developing self-sufficiency without having the tribe assume all responsibility for them. It obviously helps people to find satisfying careers with good pay, but it also prepares a future generation for leadership—an urgent concern of the current leaders, who are mostly in their fifties, have been involved in tribal government since the early 1970s, and are anxious to groom their replacements so that they can retire with peace of mind.

The tribal language program has been less successful to date but remains an urgent concern of many tribal members. With only a handful of fluent Choctaw-language speakers remaining in the community, the tribe finds itself in a common predicament in Indian country. The generation born after the Second World War and integrated into white schools grew up hearing the Choctaw language at home but lost use of it through the years. Some can still follow a conversation in Choctaw but cannot participate in one. Several efforts have been made to initiate language classes over the last two decades, and interest has been strong, but as any language student knows, learning a language is best done through intensive study or—ideally—immersion rather than weekly meetings. Very few people have the kind of free time and drive required to learn or teach a language on their own. The tribe has recently applied for grant funding to work with a linguist at the University of Oklahoma on developing a language preservation strategy, but language preservation has proved to be an overwhelming challenge for tribes, and federal recognition does not significantly help to overcome it.

The tribe is fortunate that thousands of people still speak Choctaw in Oklahoma and Mississippi, providing potential resources and partners, but they would also like to preserve their own dialect, which has subtle distinctions.[8] To capture the distinctions before the pre-war generations pass away, Christy Murphy provided the fluent speakers with tape recorders and asked them to record themselves speaking periodically and to translate and explain what they said. Murphy's generation, the children of the postwar generation, she says, was raised without knowing a single word of Choctaw. "And that's sad to say," she laments. "We are at the last straw." Without funding that will allow people to devote more time to learning the language, the outlook is bleak.

Language preservation is one of the reasons why the tribe so eagerly pursues economic development through class III gaming (casinos) rather than the less profitable class II gaming (bingo and pull tabs). Casinos have proved to be a reliable source of revenue for other tribal governments in the state, and they could help the Jena Choctaws with cultural projects such as the language project, potentially giving some people the opportunity to devote full-time attention to language revitalization.

Economic development continues apace in the absence of gaming, though, and it does aid the tribe. In 2005, for example, the tribe opened a new building for its own health clinic, which has employed tribal members in the past, though it is currently staffed by three non-Indians. The tribe is considering opening a for-profit medical clinic in Grant Parish as well, since there are none currently there, and a clinic could provide employment for tribal members and direct revenue to the tribal government. The Jena Band runs its own tribal environmental protection agency, an education program, a health department, a social services department, and a tribal construction company, which not only secures employment for tribal members but controls the costs of its services and sets priorities. The tribe paved the road to the tribal cemetery and built a small pavilion there, improving life in small but significant ways for tribal members as they continue to wait for a gaming facility. The tribal construction company recently built another clinic for a doctor in Jena, and while profits were not enormous the project did provide jobs for tribal members and helped them build their bonding capacity, which will help them secure larger projects in the future. Still, funding fluctuates significantly in a grant economy, so jobs are not always secure in the long term, and the tribe's most highly qualified workers often cannot risk working for the tribe. Cheryl Smith has been frustrated by the lack of trajectory, having "worked in every position from janitor to top dog" for the tribe over a period of more than thirty years, but still never having had a clear job description or a clear road ahead. Without casino gaming the tribe provides a safety net, but it struggles to harness the skills and energy of tribal members to achieve a national and tribal purpose.

Jerry Jackson's dream of establishing a casino immediately after recognition never materialized, and that turned out to be his downfall. He could not persuade Governor Mike Foster, a Republican, to authorize a gaming compact between the tribe and the state, and a temporary federal freeze on gaming compacts further hampered the tribe. Worse, two of the casino companies that the tribe had made deals with before recognition were suing the tribe, which prevented it from even discussing a casino plan for several years. During the years leading up to recognition the tribe had made agreements with six potential gaming partners on the premise that they would receive managerial gaming contracts after recognition in return for their providing specific forms of aid that would help the tribe to attain recognition. According to the tribe, none of the companies ever maintained their end of the bargain, so the tribe released them all. Two companies sued after the tribe was recognized, and the judge in the case ordered that the Jena Band could not negotiate anything regarding gaming until the case was settled.[9] On top of all that, the criminal prosecution of the former governor Edwin Edwards on corruption charges surrounding the issuance of state gaming licenses ensured that gaming would be political poison for the foreseeable future. Rumors and allegations about his corruption had floated around for years prior, but the FBI raid of his office and home in April 1997 began a three-year investigation and prosecution that resulted in multiple convictions on racketeering and other charges, casting a pall over the gaming industry in Louisiana in general.[10]

Jerry Jackson had pursued gaming so single-mindedly that even by his own account he did not want to bother working on other goals. When he could not produce a casino within three years after recognition, he could offer no evidence of progress to his constituents. He had not developed any other programs in that time, and so despite hard work, the tangible benefits that tribal members had been yearning for remained minimal. Still, Jackson continued to believe that the casino was the one and only endeavor that the tribe needed to pursue. As he put it, "In my opinion, we're never going to become what we could have been if we don't become economically important." Without a large population, the most logical way for the tribe to accumulate enough political power to adequately protect its interests is to become an economic force. Its votes are not enough to turn the tide in any election, but money and jobs make politicians pay attention. The only way the tribe could make enough money to be politically important, Jackson believed, would be to set up a casino in an area where it could draw a significant number of customers.

Since the Jena Choctaws had a choice in where their initial reservation would be located after recognition but could not conduct gaming on lands taken into trust after that time without clearing significant hurdles, they proposed a number of sites based on cultural and economic development considerations. Setting up a casino at a particular site involves several steps, though. First, the Jena Choctaws needed to identify several areas where they believed a casino could succeed. Initial surveys from gaming partners suggested that a location in LaSalle Parish would be least desirable because of its distance from urban areas and local opposition to gaming, so the tribe has considered a wide array of locations, both within and outside their BIA service area.

Second, the tribe needs to have the state governor approve the site, which Mike Foster, the governor at the time the Initial Reservation Plan was crafted, would only do if the people in the proposed area approved of gaming. In a statewide referendum that allowed each parish to decide whether it would allow legalized gaming in 1996, the parishes in their BIA-defined service area (LaSalle, Grant, and Rapides parishes) voted against gaming, so Governor Foster would not sign the required gaming compact for a facility in Jena, even if that was what the tribe desired.

Third, the tribe needs to have the secretary of the interior approve the gaming compact and accept the land into trust as the tribe's initial reservation. As the Jena Choctaws learned, secretarial approval is by no means a guarantee. Dozens of potentially deal-breaking negotiations accompany the process, and setting up a successful casino for the Jena Choctaws would take an enormous amount of time and resources. Jerry Jackson believed that a successful casino would make the little grants and federal programs secondary to the tribe's well-being, but he did not anticipate the massive roadblocks that the tribe encountered.

Jackson felt like a victim of circumstance and corporate profiteering at the tribe's expense:

These wolves just tore me apart. Too much greed. Like these groups suing the tribe now [in 2000], they could have done it. If everything would have worked out perfect, they could have done it. They didn't have the financial resources to do it. But see I was in a position where nobody else was coming at the time because the secretary of the interior had the compacts froze. And I was making this group pay us $10,000 a month. The ten thousand was going to the members in the form of education grants, whatever it is, it was going there. But of all the groups that came to do gaming, if any of them would have bought the land, then we would have had a partner. But what they were trying to do was nickel and dime and wait for things to get better in Washington. And they were hoping to ride us in to better times. But I wouldn't let them ride. I just kept hitting them to put up more money, do this and do that. And when you wouldn't do it, you were gone.

Cheryl Smith, Jerry Jackson's cousin and the tribal secretary for the twelve years he was in office, had a different vision for the tribe's immediate future. She saw that casino development was going to take longer than expected. She thought the tribe should seek other sources of funding at the same time as they tried to negotiate a casino deal and develop an infrastructure so that when they finally did get a casino, they would be able to put the funds to use right away. Had Jerry Jackson been able to overcome the numerous obstacles in the tribe's path and set up the casino as quickly as he had hoped, she never would have run against him in the elections of 1998, when she defeated him by fourteen votes.

The ethics of gaming were not at issue in the election, though Smith harbored some concerns about the negative impact that large per capita payments might have on younger tribal members' desire to educate themselves or work for a living. The majority of Jena Choctaws did not have significant moral qualms about establishing a casino, as other tribes had. "We can build a casino," Mary Jackson Jones offered. "If them white people crazy enough to play, we'll take their money! They took our money one time, took our land!" While a notable minority did oppose gaming, the main issue in the election was that neither the casino nor any other major tribal initiative aside from the health program had been established in the three years since recognition.

Clyde Jackson laments that Jerry Jackson "had the best intention in mind for the tribe. It was just the wrong way of doing it." If Jerry Jackson had dealt with issues other than gaming he would have been reelected, but he was too overbearing with the tribal members on the gaming issues, his cousin argues. "Plus," he adds, "you know how the newspapers are. The press kept kind of running us down. And people got aggravated because it seemed like we was a bunch of dummies sitting here, and like we didn't know what we was doing." Clyde Jackson acknowledges that it is difficult to foresee all the problems with a particular policy for the tribe, adding, "Maybe that's why I'm sitting here [at home]" instead of in the office of the chief.

Cheryl Smith and Jerry Jackson were both frustrated. Jackson felt betrayed by Smith and the other tribal members who voted him out, and he would not even be in the same room with them for a couple of years, much less participate in tribal affairs. Smith thought Jackson was a valuable leader except for his overconfidence in casino development. The tribe was stalled, and she thought she had a better way, so she ran against him. Because it is so hard to separate tribal matters from personal family matters, the tribe lost an exceptional asset in Jerry Jackson for a time, and Smith felt hobbled by the discord.

Tribal governments tend to be as riven by disagreements as any governments, but the schism at Jena is of a new kind, one exacerbated by recognition, particularly for small tribes. Suddenly the group had to have elections among siblings, cousins, aunts, uncles, and grandparents to see who would run the family. In some ways it was actually better than in the old days, in that the whole tribe agreed on a system that would democratically decide who would lead the tribe, and the tribal government has been run fairly smoothly even during tumultuous times. But the tensions created by running against a relative for a position as head of the family are immense. Hard feelings would be created in contested elections, and showing up at family gatherings after defeat could be intensely awkward while bitter feelings remained fresh. The new political system can have a powerful disunifying effect on a small tribe when the stakes are so high immediately after recognition. Even though the traditional means of making decisions and exerting social control were not perfect by any stretch, as was evident in the long-standing disputes between the Lewises and the Jacksons, they had evolved over many years to suit the needs of Choctaw families. Leadership was not ironclad, and even the chief's decisions did not have to be obeyed. Now, for better or worse, the entire tribe is bound to the actions of the chief and the council much more strongly because of the significant resources attached to their decisions.

To illustrate the difference in political forms, when much of the group decided to trek to Oklahoma in search of allotments in 1902, some of the group decided to stay in Louisiana. While the decision to go to Oklahoma seems to have been made collectively, not everyone was forced to abide by it, because the group's organizational structure was loose. No one had the authority to order a peer of another family to do anything. Since there were no significant resources or punishments attached to membership in the informal entity, male Choctaw heads of families in particular could dissent from a group decision without serious repercussions. There were not enough resources at the time to make tribal members feel as though participating in this small Choctaw community was necessary for health and prosperity. Rather, strong kinship ties and a sense of belonging to the group were forces that promoted a desire to seek group consensus. If someone dissented despite these forces, he or she was free to pursue other options. Given the long-standing rivalry between the Lewises and the Jacksons, it is apparent that dissent and separation were accepted parts of tribal life.

The situation is very different now. When the chief and the council make a decision it is a decision made for the entire tribe, and even dissenters have to accommodate themselves to it. The decisions of the elected leadership affect the health and well-being of every tribal member to a much greater degree than formerly. There is so much money (potentially) and power involved in decisions made by the tribal government that tensions are bound to run high, and the issues are so new that opinions are bound to be fractious. Almost no one wanted to be on the council before recognition because the decisions being made by the tribal government did not seem important. Moreover, it usually cost money to be on the council, since council members often had to pay expenses such as those incurred to drive to meetings in Baton Rouge. That all changed in the first post-recognition election in 1998, when more than a dozen people ran for the five government positions. Decisions made by the tribal council now will more clearly affect the lives of tribal members, contributing to the more contentious elections since recognition.

The present political form, with opponents running for election to a set term against close relatives based on minimal political differences, can foster divisions in the tribe that were weaker or not present before recognition. As noted above, the political system before formalization and recognition, based in consensus building, was not perfect, and it would not likely be sufficient to handle casino negotiations without significant problems. But it has taken time for the tribal government to develop mechanisms for dealing more effectively with internal political conflicts.

On the other hand, the creation of a tribal political entity vested with power and funding has created a new unity that offsets the divisions created by the governmental form. Cheryl Smith has noted that recognition has created a stronger bond to the tribe, particularly for the younger generation. When she was growing up there was no formal tribal entity, and the Jacksons and Lewises rarely did things together as a tribe unless there was an obligation such as a funeral, wedding, or cleaning of the tribal cemetery. Now the children grow up taking trips with the tribe to places like Washington, receiving presents and school supplies from the tribe, and generally being taken care of by the tribe, making the bond much stronger. Members feel as if they belong to the Jena Band of Choctaws, not to the Jackson or Lewis family.[11] Smith suggests that since the members have managed to build the tribe through all kinds of adversity, it should only be easier now that legal, financial, and educational prospects for the tribe are improving.

Despite some contentiousness in tribal leadership, Christine Norris finds

similar hope in the growing tendency of tribal membership to take prece-
dence over family membership. Old conflicts still exist, but they are fading
because people are being rewarded as members of a tribe. The few services
available give them a new sense of appreciation for what the tribe can mean
for them. Every tribe has some degree of internal conflict, Norris says, but the
Jena Choctaws' sense of unity keeps growing as they endure more trials
together and provide support for each other based on tribal membership.
Indeed, she says, if the tribe was to fall apart, it would have done so in the
early years of organization, not after all that the members have been through
together over the last thirty-plus years. The tribe has become an institution
now, and it would be nearly impossible to root it out of people's lives.

There have been other tribal elections since 1998 in which cousins have run
against each other for elected positions, and while losses still sting, the
current leadership feels as if détente has been reached. "We feel like we've got
a good system going, a good organization," says the current chief, Christine
Norris. "We understand each other well, and we work together well as a team
now. We haven't always in the past. Now we've got this infrastructure we're
building up, and we've got plans. We really feel like we're headed in a good
direction."[12] Rather than have one person representing the tribe or making
decisions, which would create pressure and internal tensions, the tribe has
moved toward a consensus-building model that mirrors the tribal leadership
styles of years past.

## "They'll Never Take It Away from Us"

Jerry Jackson has changed his appraisal of the tribe's situation from the year
immediately following recognition, when he said that recognition was a
disappointment. When asked if recognition had lived up to its billing five
years later, he replied, "Yeah. We haven't. We've got the recognition, but we
haven't got the most out of it. It's not anybody's fault but ours. And I take a lot
of the blame because of all the time I spent on gaming. Maybe we could have
developed something else, I don't know." He has always believed that setting
up a casino in a lucrative location, using the opportunities presented by
recognition and the Initial Reservation Plan, would be the tribe's one chance
to secure a brilliant future. "So that was my plan and I stuck with it," he says,
"right or wrong."

Federal program money and grant money do not give the tribe as much
leeway to define its own goals as its own revenue stream would do. They do
not even allow the leaders to serve the entire tribe as they define it. "The out-

of-state people are chomping at the bit wanting something out of this," Jackson says with some frustration. "They're not receiving anything from the tribe itself. With federal program money, you can only do certain things. The tribe has to develop its own money. What I wanted to do with gaming . . . is set up our own credit union. Then you could help people yourself go into business, buy homes. I don't care if they live in Arizona, California, wherever that may be. You could come up with a new vision of what a tribe is—not what it was in the 1800s, but what it could be in the future." The tribe wants to be able to serve every tribal member, but federal service area limitations that were designed to detribalize Indians now provide an impetus for relocated tribal members to return to the tribe so that they can receive the benefits of federal recognition. Those who have moved out of the area probably have more economic opportunities at this point, which balances out the reduced federal benefits, but significant tribal development will soon take place in the service area, drawing many more tribal members home. At the very least, development enabled by recognition will allow tribal members outside the service area to benefit materially from federal recognition for the first time through home loans, business loans, or even per capita payments.

Still, Jackson notes, the Jena Choctaws have come a long way since 1974 or even 1995. "It's better now," he said in 2008, "because, like I said, we're running our programs ourselves. By doing it that way, yeah, I feel a lot better. We have had good audits since day one. By doing that we were able to run our own housing—there's still rules and everything, but we get to bend them and shape them to what works for us. Times are better now, although we're still not where we should be. Times are better now than they were."

Just as Jerry Jackson argued that the tribe had to learn to think of itself as a tribe when it incorporated to obtain state recognition, Christine Norris suggests that the tribe had to learn to think of itself as a sovereign entity after federal recognition. On the concept that her extended Choctaw family constitutes a sovereign entity, she said in 2000, "I think it's been so new that it's just now beginning to sink in. Because I know I certainly myself never viewed it like that before, never really thinking about it, because it was never there before. So only until you hear that word 'sovereign' so much now when you go to meetings . . . and you hear it over and over, and it's like, that's what we really are! We are a separate entity now."

Jerry Jackson agrees that it is sometimes incongruous to think of his family as a sovereign nation:

But I think when you're a tribal leader, you have to project that image, because if you don't see it, nobody else is going to see it. And if you don't draw the line, then people are going to encroach on you. Tribal leadership has to put your arms out and keep everybody away from this . . . inner circle. So many people will cut and divide a tribe up, for whatever reason. That's why the tribal chief's main responsibility is the negotiator, the front person, with anything, everything. Because you have to develop the plan. If your plan is correct, it's great. If it's not, well, you won't be there. But somebody has to develop the plan and take the initiative. But you can call yourself a sovereign nation all you want to. If you don't act like one, if you don't go out there and fight for whatever rights . . . There's all kinds of rules and regulations, but as long as we have a right to do it, we should be doing it. We should push whatever in every direction we can legitimately go, that's where we should push . . . You've got to go get it. That's sovereignty . . . I got nephews and brothers and sisters and all looking for work. They need jobs. They need a career. They're employed, but they're underemployed. They haven't reached any potential that they could, and it's only through the tribe that's going to happen.

Whatever efforts the Jena Choctaw tribe undertakes, sovereignty will be the keystone. "There's a cultural side, there's a social side and services, and there's a business side. And you've gotta be able to jump into all three categories," Jerry Jackson notes, with the implication that the political issue of federal recognition of tribal sovereignty enables all three.

And they all have to make sense. Because you can't just stay in one and push one. And we have real dedicated people that want to keep the language going and do all that, which is fine. But see, when they wanted to get paid, well somebody had to go get the money, and that kept the culture side going. Or if somebody's kid wanted to go to college or whatever—because the BIA on the schools and most of the grants, it's for the very poor—so with us, with non-program money [from a casino development deal], we could distribute it any way we wanted to. So we never turned down anybody. We give them $500 for a part-time student, and $1,000 a semester for full-time. And then anything else that may come up, special cases, sometimes they need clothes, sometimes they need whatever. But you couldn't do that with grants, because grants tell you what you can do and what you can't do. Anyway, I think you've got these various parts of the tribe, they're all important . . . [As a tribal leader] you have responsibility for funding and developing and continuing and advancing all of these things. And they all have to march forward together. . . .

When I looked around [as tribal chief] . . . I didn't see nothing that wasn't a dollar bill. I mean they had all these wonderful ideas, but it costs money. Well, where do we get the money? Well, from the gaming people. I worked them gaming people over. I mean over. Hundreds of times.

The Jena Choctaws entered the gaming industry to support the cultural and social foundations of their tribe. They want to fund cultural and educational programs for their people who have been denied such opportunities for so long. They want to alleviate the chronic social afflictions that accompany being poor and brown in the United States. They want jobs that will allow the tribal members who live outside the service area to return. The motivation of a tribe is worlds apart from the motivation of Donald Trump or Steve Wynn, even if they are in the same industry.

As mentioned in earlier chapters, the casino developments of Indian tribes do not have the same goals as the casino developments of non-Indians. Corporate gaming interests are concerned with acquiring fantastic personal wealth and material possessions. Tribes have a broader agenda—one further ensured by the requirement of the Indian Gaming Regulatory Act that casino revenue must fund social, health, and educational programs before the remainder can be distributed per capita. The personal comfort of tribal members is certainly a consideration, but even then it is in the context of redistributive justice for a history of deep poverty and denied opportunities under racism and colonialism past and present. Moreover, the possibility of individual wealth through per capita payments for tribal members is a source of consternation more than excitement; Christine Norris and Cheryl Smith have said that they see large per capita payments as a threat to self-reliance, motivation, competence, and educational attainment, especially for young tribal members, making them potentially destructive to the tribe in the long run. Very few tribes in the country have reached that level, though, and with so much competition in the gaming market in Louisiana, it is unlikely that the Jena Band ever will.

Cheryl Smith worked on a number of projects for the tribe in her time as chief, but she ran into the same problem as her predecessor. For one, the casino project would not budge. "With Jena, nothing is fast-track for us," she lamented. She spent her first year and a half in office expanding tribal programs, but then felt as if she had to move ahead on the gaming issue. She first had to settle the lawsuit, which took several years. Then the tribe had to find a viable location that the governor and the secretary of the interior would approve for the Initial Reservation Plan, and also build local support to insure against being ambushed by opponents.

Siting a new casino turned out to be a gargantuan task. The tribe's service area, which is its "historic" home of LaSalle, Rapides, and Grant parishes, provides only minimal opportunities for profit. Furthermore, each of these parishes voted against legalized gaming in the statewide referendum in 1996, so governors of Louisiana since then have not been willing to sign a gaming compact that would allow the Jena Choctaws to operate a casino in their service area.[13] The tribe has considered locations for a casino all over the state and as far away as Tishomingo County, Mississippi, but the refusal of the governors to sign a compact for a casino in their service area has hamstrung the tribe's efforts to start gaming and to push through an Initial Reservation Plan, and it has provided embarrassing fodder for local newspapers, making the tribe appear devious for seeking a casino outside its service area.[14]

The effort to locate a casino in Vinton that began in 2001 was opposed by the Coushatta Tribe as well as the riverboat gambling interests in Lake Charles, Louisiana. Each would stand to lose considerable amounts of money if the Jena Choctaws opened a casino in Vinton, which is closer to Houston, a significant source of customers for southwest Louisiana gaming facilities. The tribe negotiated a compact with the governor to open a casino at the site, but Secretary of the Interior Gale Norton vetoed the compact in 2002. Norton argued that it essentially allowed the state to tax the tribe, which is not allowed under the IGRA, and she considered the land to be outside the tribe's historic area.[15] Following the lead of the poorly informed campaign by the Republican congressman David Vitter against Indian gaming in general and his false accusations that the Jena Choctaws had negotiated a "secret" compact with Governor Foster, the Louisiana press unleashed a furious attack against the Jena Choctaws. Vitter and the press continued to dog the tribe as it pursued gambling in Logansport, with Vitter hoping to use the issue to bolster support for his run for the governor's office in 2003 and the U.S. Senate in 2004.

The press contributed to the problem by displaying an inconsistent understanding of tribal legal and political status in the United States, often conflating issues of race and indigeneity and failing to adequately explain the unique status of tribal governments for purposes other than gaming. Newspaper

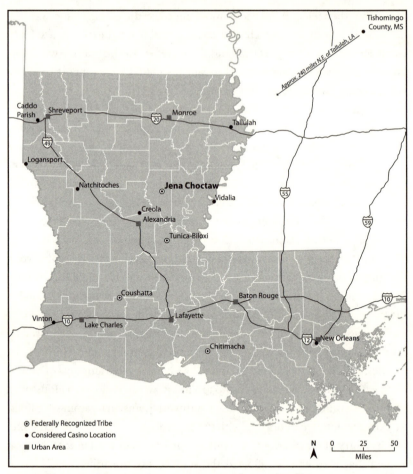

Proposed locations for a Jena Choctaw casino. Map by Derek Miller.

articles often left readers with the impression that casinos were the source of racially based handouts within the state rather than businesses that tribes had the right to establish because of the sovereignty and primacy of indigenous nations, as supported by the Constitution, Congress, and the Supreme Court. Editorials from the state's newspapers consistently opposed a Jena casino, calling it "a fourth Indian casino,"[16] as though all members of the racial group—Indians—in the state benefited from the three that were already operating. Moreover, the press failed to question the state's right to impose its will on the tribe, leaving a tacit endorsement of the colonial structure.[17]

Governor Foster's compact with the Jena Choctaws asked for a "voluntary contribution" of 15.5 percent of revenues to be paid to the state, not much less than the 21.5 percent in tax paid by the non-Indian casino operators in the state.[18] The other tribal gaming compacts in the state provide for a 6 percent tax as an offset for local services, and the higher rate is the reason why Norton claims she vetoed the compact. As long as Foster kept insisting that the Jena Choctaws must operate a casino outside their service area—because their service area included only parishes that had voted against gaming in the referendum of 1996—he continued to ask for the 15.5 percent "voluntary contribution" as payment for "permission" to operate a class III gaming facility outside the service area, creating an unwinnable situation for the tribe. Foster could trust that the compact would not likely be approved by Norton, since such a steep contribution was not asked of any other tribe in the state, and the state required the casino to be outside the tribe's three-parish service area while the federal government preferred it to be within the service area. If Foster succeeded, he would earn new revenues for the state along with a political victory over "minority interests." If he failed, the tribe would not be able to open a casino, giving him another political victory. Foster risked nothing, but the tribe repeatedly wasted its resources because it was forced to negotiate a deal with Foster in good faith.

Every year that goes by without a casino, the Jena Choctaws are losing millions of dollars for cultural programs, social services, education, and land acquisition. Tribal leaders think of this in terms of lives lost. If they had been federally recognized in the 1980s, for example, they could have developed programs to help the neediest in the community—those with severe health, mental health, and addiction problems that eventually contributed to their deaths. By 1991, when both video poker and riverboat casinos were legalized statewide, the Jena Choctaws would have been well positioned to negotiate a gaming compact, and it would not likely have been rescinded even after the referendum of 1996. Instead the tribe was forced to devote many resources to fighting with the state for what other Louisiana tribes had access to almost automatically, a battle that cost them a significant measure of public good-will along the way. Moreover, Cheryl Smith expressed concern in 2008 that "maybe the heyday of Indian gaming is gone." Entering a relatively saturated market could mean smaller annual profits or worse for the tribe even if they finally secure the necessary compact to open a class III facility.

The Jena Choctaw casino has become a touchstone in state electoral politics. Every candidate in the gubernatorial election in 2003 came out against the "expansion of gaming" and in particular against allowing the Jena Choctaws to establish a casino, indicating an alarming degree of consensus on state authority to suppress Jena Choctaw sovereignty. Though video poker is still legal in the thirty-three (of sixty-four) parishes that voted for it in the statewide local-option referendum in 1996, and gaming machines can be found in numerous establishments in those parishes, the political contentiousness of the issue has significantly impeded tribal economic development efforts, and it has become a conservative wedge issue in most significant state elections since gambling was legalized. David Vitter, elected to the U.S. Senate in 2004 on a hard-line conservative "values" campaign and later— predictably—revealed to have had a long affair with a prostitute, was perhaps the most outspoken in his opposition to the "expansion of gaming."[19] Governor Kathleen Blanco, a centrist Democrat, was not initially anti-gaming in her campaign, but she came out against the Jena Band after enduring political pressure on the issue from Vitter. Her Republican successor, Governor Bobby Jindal, continued this Louisiana tradition, using gaming as a conservative wedge issue in 2007, but like Foster and Blanco he failed to advocate the state's abolition of gaming, which would have cut off an important source of revenue for state government and numerous small business owners.[20] Jindal asked the Jena Band not to press him on the issue during the election, or he would be forced to take a public position that would likely be against them. While Jindal has renewed compacts with the other three federal tribes without any fanfare, he said he would prefer to have time to deliberate and study the Jena issue. Not surprisingly, Jindal eventually refused to sign a compact with the tribe, saying that he was against the expansion of gaming. There are already dozens of gaming facilities in the state, and the state is not willing to diminish its revenues by taking a few licenses away, but state politicians are willing to prevent the Jena Band of Choctaws from exercising their rights as a sovereign tribe and gaining access to this important source of revenue for its own government. That the state continues to operate its own gaming facilities while blocking the Jena Band's casino on supposedly moral grounds or anti-corruption grounds is the height of hypocrisy, and a clear example of unrestrained colonialism.

Gaming has a long association with political corruption in Louisiana that predates its legalization in 1991. Indeed, when Governor Edwin Edwards proposed legalizing gaming in 1986, he aroused so much suspicion that he was defeated on an anti-gaming, anti-corruption platform by Buddy Roemer in the election that year.[21] In a state known for having "the best politicians money can buy," Edwards is remembered as one of the most flamboyantly corrupt, often flaunting his acceptance of gifts and cash from lobbyists.

Nonetheless, he was reelected in 1991 when he ran against the former Ku Klux Klan leader David Duke.[22] Ironically, it was Buddy Roemer who signed into law a bill legalizing high-stakes riverboat gambling in 1991, but it was Edwards who, several years after completing his term as governor, would be convicted on multiple counts of racketeering and extortion related to the riverboat casino licensing process.[23]

Partly because of Edwards's history of corruption and the new kinds of corruption that were then rumored to be taking place with riverboat licensing, the gubernatorial election in 1995 was won by Mike Foster, a Democrat-turned-Republican whose platform centered on his opposition to gaming. That an ideology of white supremacy continues to undergird state politics is evident in the ways tribal gaming has been rolled into opposition to the "expansion of gaming" in Louisiana as a platform issue for state politicians. Opposition to gaming is now a euphemistic nod to white supremacy, in the same way that references to "conservative values" and "law and order" played to white fears of integration and black power in the 1960s. Since gaming is a supposedly race-neutral issue, it is difficult to challenge the way arguments against it are deployed, but anti-gaming rhetoric is tied to a general discourse about race, religion, and culture that challenges tribal sovereignty.

The undercurrent of race and ethnicity reveals itself in the pattern of parishes that voted for and against gaming: the predominantly Catholic, so-called Cajun parishes of south Louisiana and the predominantly black border parishes near Vicksburg, Mississippi, and Shreveport, Louisiana, all voted to legalize gaming, while the predominantly Protestant Anglo-American northern parishes voted against it. Blacks across the state were more likely to vote for it; in the racial discourse of northern Louisiana whites, the southern half of the state is associated with looser moral attitudes toward racial mixing as well as a desire for gaming, which further links the issue of gaming to notions of inherent racial morality.[24] Governor Edwards had been an advocate for communities of color in his tenure, and his political alliances have become tightly associated with gaming, corruption, and race. Add in the fact that Governor Foster supported David Duke's political aspirations on several occasions, and the white rights agenda becomes even more apparent. Even with its long history before tribal gaming, gambling has become inextricably tied to tribal casinos, and a significant element of the racial and colonial discourse includes the belief that tribal gaming operations—and even tribal sovereignty itself—are a type of affirmative action program that gives racialized minorities (rather than indigenous nations) "special" and undeserved privileges. One of the gubernatorial candidates in 2003, a former Democratic U.S. representative from Lake Charles named Buddy Leach, made this perception clear when he said, "If I'm elected governor, there will be no secret meetings about additional gaming, whether it's Indian, Chinese, Japanese, Spanish, or whatever."[25] Even if Leach has no understanding of tribal sovereignty or gaming law as distinct from racial law, his perception of indigenous sovereignty in exclusively racial terms demonstrates that racial discourses profoundly affect tribal sovereignty.

Even among those who understand the concept of indigenous tribal sovereignty, racial discourses underlie their conception of the relationship between the state and the tribes. The racial discourse and the colonial discourse share a central belief that whites, their morals, and their political institutions are inherently superior to nonwhites, their morals, and their political institutions. Even the parish government—the parish government!—in this case is given political authority over the Jena Band of Choctaws on gaming, despite federal recognition as an indigenous nation.

As it turns out, Secretary of the Interior Gale Norton's claim that she vetoed the Jena compact based on her objection to the 15.5 percent voluntary contribution may have been false. She was one of several very high-ranking federal officials to be named in the investigation of the lobbying scandal that embroiled Jack Abramoff and Michael Scanlon, and she resigned from her position as secretary of the interior in 2006, just as questions about her impartiality on the Jena issue in particular were coming to light. Scanlon, a public relations professional, had been charging the Coushattas and the Mississippi Choctaws millions of dollars to oppose the development of the Jena Choctaw casino. Scanlon had been splitting the money with Abramoff, a lobbyist who was depositing money in the account of the Council of Republicans for Environmental Advocacy, an organization founded and run for many years by Norton. The person running the CREA office at the time was Italia Federici, also the girlfriend of an assistant deputy secretary of the interior, J. Steven Griles, who tried to intervene to prevent approval of the Jena Band's Initial Reservation Plan (an issue in which he otherwise would never have been involved). Abramoff and Scanlon used Coushatta gaming money to hire the Republican leader Ralph Reed of the Christian Coalition, who was to have his members write letters expressing their moral objections to gaming, without letting anyone know he was funded by Scanlon's gaming clients. Abramoff and Scanlon thought they had figured out ways to funnel money to politicians without being caught, until some Coushatta elected officials began to question why the tribe was paying such enormous sums to them. Once the story broke, the Senate Indian Affairs Committee investigated, and a number of prominent federal politicians were brought down in one of the most significant federal corruption scandals in thirty years. The House majority leader, Tom DeLay, resigned in disgrace after the scandal, and Abramoff, Federici, and Griles each pleaded guilty to related charges. Norton was never charged in the investigation, but it seems likely that the Abramoff group influenced her decision at least somewhat on the Jena Band reservation plan and gaming compact.[26]

The Coushatta leadership involved in the scandal, like the Jena Choctaws under Jim Crow educational segregation, were complicatedly complicit in their own oppression. By manipulating the colonial structures of state and federal power to undermine the Jena Choctaws, they reinforced state power over tribes in general. Rather than fight colonial forces, they tried to participate in them. Thus they reinforced white supremacy, the presumed superiority of political institutions and practices created by whites over tribal political institutions and practices.

The tribe's Initial Reservation Plan, which included parcels of land in LaSalle, Rapides, and Grant parishes in addition to the site in Logansport, was approved in 2007—all except for the critical Logansport site. The BIA easily approved the sites in the service area, but it would only approve the Logansport site if the state governor, the newly elected Kathleen Blanco, approved it too. Citing her opposition to expanded gaming, the governor disapproved, creating another obstacle preventing the Jena Choctaws from fully benefiting from recognition.[27]

The Jena Choctaws worked hard in Logansport to build support for their casino development. They circulated petitions in support of the casino, gaining thousands of signatures. They asked the DeSoto Parish governing council (called a police jury in Louisiana) to support their project, which it did on a vote of 6–5. They had been trying to avoid the fiasco that was created by Vitter's accusations that the last compact was negotiated secretly. The majority of people in DeSoto Parish supported the casino, but a cabal of politicians and casino owners from the area surrounding Shreveport and Bossier City, fifty miles north of Logansport, opposed the project because it would drain as much as 15 percent of the business away from the gaming projects in place there. It seems like a weak argument to say that the commercial enterprises, whose profit goes mostly to the wealthy whites who own them, have some compelling right to protection from competition with a tribal entity, even though non-Indian casinos contribute more tax revenue to the state. Again, tribal casino revenues are already taxed at a rate of 100 percent, but tribal governments receive most of the tax, which most people do not understand.

The Jena Band of Choctaws had hoped to open a class II gaming facility in 2009 that would include bingo and related approved games. A class II facility does not require a state-tribal compact under the IGRA, and the parish receives no taxes or voluntary contributions from the proceeds. The venture would likely be profitable, since it would be closer to the Alexandria gaming market than any other facility, but in a state with so many other gaming attractions, revenues have proved hard to forecast.[28] The tribe needs to borrow money or find investors to build the facility, but potential investors are wary of the risk of the untested class II market in a state with class III facilities, the lack of collateral, the lack of experience, and the lack of established revenue, leading to less-than-favorable borrowing terms for the tribe. The economic recession of 2008–10 created another roadblock, with the tribe's financial services representatives saying that they did not want to take the "project to market right now," according to Cheryl Smith. "Right now, we're in limbo." A class III facility would likely be easier to finance, but even established tribal and nontribal casinos have seen revenue drop-offs.

It is hard to rally people to support the Jena Choctaws because the moral high ground remains contested, but because of state politics and intrusion into their rights on the gaming issue, it is no exaggeration to say they have lost hundreds of millions of dollars, several lives, and more than a decade of effort. Still, it would surprise no one to find that other tribes are also blocking the Jena Choctaws' casino plans behind the scenes. Just as it is hard to see how the Jena Choctaws supported white supremacy in the 1930s by refusing to attend black schools, so it is hard to see how the Coushatta and Mississippi Choctaw leadership supported colonialism (and hence white supremacy) in more recent times, but this is what white supremacy and colonialism look like: it is not always white people doing the implementation.

Most people in the country had never heard of Jena, Louisiana, before the notorious Jena Six case, in which a white district attorney charged six black teenagers with attempted murder for beating up a white student. Jena is a town of about three thousand, with 85 percent of the population white, 14 percent black, and 1 percent Indian. There had been some flare-ups of hostility toward African Americans at the school before the assault, including the appearance of nooses on a tree in the school courtyard. That a white district attorney attempted to use the power of the state to pursue a white

Jerry Jackson in his office, 2008. Photo by the author.

supremacist agenda was shocking to some, or perhaps it was just a particularly egregious example of the racism that characterizes the criminal justice system and state relations with people of color. Blacks and allies from around the country converged by the tens of thousands on Jena to protest the charges. But as has been made clear in media coverage of the event, many whites in the community still think that racism had nothing to do with the severity of the charges against the black teenagers.[29]

It is surprising that with all the media attention on the little town of Jena, none of the news organizations mentioned that Jena is home to one of the four federally recognized Indian tribes in the state of Louisiana, a tribe that has been both part of a national political scandal and the center of a statewide controversy on gaming and state rights over tribes. The continuing relevance of white supremacy to state politics has at least some relationship to the invisibility of the tribe in media coverage of the Jena Six. If the tribe had been able to flex its sovereignty, it would have been hard to miss; if the press had recognized the ordeals that the Jena Choctaws have endured in trying to secure a gaming compact with the state as symptomatic of the same racial structures, the Jena Band would have been a more important part of the story.

Speaking of the Jena Six rallies, Jerry Jackson said, "You know, I wish we had the organization that the blacks had to push our discrimination issues such as gaming. There's nobody down here rallying to help us. We don't have anybody even write good articles about us, you see what I mean. That's the difference. Whether these boys are right or wrong, I don't know what happened, but I'm just saying the difference between the way things developed, I think we had more issues over abuse than they had, but nobody rallied to help us. Now what? In fact, the other two tribes kept attacking us financially to keep us from opening up. When to me, the smart move would have been to have been our partner instead of spending all the money to stop it, be our partner, and share the revenue. It made more sense."

Indeed. The Jena Choctaws have been railroaded by colonial structures and racism under white supremacy, but the failure to see their ordeal as such has meant they have suffered alone. Under a rhetorical strategy that draws upon an ideology of white supremacy, thinly veiled as states' rights (eerily similar to segregationist rhetoric in the 1960s), the state of Louisiana has been among the worst violators of tribal sovereignty in the United States. Louisiana politicians have consistently undermined Jena Choctaw sovereignty, in part by framing tribal sovereignty as an affirmative action program—that is, as a racial entitlement program—rather than a matter of indigenous sovereignty.

The first lesson to be drawn from this, as many scholars of Native America have pointed out through the years, is that the American public has little understanding of how indigenous groups are distinct from other racialized minorities in the United States. Each tribe is its own nation, and while racial, cultural, and political alliances among them are legion, they are separate entities with the same rights as any other nation to self-government. The second lesson is that Native histories need to account for how race is deployed in the cultural discourse around Indians, because it is central to the political relationship between the United States and Indian nations. Colonialism and racism are twin practices that emerge from the singular ideology of white supremacy. When these elements are examined together, it becomes clearer how the racial climate in the Jena Six case is inseparable from colonialism in the Jena Choctaw case. With this understanding, people might rally in Jena to fight white supremacy for the Jena Band of Choctaws too.

Despite its allure, recognition creates competing forces that act on the tribe. There is pride and unity on the one hand, dissent and rivalry on the other, each amplified by federal recognition. Recognition can create unanticipated stresses on traditional community forms, and most nonrecognized tribes have not factored these stresses into their plans regarding recognition. The Jena Choctaws sacrificed decades in trying to obtain federal recognition and its benefits, and now they find that the costs are still greater and the benefits so far much smaller and slower than expected. Some benefits have begun already, but many are just out of reach. The dream of developing the local economy so that tribal members who had to leave the area to find work can return to the tribe is emerging, but slowly. While Christine Norris recognizes that entering the process slowly has the advantage of allowing the tribe to learn from the mistakes of those who have gone before them, as well as allowing them to develop a strong infrastructure to administer programs once funds are available, the whole tribe has been frustrated by the constant delays.

The Jena Choctaws seem to be following a well-worn path, and their story calls into question two important assumptions about federal recognition. On the procedural end, the story of what they had to do to achieve recognition challenges assumptions about the effectiveness of the federal recognition procedures for acknowledging even the most easily identifiable tribes. On the post-recognition end, their experiences since achieving recognition call into question its effectiveness as a means of achieving goals of community self-determination and cohesion. It has been fifteen years since recognition, so this story is still being written by the Jena Choctaws themselves. It takes time to learn the ropes well enough to be able to make meaningful changes after recognition, as the Tunica-Biloxi Tribe can attest. In the meantime, the Jena Band of Choctaws will keep pushing forward as they always have, but their story and others like it are an important corrective to perceptions of federal recognition and recognition procedures. Tribes like the Clifton-Choctaws are beginning to take these factors into consideration as they decide how to best pursue federal recognition and what they might achieve from it.

To Cheryl Smith, recognition has been the tribe's greatest feat. Whether the casino is there or not does not matter all that much, but recognition does. At one time she was at the point of abandoning the recognition project altogether. It is so much trouble, she reasoned, and Jena Choctaws truly did not need it to prove to anyone that they were Indian. But the benefits are so important that she could not justify abandoning the project. The tribe kept fighting because recognition as a tribe was its right, and to quit would be to let the federal government continue a historic injustice. Likewise, Jerry Jackson expressed frustration at times with the way everything turned out during the first decade of recognition, but he smiled with relief as he took solace in one simple fact: "The big part of it, recognition, happened. That's the most. And they'll never take it away from us."

For the time being, perseverance is the watchword. Jackson said in 2008:

The tribe has faced and is facing tremendous obstacles. We're working through it. We have come from a landless tribe with very little benefits to six parcels of land in trust, three other parcels fee status. We are running our own programs. We have had no significant findings on our audits since 1995. From that point of view, this is a success. We don't have the casino. We don't have thousands of acres of land that some other tribes may have. Okay, but we're not crying about it. We're just saying that our goal is to get to the next level. . . . The tribe is successful in a lot of different ways than what people would think—dollars and cents—because I remember when we used to meet at the courthouse. I remember when we couldn't get five people to show up for a meeting. I remember when times were tough. Now we've got a nice little gymnasium. We can seat two hundred people there. Usually, we have a big feed for them, it's jam-packed. At Christmas time we have Santa Claus. We have a black church choir that comes up and sings carols for us. We've still got programs. We've got five houses now through HUD that we have low-income [tribal members] rent. We've got ten trailers coming to help with the housing need, help with our education need. From every angle, from where we were to now, this is a very successful group, but we still have a lot of mountains to climb.

## CHAPTER 9

## On the Outside, Looking In
### Clifton-Choctaws, Race, and Federal Acknowledgment

Tunica-Biloxi and Jena Choctaw histories suggest that the federal acknowledgment process, despite being burdensome to tribes and loaded with ideological assumptions, roadblocks, and political agendas, can also lead to an array of generally positive outcomes if the United States recognizes a tribe at the end of that process. The Clifton-Choctaw case lends itself to other considerations, such as the prospect of an ongoing liminal status that accompanies the federal acknowledgment process for state-recognized groups without consistent or readily available documentation of tribal heritage. They have a different set of issues to navigate, accommodate, and plan around. The Clifton-Choctaws deserve attention because they are typical of many petitioners, in that they are a tight-knit, kin-based community with an enduring local identity as Indians. Yet intermingling, overlapping ideas about race, indigeneity, and community, interacting with legal and popular definitions of tribal existence, prompt the Clifton-Choctaws to contemplate their past, present, and future in new ways.

The recognition odyssey of the Clifton-Choctaws began in a hospital room in Alexandria, Louisiana, in 1976. A Clifton elder named Joe Thomas, frustrated with the nurse assigned to him during a stay at the hospital, said something disparaging about her to his wife in either Choctaw or Mobilian Jargon, an old Southeastern trade language, so that the nurse would not understand the insult. The person in the other bed in the room laughed out loud and responded in the same language. By the 1970s few people who

Norris Tyler at his home, 2000. Photo by the author.

spoke Choctaw lived in central Louisiana, and only a handful remained alive in the world who knew the closely related jargon, so it was quite a coincidence that two speakers would be placed in the same hospital room. The ensuing conversation between Thomas and his roommate focused on the Indian heritage of each, with the roommate suggesting that the Clifton community organize, incorporate, and seek federal recognition, as his community had done. The roommate turned out to be Joe Pierite Sr., the last traditional chief of the Tunicas.[1]

The exact sequence of events following this chance encounter is unclear in the oral tradition, but Clifton-Choctaws unambiguously recall that the meeting instigated recognition efforts in the tribal community. After returning from the hospital, Joe Pierite Sr. told a family friend, the anthropologist Hiram Gregory of Northwestern State University of Louisiana, about the Clifton community thirty miles west of Alexandria, and Gregory documented a number of the community's traditions in the years thereafter.[2] Pierite's daughter, Rose Pierite White, began to visit the community regularly to help its members organize for recognition, putting them in touch with Pete Mora, director of the Louisiana Office of Indian Affairs, Ernest Sickey, former director of the LOIA, and Emmanuel Drechsel, an anthropology graduate student documenting survivals of Mobilian Jargon.[3] The chance meeting of elders in a hospital opened a window into the Clifton world, through which they could see and be seen by other Louisiana Indians.

Following Chief Pierite's advice, Norris and Amos Tyler began the work of organizing the community for recognition in May 1977.[4] Chief Joe Pierite had died by then, but Rose Pierite White continued to visit the community and provided direction. After White's father died she went to Clifton in search of Joe Thomas, hoping to help him organize his community, but Thomas had also died. She talked with Thomas's widow: she sent White to her son-in-law, Norris Tyler, who had been a leader in the Clifton community for more than a decade as a deacon in the Baptist church.

Norris Tyler asserts that being a deacon predisposed him to becoming a community organizer, because "you know how to meet the public. . . . You just can't pick anybody [to be a community organizer]." Corine Tyler, another early community leader, confirms that this was a proper role for a deacon to take. "Back in the past," she says, "the figure of sort of like your head leaders were in your church, your deacons. Because, basically, we've always had pastors from without the community, you know that didn't live in the community. But we've always had deacons that were community men. [They continued the leadership role] up until the organization started forming as a political structure in the community." Naturally, then, according to Clifton-Choctaws, deacons such as Norris Tyler became early leaders in organizing the community for state and federal recognition.

Tribal reorganization for recognition began with the incorporation of the Clifton-Choctaw tribal council as a nonprofit entity, probably at the suggestion of Rose Pierite White or Pete Mora of the Office of Indian Affairs.[5] By 1977 incorporation was standard practice for federally nonrecognized tribes around the country, because it allowed them to compete for grants. With the help of Doug Cheatham, a non-Indian professional grant writer whom Norris Tyler had met while working with the Rapides Parish government, the tribe quickly secured a grant for $64,000 from the Administration for Native Americans (ANA) of the U.S. Department of Health, Education and Welfare. The grant was intended to help the community locate and identify its service population and conduct a needs assessment.

Norris Tyler, Amos Tyler, Corine Tyler, and a handful of other community leaders who were working for this new organization and rotating leadership duties among themselves thought of incorporation and organization as a means of securing resources that could help their community rise above the poverty they had been living in since the lumber companies moved out in the late 1950s.[6] The timber industry in the first half of the twentieth century dominated the economy of Louisiana's "piney woods" country, providing rigorous jobs with decent pay to men around the state. Clifton-Choctaw men, like other Indians in Louisiana, were particularly drawn to the industry, because it provided relatively unskilled yet accessible and honorable wage work that allowed them to stay near their home communities, validated their knowledge of the woods, and afforded a degree of independence and dignity not available to, say, sharecroppers.

Among the many groups of Louisiana Indians who were closely tied to the timber industry, the Cliftons were perhaps exceptional in moving their entire community with the Bentley company's lumber camps, mile by mile, as the treeline receded north.[7] During boom times the Cliftons were relatively prosperous, but when the end of the line arrived and the last tree was cut, the jobs were gone and the community was "left in a sea of pine stumps, on essentially barren lands."[8] The boom-bust cycle becomes apparent when descriptions of community wealth from a study in 1958 are compared with those of a needs assessment dating to 1985. The earlier study, conducted just before the lumber companies left, states that employment for men was near universal and "almost every family has a car or truck usually about three years old,"[9] whereas the needs assessment states that unemployment for men hovered above 30 percent, while the number of families living in poverty was 46 percent, and nearly one in four households did not own a vehicle.[10] The economic bust that followed the boom of the timber industry forced Clifton-Choctaws to venture out of their community in search of work, with many young people and their families departing for California and Chicago, among other destinations. Some who left stayed away, but many decided to return to Clifton when they had earned a pension or could no longer work. Some of those who returned took on leadership roles in Clifton in the 1970s, hoping to keep the community they cherished from breaking apart.

Without economic opportunity in the local area, Clifton-Choctaws faced a choice between leaving to find work and staying in Clifton and living in poverty, which became a strong motive for seeking federal recognition. "Those of us with Indian blood have been back up here for at least two hundred years," Norris Tyler noted in an interview with a local newspaper in 1978, "and we've been fairly isolated. Most of the people here don't have much education and many are in the low-income classification. We've established the Clifton-Choctaw Community Center to find out what the people's needs are. Then we'll go to the federal government and see what sorts of programs we qualify for."[11] Unlike John Barbry, who talks with a sense of irony about becoming self-sufficient by becoming dependent on federal grants, Norris Tyler asserted, "We've sat around out here too long waiting for someone to come and lead us to a better life. We've realized that if we're ever going to do something about the conditions we have here, we'll have to do it ourselves."[12] But Tyler saw possibilities for using federal grants to make permanent changes in the community, such as building a decent road and a community center and identifying community needs in order to address them systematically.

When the tribe first received the ANA grant, some people in the community did not share his vision. "Most of them didn't see the value of finding out what their needs are. They knew what their needs were and thought a little money would take care of those needs just fine."[13] But the community's long-term need for jobs, housing, education, transportation, and health care could obviously not be met with a $64,000 grant. The grant was a first step toward qualifying for federal programs. Without a needs assessment, a governing body, and an identifiable service population, the tribe could not maintain a relationship with any government body. Becoming a federal tribe, or even a state tribe, involves more than simply filling in blanks on an application form. It involves new and intensive kinds of community reorganization.[14]

The tribe incorporated as a nonprofit entity in September 1977 as the Clifton-Choctaw Reservation, Inc., beginning a new phase in community history.[15] The change represented a shift in the way the community thought of itself, reflecting its ambition and its willingness to vigorously engage the outside world. Tribal members had previously been content to manage their own affairs and keep to themselves, but when their ability to do that was threatened by deepening poverty and a sense that a lack of local opportunities to make a living might mean the gradual dissolution of their people, community leaders jumped at the proposed tribal organization.

The Cliftons took the next step in March 1978, submitting an official letter of intent to petition to the Bureau of Indian Affairs before they had even finalized new recognition criteria.[16] As with the Jena Choctaws, though, some people in the community feared that they would have their land taken away and be sent to live on a reservation if the federal government recognized them as Indians. Again, this misunderstanding was corrected by time and education, but it initially meant that some members of the community stood against the efforts for federal recognition when the letter of intent was submitted.

One month later, in April 1978, the Clifton-Choctaws sought recognition as a tribe from the state of Louisiana, stirring a controversy over the meaning and effect of tribal recognition from the state legislature. Their recognition bill was considered uncontroversial at the time it was drafted, and it easily passed the Louisiana House. When it was referred to the Senate it created a brief commotion when Senator John Saunders of Mamou called for the bill to be referred to committee, saying, "nobody in the Senate was knowledgeable enough to tell if the Choctaws of Mora [Clifton] were in fact a tribe."[17] The Senate voted the motion down 27–8 and then passed the resolution to recognize the tribe unanimously, but the commotion did not portend a smooth road ahead for the Clifton-Choctaws in state politics.[18]

Shortly thereafter, Louisiana's attorney general, William J. Guste Jr., began a campaign against recognition of tribes in the state, concerned that the state was setting itself up for land claims cases under the Indian Trade and Intercourse Acts.[19] The federal and state recognition of the Tunica tribe and their land claim were of particular and urgent interest to Guste, but he wanted to stave off potential future claims by other tribes against the state at the same time. According to Donald Juneau, he urged the Senate to scale back the wording in its recognition resolution for the Louisiana Band of Choctaws.[20] The Senate complied, changing the bill so that it provided only that the state of Louisiana acknowledged the presence of a self-proclaimed Indian community, removing all language that might be construed, however weakly, as a determination of tribal status by the state. Further, the bill retroactively amended all previous Louisiana tribal recognition resolutions to the same effect, nullifying language from the Clifton-Choctaw bill that urged their federal recognition.[21]

The conflict over the Clifton-Choctaws' recognition by the state was not limited to the Senate floor. Not surprisingly, certain Indians opposed recognizing Indian groups that they knew nothing about. The Choctaw-Apache and Louisiana (Baton Rouge) Band of Choctaws were each recognized by the state in the same year, and the Choctaw-Apaches filed a letter of intent to petition for federal recognition.[22] Ernest Sickey responded to their state recognition, asking in early 1980, "Where are all these other Choctaws coming from? I've lived here all my life and the first time I've heard of them is in the last five years. I think [the LOIA director Pete Mora] was trying to establish his own constituency and justify his existence in a state office."[23] Sickey, who is Choctaw and Coushatta, speaks both languages, and has close family ties to the Jena Band of Choctaws, was skeptical that there could be "legitimate" Choctaw tribes in the state of which he had no knowledge. Sickey had supported the Houma tribe in the past, a group with similar cultural and phenotypic markers to the Clifton-Choctaws and Choctaw-Apaches, and according to the Clifton-Choctaws he ultimately came to support their efforts as well.

The Inter-Tribal Council (ITC) of Louisiana, an independent organization composed of the Houmas, Coushattas, Jena Choctaws, Tunica-Biloxis, and Chitimachas, at that time had the authority to administer CETA funds, and it initially withheld funds from the recently incorporated groups. Defending the decision not to include the "new" Choctaw groups in 1980, the director of the ITC, Jeanette Campos, cited a "concern" that "the Southeast has sprouted Indians like it's going out of style."[24] State recognition, she contended, "gives these people a false sense of identity."[25]

While the ITC may have excluded the Clifton-Choctaws initially, many Indians in the state supported their efforts, notably the Tunica-Biloxi tribal leadership and the Louisiana Office of Indian Affairs. Pete Mora, a Chitimacha and director of the LOIA, disagreed with the Inter-Tribal Council's decision, arguing that the Clifton-Choctaws and Choctaw-Apaches had been "native to the state since the 1700s."[26] Mora fought for a share of the federal funds administered by the ITC to be given to the Clifton-Choctaws and other state Indians, but a federal representative decided that the ITC was an appropriately representative body for the management of the CETA grant.[27]

Such battles over who qualified as an Indian tribe were not unique to Louisiana. The national debate in Indian country on the matter was simply carried out on a local scale in Louisiana, with several distinct yet related features. The most common accusation since the late 1960s has been that people are identifying as Indians only now that money is available for Indians through land claims or federal government programs, or more recently through tribal gaming.[28] Within that accusation are several subaccusations. The first is that the communities are "really" white, Latino, or black. When groups are accused of being "really" white or Latino, it almost always implies that they are trying to cash in on an illegitimate Indian identity, but Indian communities with African ancestry, in addition to being accused of being financial opportunists, are also accused of trying to "pass" for Indian because that is "better" than being designated black.[29]

A second, related accusation is that although the community may have

Indian ancestry, that alone does not make them an Indian tribe. When the social, political, and cultural markers that distinguish a tribal body are no longer predominant, according to this line of reasoning, then the tribe as such has ceased to exist and should not claim tribal status for any purpose. Other Louisiana Indians sometimes hold these opinions about the Clifton-Choctaws and at other times do not. In some ways the origins of the Clifton-Choctaws remain a mystery, making it difficult for anyone to make final judgments, but their reasons for organizing and seeking recognition do not fit well with the general accusation that the "new" tribes are opportunists.

Accusations that people such as the Clifton-Choctaws only started identifying as Indians for social or financial benefits miss the point. The Clifton community had considered itself Indian throughout the living memory of tribal members. At the suggestion of an important Indian leader from a well-respected nearby tribe, the Clifton-Choctaws formally organized their community to seek resources that would help them overcome poverty. Like the Jena Band of Choctaws, they had to organize formally to gain access to programs intended for Indians. And like the Tunicas, the Clifton-Choctaws retained a core of more traditional people embedded in a large family network composed of many people of varying degrees of Indian ancestry and Indian social identification. The Clifton-Choctaws' social and political structure and ideas about Indianness became somewhat different from what they had been before organization, but the availability of funds did not create their Indian identity.

Indeed, one member of the community, Paul Thomas, wrote to an attorney in Alexandria, Louisiana, in the late nineteenth century to inquire about whether there were any "pensions" available to Indians from the federal government. Apparently unaware of the impending Dawes enrollment and allotment process in Oklahoma, the attorney responded: "I know of no law pensioning Indians, outside of the rights given and guaranteed them by the [small?] reservations of land made in their favor by the United States. These reservations, as you must be aware, are given to the various tribes and not to individuals."[30] Thomas may have heard rumors of the Dawes enrollments and sought help in securing allotments for his community, but he was unable to contact a knowledgeable representative. Then, as years later, the Clifton-Choctaws lacked access to information that might have helped them participate in federal Indian programs.

By the 1970s, like many unorganized federally nonrecognized Indians, the Clifton-Choctaws still had no idea what a relationship with the federal government might entail, what legal principles the federal-tribal relationship was based on, or how they might establish that relationship, but they wanted to help their community have their indigenous heritage recognized, and also stay together and thrive. The hope of sustaining the community remains the primary reason why many groups enter this process and continue in it despite the incredible hardships—in terms of time, effort, resources, and psychological distress—involved in petitioning.

Corine Tyler remembers that family elders always told the children they were Indian, so there was never a point when the community decided to "become" Indian. "But way back then," she says, "we didn't know anything about being special tribes or anything like that. It was a point of when other tribes started coming in. 'Cause we been—well, we're still pretty isolated—but up until the early sixties, we were what you would say really isolated." Tyler implies that the Clifton-Choctaws took their Indian identity for granted, not thinking that they could or should change their lives in any way to meet someone else's definition of how Indians should live.

Like many Indians, the Clifton-Choctaws often talked about being Indian rather than naming a specific tribe, in part because that language made sense contextually, but also because their ancestry is so mixed. They appear to have been tribally mixed, according to the tribal genealogist Theresa Clifton Sarpy, who says that the Clifton-Choctaws have ancestry from the Caddo, Choctaw, and Apache people, among others.[31] Their petition apparently claimed Creek ancestry, and tribal members have suggested that they have Virginian Indian ancestry of some unnamed type as well. Others have suggested that some ancestors of the Cliftons who were identified as "free people of color" from the Carolinas, Virginia, and Georgia were from multitribal communities such as the Lumbees, who settled among other Indians upon arrival in Louisiana in the mid-nineteenth century.[32] If all that is true, then it makes sense that the Clifton-Choctaws might generally identify as Indian rather than Choctaw, though certain community members from more distinctly Choctaw family lines would have answered that they were Choctaw if asked for a tribal affiliation.

Some Jena Choctaws have been fairly critical of the Clifton-Choctaws' claims to tribal status, but individual members of the Jena Band respond to the Cliftons in different ways. Cheryl Smith and Christine Norris have argued that while there may be Indian individuals in the Clifton-Choctaw community, the presence of Indian ancestry in some—or even all—members does not make the community a tribe. Smith noted after attending a festival in Clifton sponsored by the Inter-Tribal Council in the late 1990s that "one of the new leaders or council members or something, he looked just like a perfect old Choctaw Indian man would look like, you know just Indian. I mean, he's Indian." She feels the same way about other state-recognized tribes, acknowledging that some members clearly have Indian ancestry, but withholding support for their federal recognition. If the community as a whole could demonstrate more consistent social, cultural, and—frankly—racial markers of Indian identity, they would seem more like a cohesive Indian community to her, one that could be classified as a tribe.

Mary Jackson Jones, a Jena elder, added that it was unfair to withhold recognition from the "real" Indians at places like Clifton and Houma, but by the same token it would be unfair to recognize non-Indians with them. Her definition of what constitutes a "real" Indian was not terribly complex—she believed that anyone with any degree of Indian ancestry could be a "real" Indian. Any relation is real, she said, and ancestry cannot be cut off or erased. While she was a full-blood, her own tribe's minimum blood quantum was one-eighth, and she accurately predicted that it would drop lower still since all the young people were marrying non-Indians. The Clifton-Choctaws could have met her standards for recognition as Indians (not necessarily as a tribe) if they could document that they all had at least one Indian ancestor.

The former Jena chief Jerry Jackson believed that the Clifton-Choctaws had no Indian ancestry at all, and should have had their state recognition revoked.[33] His opinion relied on—and contributed to—a genealogical argument that erupted in 1988 between the Clifton-Choctaws and Sharon Brown, a specialist in Indian genealogy who had done fine work for the Jena Band, uncovering important documents in the Dawes enrollment files, and at the same time was doing contract work with the Clifton-Choctaws. Brown concluded after researching Clifton genealogy for six months that there was no evidence whatsoever indicating Indian heritage for the community.[34] Apparently after an argument with Anna Neal, the spouse of the Clifton tribal chairman in 1988, Brown went to the newspapers with her "revelation."

Exactly how Brown reached her conclusions is unclear. According to an article discussing the allegations, Brown "learned that some Choctaw Indians lived in the community until 1910, when they moved to Oklahoma."[35] She added that the Clifton-Choctaw tribal members were "positively not their relatives."[36] Theresa Clifton Sarpy, Clifton-Choctaw tribal administrator from 1996 to 2003, stated that Brown later brought her research to a meeting of the Inter-Tribal Council in Baton Rouge. "She wanted to put our genealogy on the table," Clifton Sarpy said, "and I know the guys from Tunica-Biloxi, Houma, and one other tribe, . . . they told her she could not. If she did, then they would sue her."

## Race, Genealogies, and the Petition

This book was not conceived of as a genealogical examination, and documentation of Clifton genealogy is not its intent, but a brief review of potential genealogical issues raised by Brown is in order. The high stakes of the acknowledgment process and the potential for publicity surrounding elements of the genealogy that are considered embarrassing to a significant segment of the Clifton population make the tribe guard its genealogy closely. Without knowing the basis of Brown's accusations, which records she reviewed, or the extent of her understanding of racial documentation, it is difficult to rebut her findings. But there are a couple of likely explanations. First, the Clifton-Choctaws may have hoped to link themselves to a number of Indians who had been living in the area in the early twentieth century, according to oral histories. A local non-Indian, Annie Parker, recalled that most of the Indians remaining in western Rapides Parish by 1900 lived at Sieper, a small town from which the Clifton community moved as the camps for Bentley Lumber Company moved north in the twentieth century, so it was entirely plausible that the Clifton families should have been descended from those families.[37] If it turned out that they were not documentably linked by blood to the Indians who left that community for Oklahoma, that would be an understandable, though disappointing, genealogical problem for a group just beginning to work out its genealogy, but it would not erase all hope of documenting its claims to Indian ancestry. While Indians had not been very numerous in central Louisiana in comparison with other groups for more than a hundred years, there were a number of other Indian individuals, families, and communities in the Louisiana countryside that could eventually be linked to the Clifton community.[38]

One indicator of a large Choctaw presence in the area is the oral testimony taken from Sesostrie Youchigant, the last speaker of Tunica, sometime in the 1930s. Youchigant refers repeatedly to Choctaws and Biloxis living at a place translated as "Pinewood" (te'ksas). The word looks phonetically like "Texas" but may refer to a settlement at Cotile Pine Woods, an area between present Boyce and Clifton.[39] Youchigant remembered attending a Choctaw celebration at this settlement where he estimated two thousand Indians attended. Although this may be a high estimate, it indicates a substantial Choctaw presence in the area that could have grown larger for important events.[40] Youchigant mentions a tantalizing but inconclusive detail, that Biloxis in this settlement "became (mixed with) various races" or, in a literal translation, "turned into different kinds of people," a possible reference to intermarriage among the Clifton families. Sharon Brown's argument that the Choctaws who lived in the Clifton community at the beginning of the twentieth century were "positively" not the relatives of today's Clifton community reveals a sort of tunnel vision, in that she only tried to make links to specific individuals and took racial designations at face value without looking at the broader picture.

An educated guess would be that Brown was trying to link the community to King Brandy, a fondly remembered local Choctaw. In the 1960s a local non-Indian, Annie Parker, recalled stories about Brandy from her youth: "Mr. Hudson from Alexandria had come to take the Indian family to the reservation and they insisted on telling my father goodbye. They were King Brandy and his family who lived in a cabin on land originally owned by Francis Henderson. . . . I remember King Brandy calling my father 'Good Bobbie Shele' as he smoked his peace pipe. This was in the early months of 1905. Chloetile and Chita were two of the children with whom I played."[41]

Parker's description of Brandy smoking a "peace pipe" and her "vanishing Indian" motif reveals the extent to which broad Anglo narratives about Indians colored her memory. That the event took place in 1905 seems fairly near the mark, however, since it was at this time that the Dawes Rolls were being recorded and all full-blood Choctaws from Mississippi, Louisiana, and Alabama were being invited to enroll in Oklahoma as Mississippi Choctaw full-bloods eligible for land allotments, the last gasp of Andrew Jackson's removal policy. Brandy apparently owned no land, probably performing wage labor, hunting, or sharecropping, as did his Choctaw contemporaries in Louisiana, so the prospect of land ownership and perhaps living in a larger Choctaw community may have appealed to him.

But King Brandy and some of his family were still in Rapides Parish in 1910, as verified by the Indian Schedules of the United States census for 1910 for Rapides Parish. More importantly, he was still in the area and active in the Choctaw community in 1924, as indicated by his participation in the coalition formed by the Tunica subchief Eli Barbry with ancestors of the Jena Choctaws and a few Biloxis.[42] If King Brandy is one of the people who Brown claims had removed to Oklahoma by 1910, this document refutes her claim.

The Clifton community currently claims descent from King Brandy for only one family line, though he is remembered by others as an important local source of Choctaw herbal and healing knowledge in the community as well.[43] The petition contains some potential genealogical stumbling blocks in the way it ties Brandy to other Clifton families. Anna Neal, formerly the tribe's primary genealogical researcher and the wife of the former tribal chairman Henry Neal, claimed that one of King Brandy's grandchildren with the last name Battiste had gone to Oklahoma and come back and changed his last name to Thomas, thus founding the Thomas family line at Clifton.[44] The story seems to be entrenched in local oral tradition, since it also appears in slightly different form in the history of the community written by two volunteers from the Mennonite Central Committee, Shari Miller and Miriam Rich, who relied extensively on oral traditions for their research in the early 1980s.[45] The "Obvious Deficiencies" letter written in response to the tribe's initial petition by OFA addresses this claim directly: "The arguments regarding the Thomas family's claim of descent from the 19th century Choctaw Indian population [of Rapides Parish] are tenuous at best."[46]

But when OFA reviewed the Jena Choctaw petition it accepted that the Gibson family "appears to be the same family later called Baptiste / Batise or Edmond in the Jena community" and that Willis Jackson had "previously been known as Willis Berry," among other unexplained name changes.[47] The reason for the easy acceptance of name changes in one case and the easy dismissal of name changes in the Clifton petition are not made clear, but the Clifton case hinges on OFA's acceptance of this long-established oral tradition.

Being able to claim King Brandy or a Battiste / Batise / Baptiste as an ancestor for even one segment of the population would be important in establishing the involvement of Clifton community members in the broader Indian community of central Louisiana, which would be helpful in petitioning for recognition. It would lend some support to the claim that the Clifton-Choctaws' recent ancestors were recognized as Indians by other Indians. But King Brandy's ties to the Clifton community alone would not make the Clifton-Choctaws an Indian tribe. They would need to document that other people in the community were Indian, that they thought of themselves as Indian, and perhaps that King Brandy thought of them as Indian.

For that reason Sharon Brown's claim that the Cliftons are not Indians would be problematic even if documents showed that they were not related to King Brandy or specifically to other Choctaws who removed to Oklahoma. The removal of several individuals in 1910 cannot have resulted in the total removal of Indians from the Clifton community if the Clifton community was tribal in the first place. If Brown's research relied solely on federal records such as the Dawes enrollment files as evidence of Indian ancestry, she would never have concluded that those who remained in Clifton were Indian, because the federal government never dealt with them. She used the Dawes enrollment records effectively to prove that the Jena Band's ancestors were full-blood Choctaws who had come from Mississippi primarily, but federal Indian records such as those would have been inappropriate for a group like the Cliftons. Being multiracial would have been cause for the federal Indian offices to exclude the people of Clifton, since only full-blooded Choctaws from Mississippi, Louisiana, and Alabama were invited to enroll in Oklahoma during the Dawes Commission. The one mixed-blood Jena Choctaw who applied was also not allowed to enroll, and he was half-white and half-Choctaw.[48] It would have been exceedingly unlikely that mixed-bloods from Clifton with or without African ancestry would have even attempted to enroll in Oklahoma. It would have been impossible for those with African ancestry to enroll as Choctaws by blood, since the Dawes Commission listed even many known tribal descendants living in Indian Territory as "Freedman" if they had discernible African ancestry.[49] Today Indians can mix with blacks after recognition and not worry too much about losing federal status, but being mixed Indian and African before a recognition decision created obstacles to acceptance by outsiders of some Clifton ancestors as Indians, making recognition in the present all the more difficult.

This leads to the second and perhaps more likely possibility that Brown accepted at face value designations of the community as "mulattos," "free people of color," or slaves in records such as the federal census. Some historical records, such as the 1910 census for Rapides Parish, list many of the families in the Clifton community as "mulattos."[50] The special "Indian Schedule" for Rapides Parish in 1910 lists none of the seven family names represented in the Clifton community in recent years, but it does list the Brandy surname, discussed above. Some of the names on the Indian Schedule appear to be associated with the Choctaw-Biloxi settlement near Woodworth that later became part of the Tunica-Biloxi Tribe, while a few seem to be related to the Jena Choctaws.[51]

The census enumerators in 1910 were instructed to use the Indian Schedules "principally for the enumeration of Indians living on reservations or in tribal relations, and also by the enumerators in certain counties containing a considerable number of Indians."[52] They were given further instructions on deciding how to group mixed communities. "Detached Indians living either in white or negro families outside of reservations should be enumerated on the general population schedule as members of the families in which they are found; but detached whites or negroes living in Indian families should be enumerated on this special Indian schedule as members of the Indian families in which they are found. In other words, every family composed mainly of Indians should be reported entirely on this special schedule, and every family composed mainly of persons not Indians should be reported entirely on the general population schedule."[53]

This presents a problem for the Clifton community. First, Jack Forbes's research into Virginia census records and Gary B. Mills's research into Cane River Creole genealogy at the very least suggest that we need to use caution in assigning any African ancestry to people listed in historical records as mulatto. It is true that people of visible African ancestry were classified as such, but so were people of undetermined racial ancestry. A designation as mulatto is not in itself confirmation of African ancestry, and certainly not confirmation of a lack of Indian ancestry.[54] We can draw only one firm conclusion: the enumerators believed that the people they listed as mulatto should not be considered white. Moreover, people of mixed black, white, and Indian ancestry were classified as mulattos by the census, undifferentiated from people of solely white and black ancestry. The surrounding population did acknowledge Indian ancestry in the Clifton community by designating them Redbones at times, but the official census record did not have a category to reflect that distinction, which would have allowed Sharon Brown to conclude that the record stated they were mulattos instead of Indians.[55]

The census enumerators' decision may also have reflected the broader American understanding that the presence or absence of Indian ancestry did not usually alter a designation as mulatto, a term that typically meant simply mixed black and nonblack ancestry in the United States. The presence of African ancestry among some Clifton families may very well have closed the enumerators' eyes to the possibility that this was an Indian community as much as anything else. The census enumerators were instructed to record the white, Indian, and black ancestry of Indians living tribally, but they were not given instructions to determine the precise mix of ancestry for any other population, so a community that did not seem "tribal" to the enumerator would have had no inquiry into the proportions of its Indian, black, and white ancestry.[56]

The Clifton community has ties with the mixed European, African, and Indian Cane River Creole communities twenty miles to its north but is still distinct from them. Identity in Clifton centers around Indianness, whereas the Cane River Creoles of color claim a unique mix of European, African, and sometimes Native heritage tied to specific places and traditions, and they celebrate the blend itself more than any particular component.[57] One of the clearest distinctions between the communities has been religion, with the Clifton community being almost entirely Baptist, while Catholicism is central to Creole identity.[58] Feelings about African ancestry in both communities vary, with some community members proud of their heritage and others who would take it as a vile offense if it were suggested that they were part "black." Neither community considers itself "black"—a distinction made abundantly clear when I discussed the Clifton-Choctaws as part "black" in early drafts of my dissertation sent to the tribe.[59]

In addition to the Cane River Creoles, the Clifton-Choctaws share genealogical ties with a number of families from surrounding towns such as Mora and Flatwoods. In fact Norris Tyler had originally recruited all people of Indian ancestry from the surrounding communities to join as one unit to receive services from the federal government, though at the time neither he nor anyone else in the area had a clear idea about what types of entities or individuals the BIA would serve.[60] Several years later the Clifton government had to cut a number of people from Flatwoods from the tribal rolls because of "genealogical problems," but the communities are quite closely connected nonetheless.

There was a time when all these communities would have been classified as "free people of color," whether they liked it or not. Despite the "one-drop rule," under which many Americans classified all people with African ancestry as black, decisions about how to classify people locally often acknowledged shades of variation, particularly in Louisiana.[61] That meant that groups such as the Cane River Creoles of color were able to achieve a remarkable degree of affluence and were accepted as peers by at least some of their non-African Creole neighbors for years. Not to say that they were unburdened by racism, but as slaveholding plantation owners of mixed ancestry they were much better positioned than blacks, especially black slaves. In effect they were a race separate from blacks and whites, and the lighter-skinned and wealthier among them were more socially mobile than the darker-skinned and poorer. According to Mills, this status began to crumble after the Civil War, when free people of color began to be designated with blacks and other former slaves as simply "colored." Without the distinction between free people of color and slaves, the distinction between Creoles of color and freed slaves lost its legal status, though it remained active in unofficial racial discourses in Louisiana. Among the Clifton-Choctaws and many others in Louisiana, Creoles of color held a status distinct from that of "blacks."

That this legal distinction from slaves and whites evaporated after the Civil War and the rise of Jim Crow laws has been cited as a factor that induced people of racially ambiguous appearance but solely black and white ancestry to falsely identify as Indians. For example, Virginia Dominguez derides the self-designation as Indian of certain Louisiana groups as simply a means of evading the "colored" label:

> Like the rest of the American South, the Louisiana countryside is dotted with special groups that Edgar Thompson has called "little races" (1972). They usually call themselves Indians and deny African ancestry. A number of former colored Creoles have moved into the various groups of this sort present in Louisiana. Many of the so-called Houma Indians have colored Creole ancestors in various generations (Parks 1974). The same is true for many of the so-called Redbones and the various "Indian" family networks of the Red River area of central and northwestern Louisiana (NSU archives at Natchitoches). The descendants of these colored Creoles who married into allegedly Indian families could, by the criterion of ancestry most often invoked in New Orleans today, qualify as Creole in the colored community. But by choice, they are "Indians" rather than Creoles.[62]

While Dominguez's book is useful in evaluating other aspects of racial identity construction, her foray into Indian identity politics is jaundiced by the tendency that Jack Forbes notes among academics to be "always finding 'blacks' (even if they look rather un-African), and . . . always losing 'Indians.' "[63] Communities such as Clifton may have as much Indian ancestry as African, but when they maintain an Indian identity, critics try to shepherd them back to their "proper" identity. Andrew Jolivette argues that Creoles of color in rural western Louisiana have similarly been discouraged from acknowledging their indigenous heritage because of their African ancestry, even though they have a history and culture set apart from those of New Orleans Creoles of color, most sharply by the presence of significant amounts of indigenous ancestry.[64]

If members of the Clifton community had identified as Creoles of color, no one would have challenged them or criticized their failure to acknowledge their indigenous heritage, no matter how black, white, or Indian they looked. But this collective erasure of indigeneity in people with African ancestry should take its place among the massive acts of genocide in United States history. Yet that the Houmas and perhaps the Cliftons could "qualify as Creole in the colored community" of New Orleans seems to make it imperative to Dominguez and similar critics that they do so. In other times and places elaborate racial classification systems acknowledged indigenous ancestry in mixed individuals through terms such as mestizo, lobo, and cambujo, but in the United States the one-drop rule has meant that African ancestry typically negates other possible classifications for legal purposes. The tendency is not solely scholarly but is informed by the white regulation of blackness and the ensuing self-regulation in the black community of people who are believed to be trying to escape their "true" identity as blacks.[65]

Perceiving the potential effects of racialization with blacks under white supremacy, Indian people in the South have at times policed the boundaries between Indianness and blackness with equal vigor. In 1984 James Merrell made the starkly illustrative statement in an article that "as recently as 1981, informants on the reservation called avoidance of and contempt for blacks 'a Catawba tradition.' "[66] Similarly, Arica Coleman discusses the Rappahannock identity of Mildred Loving, one of the plaintiffs in *Loving v. Virginia*, the famous Supreme Court case that struck down Virginia's anti-miscegenation laws. While widely regarded as an African American woman, Loving denied having any African ancestry at all in an interview in 2004, arguing that "the Rappahannocks never had anything to do with blacks."[67] Helen Rountree discusses how Virginia's "racial purity" laws, instituted immediately after the Civil War, became "a veritable cornerstone" of Indian self-identity in Virginia because they distinguished the legal rights of Indians with no African ancestry from those with African ancestry.[68] The Mississippi Choctaws, a tribe notable for its high degree of language and cultural conservatism, historically refused to associate with blacks.[69] The Lumbees, a tribe whose status has been called into question by some who see them as "mulattoes" masquerading as Indians, have historically exhibited some of the same behavior, refusing to send their children to black schools when they were not allowed to enroll in white schools under Jim Crow.[70] Each of the so-called Five Civilized Tribes of Oklahoma (Cherokee, Chickasaw, Choctaw, Creek, Seminole) has in varying degrees excluded people from tribal enrollment because of African ancestry, leading some of the remaining tribal members with African ancestry to hide their heritage behind particularly loud anti-black rhetoric.[71] The participation of the Tunica-Biloxis and the Jena Choctaws in this process has already been documented. Across the East and South, tribes and individual Indians with

African ancestry face resistance to their claims of Indianness to a greater degree than Indians with European ancestry, whether in daily life or in the federal recognition process.[72]

In fact African ancestry in the Clifton-Choctaw families may have been the reason why King Brandy was included in the pact with the Tunicas in 1924 while no other members of the Sieper/Clifton community were. Since the Tunicas banished tribal members married to blacks from the reservation by the 1930s to avoid being racialized as blacks themselves, it seems a fair guess that they would also have excluded Indians of black descent from any coalition that they hoped to form at the time. Moreover, the only two Tunicas known to have partnered with African Americans at the time were Pierites, while the Barbry family had only intermarried with whites at that time. Since Eli Barbry represented the Tunicas at the meeting to form an intertribal coalition in 1924, it stands to reason that he would have excluded anyone with African ancestry from participating.

The contemporary Tunica-Biloxi Tribe offers an interesting case for assessing the impact of federal recognition on the perception of the legitimacy as Indians of Indians with black ancestry. When Ruth Underhill initially evaluated the community for possible federal recognition in 1938, she noted that the Tunicas were "obviously much mixed with other Indians, negroes, and whites. The people of Marksville class them socially as negroes and allude to them as Redbones, or negroes with Indian ancestry."[73] Her contention that the group consisted simply of "negroes with Indian ancestry" has been invalidated in some degree by the act of federal recognition, which has since legitimated the tribal identity of Tunica-Biloxis with black ancestry, but intermarriage with African Americans did contribute to the denial of federal recognition of the community in the 1930s. Being federally recognized does not fully erase skepticism about the tribal identity of phenotypically black Indians, but it is far easier for a black Indian enrolled in a federally recognized tribe to be accepted as an Indian than it is for a black Indian from a nonfederal tribe. A number of Indian people without African ancestry have admitted both confidentially and publicly that they have much more trouble accepting as Indians people with African ancestry than people with only Indian and white ancestry, even when they know that those with African ancestry are members of federally recognized tribes. Even people who are "white as a sheet," which comes with its own set of problems, have typically been more readily accepted as Indians than those with significant African heritage have been.

Within the Tunica-Biloxi Tribe there are varying degrees of racial harmony and racism—often simultaneously—among families and individuals, but acceptance of Indians with African American ancestry as Indians is high because of known and recent family relationships. When asked about racial divisions within the Tunica-Biloxi Tribe, most tribal members concede that there is a discernible amount of racism, but that the racial composition of the tribal council, which typically has a fairly even mix of Indian and white, Indian and African American, and Indian and Latino representatives, signals that the tribe as a whole largely suppresses the racist impulses of some of its members. Of course the composition of the council also reflects the diversity of the tribe and of family alliances voting as blocs in tribal elections, but it means that the tribal council represents its diverse families well. Further, the diverse composition keeps power equally distributed among families of different racial heritages, making it nearly impossible for any single group to gain full ascendancy over the others even if it wants to do so.

The Tunica-Biloxi Tribe, perhaps informed by its own mixed racial heritage, has remained largely supportive of the efforts of the Clifton-Choctaws for federal recognition. In addition to the early role of the Pierite family in helping to organize the Clifton-Choctaws, the tribal chairman Earl Barbry Sr. has expressed support for them: "We support all the tribes who try in their efforts to get recognized. And I think each one is more or less at a different level. Some we're more familiar with—like the ones on the Inter-Tribal Council—and we have a long history of relationship dating back to the thirties, or even before that. Some of the other tribes, like Clifton and some of the other state-recognized tribes, although we have a good working relationship with them and we support each other, that relationship doesn't go that far back. But we support all Indian people."[74]

Still, for nonfederal groups such as the Clifton-Choctaws, the issue always colors public perceptions. In his master's thesis, Russell Everett reported in 1958 that the community was "known to the residents of the surrounding areas as a 'Redbone settlement,'" but he asserted that "the community considers itself a white community; only a full-blooded Negro is regarded as a Negro."[75] That people from the local community told Everett they considered the Cliftons "Redbones" was in part an acknowledgment of their Indian ancestry, but while the community almost certainly did not consider itself "Negro," Everett's report that they considered themselves "white" is misleading. Since at least some members of the Clifton community were fairly forthcoming with Everett in many ways about their Indian, white, and African ancestry, Everett likely inferred that they thought of themselves as trying to pass for being strictly European white when they were more likely interested in clarifying that they were not black, a locally rooted and very important distinction. Whiteness in the minds of the people of Clifton could encompass more than pure European ancestry, and blackness was reserved for "negroes," as distinct from themselves and Creoles of color in particular.[76] Further, in other contexts they identified as Indians explicitly. Shari Miller and Miriam Rich found that eighty-three of the eighty-six registered voters from Clifton in 1954 were listed as Indian, even though they would call themselves white for other purposes.[77] That they could register to vote at all, let alone in such high numbers, indicates that other people did not think of them as "black" either, and that the parish registrar of voters affirmed their Indian identity indicates that they were not thought of as "white."[78] And though the Clifton school was officially designated "white" by the parish school board, the superintendent of parish schools in 1988 stated that it was widely understood as a school for Choctaw Indians, and Clifton-Choctaw children were not allowed to attend white schools in Rapides Parish until 1971.[79] Being "white" and being Indian were not mutually exclusive for the Clifton-Choctaws or the people around them.

The community school in Clifton demonstrates the ambiguity and contextuality of racial identities for Clifton people.[80] According to an elderly community member, the school began when a community leader volunteered to teach school in his home for a number of years, until the home was destroyed by fire. After temporarily using another community member's home as the schoolhouse, the community built a new facility on land donated by a lumber company.[81] The new facility was used as a school for Clifton during the week and a church on the weekend. Rapides Parish paid for the teacher—who was always white rather than black or Indian—and designated the school as white. Nonetheless, the Clifton children were not allowed to enroll in the white high schools in nearby Boyce or Simpson after they had completed all eight grades at the Clifton school, although they were all part of the Rapides Parish school system. They would have been allowed to attend the black school but refused, just as Jena Choctaws, Tunica-Biloxis, and Houmas turned down similar opportunities.[82] It was more important socially and economically to the Clifton-Choctaws to avoid being considered black than to receive a high school diploma, and avoiding racialization as blacks was vital to maintaining their identity as an indigenous group.

When the Clifton school closed in 1971 students were bused to white schools in Boyce or Alexandria.[83] Had the Clifton school closed before de-segregation, the Clifton community would likely have forgone education altogether rather than attend "colored" grade schools in other communities.[84] As it was, the school was underused, with most children in Clifton only attending through the fourth or fifth grade.[85] Even by 1985 less than half of the adult community had an education beyond the fifth grade. It is possible that the Clifton children were not allowed to attend white schools because of the community's African ancestry rather than because of its Indian ancestry, but no move was ever made to designate the community school as either a "black" or an "Indian" school or to provide a secondary education facility separate from both white and black students, as in other southern Indian communities living under segregation. Though a portion of the Clifton-Choctaws had African ancestry, they maintained a strong social distinction between themselves and blacks, even if people outside their community inconsistently acknowledged the distinction.

The Clifton people and Rapides Parish officials were not alone in classifying Indians as white. Indians could be considered whites for many purposes under state law in the twentieth century. While full-blooded Indians were defined as people of color implicitly in a Louisiana Supreme Court case in 1810, there was no specific provision prohibiting Indians from marrying whites or blacks.[86] A person classified as white could possess known Indian ancestry and still be considered white, while a person with European ancestry and known African ancestry would not typically be classified as white. Thus the designation of Cliftons as "white" tends to confirm that Rapides officials did not think of them as being of African descent, especially in an area and at a time so thoroughly attuned to the subtle markers of African heritage. Indians, especially those with higher blood quanta and distinct cultural and social markers, were by no means treated as the equals of whites under the law or by the white population at large. By the same token, Indians (as long as they were not perceived to have African ancestry) were categorically distinct from people of African descent in social and often legal terms in the twentieth century, as is made clear by the Louisiana statute that made the marriage of an Indian with a person of African ancestry illegal in 1920.[87] By 1934 the Louisiana attorney general issued an opinion stating that marriage between Indians and whites was not prohibited under the state's antimiscegenation laws, confirming that Indians could be classified with whites as noncolored for many purposes.[88]

The Clifton-Choctaw community's self-designation as white for educational purposes follows this reasoning, as did the reasoning of other Indians around the state. Where they could, Indians would designate their communities as white for certain purposes when given a choice between calling themselves white and calling themselves colored. Indeed Christine Norris, a Jena Choctaw whose ancestry is half-Choctaw and half-white, recalled having to choose between "white" and "colored" on forms in her youth in the 1960s, and despite frustration at not having the option to check an "Indian" box, checked the "white" box because "colored" meant "black." The Clifton-Choctaws understood themselves as neither white nor "colored," but sometimes they chose to call themselves white because to be "colored" would imply that they were African American (and therefore not Indian).[89]

When I talked with Clifton-Choctaws between 1999 and 2004, several tribal members who had been in leadership positions told me about family ancestry that they shared with the Cane River Creoles, while some of their relatives suggested that they were not "black" at all, and that the tribe had always forbidden intermarriage with "blacks." One person went so far as to say that she and others hoped the tribe would continue to exclude tribal members who married blacks. Others were more circumspect but still distanced themselves from blacks. One elder who had served as a tribal chairman recalled that in his youth, "They'd call you Redbone, they'd call you mulatto, they'd call you everything but probably what you are. So, we always —it was a fight with us when they'd call us all these other names, 'cause we always had been taught that we was from Indian people." His narrative implies that the inaccuracy of the labels "mulatto" and "Redbone" was at issue, but the subtext suggests that the blackness of the labels caused the offense; the elder never said anything about being called white. In the context of white supremacy, asserting an Indian identity depended not only on a lack of African ancestry but also on demonstrating antipathy toward people of African ancestry.[90] Other tribal leaders, some younger and some older, have not expressed any discomfort at all with being connected to Cane River Creoles specifically, but do not accept that their ancestors mixed with "blacks" generally. Whereas under Anglo racial hierarchies any degree of African ancestry could make a person "black," in Louisiana Creoles of color and "blacks" can be distinct groups in unofficial discourses.[91] Still, the racial prejudice toward people with a large degree of African ancestry remains perceptible.

The origin of anti-black racism among southern Indians clearly rests in Anglo-American racism and colonialism, two phenomena that are so closely related that they may be better accounted for if they are understood as behaviors resulting from an ideology of white supremacy. It bears repeating that this is an ideology according to which white people and their ancestors are understood to be morally, intellectually, politically, and spiritually superior to nonwhites, and therefore entitled to various forms of privilege, power, and property.[92] This ideology was forced on southern Indian communities gradually, but surely, under the twin hammers of military conquest and assimilationism. A number of scholars have documented southern Indians' adoption of Anglo systems of racial thinking as one component of a multifaceted response to aggression by the United States; in mirroring the peculiar notions of civility held by southern Anglos with regard to race and gender, tribes hoped to protect themselves against conquest based on constructions of Indian savagery.[93] Though there was conflict within the tribes over slavery and blackness, southeastern tribes increasingly adopted Anglo-American racializations of people of African descent through the course of the nineteenth century.

Conversely, perhaps more destructive was the progressive, subconscious tribal acceptance of the Anglo-American racialization of whites, since every stereotype about people of color and indigenous nations also contains a shadow stereotype about whites and white nations. If Indians adopt the idea that blacks are inherently suited to labor, immoral, and unentitled, they are also adopting the unspoken corollary that whites are inherently intellectual, moral, and entitled. If whites are inherently intellectual, moral, and entitled, and Indians are not whites, then what are Indians? If we start thinking of race as centered on the myth of white people's inherent superiority, the system becomes much simpler to understand, and the seemingly "unique" and ever-changing racialization of people of color and indigenous groups ceases to be unique or perplexing. Rather, it becomes a permutation of the same basic idea of white supremacy, facilitating the same basic behavior of white domination.

When we understand that the ideology of white supremacy performs multiple tasks, diverting multiple resources from oppressed groups and toward whites through multiple kinds of behavior, we can see more clearly that anti-black racism, when performed by Indians, confirms a racial formation that places whites at the top of a racial hierarchy.[94] Such an ideology hardly seems to be in the best interests of Indians. Rather than pathologizing Indians, though, we need to recognize the source of Indian anti-black racism within a broader colonial project, and acknowledge its hidden impact not only on Indian resources but also on Indian senses of self. As the root of both colonialism and racism, white supremacist racial formations undermine Indian well-being through a number of practices that divert land, resources, and even culture from indigenous people.[95] But without a broader understanding of how race and colonialism emerge from and perpetuate the same ideology, we do not always see who supports white supremacy or how it affects us.

As we have seen, when the Clifton-Choctaws began organizing for recognition in the mid-1970s, it was at the urging of the last traditional chief of the Tunica tribe, who had met a Clifton elder by chance in a hospital in Alexandria. At the time the Tunicas did not allow anyone with African American ancestry on their tribal rolls. They had even banished tribal members who married African Americans from entering the reservation, though that rule had been loosened in recent years. Herman Pierite, a full brother of the last tribal chief, was able to serve on the newly organized tribal council in the late 1970s, despite having an African American wife. At the time, though, his children and grandchildren were still not allowed on the tribal rolls, because they were also African American. The tribe was in the middle of the process of petitioning for federal recognition, and the non–African American tribal members felt that it would be best for their case if they had only "Indian-looking" Indians on the rolls—those of one-quarter Indian ancestry or more and no African American ancestry. According to his grandson, Marshall Sampson, before he died Herman Pierite secured a promise from Earl Barbry, a young tribal member who had recently been elected to his first term as tribal chairman, to enroll his children and grandchildren once the tribe had attained federal recognition. Barbry followed through with his promise after the tribe was recognized in 1981, and the tribe no longer makes any official distinction between those with and those without African American ancestry.

Marshall Sampson recalls that only a few non–African American tribal members would even visit his family in his youth in the 1970s, most notably Rose Pierite White and her children. While he acknowledges that some anti-black racism remains in the tribe, he offers the repeated elections of several of Herman Pierite's descendants to the tribal council as evidence of racism's declining prevalence: "You have people that made some bad decisions," he says, "but it doesn't mean that we have to continue making bad decisions or that we have to make the same decisions that they made."

Anti-black racism in Indian communities is hardly uniform, but it is a significant presence that affects the ways people think of themselves and others. While the inherent challenges of the federal acknowledgment process put pressure on communities like the Clifton-Choctaws to distance themselves from individuals and communities with African ancestry, a different future is emerging. White supremacist racial projects divide Indian tribes from other communities of color, from other tribes, and even from other members of their own tribes, but a more equitable future—one paralleling developments among the Tunica-Biloxi Tribe—is emerging as we interrogate the past, sort out the present, and contemplate a future free from both racism and colonialism.

### "A Indian Is a Indian": Federal Nonrecognition and Tribal Life

Clifton-Choctaw families went through a period from at least the late nineteenth century to just after the Second World War during which they were particularly insular, with a number of marriages between first cousins.[96] While first-cousin marriage was also common enough among surrounding populations of whites and Creoles of color, the Clifton-Choctaws' pattern of marriage within the limited group provides further evidence that they thought of themselves as distinct. Amos Tyler, an elderly community member, believes that the high rate of first-cousin marriage is common among Indians. "I wondered, you know, a lot of my life," he says, "until I traveled, all through my days, why was it intermarriage, people marrying, you know, one another in the families. So I went to Oklahoma, and I went to work up there, and I began to visit working with a guy from Red Bird, and I began to find out that this was a natural thing with Indian people mostly. It was unusual to me, early, until I learned that it's a natural thing with Indian people."

Certain kinds of cousin marriage could be appropriate among Choctaws historically, but Tyler's continuing discussion records perhaps a more telling reason for cousin marriage:[97] "And meantime, everywhere I went, Arizona and all, I find that wherever they marry out, they stay out." In-marriage therefore seems to have been an accepted practice—if not quite a community value—because it could keep people together.[98] In-marriage within a defined ethnic community is surely valued in other southern Indian communities, though changing exogamy rules in modern southern Indian communities tend to make marriages between relatives as close as first cousins unlikely. But Clifton marriage patterns, despite the incorporation of outsiders at times, point to a strong sense of a bounded community.

Exactly when these marriage patterns developed will be an important part of OFA's assessment of the Clifton community's tribal status. In its preliminary findings concerning the United Houma Nation and its splinter groups, OFA decided that the insular marriage patterns evident from the early nineteenth century to the mid-twentieth were strong evidence of a bounded identity, but that according to earlier evidence the Houmas' ancestors were no more than a group of accidental neighbors. OFA argued that since the boundaries of Houma society were created in somewhat recent historic times, the Houmas cannot be considered a tribe with aboriginal rights on the same level as currently recognized tribes. "Since the UHN did not exist as a community until 1830, they are not a political community which is derived from a tribe existing at first sustained contact with Europeans until the present, and have not existed as a distinct political community derived from such a tribe since first settlement by Europeans in the area."[99] The Clifton-Choctaws may face a similar evaluation if they cannot demonstrate that their community gelled before the mid-nineteenth century. The most difficult hurdle for many petitioners is the need to demonstrate that there is a succession of polity. Without it they will not be acknowledged by the federal government as indigenous nations.

On some level an excessive focus on particular forms of polity ignores the political and social forces acting on Indians in Louisiana from the early eighteenth century to the present day. As discussed in chapters 2–5 on Tunica history and in OFA's report on the Houma and its offshoot petitioners, the petites nations of Indians in the area had become so small and intermingled that it was becoming difficult for administrators to distinguish one entity from another, so intermingling was becoming the norm at the time when Houma ancestors came together. Part of the problem may be that the entities were not usually as firm as the colonial administrators had hoped or imagined in the first place. All tribes are intertribal to some extent, incorporating new members through marriage, adoption, trade links, and enslavement, then naturalizing them through a process that Pauline Turner Strong and Barrik Van Winkle have called "genealogical 'amnesia.'"[100] In Louisiana the process is epitomized by the Tunica-Biloxi Tribe, whose Indian ancestors represent at least six known tribal communities, and it is safe to assume that more than those would be identifiable if the documentary record reached back far enough. Similarly, the Houma founding population consisted of an admittedly small number of multitribal refugee Indians who, for unknown reasons, formed social relations with each other in the early nineteenth century and created a new Indian social and political community. Since OFA specifically allows for the creation of new tribal entities from factions of old tribal entities, it is frustrating that they refuse to admit this instance of amalgamating people from different tribes. The lack of clear evidence that the founding population intended to create a "new tribe" when they came together demonstrates a problem with positivist historical research. What is known is that the founding families did not return to their home tribes and consistently settled next to and intermarried with other Indians, but OFA narratives suggest that because there is no positive proof of their intentions, it must be assumed that their marriage and settlement patterns were accidental. Contrary to OFA's report, this pattern seems to convey a consistent attachment to indigeneity, whether or not a polity is perceptible in the historical records. As the Houma scholar N. Bruce Duthu has noted, the criteria have tended to "universalize tribal experiences and [incorporate] non-evolving, 'fixed' visions of 'tribe' wholly inconsistent with the actual adaptive strategies and experiences of tribal communities."[101]

Lila Abu-Lughod argues that cultural theories—that is, theories which rest on the assumption that "culture" exists as a set of discernible characteristics possessed by a discrete group of people—"tend to overemphasize coherence" within "cultural" groups.[102] Thus the way ethnographers have characterized Indian communities in the past as bounded mono-"cultural" entities influences how OFA professionals conceive of what an Indian tribe can be. A multitribal community can be recognized, as the experience of the Tunica-Biloxis clearly demonstrates, but the Houma case reveals that OFA conceives of "tribal" consolidation as the consolidation of discretely bounded polities rather than an amalgamation of Indian individuals associating by choice as kith and kin, by marriage or by fictive kinship. Tribal boundaries were not always the most salient marker of identity, though—not in the same way that they are managed and maintained today under federal supervision. Consolidation into new tribes happened in both ways, but OFA only recognizes one, claiming that the polity is what must have endured since first contact to make a legitimate tribe. Nevertheless, research by numerous scholars unambiguously demonstrates that tightly bounded polities were created by years of contact with colonial authorities; they were not predominantly characteristic of aboriginal groupings at the time of contact.[103]

The precedent set in the preliminary OFA evaluation of the Houma petitions does not bode well for the Clifton-Choctaws. The Clifton people talk about having several origins, but for one reason or another those whom I have spoken with have focused on the coalescence of the community in the mid-nineteenth century with the arrival in the area of certain founding families, notably Jesse and Jane Clifton, followed by the Tyler and Neal families. Other Indians and non-Indians married into the community as the years went by, but whether the Clifton community will be considered a tribe by OFA depends on whether it can be proved that these founders were Indians, that they intentionally settled with other Indians, and that they thought of themselves as forming a primarily Indian settlement. Otherwise they will be classified as the Houma were in OFA's initial proposed finding: as just a community with Indian ancestry and no rights as an indigenous nation. The Clifton-Choctaws have speculated that most of their ancestors were mixed-blood Indians of one variety or another who sought out others of similar heritage. If they can document that these ancestors were refugee Indians from scattered Choctaw and other Indian communities, that will be a feat in itself. It will take more than that to convince OFA that such a community is entitled to federal recognition as a tribe, though, so the task before the Clifton-Choctaws is substantial.

The likelihood of finding historical records that show the Clifton-Choctaws to be unambiguously a "tribe" in the sense that OFA criteria require seems remote. What if historical documents show what has already been suggested: that the community has Indian, European, and African ancestry, and that its members came together as people do, and went on living with some contribution to their current form from each of these heritages, even while maintaining—for whatever reason—a predominantly Indian identity? This presents a difficult question for federal policy. Can a community with distinct boundaries and a distinct Indian identity and heritage be considered not a tribe but still an indigenous community? The conundrum is symptomatic of the larger problem with federal recognition policy and racial discourses: they contribute to the deprivation of communities such as the Clifton-Choctaws of social and cultural recognition of their indigenous heritage and their right to self-rule as indigenous peoples.

Indigeneity has survived in many forms. The question is whether those forms should be treated differently in terms of political status in the United States. Rather than nurturing indigeneity where it is found, federal recognition policy induces Indians from federal tribes to participate in a genocidal project, pressuring nonfederal groups to identify as non-indigenous. For this reason alone state recognition ends up being a vital source of support for indigeneity, as does membership in intertribal organizations such as the National Indian Education Association and the National Congress of American Indians that accept nonfederal tribes case by case. The federal government has ways of supporting nonfederal tribes by distributing some benefits to tribes not recognized by the BIA, particularly under the Johnson-O'Malley Act. They can each affirm indigeneity in its many forms in ways that the BIA refuses. Nurturing indigeneity where we find it rather than excluding or demeaning it, whether the tribal hearth is a warm and nurturing blaze or is down to dim embers, can help us all to heal ourselves.

OFA regulations and the pull of federal recognition have changed the course of Clifton-Choctaw history. The Clifton-Choctaws have been Indian for as long as anyone in the community can remember, but their identity is moving in new directions because of the complex interplay between federal recognition requirements, racial discourses, local and regional Indian cultural markers, interactions with other Indians, and community-defined needs and goals.

That some of the tribe's goals are economic ought not be held against them. J. Anthony Paredes argues that tribes should not hesitate to assert their Indian identity as an economic asset. Citing his own paper from 1973, Paredes noted in 1992 his prediction that "given the special governmental status of reservation Indians and the romantic thirst of the American public for things Indian, identity as Indian ultimately may be the most important economic asset held by the poorer, smaller [federally nonrecognized] Indian communities."[104] While such an indelicate proposition as cultivating a community's tribal heritage for "blunt economic motivations," as Paredes puts it, might seem unsavory, it was the most valuable asset that the Clifton community had in 1976. The Clifton-Choctaws were not alone in this practice; indeed the Indian community that does not seek the benefits of federal programs or market its identity in any way would be the rare exception. Rather than simply reap some imagined windfall by "marketing" themselves as Indians, though, the Clifton-Choctaws think of economic development as a way to uplift the community by meeting its most pressing needs. They had heard that education funds were available for Indians, in addition to funds for health and social programs. They wanted a way to create jobs so that people would not have to leave to find work, a practice that they saw as tugging at the seams of the community. They wanted some land so that people could have a place to live if they decided to return.[105]

Scrutiny from the federal government, social scientists, neighbors, and other tribes has different effects on different people in the community. People in the leadership circle seem confident and comfortable in their Indian identities, but also aware that there is a degree of skepticism about their Indianness. The skepticism rankles some people, while others more easily shrug off suggestions that they might not be Indian. The federal recognition process, and even the state recognition process to some extent, have created a situation in which the Clifton people have had to defend their Indian identity in a new way: publicly, as a group. For the first time they had to be able to demonstrate what exactly made them Indians other than having been told by their parents that they were Indians. For a group with limited cultural distinctions, even an entirely legitimate Indian community, the need to do this can create some embarrassing moments and potential feelings of inadequacy.

It is difficult to distinguish between compensating for feelings of inadequacy in Indian identity and genuinely seeking knowledge about one's ancestral traditions or other Indian traditions. The Clifton community has a number of crafts traditions that are ambiguously Indian but are shared by a number of backcountry black and white communities across the South, such as making white-oak basketry, turkey-tail fans, and carved gourd dippers. Some of their techniques suggest Indian influences, especially those used for tanning deer hides and the burn-and-scrape methods used to carve tupelo wood bowls, but none is sufficient to establish a definitive link, according to the anthropologist of Louisiana cultures Hiram Gregory.[106] Some Clifton-Choctaws began making pine-needle baskets in the 1970s as a means of connecting with something more generally considered a Native American craft in Louisiana, since the nearby Coushatta women have developed basket making into a sought-after art form. Others have begun making beaded earrings and quilts with designs that reflect a blend of popular Indian imagery and the traditional African American and Native American quilting techniques.[107] These new crafts rest next to the older crafts produced by community members in a display case in the tribal center, the closest thing to a tribal museum in Clifton. The newer, more distinctively "Indian" items seem a bit self-conscious, though not entirely awkward, next to the more traditional, though less distinctively Indian, wooden furniture, cross-stitch items, and a turkey-tail fan.

Neither the display case nor the tribal center itself would exist were it not for the organization of the community for state and federal recognition. In that lie a benefit and a drawback of recognition requirements. The display case captures the trajectory of the community's material culture and reflects the shifting identity of a community that must—and wants to—prove its Indianness in a way that it would never have had to do in the past. The people at Clifton no longer practiced crafts such as split-cane basket weaving that distinguished other Choctaw communities. Without the demanding recognition

Corine Tyler next to the display case at the Clifton-Choctaw community center, 2000. Photo by the author.

criteria and benefits attached to state and federal Indian programs, only the broader movement of the Indian renaissance would corral them toward what might be considered more "Indian" traditions, and that entails an interesting dilemma. The people at Clifton evolved to approximate socially and culturally many of their non-Indian neighbors, partly by force of entrenched systems of racism and ethnocentrism and partly through the natural development of varied cultural influences in a multicultural community. Since the 1970s people of Indian descent in Louisiana have become more vocal and organized in their assertion of Indian heritage, mostly in response to the Indian renaissance itself, but also because of an increased acceptance—even embrace—of things Indian among southerners and Americans in general and the expanded federal and state benefits (legal and economic) available to Indian communities.[108] Each of these inducements contributed to the Clifton-Choctaw recognition project and led to the creation of a community center and construction of the material culture display case.

Still, the display case stands as an apt metaphor for the impact of pressures to meet the federal recognition requirements. In one sense it is a somewhat contrived attempt to display the community's identity. The newer "Indian" crafts sit alongside the older ones as if they sprang from the same creative well and made for a natural fit. Their pragmatic and increasingly acculturated ancestors maintained only those traditions that they needed, such as hide tanning and the burn-and-scrape method of bowl carving, scuttling crafts such as the making of cane and white-oak baskets as cheap manufactured replacements made them less practical. In the early twentieth century small pine-needle baskets and beaded earrings might have been extravagant or simply unfashionable, though Clifton-Choctaws would likely have made them if doing so would have put food on the table. Federal recognition criteria pressure members of the modern Clifton community to perform their Indianness in a way that their ancestors did not: in overt displays of unique material culture in the tribal center, for example. The display case highlights the disjuncture between the "traditions" in which modern Clifton-Choctaws have begun to take part and what their more recent ancestors did in their daily lives. The older traditions have slight Indian influences apparent in crafts that were not entirely unique to the community, while some of the newer crafts more clearly reflect popular American conceptions of Indianness, such as the set of plastic Indian dolls outfitted by tribal members, and contemporary Indian crafts such as beaded earrings.

At the same time, while I cannot represent the motivations of every person in the community, the modern Clifton community craftspeople, as participants in this tribal cultural movement, are simply finding ways to connect with their Indian heritage, even if they know that their grandparents never made beaded earrings. Rather than make them poseurs, this makes them part of a nationwide movement to revitalize Indian culture that took root in the 1960s. Similar items with similar amounts of cultural borrowing and invention are made and marketed in federal and nonfederal communities around the country.

A number of community members had opportunities to visit other Indian communities often as they traveled while looking for work. The former tribal chairman Roy Tyler remembers wishing that the Clifton people had been able to retain traditions in the same way as the tribes he saw in Arizona, Alaska, and New Mexico. "We didn't have a lot of the [ceremonial and social] activities that I have seed on different reservations, what Indians did have, you know." Far from rejecting their ancestors' more recent traditions, however, members of the Clifton community have attempted to revitalize even the crafts traditions that were not specifically Indian, such as fan making,

Roy Tyler at the Clifton-Choctaw community center, 2000. Photo by the author.

building log cabins, and quilting. These are the traditions handed down from people who used essential skills and let unessential ones fade into obscurity. The craft traditions of the Clifton-Choctaws' ancestors more clearly reflect the pragmatism and resourcefulness that marked the lives of multiracial, multicultural people in rural Louisiana than they do any specific tribal material culture tradition.

Material culture survivals are valued by Indians and non-Indians today as tangible manifestations of Indian cultural heritage. Unique artistic traditions are easier to exhibit as boundary markers than cultural values such as pragmatism and resourcefulness, and therefore make more satisfying examples of the unadulterated proof of tribal heritage when language and religious traditions have faded. But Denise Ferreira da Silva writes of this phenomenon, "As postmodern accounts sent the earlier formulation of the cultural to join the racial in ethical exile, the others of Europe embraced another doomed strategy of emancipation, namely, the project of producing and interpreting crafts that communicate their particular sociohistorical trajectories as subaltern travelers on the road to transparency."[109] For the Clifton-Choctaws it is not clear whether their recent ancestors practiced the kinds of traditions that OFA would consider Native American, and that is exactly the kind of problem that

OFA creates for petitioners. It leads petitioners to doubt the legitimacy of their ancestry, their social identity, and their heritage.[110] It fuels the tendency among southern Indians, suggested by J. Anthony Paredes, to "leapfrog over their genuine but unexotic 'folk culture'" of more recent ancestors "and attempt to revivify and enshrine [contact-era tribal cultures] in their quest to legitimate their political separateness."[111]

The display case at the Clifton-Choctaw tribal center, with chairs, wooden biscuit trays, and gourd dippers alongside newer, more obviously "Indian" crafts, reveals that the Clifton-Choctaw people did not "leapfrog over their genuine but unexotic folk culture" entirely. Rather, they seem to cherish their known crafts at least as much as the introduced crafts. Most of their known crafts are not particularly unique to them, but the occasional "humble detail of habit or custom traceable to indigenous roots"[112] satisfies their desire to display their Indianness. At the same time, the introduced crafts, such as beadwork and pine-needle basketry, suggest a longing for boundary markers that more clearly coincide with American and Indian expectations of tribal people. Federal recognition requirements may not have created this longing but they clearly exacerbate it, promoting an intense concern with demonstrating authenticity. This problem is not written into the criteria themselves, and in fact OFA would not consider knowledge of recently introduced crafts as a demonstration of Indian heritage.[113] Rather, the very existence of a dividing line between federally recognized and federally nonrecognized tribes fuels a crisis of legitimation that leads to a sometimes misguided search for authentication.[114]

Folklife professionals strictly adhering to rigid criteria might question the authenticity of the Clifton-Choctaw community's effort to resume broken traditions or participate in newer, broader Indian artistic movements, but Clifton community members are doing the same kinds of things that other Indians, federally recognized and not, are doing around the country. Living cultures innovate and borrow and even recreate the past. Even the thoroughly Choctaw members of the Jena Band have recently undertaken a project to reintroduce cane-basket weaving into the community after an extended period of dormancy.[115] But since the Clifton people are not federally recognized, a shadow is cast over their right to claim introduced and reintroduced crafts such as beading and basket weaving as part of their proper "tradition." Individual Indians and anthropologists have different expectations for, and attach different meanings to, displays of Indian crafts as identity markers, and meanings are heavily influenced by their understanding of the authenticity of the group producing the crafts. Federal recognition status can be and often is determinative in such cases, making the outcomes of federal recognition decisions exceedingly important in the arts and crafts arena, even though the Indian Arts and Crafts Act of 1990 legitimates state-recognized tribal artisans to some extent.[116]

At the same time as it reveals the pressures of the petitioning process, the display case of Clifton material culture represents the opportunity that dwells in the federal recognition procedures. The desire to meet the federal requirements at Clifton led to an intensive community effort to document history. The initial needs assessment conducted by Norris Tyler and others in the late 1970s was the first phase of the effort, followed by the two-year project by Mennonite volunteers to help document oral histories, genealogies, craft traditions, and knowledge of herbal medicine for a federal petition. A later needs assessment conducted by the sociologist John R. Faine for the Institute for Indian Development of Louisiana further documented the Clifton-Choctaws' status and oral traditions.[117] The community has also conducted its own extensive genealogical research, with further research yet to be completed.

Without federal recognition requirements much of the community's oral history, craft traditions, and herbal knowledge might have gone undocumented, and considerable knowledge would have been taken to the grave with each passing elder. The impetus for doing this research would not have been as strong without the petition as a goal, and the funding for conducting the research would not have been as readily available without the presence of such a measurable goal. Conducting this valuable research, even arguing about the accuracy of the research, creates a stronger sense of Clifton peoplehood; as tribal members struggle to document their heritage, with all the excitement and disappointment that can entail, Clifton people develop an even more thorough understanding of themselves as a bounded people, "a 'we,' as it were."[118]

The tribal center might never have been constructed without a federal recognition project under way, and the center similarly reinforces Clifton conceptions of themselves as a people. Regular events at the tribal center, such as weekday meals for the elderly, wedding and graduation parties, crafts projects, tutoring sessions, and quilting bees integrate the center into people's daily lives and identities. The center and its activities, the historical and cultural research conducted in support of the recognition petition, the tribal government in its relationships with other government entities, and even the display case formalize and institutionalize tribal identity in a way that substantially promotes long-term tribal persistence, even if the community is never federally recognized.

The Clifton-Choctaws, like most other tribes, consider federal recognition a vehicle for pursuing other community goals—community empowerment through economic development, educational assistance, accessible health care, housing improvements, and cultural programs, as well as affirmation of Indian heritage—and the tribe has been pursuing these goals even while conducting research for the petition. Tribal members hope that federal recognition will make these endeavors more fruitful, but they will not wait until they have federal assistance to pursue them.

Since its organization in the late 1970s the Clifton-Choctaw government has always been dependent on finding small grants to take care of its programming needs. The tribe has already initiated successful housing improvement, educational support, and cultural programs using the resources available to it, though of course it would welcome the added support that federal recognition would bring. Health care remains a substantial need, but community members have access to state and federal medical programs that are not specific to Indians, in addition to employment-based health insurance for some members.

Economic development has presented a difficult and frequently cursed obstacle for most federally nonrecognized tribes. Even tribes with federal status can have a difficult time developing their economies, but federally nonrecognized tribes face the same burdens, such as lack of capital, low educational attainment, racism, colonialism, geographical isolation, and cultural barriers, with none of the benefits of federal recognition, such as land held in trust status, tax exemptions, eligibility for grant programs, and potentially the ability to run a tribal casino. On top of that, most of the Clifton-Choctaws' spare time and material resources are dedicated to the federal recognition project itself.

The Clifton-Choctaws, though not bucking trends entirely, have had some modest success with economic development. While an attempted tribal crafts shop failed in the mid-1990s, the tribe did develop a tree seedling nursery that has been producing hundreds of thousands of containerized long-leaf pine seedlings for the Kisatchie National Forest every year since 1994. In a related project, tribal members rake and bale pine straw in the Kisatchie National Forest and sell it for use as mulch in landscaping. While the venture provides year-round part-time work for only a handful of people

New Clifton-Choctaw sign, 2008. Photo by the author.

and seasonal work for a dozen more, it has provided the community with a successful business endeavor that provides sorely needed income to several tribal households and funds for the operating costs of the tribal government. It allows the tribal employees to work near their homes and with their people. Further, the work is culturally appropriate for the Clifton-Choctaws, who know and treasure the woods as part of their heritage. Working seasonally in the woods, in fact, is perhaps one of the most firmly established of the Clifton-Choctaws' traditions, and the seedling nursery and pine straw project allow the tribe to nurture that tradition. The U.S. Department of Energy has featured the Clifton-Choctaws' operation as one of twenty-eight success stories that provide sustainable development models for other rural communities.[119] The Regional Rural Development Center at Iowa State University also heralds the Clifton forestry project for its environmental and social sustainability and its "increased use of the skills, knowledge and ability of local people."[120] Perhaps the most telling compliment for the program came from the Jena Choctaw council member Cheryl Smith, who has cited the Clifton forestry project as a project worth emulating in her own community.

The rapidly growing model for economic development among unrecognized tribes has been to market to an established gaming interest the poten-

Theresa Clifton Sarpy and her son Les in her office at the Clifton-Choctaw community center, 2000. Photo by the author.

tial right to operate a gaming facility, in exchange for payments for research and tribal operations, a model the Clifton-Choctaws have been reluctant to use. The Jena Choctaws improved their lot for a few years using this model, as have federally nonrecognized tribes elsewhere. But the Clifton-Choctaws have shied away from the gaming business, primarily because the community has a deeply Baptist element that frowns on gambling. "The casino ain't ruled out for me," Roy Tyler says, "but you got just a little small community [of about five hundred tribal members] here and you got three churches in it, so now you know about what chances you have of getting them to say you want a casino! [laughs]."

A representative of a gaming corporation asked to make a presentation at a council meeting in 1999. "What he kept telling them," Theresa Clifton Sarpy reports, "[was] that he could really make them recognize them right 0away if they would be willing. [But] most of our people here are diehard Baptists, and the word bingo—anything with gambling—is out. So they kind of turned him down right there." The tribal council unanimously opposed his proposition. One council member, Corine Tyler, explains why she opposes gaming at Clifton: "If I won a bunch of money," she says, "I know somebody else lost a lot in order for me to win. So I could not say I was happy. Yeah, I know it brings a lot of jobs, and it brings the community up a lot, because Marksville, I can remember when it was hardly nothing. And now they got nice homes and everything. So it do bring progress, but at that expense, I don't think I could ever say I really approve of the progress it makes. Because where there's some progress, other people has hurt a whole lot in order for it to advance. But it appears that that's where the biggest money will be circulating, is where there is a casino. But there should be something else that you could get started that would bring jobs and stuff without it being a casino."

But even some of the older leaders were beginning to soften their stance on pursuing a casino by 2000. Roy Tyler, for example, would approve a casino project if that is what it took to achieve federal recognition. He argues that people have a choice about whether to enter a casino, so he would feel no moral responsibility for profiting from adults who walk through the front door knowing the risks they are taking. He would rather make money for the tribe and put people to work at a country store and gas station, or perhaps a small motel unit, than a casino, but he understands that a casino has much to offer.

Amos Tyler fully supports developing a casino. Referring to the gaming corporation representative who proposed a partnership with the tribe, he says, "They tried to put one up out here on some land they have out here on the highway. And in my mind, that would have been the quickest way to get federally recognized. Because the guy guaranteed, he said, 'If y'all will let me build a casino' . . . he says, 'I'll guarantee you you'll get federal recognized.' . . . I think that would have been our quickest way if we would have accepted the casino, but my wife and them, man, you mention casino, they . . . [laughs pointedly]. I said people go gambling if they got to go thousands of miles. They used to fly right out [of] here and go to Las Vegas. I mean they going to gamble no matter! They had gambling right here in town [Alexandria] in my days!" He downplays the moral dilemmas of other tribal members and feels that gaming represents the best opportunity for the tribe to achieve recognition.

The younger generations of Clifton-Choctaws, according to some tribal leaders, seem to agree with him. Everyone has seen the success that casinos have brought to the Tunica-Biloxis and the Coushattas, and as the younger Clifton-Choctaws move into leadership roles, the casino issue will undoubtedly be revisited. "Our council keeps getting younger and younger," Theresa Clifton Sarpy noted in 1999. "And we never know, [the casino representative] may re-approach. The younger ones may say, 'Well, we've tried everything else. This may be the way to go.'" The gaming landscape has changed markedly in the last ten years, as the Jena Choctaw story attests, but gaming always remains a consideration in tribal economic development efforts.

The Clifton-Choctaws will continue to grapple with community development whether or not they ever achieve federal recognition. If they do attain recognition, they will revisit the gaming issue and will have several more avenues to pursue for economic and social programs to benefit the community. Doubts about their identity will be largely put to rest. The impact that the gaming dispute might have on the unity of the Clifton-Choctaw people remains to be seen. Magnificent success and exhausting disappointment are equal possibilities as tribes try to enter the gaming industry, and numerous internal and external factors will ultimately come into play to determine that possibility for the Clifton-Choctaws.

If the Clifton-Choctaws were denied federal recognition, it would be a painful psychological blow that would test the group's endurance. Jerry Jackson, a Jena Choctaw, advocated revoking the state recognition of any tribe that had been turned down for federal recognition. "Once you do a petition and your petition in Washington is rejected, then what are you? You're not an Indian tribe," he argued. The Clifton-Choctaws would surely contest that assertion if they were denied federal recognition. Even OFA says that its process does not decide who is Indian or not Indian, merely who qualifies as an Indian tribe under federal law.[121] So the Clifton-Choctaws would likely continue many of the same programs and activities that they are operating now as a state-recognized Indian tribe. They would continue to pursue their goals of economic and social development using resources available to them, but they would be denied access to many vital federal programs and tribal privileges in federal law that have the potential to help them achieve those goals faster, more easily, and more completely. They would continue to be a racialized group and an indigenous group, but without recognized sovereignty to protect them.

Paredes notes that tribal museums and cultural centers, which are dependent on tourism, various funding sources for Indians, and tribal revenues, "serve to formalize, compartmentalize, and enshrine tribal distinctiveness. . . . [creating] an increased probability for long-term survival of institutionalized cultural Indianness in a way that would not be very likely for a truly tribal society in the modern world."[122] Along those lines, state recognition further institutionalizes Clifton identity. A decision against federal recognition would be a setback, but Clifton-Choctaw identity and social boundaries would continue to exist then as now, though they might shift to accommodate the Clifton-Choctaws' understanding of themselves as people of Indian descent living permanently outside the federal realm. State recognition has already been institutionalized, as have all the activities pursued as part of the community revitalization project that included the federal recognition petition. Federal recognition would strengthen that position, but federal nonrecognition would not undo all that has been built since 1977.

Roy Tyler maintains perspective on the federal recognition project, noting that the Clifton-Choctaws had very little to lose in petitioning for recognition. He asserts that the only direction their fortunes could have turned in the beginning was up, so the risks were felt to be minimal. In the meantime, the Clifton-Choctaws have been able to use the prospect of federal recognition as a vehicle to promote revitalization of their community, not only by attracting funds but by fostering pride and spirit in the community's indigenous heritage.

As for the bias against federally nonrecognized Indians that might remain with the Cliftons, Roy Tyler dismisses the possibility that the Clifton-Choctaws would feel somehow diminished by continuing nonfederal status. When asked if he has ever felt as though nonrecognition made him a "second-class Indian," an expression heard in recognition movement circles since the 1970s, he pauses. "Not really," he says, considering the wording. He smiles, and turns the phrase around in a way that simultaneously characterizes would-be detractors as pompous and self-important, humorously forgives them for this sin of the Indian world, and highlights the absurdity of the label itself. "I feel like a Indian is a Indian," Tyler says, "if he's first class or second class."

## CHAPTER 10

## Conclusions and Implications

Federal recognition contains a constellation of rewards, tensions, and contradictions: recognition overflows with potential benefits and yet also bears hidden risks to what might be called traditional tribal configurations; federally nonrecognized tribes do not have access to the political status of tribes recognized under federal law and are therefore exposed to serious threats to their self-governance, but they also do not face the same regulatory intrusions and risks that federally recognized tribes do; casino development can have an enormous economic impact and can enable tribal members to move back to the home community, but it can also exacerbate class stratification and tilt the focus of tribal members toward materialism and the kind of economic system that kept them impoverished in the past; recognition procedures and tribal decisions to pursue recognition have provided surprising benefits to federally nonrecognized tribes, while at the same time weighing heavily on community resources; and the nearly powerless but unregulated "self-determination" of tribal existence outside the federal domain can only be exchanged for the vagaries of exercising "self-determination" within the "domestic dependent nations" formulation of sovereignty in the federal-tribal relationship.

Examining how these tensions reveal themselves in the histories of the three tribes discussed in this book clarifies the material and discursive impact of federal recognition on a national scale. Economy, culture, political strength, and social health have been cited as perceived areas of benefit that should accompany federal recognition; analyzing each of these realms, which overlap extensively with each other, yields important findings. Beyond these narrower considerations, federal recognition must be considered within the broader frame of racial and indigenous issues in the United States, where its origins and effects are more complicated.

*Economic Realm*

Perhaps the most publicized benefit of federal recognition has been its economic impact. The Tunica-Biloxi Tribe provides a clear and dramatic example of economic improvement following recognition. The tribe moved from considering the leasing of part of the reservation to the city for use as a garbage dump in the 1970s to running a failed pecan-shelling factory in the 1980s to running a fantastically successful casino and several other lucrative business ventures since the 1990s. The reverberations of the economic success have been strong and widespread for Tunica-Biloxi tribal members, ranging from the simple economic boost of monthly per capita payments to the straightforward cultural benefits of funding for the tribal museum and annual powwow to the socially cohesive impact of economic development that draws distant tribal members to the reservation to the adequate funding of social services programs.

At the same time, economic development carries its own problems. While no Tunica laments the tribe's economic success overall, some tribal members have expressed concern that the values maintained by tribal families who stayed in Marksville are being overwhelmed by the values of less culturally attuned tribal members who have returned to the tribal home for primarily economic reasons, and that perhaps the coming generations will be more concerned with money than family and culture. Unchecked materialism, after all, would shift Tunicas toward the same economic systems of domination through unequal exchange that kept them outside the loop of prosperity in years past. Most tribal members have faith in the ability of the tribe to reintegrate family members into the reservation community and are excited to have so many people returning, but that is counterbalanced by a concern about the preoccupation of tribal members with profit and money-making that accompanies a large casino. Economic development has fostered a degree of class stratification in the Tunica tribe that has the potential to create antagonisms previously absent.

Once regarded as small and pitiable, the tribe now has wealth and power that rest on its participation in an industry considered by some to be predatory.[1] While the Tunicas were relatively disempowered before economic development began, because white racial and colonial projects diverted resources from them, they had a moral claim to public political support through a sort of noble and vanishing Indian discourse. Thus although money and industry generally attract political support, in the public mind there has been a reduction in the Tunica-Biloxis' moral claims for continued trust status (claims that may admittedly have been based in the notion of the "white man's burden"), along with the rise of new stereotypes about rich and undeserving Indians (still obviously rooted in an ideology of white supremacy). Success has bred occasional hostility against the Tunica-Biloxis as they continually assert their political independence from the state, but they have endured hostility in the past, so they are probably better positioned to endure it while standing on solid financial ground. Even in this climate, they have effectively fostered good public relations and political alliances.

The economic success of the Tunica-Biloxis and other gaming tribes has in fact contributed to the backlash that the Jena Band of Choctaws have experienced in trying to establish their own casino. While much of the anti-gaming movement in Louisiana is based in religious conservatism and in the anti-corruption activism that followed the conviction of Governor Edwin Edwards, a significant part of the opposition arises from racial ideology, both the resentment of whites toward what they perceive as unfair "racial advantages" and the assumption of superiority of colonial and white political institutions. Politicians and newspapers have fueled white resentment against gaming in general and Indian gaming in particular in Louisiana, making the state's cooperation with the Jena Band's casino development efforts a difficult and very public battle for the tribe. More than a decade after recognition, legal and political roadblocks have prevented the tribe from achieving the economic prosperity that would come from a class III gaming facility, and even other benefits of federal recognition have been slow to develop because the casino issues have substantially impeded the land-into-trust process. While other tribes, such as the Mohegans in Connecticut, have been able to institute gaming operations relatively quickly after recognition, the Jena Band has faced considerable obstacles to economic development.[2] Economic benefits may be fewer, may take longer to arrive, and may take different forms than originally imagined.

Some federal benefits are coming to the tribe for now, though. The Tunica-Biloxi Tribe's economic development only began in earnest thirteen years after recognition, so the Jena Band of Choctaws may simply be working through a period of negotiating and becoming familiar with the intricate details of the federal-tribal-state relationship that are evident in other recently recognized communities as well. Of course the right of tribes to operate casinos was not firmly established and protected until the passage in 1988 of the Indian Gaming Regulatory Act, which would seem to make unreasonable a direct comparison of the two tribal development timelines, but it was six years after the passage of the IGRA before a Tunica gaming facility opened its doors, and high-stakes bingo had been a possibility since the U.S. Supreme Court decision in *Seminole v. Butterworth* (1981), the same year the Tunicas were recognized.[3] The Chitimacha tribe in southern Louisiana, which had been federally recognized since the early twentieth century, in the 1980s was able to open a high-stakes bingo facility occupying thirty thousand square feet, suggesting that familiarity with the domain of federal tribes allowed them to seize opportunities more quickly.[4] Given the added scrutiny focused on the Jena Band and that it did not have land taken into trust until 2007, there is reason to believe that the Jena Band's current economic outlook will improve in the near future. By 2008, thirteen years after recognition, the Jena Band had made significant progress, with a slew of development plans in various stages that may lead to a similar surge in economic growth, but it faced unique impediments that the Tunica-Biloxi Tribe did not.

The Jena Band's petition for federal recognition, like that of the Clifton-Choctaws and all other currently federally nonrecognized tribes, was heavily influenced by the arrival of gaming in Indian country. Tribes in the 1990s had the opportunity to form partnerships with wealthy gaming companies looking for prospective management contracts in new markets, an opportunity that brought with it a host of benefits and risks. Gaming money was welcomed by the Jena Band and facilitated its drive for federal recognition—even enabled it, according to some tribal members. But as with the Tunicas, the moral construction of the tribe as worthy recipients of protections from the federal government was challenged by the public construction of recognition as an avenue to casino development rather than a political or even ethnological decision. Partnerships with gaming corporations came with new sets of problems for the Jena Band and others.[5]

For the Clifton-Choctaws the goal of recognition has not yet been achieved, but a look at the economic impact of petitioning for recognition demonstrates that the gambling begins long before the casino arrives. The Clifton-Choctaws have expended a sizable amount of personal and community resources in the quest for recognition, and there is no telling whether that gamble will result in recognition. While Jerry Jackson notes that the Jena

Choctaws did not have to pay for their recognition efforts because of the grants and gaming capital that the tribal government was able to attain after 1991, the Clifton-Choctaws' hesitance to enter the gaming industry means that they are heavily reliant on grants, which are highly restricted and provide only marginal economic benefit, mostly for the few people whom the tribe employs directly. Still, being able to bring grants to the community in support of recognition has provided an economic boost that cannot be ignored, and the long-term economic impact of educational and other programs available to the Clifton-Choctaws as a state-recognized Indian tribe will surely pay dividends down the road.

While federal recognition has also been seen as the most viable means to achieve economic prosperity, the Clifton-Choctaws are not waiting for recognition to arrive before starting independent economic development programs. While the forest industries that they have initiated do not provide millions of dollars a year (unlike the Tunica casino), the tribe, which has no plans to develop a casino, sees these industries as a stepping-stone. Recognition, if achieved, would only help the tribe, but mobilizing the tribe for recognition is what enabled its economic development program in the first place. Even if OFA eventually decides against the Clifton-Choctaws' petition, they will have a modest economic development plan in place that can persist regardless. Envisioning economic development as completely dependent on recognition would have constrained the tribe's planning efforts.

Thus the history of the economic impact of recognition needs to be broken into at least four phases. In the first phase, pre-recognition, the tribes had not yet organized to seek federal recognition, so the economic impact could be measured by recognition's absence. When the AIPRC conducted surveys of federally nonrecognized tribes in the mid-1970s, it found that federally nonrecognized tribes clearly suffered economically when compared to federally recognized tribes.[6] All three tribes discussed here were deeply impoverished in this phase.

In the second phase, the petitioning phase, the tribes began expending time and resources in support of research and other requirements for completing a petition. For most of the people involved in this effort there was no immediate monetary compensation. Some tribal members—generally only two or three at a time for each tribe—had employment in grant-funded positions beginning in the 1970s. Grant money typically supported small projects and petition research, and it was spent almost as fast as it arrived. Most petitioners see their investment at least in part as a matter of justice rather than an economic investment, and the dividends are paid in the form of increasing knowledge of tribal and family histories and the hope for federal recognition of the tribe. The Clifton-Choctaws are in this phase, but they are also instituting small-scale economic projects in advance of recognition, a strategy that attempts to circumvent recognition as the sole enabling tool for the benefits of economic development, and at the same time provides funds to support the recognition effort.

The Jena Choctaws could be said to occupy a third phase, the immediate post-recognition phase, as they continue to familiarize themselves with the federal-tribal relationship and negotiate their political status with and within the state of Louisiana. While tribal economic status is always in flux, this third phase could best be described as an intermediate state of learning and negotiation. Immediately after recognition federal funds are especially slow to arrive, but some, such as health funds, eventually become established and institutionalized. Federal housing and health programs and other sources of funding have boosted tribal standards of living, but the period following recognition has hardly been one of unchecked financial prosperity. Many tribal members, especially those outside the service area, have not yet experienced any significant economic impact from federal recognition, but the tribe is beginning to put the pieces into place for a stronger tribal economy.

The fourth phase is the long-term post-recognition phase, in which a tribe may or may not ever achieve economic independence or prosperity, but in which uncertainties in the federal-tribal-state relationship becomes less central to the tribe's economic status than in the years immediately following recognition. The Jena Band of Choctaws is moving slowly into this phase, and the Tunica-Biloxi Tribe is already in it. Through over a decade of work as a federal tribe, the Tunica-Biloxis established a series of appropriate political and economic institutions that laid a foundation for successful economic development and maximized its impact once the casino opened.[7]

But successful economic development is a possibility, not a promise. Recognition creates opportunities, but for various reasons, not the least of which are racism, colonialism, isolation, lack of appropriate education, and lack of adequate land bases, most tribes have not yet achieved sufficient economic development. In both gaming and non-gaming tribes individual income on reservations in 2000 stood at less than half that of the American population as a whole.[8] Furthermore, investing in recognition itself is a massive and risky undertaking that typically does not pay off well economically unless a tribe achieves recognition in the end. Tribes need to consider economic development as part of a holistic plan for the tribal future, to ensure that it does not become its own justification, to the detriment of tribal values with which it may ultimately be incompatible.

## Cultural Realm

Thinking of culture only in terms of aboriginal cultural survivals can be limiting, but a discussion of persistence is appropriate to the colonial context in which Native American cultural change has taken place, and it is a discussion that tribes typically invoke as they pursue federal recognition. In abstract terms, change is a perpetual process in every culture, in every people's history. The interplay of events, ideas, and actions creates a never-ending drama in which people reemerge from history with every passing day. But the imbalances of power in the American Indian context have meant that Indian people have historically been forced to change against their will, and even recently have struggled to achieve any kind of potency in redirecting cultural change away from acculturation with surrounding populations. For this reason it is important to interrogate the utility of federal recognition as a tool to counter the forces of assimilation, which is how it is often imagined.

For all three tribes the research phase of the petitioning process, while burdensome, also came with cultural benefits in terms of the knowledge it preserved and produced. Research and investigation have provided new insights into tribal history and cultures and made them available to the broader community. Moreover, petition research intensified emotional connections to tribal pasts and distant cousins, making a stronger bond to the tribal future.

The impact of petitioning for recognition on tribal culture is difficult to unravel from what might be called the "long" Indian renaissance of the last half-century,[9] since the pursuit of federal recognition is a product of the Indian renaissance and at the same time a catalyst for revitalization in its own right. Surely the petition for recognition highlighted tribal identity for nonfederal tribal members who took up crafts, for example, but crafts also highlighted tribal identity and made the pursuit of recognition more important. Similar kinds of crafts revitalization efforts developed with and without federal recognition projects under way, but the interconnection of crafts, revitalization, and the recognition movement intensified the extent to which nonfederal communities embraced all three.

The Jena Band of Choctaws enriched their understanding of their history by compiling a petition for federal recognition, and the tribe's genealogical documentation helped tribal members visualize how closely they were all related, helping to alleviate some of the interfamily tensions of earlier years. The elation upon receipt of recognition and the growing bond to the tribe—rather than the family line—after recognition augment Jena tribalism. Deepening emotional attachment to the tribal unit has clear implications for tribal revitalization, and that process of deepening begins with petitioning, grows with recognition, and grows still more in the years after recognition, as tribes develop internal support mechanisms that did not exist before recognition.

Programs designed to introduce or reintroduce a craft into a community do not rely on federal recognition, again making it hard to disaggregate the effect of recognition from the influence of the broader Indian revitalization movement. In 2000, for example, Rose Fisher Blassingame, a Jena tribal member, began a project to teach other tribal members how to make traditional Choctaw split-cane baskets. The project was sponsored by the U.S. Forest Service and the Louisiana Regional Folklife Project, funding sources that the tribe could have pursued with or without federal recognition.[10] Basket making had been dormant in the community for some time until Fisher Blassingame revived it. A similar Clifton-Choctaw basket-making revitalization took place twenty years earlier, but without recognition.[11] So even though the Jena basketry project was initiated after recognition, it can hardly be said to be a direct result of recognition.

On the opposite end of the spectrum in terms of ease of implementation, the Jena Choctaws have made several attempts to initiate a language revitalization program so that the community can regain universal fluency in Choctaw, but such efforts began before recognition and have still not been institutionalized since recognition. Similarly, there has not been a fluent Tunica speaker for more than fifty years, and though one family has shown particular interest in bringing back the language, even federal recognition with massive economic development has not been able to make that happen yet. Language revitalization has proved to be one of the most exasperating challenges for tribes, and recognition has had surprisingly little impact on it. Indeed the Miami Tribe of Indiana has created one of the most successful language revitalization programs in the United States, despite having been repeatedly denied federal recognition.[12] Jessica Cattelino's caveats about the bureaucratized transmission of culture merit consideration, but one hopes that as more tribes work on language revitalization projects in consultation with other tribes and language professionals, they will figure out how to more effectively implement these programs.[13]

For the Tunica-Biloxi Tribe there have been very visible cultural benefits associated with recognition, though some are more clearly connected with the ensuing economic development that recognition facilitated. The return of the Tunica Treasure, an event of enormous importance culturally and politically, would likely have been much more difficult without federal recognition, and the creation of the archaeological conservation lab and museum projects would have been similarly hampered. The casino has driven tribal economic prosperity, which allows a critical mass of tribal members to live and work together in the home area, as well as providing unencumbered funding for research, education for tribal members, cultural events and homecomings, and a broader array of social services to tribal members, whose allegiance to the tribe strengthens as a result. Casino development obviously depends on federal recognition, so federally nonrecognized tribes do not have access to this potential windfall for their cultural revitalization programs. But as the example of the Jena Choctaws demonstrates, federal recognition hardly guarantees access to the gaming industry. If one isolates the impact of recognition from that of successful class III gaming development, the cultural advantages of recognition seem to lie in the deepening bond between the tribe and the tribal members and the sovereignty that allows tribes to protect significant cultural resources.

Federal recognition before the era of self-determination that began in the late 1960s had different effects on tribes. Rather than protect tribal cultures, involvement with the federal government led to more focused assimilationist efforts and often removal and dispossession. For the Tunica in the nineteenth century federal recognition might just as easily have led to removal to Oklahoma as to protection of tribal land near Marksville. Similarly, federal nonrecognition of the Jena Choctaws in the early twentieth century allowed the community to retain its use of the Choctaw language, since the children were never sent to a boarding school where speaking Choctaw was forbidden. Even today federal programs have somewhat hidden acculturative effects, such as housing programs that do not support kin-based housing patterns, health programs that force tribes to distinguish between tribal members who live in the service area and those who do not, and bureaucratized conceptions of community belonging that exclude people who would not previously have felt excluded, revealing recognition to be a sometimes contradictory force in the cultural realm.

*Political Realm*

One of the clearest transformations that takes place as a result of the demands of recognition is in the political realm, which might be considered an extension of the cultural realm. Transformation in the political realm begins early, as tribes incorporate before recognition to be able to receive funding. The Tunica-Biloxis had been electing leaders and trying to establish consensus under their own system for many years before incorporating and electing a tribal council to set terms in 1974. For the Jena Choctaws and the Clifton-Choctaws, leadership had primarily been informal before incorporation, with reliance on elders and family heads to help make, enforce, and represent community decisions. Incorporation meant that two forms of group decision making existed alongside each other, with important religious and cultural decisions still made by elders and by group consensus, and economic and group political decisions made increasingly by the elected leadership, albeit normally with some say given to the rest of the tribe.

Decision making became formalized after recognition and fell more often into the hands of a younger set of leaders. Conflicts inevitably arose as communities negotiated the addition of a new political structure to an existing extended family structure. After federal recognition the newly created tribal governments had more power than the informal leadership of the past because of the new resources attached to their decisions, sometimes exacerbating gender and family-line inequities. The Jena Choctaws have elected women to the tribal chair in each election since 1998, and others have consistently served on the tribal council. Family ties have been affected by tribal political issues connected to formalization in all three tribes. Without romanticizing "traditional" government forms, which would not likely be adequate for conducting a contemporary federal-tribal relationship, it must be conceded that the internal changes in social structure arising from the new political structures accompanying preparations for federal recognition amount to a significant cultural reorganization.

Despite the commotion that it brings to internal tribal structures, recognition needs to be understood in context, as part of a strategic decision that the tribes have made to gain greater control over internal and external political matters. While there are examples of federal Indian policy intruding on internal tribal values, the significant fortification of external tribal sovereignty that comes with recognition gives tribes a greater control over other internal tribal decisions, such as land use, access to tribal resources, regulatory matters such as gaming and hunting, protection of ancestral remains and items of religious significance under NAGPRA, and religious observance. Perhaps most glaringly, federal recognition made it much easier for the Tunica-Biloxi Tribe to protect and gain custody over the Tunica Treasure even before NAGPRA was implemented, with compelling cultural ramifications for the tribe. Federally nonrecognized tribes have none of these important political and cultural protections in place.

*Social Health*

Validation of the tribal political entity through federal recognition brings several immediate benefits to tribal social health. The first is the psychological impact on the tribe. Federal nonrecognition carries a stigma in Indian country, making tribal members feel like "second-class Indians" and "snotty-nosed stepkids" even when their Indian ancestry is not in doubt. The stigma of being a federally nonrecognized Indian trying to achieve recognition centers on accusations of lying about tribal ancestry, opportunism, and worst of all, preying on "real" Indian people by attempting to take benefits intended for them. Moreover, federal nonrecognition of tribal identity invalidates the historical trauma that tribal members and their ancestors have had to endure because they were Indians. Stigma and invalidation are persistent problems for nonfederal tribes. Since identity is so central to the mental health of Indians, the stigma of federal nonrecognition creates community-wide distress. Members of tribes who have received federal recognition often feel that recognition carries at least some redemption for the injustices that their ancestors endured and that they continue to endure as Indians, as well as simple acceptance of their identity.

Federally nonrecognized Indians often feel compelled to reassure themselves that they are Indian with or without recognition. The Jena Choctaws usefully illustrate the problem. Even though no one who met them harbored doubts about their Choctaw identity, federal nonrecognition remained a constant thorn in their side, suggesting they were somehow less Indian than others, or had given up their tribal connections. They were "just" descendants. Tribal members expressed frustration with having to prove their identities repeatedly, and part of the euphoria following recognition reflected their relief that this travail had ended. For tribes that remain federally nonrecognized, constant self-assurance is absolutely necessary for self-preservation, but it will never be able to fully neutralize the indignity of federal nonrecognition.

Thus the return of sovereignty needs to be understood as a matter of restorative justice. The emotional, psychological, and spiritual rewards attending events that redress historical trauma—events such as Jena Choctaw recognition and the return of the Tunica Treasure—have a powerful effect on the well-being of Indian communities. Further, federal recognition can at least relieve the anxiety associated with the stigma of federal nonrecognition. Given the pervasiveness of problems related to mental health in Indian communities—suicide, substance abuse, depression, domestic violence—the impact of recognition and nonrecognition on community mental health should never be dismissed as incidental to the more visible economic and political impacts.[14]

Federal recognition affords to tribes several observable advantages in addressing community social health. Funds from the Indian Health Services alleviate the intractable problems of access to health care for the predominantly rural Indian poor in the service area. Federal status makes tribes eligible for programs and jobs under the auspices of the BIA and a number of other federal programs that serve federal tribes exclusively. Tribal crime victim grants of the Department of Justice, certain environmental programs of the Environmental Protection Agency, some commodity food distribution programs of the Department of Agriculture, protections under the Indian Child Welfare Act, and some tribal programs of the Department of Housing and Urban Development, for example, are limited to federal tribes.[15] Needless to say, the resources available to federal tribes make recognition potentially very valuable for implementing important social service programs. Moreover, recognition enables the kinds of economic development that can adequately fund all of a tribe's social programs, creating a new reliance on the tribe. Yet the social services and economic development opportunities have not been enough to bring the social health indicators of most federal tribes into a range comparable with those of white Americans, a point often overlooked by petitioners for federal recognition.

Nonfederal tribes do have limited access to federal programs. They can qualify for certain HUD funding, programs under the Administration for Native Americans administered by the Department of Health and Human Services, and, if they are state-recognized, funding from the Department of Education and protection under the American Indian Arts and Crafts Act. Federally nonrecognized tribes have been forced to find ways to obtain social services and pursue economic development without recognition. The Jena Choctaws' list of local social service agencies, to which they referred tribal members in need of support before recognition, provides an example of the resourcefulness required of nonfederal tribes, while the Clifton-Choctaw forest industry development project provides an example of a nonfederal tribe committed to sustainable and culturally appropriate economic development to support tribal well-being and provide jobs to individual tribal members. The Clifton-Choctaws have demonstrated resourcefulness and tenacity, having participated in state housing insulation programs, developed a successful tutoring program for tribal youth, provided a meal program for elderly community members, and built a community center using combinations of federal, state, foundation, church, and personal funds. Such efforts are common among nonfederal tribes, and they demonstrate that tribal energy is focused on community health, writ large, rather than recognition per se. Federal recognition is another means to the same end.

The Clifton-Choctaws organized for recognition in the late 1970s after Tunica-Biloxi tribal leaders urged them to do so, just as the Jena Choctaws organized at the suggestion of a Coushatta leader, Ernest Sickey. The Tunica-Biloxis were leaders in the movement for recognition of tribal sovereignty in Louisiana and possessed an unusual degree of formal organization before reorganizing the tribal government in 1974. Their degree of organization undoubtedly contributed to their success in the process, years before similar success was achieved by the Jena Band of Choctaws and the Clifton-Choctaws. In all three communities the process of organizing for recognition created benefits for the tribes before recognition was achieved. Organization and incorporation brought in funding and focused community efforts to revitalize each tribe's social health and culture.

### The Politics of Federal Recognition Policy

As a racial project that seeks to define the boundaries of Indian identity, federal recognition policy has heavily influenced the direction of social, cultural, economic, and political change among Louisiana Indians.[16] But federal recognition needs to be framed as a particularly empowered part of a much broader structure of racial and colonial relationships. Rather than the single determining factor in a tribal history, it is one of many in the transformation of tribes with and without federal recognition. Social, cultural, economic, and political change among tribes needs to be seen as a normative, continuing —if uneven—process, which reveals the effect of recognition policy and recognition itself to be gradual rather than precipitous, contradictory rather than wholly positive or negative, unsettled rather than clear-cut. Tribes have been subject to the same kinds of racial projects on both sides of the recog-

nition divide, making recognition policy in some ways an ideological extension of other kinds of racial and colonial thinking rather than a policy that
stands alone.

Federal recognition policy marks the boundaries of Indian identity for the
BIA, but it cannot mirror the complex shifting boundaries of Indian identity
that are created, recreated, and policed in the minds of individual Indians and
non-Indians every day. The issue of what constitutes a tribe is often not
resolved in any concrete way in the minds of individuals, much less throughout a community, so it cannot be expected that the issue would be fully
resolvable in any federal policy formulation.

OFA contends that groups capable of being considered tribes in an ethnological sense may be turned down for federal recognition because they do not
meet the definitions established by OFA criteria. The essence of the *Passamaquoddy* decision and of the federal recognition reform movement leading to
the creation of OFA was that the federal government had a responsibility to all
tribes, whether ethnologically or legally defined. In fact, the basis of the
decision was that the distinction between the two was spurious in the first
place. Now the federal government attempts to use academic assessments to
draw a legal and administrative line between tribal and nontribal people, but
it will be instructive to remember examples discussed in chapter 1 of earlier
attempts by the federal government to use anthropologists to "have the
illusion provided by expert opinion that all decisions, however complex, are
fairly and logically made."[17]

The former OFA historian William Quinn stands by the validity of the
distinction. "To be sure," he writes, "the various other definitions of 'tribe' as
they relate to Native American Indian societies are no doubt valid in their
own rights, and [the definition of tribe] found in [the regulations] was never
intended to preclude or preempt these other definitions from currency or
their own particularized applications. The one thing which must be kept in
mind . . . is that [the regulations] define tribe *within the meaning of federal law*"
(Quinn's emphasis).[18] Because they determine a group's status as a federal
tribe, OFA regulations were intended to preclude other definitions of tribe, or
else the BIA would stand in direct violation of the judge's ruling in *Passamaquoddy* that the federal government had a responsibility to all Indian tribes,
regardless of their standing with the federal government.

As much as the bright line dividing federal and nonfederal Indians is an
illusion ethnologically speaking, in the end there must be some way of
deciding who qualifies as a tribe. The federal government, federal tribes, and

nonfederal tribes do not have the luxury of leaving the issue unresolved. The federal government has both an obligation to recognize Indian tribes and an obligation to protect the rights and resources of Indian tribes from non-Indians who want to be recognized as Indians. The federal government and Indian tribes alike want access to federal resources designated for Indians to be limited to legitimate Indian tribes. On the surface this is entirely reasonable, but many of the people denied recognition have some Indian ancestry and cultural characteristics, and many people in recognized tribes have non-Indian ancestry and cultural characteristics. Creating an immutable, constant dividing line between tribal and nontribal is an ethnological impossibility heavily informed by racial thinking, what Peggy Pascoe has called the "imperative of race classification."[19] The federal government has not been able to consistently identify persistent indigenous sociopolitical groups. As a practical matter, the federal government cannot simply cease making decisions, but it must continue to reevaluate the process of how those decisions are made.

*Yes or No: Making Decisions at OFA*

Patterns emerge in OFA decisions that give us a clearer image of the BIA's ideas about which Indians it has a responsibility to serve. OFA staff members have stated that they expect to recognize about 30 percent of petitioning tribes, which implies that they make up their minds about whom to acknowledge well in advance of reviewing the applications.[20] When they make up their minds in advance without specifying a reason, their decisions must be based in large part on the "common sense" of the racial and colonial gaze. As James Clifford has argued in a similar context, recognition decisions are "constrained not simply by the law, with its peculiar rules, but by powerful assumptions and categories underlying the common sense that supported the law."[21] As a result of these "powerful ways of looking,"[22] issues such as the petitioner's degree of cultural change and retention since contact, the degree of racial mixing, the degree to which a petitioner fits the social construction of Indianness and the word "tribe"—with all of its racial and cultural baggage—will all creep into the evaluations, despite OFA's denials. The criteria are applied differently to each group, and OFA denies or severely limits the precedential value of its decisions, which Gerald Sider has argued "loosens some of the constraints on power, making it even more arbitrary and total."[23] Indeed, variable application of the criteria suggests that the racial and colonial gaze is driving OFA decisions more than its administrators realize, allowing them to arrange the "facts" to match up with the decisions.

The constant conflict between the petitioners' interpretations of records and OFA's interpretations exposes the weakness of the quasi-adversarial, quasi-judicial nature of the acknowledgment procedures. The historian Francis Jennings captured the essence of the problem in a letter he wrote in response to OFA's original proposed negative finding for the Gay Head Wampanoags: "The writers of this report have not surveyed the evidence with judicial detachment. Instead they have produced . . . a prosecutor's brief in which facts favorable to the tribe are omitted and the facts included are twisted about to look somehow bad." Jennings went on to note that he had been going to Martha's Vineyard for years, and only after the lawyers arrived did anyone question their status as a tribe. "The Gay Head Indians are a tribe in social fact, regardless of legal fiction, and should be recognized for what they are."[24]

Other examples of this pattern can be found in OFA decisions against the MOWA Choctaw, the Ramapough, and the Paugusset, which dismiss all evidence that supports the petitioners' claims to Indian ancestry and read like "a prosecutor's brief in which facts favorable to the tribe are omitted and the facts included are twisted about to look somehow bad." Only after a final decision is confirmed is there an opportunity for the tribes to force OFA to defend its findings in front of a supposedly impartial review board—the Interior Board of Indian Appeals (IBIA)—or a federal court. OFA is both the adversary and the judge for nearly the entire process, an obvious conflict of interest. Tribes are placed in a situation that has all the shortcomings of an adversarial process, without the benefit of an impartial judge. The adversarial nature of the process forces OFA to defend its findings, and it does so in a way that makes its findings look unquestionable and objective, rather than ambiguous and subjective as they are.

In that sense the federal recognition process stands as a conspicuous example of the concept of judicial "masks" developed by John T. Noonan and applied to Indian law by David Wilkins.[25] Noonan discusses two kinds of masks in the legal system: "masks" voluntarily worn by judges or other governmental officials that give them the appearance of objective authority and "masks" imposed on others to alter their identity so that official treatment of them is consistent with social mores. In recognition decisions OFA not only dons the mask of impartial, objective authority but also places masks on those upon whom it confers judgment by labeling them either Indian or non-Indian. Since it would be morally unacceptable to deny acknowledgment to a group of Indians with a legitimate claim to tribal status, OFA has historically attempted to portray each group that it denies as non-Indian and each group that it acknowledges as Indian, officially placing an unambiguous conceptual mask over the faces of all petitioners to cover the complex reality of their multicultural identities.

Lila Abu-Lughod, expanding on James Clifford's work, argues that ethnographic representations are always "partial truths," but what has not been particularly recognized is "that they are also positioned truths."[26] Never is this more clear than in an OFA review of a petitioning community. As bureaucratic academics, OFA staff members use academic research methods to evaluate materials before deciding who qualifies as a tribe under the regulations, and then write positioned ethnohistories disguised as objective legal and administrative discussions that defend their decisions.[27] Such mystification of positionality cannot produce sound ethnohistory, if for no other reason than because it is unable to question the bright line between tribe and non-tribe. Russel Barsh poses this as an ethical issue arising out of the design of the petitioning process, in which "the anthropologist is no longer merely an advisor to the government, but a decision maker employed to research and adjudicate the rights and claims of studied groups."[28] The whole recognition process is based on ethnohistorical tenets, and yet it requires that the researchers abandon what accuracy the field has because it only allows for two possible findings: yes, they are an Indian tribe, or no, they are not an Indian tribe.[29]

Evidence in ethnohistorical texts suggests that "tribes" as formally bounded, cohesive, meaningful geopolitical and ethnonational entities were not typical as such at first contact with Europeans but were created in response to colonial intrusions, especially in the Southeast, which Greenbaum and others have identified as a problem with OFA's expectations of tribal leadership and cohesion.[30] The rules favor "distinct, bounded communities with relatively centralized leadership," which has been characteristic of recognized tribes only since they began relations with the colonial governments. Group leadership and identity in the early years of contact between Indians and whites only occasionally and situationally transcended local village and kin-based identities.[31] To expect that unrecognized tribes with no political relations with the federal government or other bureaucratic entities should fit this mold and demonstrate authority over membership is of questionable value as a recognition criterion, since it is a product of a federal relationship which nonfederally recognized tribes, by definition, have not had throughout their histories, if they ever had it at all. OFA claims to take into account the difficulties of maintaining influence among unrecognized tribes, but it insists that "more than a trivial degree of political influence be demonstrated," without specifying what would be considered "trivial."[32]

As Alexandra Harmon notes about trials over tribal membership of various people in late-nineteenth-century and early-twentieth-century Puget Sound, "the official formulations of Indian identity emerged from complex cross-cultural and intracultural dialogues."[33] Neither whites nor Indians could come to any kind of consensus about what constituted tribal membership among Puget Sound Indian communities. Various discussions were held among Indians, among whites, and between Indians and whites that helped people arrive at provisional decisions in various cases. What emerges from this discourse is that tribal identity is flexible, situational, and contestable, even when blood quanta are high, and that although the political influence of a tribe over its people could be slight, that does not mean that they were not members or that the tribe did not exist. The multiple and shifting "tribal" identities of Puget Sound Indians demonstrate that the concept of tribal cohesion and even political influence is not always compatible with indigenous senses of identity. Many Indians in the area "did not stay put [on their reservations or allotments], identify consistently with a single group, or restrict their social relations to treaty Indians."[34] Political cohesion as it is imagined in OFA criteria does not always reflect the worldviews of indigenous groups.

The Tunica-Biloxis easily met the political cohesion requirement of OFA criteria, since they were able to document a long succession of tribal chiefs. The Jena Choctaws essentially granted authority to family elders, but they were a small enough community that such an arrangement could be described as a cohesive political system. Even they were close to being considered a descendant community, though, since OFA at times argued that there was no obvious intent to create a new political unit. An evident commitment to maintaining ethnoracial boundaries provided the strongest evidence of the Jena Choctaws' tribalism; that they maintained their culture and language and married primarily within the nexus of family relationships that would emerge as "the tribe" was eventually taken as indicative that the Jena Choctaws thought of themselves as a separate people bound by common agreement to uphold their Choctaw identity in Louisiana, apart from the Mississippi and Oklahoma Choctaws. Like the Jena Choctaws, the Clifton-Choctaws have had family leaders and community leaders over the last 150 years, but the emergence of a tribal entity from a nexus of family relationships will likely create problems for them if they cannot document a predecessor tribal entity from which these families emerged. In contrast with the Jena Choctaws, the Clifton-Choctaws do not retain the Choctaw language and high blood quanta as distinct markers of identity, which makes it harder for them to document that their ancestors continued to identify as an Indian people generation after generation, regardless of the political structure of the community.

The persistent conflation of blood quantum, culture, and tribal and national identity has been troubling to Clifton-Choctaw recognition efforts. The anthropologist Karen I. Blu argues that the domination of blood quantum and obvious aboriginal cultural markers in discussions of Indianness and eligibility for federal recognition, at the expense of more subtle cultural and social ties to an Indian entity, ignores the acculturative social forces acting on nonfederally recognized tribes. Without documentable blood quanta that arise from federal interaction or aboriginal cultural markers, tribes like the Lumbees and the Clifton-Choctaws face challenges to their claims to status as recognizable Indian nations.[35] As Blu testified on behalf of the Lumbees, "Indian identity . . . is not lost when Indians change their ways of making a living or use a different language."[36] The ancestors of the Clifton-Choctaws reproduced a sense of themselves as a distinct Indian people from one generation to the next, and surrounding communities recognized that distinction, but under the grinding assault of everyday colonialism and racism, the community slowly surrendered many of the distinct traditions that would mark it as "authentically" Indian.[37] On the surface the Clifton-Choctaws are not as easily identifiable as the Jena Choctaws, but their sense of themselves as an Indian people is just as strong.[38]

*Interventions: Policy Reform at OFA*

Commenting in 1991 on the numerous Congressional hearings that had had only minimal effect on federal recognition policy, Rachael Paschal wrote that "interminable oversight hearings resulting in studies, reports, and proposed legislation are insufficient."[39] Indeed, since that time there have been considerably more studies, hearings, lawsuits, proposed legislation, and investigations by the Government Accountability Office (GAO).[40] Perhaps this book simply adds to those, though with the hope that the accumulation of evidence will tip the process toward a more favorable pattern for nonfederal tribes. The bigger intervention that this book can make is ideological more than policy-oriented. If policy indeed flows from ideology (even if the relationship is mutually constitutive to an extent), then ideology is also an appropriate place to direct our attention.

Nonfederal tribes, federal tribes, states, and municipalities have pressed for changes in the recognition process, resulting in minor modifications. Some of the more commendable aspects of OFA's work must be acknowledged, because OFA is in many ways intended to benefit tribes. Technical advice letters, detailed and level-headed guidelines, and workshops that OFA formerly provided for petitioners have all been important in helping tribes to look in the right places for documents that would give them the best chance at presenting their case. OFA has been willing to overturn initially negative proposed findings regarding the Mohegans and the Gay Head Wampanoags, thus admitting the limitations of its initial recommendations. It has allowed tribes to appeal decisions at several points, and to rebut comments of so-called interested parties. It has tried to correct some of the more grievous errors of the regulations by inviting commentary on revisions to the process in 1994. And most importantly, it has created a somewhat accessible process that provides significant new opportunities for the tribes that it does recognize.

OFA says that tribes have other avenues to recognition. While it is true that tribes can be acknowledged by Congress, executive order, or judicial authority, since the procedures were established in 1978 presidents and members of Congress have been reluctant to acknowledge tribes without first consulting OFA, judges have been deferring recognition decisions to the executive and legislative branches, and the phrasing in legislative acts of recognition can place limits on the sovereignty of legislatively recognized tribes—limits that tribes recognized through other means do not face.[41] Seven petitioners have been recognized by Congress since 1978, not counting any of the terminated tribes that had their federal status "restored." The Mashantucket Pequots were recognized by Congress as part of the settlement of their land claims. Others were recognized only after Congress consulted with OFA on the likelihood of recognizing them. The Jena Choctaw recognition bill was approved by Congress, but President George H. W. Bush refused to sign it after consulting with OFA, stating that he would rather see the tribes go through the standard administrative process.[42] Ben Nighthorse Campbell, at the time the chairman of the Senate Indian Affairs Committee, also expressed his opposition to legislative recognition without extenuating circumstances, establishing a roadblock that makes legislative recognition an unpromising option for most tribes.[43] With very few exceptions tribes will continue to be forced to go through OFA to get federal recognition, and some like the Samish Tribe, the Miami Tribe of Indiana, and the Schaghticoke Tribal Nation will be forced into the courtroom to sue OFA if they are denied acknowledgment. Tribes are constantly seeking better alternatives to this process.

OFA is in a bad position, of course, and it makes an easy target. Because of the many complex conceptions that people hold about the boundaries of Indianness, there is no way meet the expectations of every interested party. Further, OFA remains underfunded and understaffed. In May 2000 Kevin Gover, the head of the BIA, tried to persuade Congress to take the process away from the Bureau of Indian Affairs.[44] At the time Congress was again considering whether to take that action, but ultimately did nothing. Gover was trying to make the point that OFA will never receive the funding it needs because it has such a low priority in the BIA funding hierarchy, particularly now that its decisions have become so contentious with the advent of Indian gaming. The BIA is not overly inclined to spend money on a program that many in the bureau think is for "fake" or less deserving Indians anyway. The more money is given to that program, the more quickly tribes will be recognized, which will lead to further budgetary requirements, and the BIA is already a low priority in the Department of the Interior. If OFA were funded separately, Gover argues, it would have a better chance of receiving appropriate funding. Gover's statement tiptoes around the contradiction that he had the power to appropriately fund OFA, but only at the expense of other important programs. That he suggested taking recognition responsibilities from BIA and that this has been suggested so many times before are important keys to understanding OFA's history. The office has never been accepted as a competent unit of government, even by those overseeing it.

There can be no hope that OFA will ever work to everyone's satisfaction, but critical issues can be addressed, as Gover and others have suggested. Lee Fleming, an Oklahoma Cherokee who joined the office as a genealogy specialist in 1997 and became director in 1998, contended in 2000 that his biggest problem continued to be a lack of resources. He estimated that 60 percent of staff members' time was spent dealing with administrative duties, such as requests for copies of petitions under the Freedom of Information Act (FOIA), instead of evaluating petitions. FOIA requests involve an incredible amount of tedious work for professional staff, such as blacking out social security numbers, genealogies, and other protected information on up to twenty thousand pages of documents for each request. Everyone wants the process to move faster, but unless more funding is allocated to the program, the easiest way to make things move faster is to devote fewer hours to each case and less attention to each petitioner's research problems.

One of the key criticisms of the process has been that it is too slow, leading OFA to change its internal regulations. While petitioners had hoped that these criticisms would lead to the allocation of more resources to the program, the result instead was fewer resources devoted to each petitioner as staff members were discouraged, by an internal decision, from doing even the smallest amount of original research to fill in apparent gaps in petitions. Technical assistance was given a lower priority than working on final determinations. The research burden had always been on the petitioners, but OFA staff would previously walk down the street to the National Archives to copy documents that they could locate in thirty minutes but that might take several months for the petitioner to find.[45]

As a result of criticisms from Congress, the GAO audit in 2001, and a federal court order in the Schaghticoke case, OFA developed a new database to reduce the burden of FOIA requests and make the analysis of research materials faster for the researchers and more transparent for third parties. The Federal Acknowledgment Information Resource (FAIR) database catalogues, cross-references, and scans all documents relevant to a petition and makes them available for review. Data entry was contracted out to allow professional staff to devote more time to evaluation.[46] The FAIR system is a significant improvement in OFA procedures that has increased transparency and freed the researchers to devote more time to petitions.

Even without the FOIA requests, the amount of time needed to process and evaluate petitions is overwhelming. For the petition of the United Houma Nation alone, OFA needs to document the genealogies of seventeen thousand tribal members, in addition to evaluating historical and anthropological reports. Staffing for OFA peaked at seventeen around 1994, when the BIA director Ada Deer confidently stated that the office was "fully staffed" and petitioning tribes would "have a much speedier action on their petitions."[47] While Deer's initiative significantly increased OFA staffing after a policy review in 1993, Fleming has suggested that to function at expected levels, OFA would need to double or triple its professional and administrative staff. Currently the office has three research teams, each consisting of an anthropologist, a historian, and a genealogist, plus a secretary and the director, for a total of eleven full-time staff members.[48] Despite attempts to speed the process through outsourcing, the rate at which OFA produces final determinations has not changed significantly in its thirty-year history; it still averages about two final determinations a year. With 331 letters of intent to petition received between 1978 and 2008 and only 66 resolved cases, if even half the remaining petitioners follow through the process to the end, it will take until 2075 to complete them at the current rate.[49] In the unlikely event that all groups follow through with the entire process, assuming no new petitioners are added, the last case will be completed in 2141.

In 2002 the BIA's director, Neal McCaleb, proposed elevating the Branch of Acknowledgment and Research (as OFA was previously known) to the status of a division within the BIA, tripling its staff from eleven to thirty-three and raising its budget to $3.18 million.[50] While the funding and staffing proposals were not implemented, the Branch of Acknowledgment and Research was moved from its previous home in the Office of Tribal Services and renamed, and the new Office of Federal Acknowledgment now reports directly to the assistant secretary for Indian affairs.[51] Despite apparent problems with OFA and its regulations, increased funding would allow for a repeal of the order to avoid doing any extra research for petitioners. It would probably alleviate the problem of timeliness, but a greater priority should be providing more technical and research assistance to help petitioners again. Increased funding to OFA would not be a complete solution, but it would not likely create any new problems for the petitioners either.

As it now stands, the backlog of petitions awaiting review because of inadequate staffing at OFA is only part of the timeliness problem. Another formidable obstacle has been the amount of time and resources that it takes to prepare a defensible petition in the first place. Legitimate tribes with incomplete research are prevented from receiving federal benefits and protections, and the amount of time that it takes to complete a petition has just as much to do with their inordinately long delays in justice.[52] To that end, increased funding for the research support program of the Administration for Native Americans for nonfederal tribes would be more productive for the tribes than increased funding to OFA, as long as OFA maintains its current hands-off approach to petition research.

The process as it is currently configured at least gives tribes some advantages over the previous, poorly defined ad hoc system. Since the BIA formerly made decisions without offering any recourse to petitioning tribes, the current process is a step in the right direction. Tribes are allowed to compile or oversee their own research and develop the best case they can before entering the "Active Consideration" phase. OFA has set up a process that allows tribes to pursue an avenue other than Congressional recognition or court action, neither of which has been particularly successful in the past. Congress remains leery of any tribe that feels the need to circumvent the OFA process, despite the flaws that Congress has asked OFA to remedy, and Congress and judges alike would be more likely than OFA staff to rely on highly racialized and stereotypical understandings of what a tribe is.[53]

A revealing quirk in the process developed in 2000, when the BIA director Kevin Gover went against OFA staff interpretations of petitions and ordered findings in favor of acknowledgment for the Chinook tribe of Oregon, and his successor, the acting BIA director Michael Anderson, did the same with the petitions of the Nipmuc tribe of Massachusetts and the Duwamish of Washington.[54] While in the past, BIA directors have always approved staff findings, Gover and Anderson bucked tradition by rejecting what they viewed as erroneous findings in the final weeks of President Bill Clinton's administration. Unfortunately for the petitioning tribes, George W. Bush's administration reversed those findings under Neal McCaleb, but the initial actions on the part of Anderson and Gover point to a lack of faith in the ability of the OFA to adequately evaluate petitions with its current criteria and practices. Rejected petitioners and the scholars working with them had expressed such sentiments previously, but their statements were always questionable because they could be too easily dismissed as biased. The actions of Gover and Anderson helped to validate their complaints, and pointed to the highly political nature of the decisions. Similarly, under Bush several final determinations in favor of recognition were overturned after a furious lobbying campaign by Connecticut officials, and likely by the significant anti-gaming and anti–tribal sovereignty lobby associated with Jack Abramoff. The nature of recognition decisions, much like the decision to recognize any government, is fundamentally political. Ethnology, race, and notions of territorial sovereignty play greater roles in tribal recognition decisions than in decisions about the recognition of nations considered external territories (such as, say, Taiwan), so heavily politicized racial and colonial ideas remain deeply embedded in the tribal recognition policy of the United States.

OFA officials have stated that one of the main reasons for establishing its procedures was to remove politics from the acknowledgment process. In theory this is a noble goal, one intended to make the process fair for both the government and the tribes. The "facts" are supposed to determine the outcome of these cases, but just as the "facts" are hardly objective, so politics is hardly removed from the process. Political judgments about what constitutes a sovereign Indian entity are written into the procedures themselves. In addition, the procedures allow "interested parties" to participate in the process. Interested parties include any "parties which may have a legal or property interest in a decision, such as recognized tribes or non-Indian governmental units."[55] Some interested parties are allowed to participate not because they have any knowledge of what constitutes a sovereign Indian entity, but because they stand to "lose" property if a tribe gains recognition (though if it is established that a group has aboriginal title, then "interested parties" never had a right to the property in the first place). If this procedure was established solely to determine whether a group is a tribe, then it is unjust to allow antagonistic entities to attack the credibility of petitioning tribes because of financial and political motives. Interested parties even have the right to appeal positive decisions,[56] thus making tribes jump through even more bureaucratic hoops and possibly lose their trust status. OFA claims that its procedures are free of political influence, but in truth the procedures invite politics into every decision. If these are not political decisions, then so-called interested parties should have no special status within the procedures.

Under the revised procedures, OFA differentiates "informed parties" from "interested parties." Informed parties are third parties who lack any significant property or legal interests in the petition but who can contribute valuable information. OFA has determined that these parties should not be allowed to participate in the process to the same extent as interested parties because they have no property at stake. Property interest is weighted more heavily than actual knowledge of the petitioning group in determining the extent to which a party can participate in the process. This is a minor distinction, though, as informed parties should not be granted unlimited participation in the process either: if they were, tribes might be bogged down even more. Both informed and interested parties should be allowed to submit relevant information, but neither should be allowed to appeal OFA decisions.

The legal scholar L. R. Weatherhead argues for a liberal interpretation of the statutes in favor of petitioners, noting that the deck is stacked against them in the first place.[57] The canons of construction for Indian law in the United States have established "that treaties, agreements, statutes, and executive orders be liberally construed in favor of the Indians,"[58] given the lack of control that they have over federal processes related to their tribal well-being. Perhaps this was the sentiment of Kevin Gover and Michael Anderson when they overruled OFA's findings in the three cases mentioned above. Considering OFA's resistance to criticism, the retraction of the decisions of Gover and Anderson in the Chinook and Duwamish cases, and the overturned positive determinations in the Schaghticoke and Eastern / Pauckatuck Pequot cases, petitioners could not expect Weatherhead's suggestion to be honored under Bush's administration. The success rate of petitioners plummeted from roughly 50 percent in the pre-Bush years to only two of fifteen final determinations in favor of recognition for petitioners between 2001 and 2009.[59] President Barack Obama's administration may pursue a more measured approach and appoint a sympathetic head of Indian affairs again, but OFA officials remain the same from one administration to the next. Tribes still have to wait for recognition until they have irrefutable research supporting their petitions, which demands extensive resources, the deep commitment of the tribal leadership, and exorbitant amounts of time and energy. The burden on the tribes is immense, and the tribes are often poorly equipped to handle the burden.[60] Consultation with professional researchers is absolutely required for success, but even that hardly guarantees federal recognition, because the increasing politicizing of the process has made the decisions increasingly arbitrary.

Perhaps the key to success for petitioners will be to understand federal recognition policy as a thoroughly political process and engage it on those terms, as the Jena Choctaws did and even as the Tunica-Biloxis did to some extent. There has to be truth to tribal claims for the political process to be either just or successful, but the actions of Gover, Anderson, OFA researchers, BIA officials, "interested parties," and federal, state, and municipal politicians from presidents to local aldermen have revealed the extent to which these decisions are fundamentally political, despite all the academic and legal trappings. If petitioners frame recognition decisions in political terms, then the racially and colonially empowered language of "objectivity" becomes more visible.

### On Federal Recognition and White Supremacy

Indigenous identity can persist even when racial and cultural markers of aboriginal heritage have receded significantly. When an indigenous community also has African ancestry, racial thinking spurs suspicion of ulterior motives, and outsiders often suspect that the community is trying to "pass" for Indian to explain away its nonwhite features.[61] The practice of anti-black racism under white supremacy has trained generations of people from all racial and cultural groups in the United States to be vigilant about racial boundaries in general, and signs of African ancestry in particular. On one level it is clear that anti-black racism contributed to the staunchly Indian and anti-black identity of Clifton-Choctaws and Indian communities like them, rather than to a more open acknowledgment of the African ancestry of some tribal members. This is hardly surprising, since people around the world have tried to hide attributes that mark them as socially inferior, and African ancestry in the United States is such an attribute. But this does not mean that the Clifton-Choctaws and groups like them are not Indian. The "passing" explanation is incomplete in that it tries to make Indian ancestry a non-factor because of the simultaneous presence of African ancestry.

The end of the legal distinction between free people of color and black slaves after emancipation did not mean the end of a viable identity for people of mixed black and white ancestry, and most free communities of color never asserted any Indian identity at that time, even if they had known Indian ancestry. If they were not Indian they generally did not try to assert an Indian identity. In rural Louisiana, Creoles of color continued to identify as such even though many had significant indigenous ancestry, and continued to distinguish themselves from blacks even if the distinction was validated barely or not at all by surrounding whites and blacks. From the tangled roots of the Clifton-Choctaw community, on the other hand, evolved a distinct, local, mixed-race Indian identity that ought to be understood as an ethnonational or tribal identity. Though other peoples and traditions were incorporated into that body of real and imagined kinship, Indian identity persisted as the predominant self-characterization of the group through a multitude of social forces—including but not limited to anti-black racism—and succeeding generations were born into it. National identity is a slippery creature that cannot always be explained "rationally."[62] All the reasons why the Clifton-Choctaws clung to an Indian identity cannot be known, and yet outsiders are quick to mark them as poseurs in large part because of African ancestry in the community.

Ascriptions of false identity to petitioners with African ancestry create obstacles for tribes in the petitioning process, even though OFA claims that "triraciality is a non-issue."[63] Susan Greenbaum identifies the precise locations where blackness enters the recognition criteria. First, the criteria require that the group be identified by outsiders and academics as Indians. That has been a problem for many of the petitioning groups with black ancestry, which have occasionally been identified as "black" communities masquerading as Indians, and therefore have often been identified as non-Indian by some of their neighbors and academics, even as they have been identified as Indian or triracial by others. Second, in privileging groups that have previously been recognized as Indians by the federal government, OFA disadvantages groups such as the Shinnecocks, Lumbees, Tunicas, and Houmas, who were denied federal assistance in the past primarily because some of their members were perceived to have mixed with blacks in any degree. If we think of racism and colonialism as centered in white supremacist ideology, then it is hardly surprising to find that BIA officials, deeply invested in assimilationism as they were, should also have supported other aspects of white supremacy, such as the one-drop rule. Third, in the archival record any person who was documentably enslaved is assumed to have had entirely black ancestry, even though Indian slavery has been well documented in the South into the nineteenth century, a number of slaves were of mixed Indian and black ancestry, and a number of blacks have genetically documentable Native American ancestry.[64]

Finally, a former OFA historian, William Quinn, revealed his own stunning justification for prejudice against petitioners with African ancestry: "At times . . . the data . . . can be interpreted in opposite ways, with a proportion of the evidence indicating the existence of an Indian entity and another equal or greater proportion indicating the existence of some other kind of hybrid community with undetermined antecedents and ancestry."[65] Quinn uses the phrase "some other kind of hybrid" to conceal that he is talking about groups with black ancestry who, he suggests, are trying to pass for Indian. Quinn continues, "To have to decide in which direction the preponderance of evidence leans in such instances is often extremely difficult . . . A principal component of the matter of establishing Indian identity for purposes of federal acknowledgment as an Indian tribe is the *reasons* [Quinn's emphasis] Indian groups seek to establish it." He lists the economic and legal benefits and mentions validation, then implies that an insidious and disqualifying motivation lurks undetected among "groups whose identification as Indian has not been consistent or unquestioned. . . . [Such] socially marginal communities which are acculturated to the 'mainstream' of modern America and which exhibit evidence of racial mixtures seek identification as Indian owing to the fact that they perceive such identification as superior to the way they have been identified by the surrounding population." Quinn continually avoids using the word "black" or "African," only using "triracial," an ethnologically loaded term that refers to a specific set of literature which characterizes groups such as the Houmas, Lumbees, and Clifton-Choctaws as nontribal and simultaneously allows Quinn to leave the question of blackness somewhat removed from the picture he is painting.[66] Partial African ancestry has resulted in skepticism from OFA toward every petitioner who possesses it. Partial white ancestry does not impose the same barriers.

Federal recognition, while in many ways a project intended to be supportive of indigeneity, carries white supremacist racial projects within it. First, it induces Indians to distance themselves from blacks by rewarding tribes that have maintained strict racial boundaries with peoples of African descent and punishing those that have not. When Indians internalize implicit racial hierarchies and distance themselves from blacks but not whites (or distance themselves from blacks more than from whites), they are supporting white supremacy. Second, federal criteria, which create a powerful discourse of objectivity and authority, create the illusion of a bright line between groups that are definitely tribal and groups that are definitely not. Through definitional authority, recognition policy drives a wedge between federal and non-federal Indians, and prompts communities composed of related people with common indigenous ancestry and a persistent social identity as Indians to question themselves as bearers of indigenous heritage. This is not a call for blanket acknowledgment of every group claiming tribal status, because the federal government cannot acknowledge groups without evidence of tribal heritage. Rather, it is a reminder that indigeneity has survived in more than one form, and that we should be careful to nurture it in communities where it persists rather than participate in its final annihilation, for that is surely a colonial and white supremacist racial project.

Beyond its implications for federal recognition policy, the adoption by communities of color of white supremacist notions about each other provides us with new insights into how race works, whether their adoption of these notions is unwitting or calculated. Educational segregation under Jim Crow provides a useful example. While there were simultaneous—albeit weaker—impulses toward isolationism from whites, when southern Indians with and without African ancestry wanted access to education, they fought to have their children enrolled in white schools and refused to send them to black schools. Rather than challenge the existence of the color line, most tried to position themselves on the right side of it. By saying that they would not go to school with blacks, Indians were complicit in the segregation and oppression of blacks. Even though this was partially an act of self-defense intended to ameliorate racial discrimination against Indian people and maintain a distinct indigenous identity (with its attendant legal, moral, and political claims), refusing to attend black schools affirmed the white racialization of blacks.[67] While in some cases this stance eventually led to the integration into white schools in the 1940s of even full-blooded Indians who spoke little English, it simultaneously reinforced the foundations of white supremacy. The stance of Indians who refused to attend school with blacks affirmed the existence of a color line, but did not give these Indians access to whiteness itself or free them from racism or colonialism. Whites continued to divert resources from indigenous groups. Anti-black racism undermines the best interests of tribes in its support for white supremacy.

Phil Deloria's exploration of the outcomes of a single idea is instructive. "The stereotype of Indian savagery, for example, worked in a number of different contexts—the 'kill or be killed' hatred of the frontiersman, the scientific racism of the intellectual, the evangelical demand of the missionary, the sympathetic disdain of the reformer, the justified expediency of the politician. The idea of savagery undoubtedly enabled white Americans to exercise multiple kinds of power over multiple kinds of Indians."[68] Similarly, the idea of Indian savagery contains a shadow stereotype about whites—if Indians are savage, then whites as the unnamed norm are by implication civilized. If we think about the multitude of shadow stereotypes about people of color, a single, very simple idea, hidden where the shadows converge, becomes visible: white racial superiority and the right to dominate that accompanies it. In short, white supremacy.

When white supremacist ideology is placed at the center of our under-standing of racism and colonialism, it becomes easier to understand as an ideology that structures and justifies social relations through multiple proj-ects, multiple outcomes, and commonsense behaviors and thoughts. Using this model, we can better understand the extent to which Indian anti-black racism undermines tribal sovereignty in its support for white supremacy. If racism and colonialism both emanate from a singular ideology of white supremacy, then the struggle for indigenous sovereignty has to be a struggle against racism in all of its forms as well. This model is crucial to understand-ing how racism and colonialism are perpetuated. Too often racism is ex-plained in terms of intentional, hateful acts committed against individuals, and colonialism is seen as as only partially racial and always extraterri-torial for the United States. Certainly such behavior is the outcome of a white supremacist ideology, but the root idea—that whites and their ances-tors are morally, intellectually, politically, and spiritually superior to non-whites, and therefore entitled to various forms of privilege, power, and property—remains even in the absence of physical violence and legal segregation. Part of the reason why this notion has been able to thrive is that we have not been able to describe how something so passive and reflexive could structure relationships between both social groups and nations. White supremacy is not something that typically people choose actively in the modern era. Rather, it is something in which we are raised without knowing it, without being able to see every iteration of it.

The insights derived from this history suggest a need to bring scholars of race and indigeneity into closer conversation. As I have mentioned, within ethnic studies in the United States an appreciation for the distinction between indigenous groups and racial groups is sorely lacking. That said, Native American studies would greatly benefit from an infusion of racial theory into the field, because Indians are part of a racial system that goes beyond simple binary relationships. We understand, for example, that white racializations of Indian people affect everything from the government-to-government relationship to the way Indian children are socialized in educational systems, and we understand the colonial nature of Indian tribal relations with the United States. But scholars in the field have spent so long focusing on how tribal sovereignty makes Indians unique that we have frequently lost sight of how Indians are part of, and participate in, a global discourse about race. Moreover, without racial theory we do not recognize that unflattering stereotypes about blacks contain unspoken, flattering stereotypes about whites that play heavily in the relationship between Indians and whites, as well as between Indian tribes and the United States government.

Like Indian educational integration activism, federal recognition activism carries multiple racial projects within it. On some level federal tribal recognition policy has the potential to be just and emancipatory, because it is the most accessible process by which tribes can ask that their sovereignty as indigenous nations be honored by the federal government, and it is rigorous enough to ensure that non-Indians do not have access to Indian resources. But contained within the promise to honor the sovereignty of legitimate tribes is an assertion of colonial authority, and the process has often undermined documented indigenous groups. As Glen Coulthard has commented, building on Elizabeth Povinelli's work, "colonial powers will only recognize the collective rights and identities of Indigenous peoples insofar as this recognition does not throw into question the background legal, political and economic framework of the colonial relationship itself."[69] As a practical matter the OFA process is virtually unavoidable for tribes seeking recognition of their sovereignty, but it must be understood as a process that also props up colonial structures—a process fraught with racial and colonial baggage.

Federal recognition cannot free tribes from various colonial and racial projects. Emancipation does not arrive by fax from the Bureau of Indian Affairs. Oppression of the Tunica-Biloxi, Jena Choctaw, and Clifton-Choctaw peoples has come in equal measure from the federal government and from local people. Federal recognition gives tribes more power to chart their own future, even as states and other localities contest their sovereignty, on issues such as gaming, environmental regulation, education, and law enforcement. Federal policies of assimilation that nonfederal tribes had been able to avoid through nonrecognition, with regard to areas such as boarding schools and relocation, were merely the logical extension of an ideology that reached Indians whether they were under the thumb of federal agents or of local plantation owners and school superintendents. Federal recognition gives tribes new and enforceable powers to protect themselves from local forces, even while it creates what might be called a buy-in for the federal-tribal system and for bureaucratized conceptions of tribal existence.

Perhaps the greatest power of recognition is discursive, though. A decision to recognize a tribe gives that tribe a new sense of license, of righteousness, of ownership, of sovereignty, of justice—all things that seem absent under non-recognition. It reminds surrounding polities of their status as well, and fundamentally alters legal and political relationships. At the same time, for tribes that are turned down the feeling of injustice and disempowerment can be overwhelming. The discursive power—the power to define—that participation in this process cedes to the federal government levies an enormous cost.

*Recognition Policy and Tribal Life*

No matter how cut and dried the laws of blood descent may
seem to make Cherokee identity, the reality of lived experience
is infinitely more complex.[70]—CIRCE STURM

It is important to avoid thinking of petitioners only in terms of whether they have been validated by a colonial tool of the government, because Indian identity is so complex, contestable, and constantly shifting depending on the context, and yet the power of the state in constructing social relations and racial discourses should not be underestimated. Federal recognition policy shapes and constrains discourses on Indian identity, and provides an important public domain in which the boundaries of Indian identity are expressed, formed, policed, and contested.[71] The people involved in the debate are unified by their concern for the survival of Indian peoples as Indians, and divided by their perceptions of exactly how to ensure that survival. Vital resources and rights are at stake, and some Indians on both sides of the recognition divide feel that their rights are being encroached upon in this process, both by tribes of the opposing category and by the federal government. Many people are misinformed about the process of petitioning and the effects of recognition. The widespread notion that the federal guidelines, though rigorous, will allow for "legitimate" tribes to be recognized masks the shortcomings of the OFA process as a means of identifying and aiding tribes entitled to federal recognition.

The histories of federally nonrecognized tribes and tribes that were only recently recognized reveal that tribal persistence and even revitalization are entirely possible without recognition, an important point that is often lost in the federal recognition debate because it is so focused on the "actionable justice" of federal policy.[72] The very existence of the federal acknowledgment procedures, in fact, has in some ways helped to preserve and reinvigorate tribal entities throughout the country who have used it as a rallying point for revitalizing and consolidating tribal goals, despite the significant drain that it can place on tribal resources and the psychic cost of not being a federally recognized tribe.[73]

Recognition does, however, elevate the opportunities for revitalization, as documented by the cases of the Tunica-Biloxi Tribe and the Jena Band of Choctaws, among others.[74] Tribal sovereignty under federal law continues to be indisputably the greatest weapon that Indian tribes have for their defense. And yet, because sovereignty in the federal-tribal context involves coming *under* federal law in many ways, it makes for a limited self-determination within a colonial relationship.[75] Nonetheless, access to federal resources and federal definitions is enormously important for tribes.

The Tunica-Biloxi Tribe, the Jena Band of Choctaws, and the Clifton-Choctaws sought federal recognition because they saw it as a tool that would help them pursue political and economic self-determination, cultural revitalization, social services, and protection against intrusion. They hoped that it would help their people survive together, as a tribe. Many lessons have been learned along the way as the shortcomings, pleasures, tensions, and contradictions of recognition and nonrecognition have become more apparent.

Despite the constant assault on tribal identities, the tribes retain the knowledge with which they began:

A Indian is a Indian, if he's first class or second class.
ROY TYLER, CLIFTON-CHOCTAW

Indian tribes shouldn't even be federally recognized.
Indian tribes are Indian tribes. It's just that.
—CLYDE JACKSON, JENA CHOCTAW

We have a promise from the sun. As long as there is the sun,
there will be Indian people.
—JOSEPH PIERITE SR., TUNICA-BILOXI

# Appendix

25 CFR Part 83, Procedures for Establishing That an American Indian Group Exists as an Indian Tribe

83.7 Mandatory criteria for Federal acknowledgment

(a) The petitioner has been identified as an American Indian entity on a substantially continuous basis since 1900.

(b) A predominant portion of the petitioning group comprises a distinct community and has existed as a community from historical times until the present.

(c) The petitioner has maintained political influence or authority over its members as an autonomous entity from historical times until the present.

(d) A copy of the group's present governing document including its membership criteria. In the absence of a written document, the petitioner must provide a statement describing in full its membership criteria and current governing procedures.

(e) The petitioner's membership consists of individuals who descend from a historical Indian tribe or from historical Indian tribes which combined and functioned as a single autonomous political entity.

(f) The membership of the petitioning group is composed principally of persons who are not members of any acknowledged North American Indian tribe.

(g) Neither the petitioner nor its members are the subject of congressional legislation that has expressly terminated or forbidden the Federal relationship.

# Notes

*Abbreviations*

AIPRC—American Indian Policy Review Commission

BIA—Bureau of Indian Affairs (formerly Office of Indian Affairs)

CENA—Coalition of Eastern Native Americans

DOI—Department of the Interior

IGRA—Indian Gaming Regulatory Act

LOIA—Louisiana Office of Indian Affairs

NARA—National Archives and Records Administration

NCAI—National Congress of American Indians

OFA—Office of Federal Acknowledgment
(formerly known as Branch of Acknowledgment and Research)

*Introduction*

1. The Office of Federal Acknowledgment began as the Federal Acknowledgment Project and later became the Branch of Acknowledgment and Research. The present name was taken in 2003 after a reorganization of its duties and reporting hierarchy. For simplicity's sake I refer to the office as OFA throughout the text rather than meticulously matching the name to the date of the interaction. Fleming, "Testimony of R. Lee Fleming, Director, Office of Federal Acknowledgement for the Hearing before the Committee on Indian Affairs, United States Senate, on the Federal Acknowledgement Process."

    Documents from OFA referred to in the text without publication information were either obtained directly from the OFA through the Freedom of Information Act or downloaded from the OFA web site, http://www.bia.gov/WhoWeAre/AS-IA/OFA/index.htm. Several were downloaded and printed by the author in 1998–99.

2. Indeed, a significant number of tribal governments were created as convenient

administrative units that did not tightly correspond with tribal boundaries. Examples include the multiple Ojibway / Chippewa tribal governments recognized by the United States that do not necessarily correspond neatly to any previous tribal body, and the many tribal governments created for "confederated tribes" that were simply placed on reservations together, such as the Confederated Tribes of Grand Ronde.

3. See Felix Cohen's list of criteria for determining whether a tribe has been previously recognized. Cohen, *Handbook of Federal Indian Law*, 270–71.

4. Ironically, the threat of termination in the 1950s focused attention on the significance of federal recognition for tribal prosperity and persistence, helping to establish a booming recognition movement in the following years that ultimately forced the BIA to create formal channels through which nonfederal groups could seek recognition.

5. Such allegations have been made time and again by scholars. Tribal leaders from federal tribes have been supportive of OFA for the most part, arguing that it is necessary and offers the most viable structure available for making such determinations. Among the most salient essays dissecting OFA have been the following: Paschal, "The Imprimatur of Recognition"; Duthu, "The Houma Indians of Louisiana"; Greenbaum, "What's in a Label?"; Starna, " 'Public Ethnohistory' and Native-American Communities"; Garroutte, "What If My Grandma Eats Big Macs? Culture," *Real Indians: Identity and the Survival of Native America*, 61–81; Campisi, "New England Tribes and Their Quest for Justice"; Greenbaum, "In Search of Lost Tribes"; McCulloch and Wilkins, " 'Constructing' Nations within States"; Wilkins, "Breaking into the Intergovernmental Matrix"; Meyers, "Federal Recognition of Indian Tribes in the United States." Book-length treatments include Cramer, *Cash, Color, and Colonialism*; Grabowski, "Coiled Intent"; Miller, *Invisible Indigenes*; Miller, *Forgotten Tribes*; and Tolley, *Quest for Tribal Acknowledgment*. Tribal statements can be found primarily in Congressional testimonies included in recognition reform bills. For examples of OFA staff defending the process see primarily Roth, "Comment in Reply [to Russel Barsh]"; Quinn, "Southeastern Indians"; Quinn, "The Southeast Syndrome"; and Quinn, "Federal Acknowledgment of American Indian Tribes."

6. Opposition to tribal recognition in Connecticut has been bipartisan: the Democratic state attorney general Richard Blumenthal, U.S. Representatives Robert Simmons and Chris Shays (Republicans), and U.S. Senators Joseph Lieberman (Democrat, later Independent) and Chris Dodd (Democrat) have all opposed further recognition of Connecticut tribes on the grounds of opposition to gaming and tribal sovereignty rather than on the merits of any given case.

7. Toensing, "Schagticoke Files 2nd Circuit Appeal for Acknowledgment Restoration."

8. Green, "Dodd Drops Tribal Recognition Reform Plan"; Robinson, "Senate Committee Hears Criticisms of Indian Recognition Process"; Blumenthal, Statement of Attorney General Richard Blumenthal before the Senate Indian Affairs Committee.

The Dodd and Lieberman legislation, attached as a rider to an Interior appropriations bill, never had widespread support, and "went down in a crushing defeat in an 80 to 15 Senate vote Sept. 23 [2002]." Adams, "Department of Interior Official Floats Reform Plan for Tribal Recognition." A key catalyst in this movement was Jeff Benedict's poorly researched backlash against the Mashantucket Pequots, taken as gospel by Connecticut's antitribal movement. Benedict, *Without Reservation.* Benedict is a local author of exposés, including several books on professional and college athletes who were criminals.

9. See note 3, above.

10. Omi and Winant, *Racial Formation in the United States from the 1960s to the 1990s*, 55–56.

11. Saunt, *Black, White, and Indian*; George Lipsitz, "Like Crabs in a Barrel: Why Interethnic Anti-racism Matters Now," *American Studies in a Moment of Danger*, 117–38; Miles and Holland, eds., *Crossing Waters, Crossing Worlds*; Brooks, ed., *Confounding the Color Line*; Foley, *The White Scourge*; Forbes, "The Manipulation of Race, Caste and Identity"; Miles, *Ties That Bind*; Prashad, *Everybody Was Kung Fu Fighting*; Sturm, *Blood Politics*; Chang, *The Color of the Land*.

12. I use "ethnonational groups" because the term describes the ways the ideology shapes relations between tribes as self-aware groups with a sense of both political and ethnic self-differentiation from their neighbors (nationhood versus racialized minority status) and Anglo-Americans, who constructed the United States as a political body and continue to be considered most representative of that political body despite increasing racial and ethnic heterogeneity in the government and the population as a whole. That the Anglo "founding fathers" and later white politicians differentiated themselves as a distinct political and ethnic body is evident in the number of restrictive ethnically and racially based laws through the years. My use of this term follows Connor, *Ethnonationalism.*

13. I do not know who first used the term in this way, but my first encounter with it was the documentary *The Color of Fear* (1994), in which Victor Lewis, a racial activist of African American and Native American ancestry, deployed the term in this way. Wah, *The Color of Fear.* For a general discussion of white racial ideology and material advantages in the United States see Rothenberg, ed., *White Privilege*; Lipsitz, *The Possessive Investment in Whiteness*; Roediger, *The Wages of Whiteness.* On unconscious racism see Lawrence, "The Id, the Ego, and Equal Protection."

14. White supremacist *ideology* contrasts with what I would call the *doctrine* of white supremacy, which is an unambiguously articulated belief in white superiority and entitlement that would typify groups like neo-Nazis, or explicit state and federal government policies of segregation under Jim Crow in years past or assimilationism in federal Indian boarding schools. The ideology of white supremacy produces the doctrine of white supremacy, to be sure, but it operates in broader and more subtle ways that continue to structure racial and ethnonational relations. The ideology continues to have power after the doctrine has been largely renounced because it is so often expressed obliquely and justified as a reflection of racial and

colonial relations as they are now, after centuries of living under white supremacy. On the expression of race and race relations as "natural" see Pascoe, *What Comes Naturally*.

15. See Deloria, *Indians in Unexpected Places*, 2–14.

16. See Harris, "Whiteness as Property"; Rothenberg, ed., *White Privilege*; Lipsitz, *The Possessive Investment in Whiteness*.

17. Native American here is inclusive of Alaska Native and Hawaiian peoples. Chamorro and Samoan grievances and experiences are similarly based in indigeneity and nationhood, but these peoples' homelands are in what are considered "unorganized territories," and this distinguishes them somewhat from other indigenous groups in the United States.

18. See note 11, above.

19. Trask, "Settlers of Color and 'Immigrant' Hegemony."

20. Warrior, "A Room of One's Own at the ASA," 686. The "miner's canary" quote cited by Warrior, as scholars in the field will recognize, is from Cohen, "The Erosion of Indian Rights," 390.

21. Miller, *Forgotten Tribes*, 39–46.

22. Official and unofficial discourses discussed in Strong and Van Winkle, " 'Indian Blood.' "

23. See for example Benedict, *Without Reservation*.

24. Note that the Louisiana Purchase Treaty and the Indian Trade and Intercourse Acts did oblige the United States to protect tribal land and sovereignty, but the United States failed to uphold its obligation. See chapter 2.

25. Records of the American Indian Policy Review Commission, Record Group 220, National Archives and Records Administration, College Park, Md., unidentified records, box 315. Transcript of hearing in Baton Rouge, March 1976. Document title: "Baton Rouge, Louisiana; TF 5, 10; vol I, copy 1," 23.

26. Under the Indian Gaming Regulatory Act, class III gaming includes games such as poker, blackjack, craps, and roulette, as well as the highly profitable slot machines, and requires a state-tribal compact to govern the terms of its operation. The much less profitable class II games include bingo and pulltabs, and do not require a state-tribal compact. See chapter 8.

27. For an excellent analysis of the variety of conceptions of Indian identity see Garroutte, *Real Indians*.

28. The oral histories and ethnographic research were conducted in May 1998; May 1999; a nine-month period from September 1999 to May 2000 during which I lived a few miles from the Tunica-Biloxi reservation; August 2004; July–August 2007; May 2008; November 2008; April 2009; and July 2009. I conducted archival research at the Louisiana State Archives in Baton Rouge, the Rapides and Avoyelles Parish school boards, and in Washington at the National Archives and the Smithsonian Institution's National Anthropological Archives from June 2000 to August 2000. Various tribal members provided me with access to personal archives and copies of documents found in their own research, including Brenda Lintinger, John Barbry,

Norris Tyler, Cheryl Smith, and Christine Norris, and I am deeply indebted to them for their assistance.

29. I conducted formal interviews with fifteen Tunica-Biloxi tribal members, seven Jena Choctaw tribal members, and nine Clifton-Choctaw tribal members, in addition to informal conversations with others. I conducted formal and informal interviews with members of several other Louisiana tribes (Choctaw-Apache, Caddo-Adai, Apalachee, Houma, and Coushatta), local anthropologists, officials, non-Indian neighbors, and Lee Fleming, head of the Office of Federal Acknowledgment. Any quotes that are not attributed to some other source come from these formal interviews.

30. One graduate professor of mine called this an "élite" history, which might also work, but it is hard for me to justify using that term to describe Louisiana tribal people, no matter their positions within their tribes.

31. Not everyone who received materials responded.

32. Indeed, the idea that it is possible to represent the views of an entire tribe is based on the false premise of complete homogeneity of opinion within a tribe, something that would not normally be expected of, say, European nations. Lila Abu-Lughod discusses this issue in "Writing against Culture." I address this issue in more depth elsewhere. Klopotek, "Dangerous Decolonizing."

33. See for example Miles, *Ties That Bind*, xiii–xvi; Valerie Philips, Epilogue, *Confounding the Color Line*, ed. Brooks; Saunt, "Profile: A Symposium at Dartmouth College," *Crossing Waters, Crossing Worlds*, ed. Miles and Holland, 6–9; Miles, "Preface: Eating Out of the Same Pot?," *Crossing Waters, Crossing Worlds*, ed. Miles and Holland, xv–xviii; and Warrior, Afterword, *Crossing Waters, Crossing Worlds*, ed. Miles and Holland, 321–25.

34. Thiong'o, *Decolonising the Mind*, xii.

## Chapter 1: Origins of Federal Acknowledgment Policy

1. Wheeler-Howard Act (Indian Reorganization Act), § 479, emphasis added. This phrase recently became central to the U.S. Supreme Court's decision in Carcieri v. Salazar, particularly the issue of Congressional intent around the phrase "now under federal jurisdiction." I agree with the position of the National Congress of American Indians (NCAI) on this matter, which is that any tribe that has been recognized since that time is recognized to have been a tribe under the meaning of federal law at all times previously, whether the federal government acknowledged that obligation or not. Therefore, according to the National Congress of American Indians, "Any tribe recognized pursuant to part 83 [OFA procedures] has already received a factual determination that the tribe was under federal jurisdiction in 1934," and further, "there are no federally recognized tribes which were not 'under federal jurisdiction' in 1934." "Testimony of the National Congress of American Indians on the Supreme Court Decision in Carcieri v. Salazar and Executive Branch Authority to Acquire Trust Land for Indian Tribes." This in fact was the thrust of

the *Passamaquoddy* decision, which states that the federal government has an obligation to protect all tribes under the terms of the Indian Trade and Intercourse Acts. If a tribe exists within the boundaries claimed by the United States at a given point in time, it is "under federal jurisdiction." On this, more later in the chapter. One Tunica-Biloxi tribal council member, Brenda Lintinger, has further noted that a discussion at the meeting of the United Southern and Eastern Tribes organization in 2009 included the observation that the term "recognized" did not have its current formal and legal meaning in 1934, but rather an informal meaning implying that a group is "recognizably Indian." It only came to have its present meaning through formal legal interpretation of the Act.

2. Document as cited in Sider, *Lumbee Indian Histories*, 135–36. Sider does not cite the location of the document (the book does not have notes), but states that the memorandum is dated 22 September 1935.

3. Story as recounted here is taken primarily from Sider, *Lumbee Indian Histories*, 135–37. Only a lawsuit filed in 1971 ever brought any benefits to the twenty-two Lumbees designated 50 percent Indian or more by blood. See Morton v. Maynor. See also Blu, *The Lumbee Problem*.

4. Under the Dawes Act and the Clapp Rider.

5. See Beaulieu, "Curly Hair and Big Feet"; LaDuke, *All Our Relations*; Meyer, *The White Earth Tragedy*, 203–24. For a general discussion of conceptions of race in anthropology at the turn of the century see Hoxie, "Frozen in Time and Space," *A Final Promise*.

6. The eugenics movement, popular in the early twentieth century, sought to control human evolution by controlling gene pools. One of the core tenets of the movement was that whites constituted a biologically, measurably superior set of humans, and as such needed to be separated from genetically inferior humans for the good of humankind. In this endeavor eugenic scientists sought to classify, catalogue, and rank various physical attributes as belonging to particular genetic populations to support their theories. See note 5, above, for sources on application to Indians. See also Pascoe, *What Comes Naturally*, esp. chapter 4, for an understanding of other ways these beliefs played out in the law.

7. Beaulieu, "Curly Hair and Big Feet," 305.

8. See Porter, "Nonrecognized American Indian Tribes"; Weatherhead, "What Is an 'Indian Tribe'?" For a list of relevant citations of the development of the legal concept of federal recognition of Indian tribes see Quinn, "Federal Acknowledgment of American Indian Tribes," with the caveat that Quinn's unnuanced readings suggest a lack of awareness of Indian perspectives on federal law and policy and of how they were often designed to empower whites at the expense of Indians. He has read the case law, solicitor's opinions, and commissioner's reports but does not seem to understand the historical forces or prerogatives of power behind them.

9. The foundation for this set of laws dates to colonial times and is expressed first in the Constitution of the United States, which states that "treaties shall be held as the supreme law of the land" and empowers Congress to "regulate commerce . . . with

Indian tribes." Further, the Indian Trade and Intercourse Acts of 1790–1834 established that only the federal government was allowed to conduct treaties and transactions with Indian tribes, a restriction meant to bring all interactions with Indian tribes under unified federal Indian policies (rather than various state Indian policies), except where treaties carried special stipulations. Of course this policy is not fully in effect to this day, even after Passamaquoddy v. Morton restated the federal government's responsibility to all tribes regardless of whether they were federally recognized, as the Jena Choctaw gaming conflict reveals.

10. John Borrows suggests that traditional Ojibwe law, for example, is contained in the examples of proper and improper behavior and appropriate responses in stories from oral tradition, giving tribes more flexibility and authority than written codes do in determining how to respond to improper behavior. Borrows, *Recovering Canada*, esp. 13–28.

11. The twin policies of termination and relocation dominated federal Indian policy in the 1950s and early 1960s. Over a hundred tribes were "terminated," meaning that the United States ceased to acknowledge their existence as tribes. Most of the terminated tribes were small tribes in western Oregon and California, though the best-known cases were the Klamath Tribes in Oregon and the Menominee tribe in Wisconsin. The results of termination were devastating, destroying tribal economies and political structures, and dealing serious blows to tribal cultural integrity and identities in many cases. Most tribes felt the threat of termination, whether they were terminated or not. While termination was aimed at tribes as a whole, relocation policy sought to remove individual Indians and families from tribes with the same genocidal intent. The relocation program was designed to move reservation Indians to urban centers, where they typically traded rural poverty for urban poverty, with the goal of reducing the tribal service population through a war of attrition. See Deloria, *Custer Died for Your Sins*, chapter 3 ("The Disastrous Policy of Termination"); Fixico, *Termination and Relocation*; Lewis, "Termination of the Confederated Tribes of the Grande Ronde Community of Oregon." For a personal narrative of relocation see Mankiller and Wallis, *Mankiller*.

12. Informed and reinforced by the fundamental transformations in political dissent and race relations coming out of the African American civil rights movement of the 1950s (even if a key strategy of established tribal leaders was to distance themselves from African American protest tactics—see for example Vine Deloria's at times disturbing comparison of Indian and black political efforts in *Custer Died for Your Sins*, 168–96, 254–55), tribal and nationwide Indian activism pushed the federal government out of termination policy and into the so-called self-determination era. Indian activism continued and even grew despite (and in response to) the assault on tribal sovereignty.

13. The Tunicas led a statewide movement for federal recognition from the 1920s to the 1970s. See chapter 2. The Lumbees had been pursuing recognition since the late nineteenth century and led a regional movement in the Carolinas that inspired the Haliwa-Saponi to organize and seek recognition. Haliwa-Saponi Tribe, Haliwa-

Saponi Petition for Federal Acknowledgment, 117–18. Chief Calvin McGhee of the Poarch Creeks led a regional movement for federal recognition of Indians in Alabama and Florida for many years. Paredes, "Federal Recognition and the Poarch Creek Indians."

14. American Indian Chicago Conference, "The Voice of the American Indian." Copies of the report are scattered across the country; the copy I consulted was in National Archives and Records Administration II, College Park, Md., Record Group 220.17.8, AI / entry 38060, AIPRC Transcripts of Task Force Hearings, stack 650, 31:5:1–3, box 35, "Special, Draft & Final Reports of the Commission: Historical Indian Policies & Priorities Report: Background Information." See also Hauptman and Campisi, "There Are No Indians East of the Mississippi." Abridged version available in Albert L. Hurtado and Peter Iverson, eds., *Major Problems in American Indian History*, 2nd edn (New York: Houghton Mifflin, 2001), 461–72. Keep in mind Chadwick Allen's critique of the AICC, *Blood Narrative*, 103–6.

15. The relationship between federal and nonfederal Indians at the conference was not altogether genial, but the final document's strongly worded advocacy for nonfederal tribes could not have been made without widespread support that developed through interactions at the Chicago meeting.

16. Statement to Nancy Lurie cited in Campisi and Hauptman, "There Are No Indians East of the Mississippi." 106. Cited as Nancy O. Lurie, personal communication, 7 July 1985.

17. In this vein see an earlier criticism of Wilcomb Washburn's similar assertion that Tax and the AICC created Indian radicalism and forced Indians to accept the opinions of marginal Indians as part of the "voice of the American Indian." Straus, Bowman, and Chapman, "Anthropology, Ethics, and the American Indian Chicago Conference."

18. Deloria, *Custer Died for Your Sins*, 245.

19. Ibid., 245–46.

20. The Coushatta tribe had its federal recognition reaffirmed in 1973, after twenty years of administrative termination. Their recognition case provides an interesting counterpoint to cases that went through after the ad hoc process was formalized in 1978, especially the highly comparable Jena Choctaws. Formerly a component tribe of the Creek Confederacy, the Coushatta moved to the area in the 1790s to escape the violence in their homeland in Alabama and have maintained a fairly insular community since that time. Their language was almost universally spoken by tribal members at the time, and many of their cultural traditions had remained viable as well, which certainly made their case easier for the BIA to decide. Some members still had land-in-trust status—a distinguishing factor—and the tribe had been receiving federal funds designated for Indian health and education as recently as the 1950s, at which point the BIA simply decided that it could stop recognizing the tribe, administratively terminating the members against their wishes. When Coushatta political activity resurged in the late 1960s the tribe began pursuing federal services again. The Coushattas created a corporation in 1965 for the purpose of

marketing crafts that quickly became a forum for leadership to gather to discuss tribal politics. The Coushatta tribe's official web site discusses this development in its history section, http://www.coushattatribela.org/history.html. The tribe quickly achieved recognition from the state of Louisiana in 1972, incorporated as a tribe in March 1973 under the guidelines of the IRA, and secured federal recognition in June 1973 under the leadership of Ernest Sickey with the assistance of the Louisiana commissioner of Indian affairs, David Garrison, and the Association for American Indian Affairs. Johnson, *The Coushatta People*, 90–96. Raymond Butler, acting director, Office of Indian Services, to secretary of the interior, 13 June 1973; Marvin L. Franklin, assistant secretary of the interior, to David Garrison, Louisiana commissioner of Indian affairs, 27 June 1973, available in records of the American Indian Policy Review Commission, 1975–77, "Unidentified Records," box 315, folder: "A Report on the Landless Tribes of Washington State." The Coushattas were granted educational funding through the BIA's Mississippi Choctaw Agency and the State of Louisiana. For documentation of federal funds for Coushatta pupils see File 68776 -1931-800, part I, National Archives, Record Group 75.

The Coushatta leadership in general and Ernest Sickey in particular became leaders in the fight for federal recognition in Louisiana after achieving that status so quickly. Other Louisiana tribes followed their lead in many ways, hoping to emulate their success, with mixed results. In contrast to the Coushattas, the Jena Choctaws had many similar characteristics and relationships with the federal government and were even related to Ernest Sickey by blood, but they had a much harder time being recognized under new OFA policy. Instead of the yearlong informal process that the Coushattas had gone through, the Jena petition took sixteen years, demonstrating the considerable added burden entailed in the new process.

21. LaFollette Butler, acting deputy commissioner of Indian affairs, to Henry M. Jackson, chairman, Senate Committee on Interior and Insular Affairs, 7 ?September 1974, records of the American Indian Policy Review Commission, 1975–77, "Unidentified Records," box 315, folder: "A Report on the Landless Tribes of Washington State." Tribes recognized by BIA: Original Band of Sault Ste. Marie Chippewa Indians, 27 February 1974; Nooksack Indian Tribe of Washington, 13 August 1971; Burns Paiute Indian Community, 16 November 1967; Upper Skagit Indian Tribe, 9 June 1972; Sauk-Suiattle Indian Tribe, 9 June 1972; Coushatta Indians of Louisiana, 27 June 1973; Miccosukee Tribe of Indians of Florida, 11 January 1962. Congress recognized the Yavapai-Tonto Apache Tribe on 6 October 1972, P.L. 92-470 (36 Stat. 763), and restored the Menominee Indian Tribe of Wisconsin on 22 December 1973. Deloria further notes that the Ysleta del Sur Tiguas were Congressionally recognized in 1968, but that their recognition bill immediately ceded responsibility for their services to the State of Texas. Deloria, *Custer Died for Your Sins*, 244.

22. LaFollette Butler, acting deputy commissioner of Indian affairs, to Senator Henry M. Jackson, 7 September 1974, American Indian Policy Review Commission, "Unidentified Records," box 315, folder: "A Report on the Landless Tribes of Washington State."

23. Again, since recognition of a tribe determined that a tribe had existed continuously at all times previously, it implied that the tribe had been under federal jurisdiction at all times previously, whether the federal government had previously acknowledged that jurisdiction or not, contrary to the Supreme Court decision in *Carcieri*. See note 1, above.

24. While the Solicitor's Mole Lake Opinion cites United States v. Sandoval (1913) as the authority acknowledging the right of the executive to extend recognition in the absence of a clearly stated Congressional recognition of a tribe, a solicitor's opinion from 1974 states that the right is more clearly argued in United States v. Holliday (1865): "The facts in the case certified up with the division of opinion, show distinctly 'that the Secretary of the Interior and the Commissioner of Indian Affairs have decided that it is necessary, in order to carry into effect the provisions of [a certain] treaty, that the tribal organization [of the affected group] should be preserved.' In reference to all matters of this kind, it is the rule of this court to follow the action of the executive and other political departments of the government, whose more special duty it is to determine such affairs. If by them those Indians are recognized as a tribe, this court must do the same."

    Citation from "Memorandum: Secretary's Authority to Extend Federal Recognition to Indian Tribes," Reid P. Chambers, associate solicitor, Indian affairs, to solicitor, Department of the Interior, 20 August 1974. Copy in American Indian Policy Review Commission, "Unidentified Records," box 315, folder: "A Report on the Landless Tribes of Washington State."

25. Cohen, *Handbook of Federal Indian Law*, 270–71.

26. LaFollette Butler, acting deputy commissioner of the Bureau of Indian Affairs, explained the "informal" process of determining federal recognition to Senator Henry M. Jackson (D-Washington), chairman of the Senate Committee on Interior and Insular Affairs, in response to a letter of inquiry seeking clarification of the process. Senator Jackson himself wrote the letter of inquiry in December 1973 in response to a request from an organization called Small Tribes of Western Washington (STOWW), which asked him to help clarify the recognition status of its member tribes. This chain of events was initiated by the federally nonrecognized Indian groups themselves in response to the developing treaty fishing rights case in Washington, since "if these Tribes had not sought to preserve their treaty right on their own, the United States would have gladly continued to ignore it." LaFollette Butler to Senator Henry M. Jackson, 7 ?September 1974, American Indian Policy Review Commission, "Unidentified Records," box 315, folder: "A Report on the Landless Tribes of Washington State." The date at the top of the letter is smudged, and the AIPRC Task Force 10 report gives the date 7 January 1974. The letter cites administrative recognition of the Sault Ste. Marie Chippewas on 27 February 1974, however. The date is significant because it indicates a baseline at which the BIA began to reevaluate its recognition procedures. A report from STOWW further indicates that "the Department of Interior first denied its existence and then disavowed any

responsibility for its contents." Bishop and Hansen, "A Report on the Landless Tribes of Washington State," 3. Butler's letter indicates this chain of events on page 2 of the letter, citing an enclosed letter from the STOWW executive director, Dewey Sigo, dated 13 November 1973, but I have not seen the original letter from Senator Jackson. It may be held with the Henry M. Jackson Papers at the University of Washington, accessions 3560-5, "Senate Papers, 1973–1983," and 3560-19, "Microfilm of Outgoing Correspondence." For more information on STOWW see Ruby and Brown, *Esther Ross*, esp. 96–98, 172–87. The statement "If these tribes . . ." is quoted from Bishop and Hansen, "A Report on the Landless Tribes of Washington State," 10.

27. See note 28, below.

28. Reid Peyton Chambers, associate solicitor, Department of the Interior, Division of Indian Affairs, to Mrs. Karleen F. McKenzie, chairperson of the Tchinouk Indians, 14 February 1975, AIPRC box 76, "Submissions for the Records of Task Force Hearings, Oklahoma to Oregon," folder: "Salem, Oregon, Supportive Document."

29. Frizzell's statement seems to indicate a longer process of two phases. The first phase involved inquiry into the right of the secretary to extend recognition, a right being reconsidered at some point after 27 February 1974, when BIA formally recognized the Sault Ste. Marie Chippewa tribe. The solicitor's opinion of 20 August 1974, arguing that the Department of the Interior did have authority to grant recognition as an extension of the "political branches" of the government, seems to represent the culmination of that phase of the research. The second phase concerned the development of proper procedures for extending recognition. Kent Frizzell, acting secretary of the interior, to Senator Henry M. Jackson, 22 May 1975, in Bishop and Hansen, "A Report on the Landless Tribes of Washington State," appendix viii.

30. Joint Tribal Council of the Passamaquoddy Tribe v. Morton. For more detailed information on the development of case law regarding the Eastern Indian land claims see Canby, *American Indian Law in a Nutshell*, 348–52. When Reid Peyton Chambers, author of the solicitor's opinion of 1974 supporting the right of the Interior to recognize tribes (see note 28, above), indicated in correspondence three days after the final decision was handed down that review of recognition standards was under way, it was almost certainly in response to the Passamaquoddy decision. Reid Peyton Chambers, associate solicitor, Department of the Interior, Division of Indian Affairs, to Mrs. Karleen F. McKenzie, chairperson of the Tchinouk Indians, 14 February 1975, AIPRC box 76, "Submissions for the Records of Task Force Hearings, Oklahoma to Oregon," folder: "Salem, Oregon, Supportive Document."

31. The decision also eventually led to a settlement acknowledging that the State of Maine and the federal government were both responsible for compensating the tribe for losses.

32. Abourezk had been planning such a review in 1972, but the Wounded Knee occupation accelerated the program. See Thompson, "Nurturing the Forked Tree"; U.S. Congress, Joint Resolution to Provide for the Establishment of the American

Indian Policy Review Commission. Jeffrey Wollock suggests that Kickingbird and Deloria proposed the legislation to Abourezk in the first place. Wollock, "On the Wings of History," 26–27.

33. See Quinn, "Southeastern Indians." Quinn was an ethnohistorian for OFA when he wrote the paper.

34. American Indian Policy Review Commission, *Report on Terminated and Nonfederally Recognized Indians*, 1701.

35. Jojola, Foreword, xv.

36. American Indian Policy Review Commission, *Final Report of the American Indian Policy Review Commission*, vol. 1, 461–84.

37. Ibid., 461.

38. Task Force 10 did make one important recommendation that was never seriously considered by the BIA: the creation of an independent Congressional body to determine tribal eligibility for federal programs. This body would have been charged with recognizing tribes, immediately supplying them with resources, and then directing their transition into the federal-tribal system. The approach was intended to negate the anticipated conflict of interest that would arise if the BIA were left in charge of deciding which tribes it would serve, and to offset the delays in service delivery that tribes experience as their eligibility for programs is determined after recognition. While staff members of the current OFA have made the debatable claim that they never feel any pressure to decline to acknowledge a tribe that would significantly burden the BIA's already strained budget, there is certainly a conflict of interest in that OFA will never be adequately funded as long as it must draw its resources directly from the budget of a parent agency that prefers to allocate resources to established tribal groups. See statements of Kevin Gover regarding S. 611, Indian Federal Recognition Administrative Procedures Act of 1999, and H.R. 361, Indian Federal Recognition Administrative Procedures Act of 1998, each of which attempted to create an independent commission to replace OFA. Benjamin, "Bureau of Indian Affairs Getting Out of Recognition Business"; "Native American Agency Wants to Give Up Key Role"; Barry, "Agency Willing to Relinquish Power to Recognize Tribes."

39. American Indian Policy Review Commission, *Final Report of the American Indian Policy Review Commission*, vol. 1, 479.

40. The Stillaguamish Tribe, which had been petitioning for recognition for several years before the Passamaquoddy decision, forced the issue of federal responsibilities to Indian tribes. The tribe had been a plaintiff in the landmark case concerning tribal fishing rights, United States v. Washington (1975), in which Judge George Hugo Boldt ruled that the Stillaguamish and other tribes who signed the Treaty of Point Elliot (1855) had unextinguished treaty rights to fish since they had never ceased to be organized as a tribal body. In recognizing their treaty rights Boldt acknowledged the federal relationship with the tribe. The BIA was slower to come around, however, so the tribe filed suit against the Department of the Interior in October 1975. The suit, Stillaguamish v. Kleppe (1976), demanded that the

federal government make a decision on the petition. The Stillaguamish, it seems, had been caught up in the wave of federal indecision and confusion over recognition that led to "an unofficial moratorium on acknowledging tribes" (Quinn, "Federal Acknowledgment of American Indian Tribes," 363), and the judge in the case held that the DOI's "unexplained failure to act on plaintiff's petition for almost two and one-half years is arbitrary and capricious and an abuse of their discretion" (Stillaguamish v. Kleppe). The court order eventually led to an equivocal statement of recognition in October 1976 acknowledging only that certain aspects of a trust relationship existed, while still claiming that Interior lacked authority to fully recognize tribes without Congressional consent (Ruby and Brown, *Esther Ross*, 158–77, 185–86). While the BIA eventually fully acknowledged its trust responsibility to the tribe, the case was crucial for all nonrecognized tribes in forcing the BIA to quickly develop procedures to make decisions on petitions, rather than stonewalling and claiming to lack authority to decide on issues of recognition. Quinn, "Federal Acknowledgment of American Indian Tribes," 363. Stillaguamish v. Kleppe cited in Ruby and Brown, *Esther Ross*, 175.

41. For example, the Mashpee Wampanoag Tribe, the Narragansett Tribe, and the Mashantucket Pequot Tribe. See Canby, *American Indian Law in a Nutshell*, 348–52; Quinn, "Southeastern Indians."

42. David E. Lindgren, deputy solicitor, Department of the Interior, memorandum to undersecretary, 27 February 1976, extensively quoted in Bishop and Hansen, "A Report on the Landless Tribes of Washington State," 4.

43. Bishop and Hansen, "A Report on the Landless Tribes of Washington State," 5.

44. Proposed acknowledgment regulations published 16 June 1977, 42 Fed. Reg. 30647.

45. Quinn, "Southeastern Indians"; Anthony Paredes and J. Leitch Wright, Jr., eds. *From Big Game to Bingo: Native Peoples of the Southeastern United States: A Retrospective Occasioned by the Sesquicentennial of the Great Removal*, Proceedings of a conference conducted at Florida State University, 5–7 March 1987, 255–74. John A. "Bud" Shapard Jr. notes the same sequence of events in supplementary information provided with the proposed regulations, 43 Fed. Reg. 23743, 1 June 1978. The final regulation notice observes that the BIA took into account information gathered from four hundred meetings, discussions, and conversations with outside groups and sixty written comments, followed by a national conference on recognition, all of which contributed to the initial revision, and thirty-four more written comments on the second proposed regulations. 43 Fed. Reg. 39361, 5 September 1978.

46. Initially codified as 25 CFR § 54, later redesignated 25 CFR § 83.

47. 43 Fed. Reg. 39361, 5 September 1978.

48. The idea of an "American Indian renaissance" is generally attributed to the white anthropologist Nancy Lurie, who in 1964 asked whether a "renascence" was under way in Indian communities. The question framed a special issue of the *Mid-Continent American Studies Journal* that eventually became the popular book *The American Indian Today*. Levine and Lurie, eds., *The American Indian Today*. See espe-

cially Walker, "Some Limitations of the Renascence Concept in Acculturation," 235–56; and Nancy O. Lurie, "An American Indian Renascence?," 295–328. Kenneth Lincoln, professor of Native American literature, uses a narrower definition in his book *Native American Renaissance*, limiting the renaissance to scholarly and literary production. This book argues for a broader definition, one in which the Indian renaissance continues today.

49. Roger Jourdain to Noah Allen, 31 July 1975, records of the American Indian Policy Review Commission, Record Group 220.17.8, box 123, "Task Force Administrative Records, Unsorted Records," folder: "Indian Eligibility." In the copy in my possession, an unknown person has underlined "land based, federally recognized Indians," but it does not seem likely that the emphasis was in Jourdain's original letter.

50. Ibid.

51. George Tomer, Task Force 10 specialist, to Ernest Stevens, director, American Indian Policy Review Commission, 5 December 1975, American Indian Policy Review Commission, box 124, "Task Force Administrative Records, Unsorted Records," folder: "Inter-Task Force Communications."

52. National Congress of American Indians, Resolution no. 75–46, "Opposition to Federal Recognition of the Lumbees," cited in correspondence, Terry Polchies and Edward Bernard, Federal Regional Council of New England, Indian Task Force, to Mel Tonasket, president, National Congress of American Indians, 3 June 1976, American Indian Policy Review Commission, box 117, "Task Force Administrative Records, Task Force 10."

53. Sider, *Lumbee Indian Histories*, 268–69.

54. Charles Trimble, "Commentary," NCAI *Bulletin* (spring 1976), cited in correspondence, Terry Polchies and Edward Bernard, Federal Regional Council of New England, Indian Task Force, to Mel Tonasket, president, National Congress of American Indians, 3 June 1976, American Indian Policy Review Commission, box 117, "Task Force Administrative Records, Task Force 10."

55. See for example Delphine Red Shirt's editorial on Connecticut Indian tribes, "These Are Not Indians." Elisabeth Pierite, a Tunica-Biloxi tribal member, noted during a conversation in 2008 that a recruiter she spoke with at Haskell Indian Nations University initially doubted that the Tunica-Biloxi Tribe was federally recognized and had to look the information up on the internet, and that even the officials at the Alabama-Coushatta powwow in not-too-distant Livingston, Texas, did not believe the Tunica-Biloxis were a "real" federal tribe, and initially tried to prevent her from participating in their powwow on that basis, though she is close to half-Indian by blood.

56. Cited in Ruby and Brown, *Esther Ross*, 177–78, "from an unidentified and undated clipping in Esther [Ross]'s files."

57. Green, "Chief Seattle's Tribe Clings to Its Identity."

58. Testimony cited in Bordewich, *Killing the White Man's Indian*, 82.

59. Information submitted to the AIPRC by the landless tribes of Washington state suggests that the BIA introduced and fostered the concern about recognition of more

tribes among the Tulalips and the Swinomish in the 1970s. These tribes felt strongly that their political influence, their share of the state's salmon run, and their federal services would all be diminished significantly by extending recognition to the federally nonrecognized tribes in the area. The usefulness of this "grave" concern is questionable, since the tribe they spent the most time fighting, the Stillaguamish, had about a hundred members. Based on these suggestions, the Tulalips expended "tens of thousands of dollars in legal fees" fighting federal recognition of Puget Sound tribes. The fight proved imprudent: several of the groups that they opposed were recognized by the federal government, and the Tulalips eventually accepted them as recognized Indians. Bishop and Hansen, "A Report on the Landless Tribes of Washington State," 13–14.

60. National Congress of American Indians, "Indian Recognition."

61. Ibid. Indians are racially and culturally idealized subjects in the American imagination, and the degree to which petitioners fit popular constructions of Indians matters. Popular American constructions of Indians come to bear on the issue because of concerns over public opinion and Congressional support for tribal sovereignty. Congress is representative of the American people in both the degree to which it holds dear myths about Indians and the extent to which it must respond to the wishes of constituents who also hold these myths dear. When tribes fail to match these popular constructions of Indianness, certain tribes are concerned that public backlash will lead to Congressional backlash against tribal programs and tribal sovereignty. The ways politicians in Connecticut have assaulted the sovereignty of Indian tribes in race-baiting campaigns stands as a clear example of the potential dangers that some recognized tribes see in the recognition of Indian tribes with fewer racial and cultural markers. Opponents of further acknowledgment of Indian tribes would argue that recognition of tribes that are not easily "recognizable" (in the nonlegal sense) as Indians deepens the threat of backlash, making non-Indian popular conceptions of Indians consistently important in the ongoing discourse about Indian identity and federal recognition. See McCulloch and Wilkins, " 'Constructing' Nations within States," among others.

62. National Congress of American Indians, "Indian Recognition."

63. See Eva Garroutte's exceptional examination of the many issues, perspectives, and stakes involved. Garroutte, *Real Indians*.

64. Fogelson, Review of *Indians of the Southeastern United States in the Late 20th Century*, 501.

65. Setting aside the question of whether any individual of Indian descent in any degree ought to qualify as an Indian, which is certainly a sticky wicket in its own right, the question at hand is about sovereignty of a group rather than racial identity of an individual. There is another question to be asked. Does the federal or colonial government have obligations to all Indian descendants who want to call themselves Indian that might be in addition to or separate from its obligation to tribal nations? The IRA suggests that this is so, but limits the service pool to those who are half-Indian or more, though it is difficult to imagine that someone could be half-Indian or more and not have a tribe.

66. For example, the petitioner identified as "Federation: Moorish Science Temple of America, Inc." did not even claim to be Native American. U.S. Office of Federal Acknowledgment, "List of Petitioners by State as of September 22, 2008."

67. Clifford, *The Predicament of Culture*, 338.

68. Vine Deloria Jr., Statement from Senate Hearing 100-881 on S. 2672, 93. Quoted in U.S. Congress, *Federal Recognition Administrative Procedures Act*, 135.

69. See McCulloch and Wilkins, " 'Constructing' Nations within States."

70. American Indian Policy Review Commission, *Report on Terminated and Nonfederally Recognized Indians*, 1684. Though statements describing treatment as second-class Indians are ubiquitous, an AIPRC hearing in Virginia includes typical testimony about disputes between federal and nonfederal tribes. The statement, which is terribly transcribed, is presented by "Chief Ackins" (probably Chief Ozias Oliver Adkins) of the Chickahominy Tribe, and it demonstrates the frustrations of each side, the certain identity of most petitioning tribes, and the simple desire for unity on the part of federally nonrecognized tribes. Adkins states: "I know that Western Indians are not too happy about the possible that in days to come we might be receiving those services. I have meet with the Indian people in many areas of the nation and I find that many of those tribes are concern are deeply concern about the Indian here because when I was in Phoenix, Arizona quite recently the Housing and Urban Development those Indians could be deeply concern about the Indian of the East and many of those Indian told me say now look Chief you know we are not feed from the silver platter either, we have to pay for services, it not all given to us. And I find that if the Indian are United in which I am not hopefully, I hope our government would be in full court [accord] with the Indians, being united together and surely if we are united as a group of Indians nationally then there can be a lot of progress for the American Indians which is so greatly needed and it is a great concern for them as well." American Indian Policy Review Commission, box 59, "Testimony from Virginia," 8.

71. Gone, "Mental Health, Wellness, and the Quest for an Authentic American Indian Identity."

72. American Indian Policy Review Commission, *Report on Terminated and Nonfederally Recognized Indians*, 1695.

73. Ibid., 1684.

74. Momaday, *House Made of Dawn*, 58.

## Chapter 2: Early Recognition Efforts

1. Downs, "Documentation of the Tunica-Biloxi-Ofo-Avoyel Community Near Marksville, Louisiana," 202–3. At the time he wrote this report, Downs was working for the Institute for the Development of Indian Law, a group formed by Vine Deloria Jr. and others to research and interpret the relationship between Indians and the federal government.

2. Tunica history until about 1970 has been well documented elsewhere, particularly

in the materials produced as part of the Tunica-Biloxi petition for federal recognition in 1978 and in the federal review of these materials in 1980. I will reexamine their compelling history to that time before moving into more recent events that deal directly with the impact of OFA's recognition process and recognition itself. Native American Rights Fund, *Petition for Recognition of the Tunica-Biloxi Indian Tribe in Compliance with 25 CFR Part 54*; U.S. Office of Federal Acknowledgment, "Recommendation and Summary of Evidence for Proposed Finding for Federal Acknowledgment of the Tunica-Biloxi Indian Tribe of Louisiana Pursuant to 25 CFR 54." Analysis of Tunica history in the French and Spanish colonial eras can be found in Brain, *Tunica Archaeology*.

3. Jean O'Brien painstakingly illustrates the ways such dispossession happened through daily life among Massachusetts Indians in *Dispossession by Degrees*.

4. U.S. Office of Federal Acknowledgment, "Historical Report on the United Houma Nation, Inc.," 9. Merrell documents similar tribal amalgamations elsewhere in the South in *The Indians' New World*. For more information on the nature and extent of tribal mixing in Louisiana see also Kniffen, Gregory, and Stokes, *The Historic Tribes of Louisiana from 1542 to the Present*, 83–121. Patricia Galloway suggests that the Choctaw nation itself comprised many distinguishable groups, a "multiethnic confederacy of autonomous towns" that came together in the protohistorical period, sometime between the arrival of DeSoto in 1539 and the later European ventures in the area beginning in the late eighteenth century. Galloway, " 'So Many Little Republics.' "

5. Thwaites, ed., *The Jesuit Relations and Allied Documents*, 335–38, cited in U.S. Office of Federal Acknowledgment, "Recommendation and Summary of Evidence for Proposed Finding for Federal Acknowledgment of the Tunica-Biloxi Indian Tribe of Louisiana Pursuant to 25 CFR 54," 2. There is some debate among scholars over whether DeSoto's expedition encountered the Tunicas at the town of Quizquiz in 1541. The debate centers on whether Quizquiz was a Tunica town, since it was above the confluence of the Arkansas and Mississippi Rivers, far north of the site near Vicksburg, Mississippi, where the Tunicas were located in 1694. See Downs, "Documentation of the Tunica-Biloxi-Ofo-Avoyel Community near Marksville, Louisiana," 193, for details. Downs cites 1698 as the year of the encounter with the French. For a discussion of historical and archaeological evidence see Brain, *Tunica Archaeology*, 21–25.

6. Documentation of Tunica arrival by this date comes from an order from the Spanish governor general Miro to the commandant of the Avoyelles Post to protect Tunica rights to their lands in Avoyelles Prairie after the Tunicas had protested to him an attempt by a pair of colonists to gain title to their land. Miro to Gognard, 6 October 1786, *American State Papers: Public Lands*, vol. 2 (Washington: U.S. Government Printing Office, 1832), 243, cited in Downs, "Documentation of the Tunica-Biloxi-Ofo-Avoyel Community near Marksville, Louisiana," 201.

7. Article VI of the Louisiana Purchase Treaty states: "The United States promise to execute Such treaties and articles as may have been agreed between Spain and the

tribes and nations of Indians until by mutual consent of the United States and the said tribes or nations other Suitable articles Shall have been agreed upon." Spain's clear policy was to grant to the Indians one league square around their villages, and both Tunica land and the Spanish intention to protect it are specifically mentioned in Spanish colonial documents. See note 6, above. According to one source, a Spanish league consisted of 4,439 acres, or about seven square miles. Hager, "Tunicas Still Await Recognition." The Indian Trade and Intercourse Act in force at the time is cited by Donald Juneau as follows: Act of March 26, 1804, ch. 13, 2 Stat. 139, *amending* Act of March 3, 1799, ch. 46, 1 Stat. 743, *amending* Act of May 19, 1796, ch. 30, 1 Stat. 469, *amending* Act of March 1, 1793, ch. 19, 1 Stat. 329, *amending* Act of July 22, 1790, ch. 33. The present version of the Intercourse Act is the Act of June 30, 1834, ch. 161, 4 Stat. 729. See Rev. Stat. § 2116 (2d ed. 1878), now codified as 25 U.S.C. § 177. Juneau, "The Judicial Extinguishment of the Tunica Indian Tribe."

8. Juneau, "The Judicial Extinguishment of the Tunica Indian Tribe." I will not go into detail on the precise means of usurpation, since I would merely be reiterating Juneau's research.

9. State Land Office, Baton Rouge, *Pintado Papers*, vol. 20, 219–20, cited in Downs, "Documentation of the Tunica-Biloxi-Ofo-Avoyel Community Near Marksville, Louisiana," 202.

10. Decision of the Register and Receiver, Opelousas, Louisiana, 26 September 1826. Recorded in Works Progress Administration, *Survey of Federal Archives in Louisiana*, 74–75, cited in Downs, "Documentation of the Tunica-Biloxi-Ofo-Avoyel Community Near Marksville, Louisiana," 202–3. The basis for the accusation of savagery is unknown, since the Tunicas were predominantly agricultural and by 1813 had "adopted the manners and customs of the French." Darby, *Immigrants Guide to Western and Southwestern States and Territories*, cited in U.S. Office of Federal Acknowledgment, "Anthropological Report on the Tunica-Biloxi Indian Tribe," 8. Still, the tribe still spoke its own language and surely practiced certain customs alien to its French neighbors, so while Mr. Bordelon's motivations for the accusation are obvious, the accusation itself is not clear. The decision may be based on the U.S. Supreme Court decision in Johnson v. M'Intosh, which gave force of law to the so-called doctrine of discovery, entitling Europeans to "take possession [of land] notwithstanding the occupancy of the natives, who were heathens." Johnson v. M'Intosh, 576–77.

11. Juneau, "The Judicial Extinguishment of the Tunica Indian Tribe."

12. Moreau v. Valentine, discussed in Juneau, "The Judicial Extinguishment of the Tunica Indian Tribe," 60–73.

13. Downs, "Documentation of the Tunica-Biloxi-Ofo-Avoyel Community Near Marksville, Louisiana," 205–6.

14. Juneau, "The Judicial Extinguishment of the Tunica Indian Tribe," 72.

15. Brenda Child makes a similar argument about the ways Indians blame boarding schools for their cultural and language loss, to the point where boarding schools become a metaphor for all the other less easily identifiable forces of assimilation

(television, popular culture, local day schools) that have perhaps contributed more than boarding schools to language loss. Boarding schools certainly contributed devastatingly to assimilation, but they have become a shorthand way of talking about and naming grief over cultural loss. Child, Preface, *Boarding School Seasons*, 2nd edn.

16. Downs, "Documentation of the Tunica-Biloxi-Ofo-Avoyel Community Near Marksville, Louisiana," 207. Downs spells the name Chiki, while the OFA report uses the same spelling as the court case. U.S. Office of Federal Acknowledgment, "Recommendation and Summary of Evidence for Proposed Finding for Federal Acknowledgment of the Tunica-Biloxi Indian Tribe of Louisiana Pursuant to 25 CFR 54," 11. The OFA report cites the case as State v. Chiqui, 49 La. Ann. 131, 21 So. 51 [*recte* 513] (1897).

17. D. W. Browning to S. D. McEnery, 9 December 1896, Letters Sent, Land, vol. 172, pp. 112–13, Record Group 75, National Archives, cited in U.S. Office of Federal Acknowledgment, "History Report on Tunica-Biloxi Indian Tribe," 11. This section of the letter is also cited in State v. Chiqui.

18. State v. Chiqui; U.S. Office of Federal Acknowledgment, "History Report on Tunica-Biloxi Indian Tribe," 11.

19. 23 U.S. Stat. 62; Baca, "The Legal Status of American Indians," 236.

20. See Harring, *Crow Dog's Case*, esp. chapter 4 ("Crow Dog's Case"), 100–141, for a discussion of the development of the Major Crimes Act. The act was not extended over the Five Civilized Tribes (see Talton v. Mayes).

21. Downs, "Documentation of the Tunica-Biloxi-Ofo-Avoyel Community Near Marksville, Louisiana," 207. This information was also relayed to me in an interview, but it is unclear whether the person who told me learned about it from Downs's work or from tribal oral history, which was Downs's original source anyway.

22. Youchican v. Texas & Pacific Railway. There are several spellings of Sesostrie Youchigant's name. I have chosen that used by the linguist Mary Haas, since her trained ear probably recorded the most accurate spelling of his name. Haas, *Tunica Dictionary*.

23. See Harris, "Whiteness as Property."

24. See d'Oney, *A Kingdom of Water*.

25. Juneau, "The Judicial Extinguishment of the Tunica Indian Tribe," 86–99; Downs, "Documentation of the Tunica-Biloxi-Ofo-Avoyel Community Near Marksville, Louisiana," 207–8.

26. U.S. Representative J. B. Aswell to Charles H. Burke, commissioner of Indian affairs, 22 December 1925, Record Group 75, 78634-1925-Genl Service File No. 3074.

27. Charles H. Burke, commissioner of Indian affairs, to U.S. Representative J. B. Aswell, 28 December 1925, Record Group 75, 78634-1925-Genl Service File no. 3074. Chitimacha Tribe recognized by the Act of 18 May 1916 (39 Stat. 123).

28. Sibley, "Historical Sketches of the Several Indian Tribes in Louisiana, South of the Arkansas and between the Mississippi and River Grande," 725.

29. Jean O'Brien also notes that the trope of Indian disappearance was consistently used to dispossess Indians in New England. O'Brien, *Dispossession by Degrees*.

30. The switch to a two-chief system may have been due to conflicts between the Pierite and Barbry-Chiki-Youchigant family lines.

31. In an unpublished paper completed as a requirement for a master's degree in history at the University of New Orleans, John Barbry cites a letter kept in the private collection of Mary Vercher, Tunica-Biloxi Reservation, Marksville, Louisiana: C. F. Hauke, Department of the Interior, to Elijah Barbry, 2 November 1922. Barbry, "Tunica-Biloxi Tribalism and Indian Policy Reform, 1922–1947," 16.

32. Document included in Native American Rights Fund, *Petition for Recognition of the Tunica-Biloxi Indian Tribe in Compliance with 25 CFR Part 54*, though its source is unclear. Header reads: "State of Louisiana—Parish of Rapides." OFA cites the document as "Biloxi Tribe, et al., 1924, Signed copy of statement by Biloxi Indian tribe and members of the Choctaw Indian Tribe residing in different parts of the State of Louisiana. October 9, 1924, Woodworth, Louisiana." For purposes of continuity I will use the same citation.

33. "Biloxi Tribe, et al., 1924."

34. John Barbry notes that Eli Barbry attempted similar coalitions with the Coushattas and Chitimachas. The Coushattas signed the document but the Chitimachas apparently refused, since they had already been federally recognized as a tribe in 1916. Barbry, "Tunica-Biloxi Tribalism and Indian Policy Reform, 1922–1947," 15–16.

35. According to statements made to OFA during the review of the Tunica-Biloxi petition, "the attitude of the Marksville community, judging by current informants, was not so much that they opposed this but that Barbry, who was only sub-chief, was overstepping himself." U.S. Office of Federal Acknowledgment, "Anthropological Report on the Tunica-Biloxi Indian Tribe," 17. Barbry's actions suggest that the appointment of Ernest Pierite as chief may have been contested or age-based and honorary, and Barbry may have been acting according to reasonable expectations.

36. The earliest Indian policy reform efforts of the 1920s began with the Bursum bill in 1922, which Margaret Connell Szasz describes as a cause célèbre of the day. The issue catalyzed the Indian reform movement that fairly engrossed public sentiment of the 1920s and perhaps peaked with the release of the so-called Meriam Report in 1928. See Szasz, *Education and the American Indian*, 13–15; Brookings Institution, Institute for Government Research, *The Problem of Indian Administration*, widely known as the Meriam Report. Letters from supporters of Louisiana Indians are too numerous to cite individually but can be found in the following files: General Service File 67669-1931-053, General Service File 78634-1925-307.4, File 68776-1931-800, all in Record Group 75, National Archives.

37. Ray Lyman Wilbur, secretary of the interior, to T. H. Harris, Louisiana state superintendent of education, 3 March 1932, File 68776-1931-800, part I, Record Group 75, National Archives.

38. Ibid.

39. George Roth, anthropologist for OFA, discusses some of these attitudes toward "recognizing" tribes elsewhere in the South in the early twentieth century, citing a report from the Commissioner of Indian Affairs in 1912 which stated that "in many

cases these Indians have worked out for themselves problems which the service has still to meet in other parts of the field," thereby excusing the federal government from taking responsibility for these tribes. Commissioner of Indian affairs, *Annual Report of the Commissioner of Indian Affairs to the Secretary of the Interior for the Fiscal year Ended June 30, 1911*; Roth, "Federal Tribal Recognition and the South," 52.

40. This policy began in 1891 and continued until the Johnson-O'Malley Act in 1934 empowered the bureau to contract with states, which would then oversee distribution of federal Indian funds to school districts with Indian students. Szasz, *Education and the American Indian*, 89–92.

41. Several Coushatta individuals had allotted land in trust, but there was no communally held trust land, so the government reasoned at this time that no action was needed.

42. Even the Chitimacha reservation, at 225 acres, was not big enough to have any sizable negative impact on the St. Mary's Parish tax revenues, though, and since parish schools would not admit Chitimacha children to white schools and they would not attend black schools, the commissioner of Indian affairs, C. J. Rhoads, saw no reason to offer to make payments to the parish for their education. In that light it is clearer why federal officials denied aid to the Tunicas, whose reservation was not held in trust by the federal government, and who faced the same segregation issues. C. J. Rhoads to Senator Huey P. Long, 26 April 1932, File 68776-1931-800, part I.

43. Some have argued that Indians and other people of color lived in a constant state of economic depression, so the Great Depression brought no new hardships to them and even brought in new jobs under Roosevelt's "alphabet" programs, such as the WPA and the CCC. My point, however, is that under white supremacy people of color would generally be last hired and first fired, except in situations where their willingness to work for low wages out of desperation was being exploited.

44. At one point Indians provided the bulk of temporary migrant labor on American farms. See Littlefield and Knack, eds., *Native Americans and Wage Labor*.

45. William A. Morrow to John Collier, 16 May 1933; John Collier to William A. Morrow, 1 June 1933; William A. Morrow to John Overton, 19 January 1934; Senator John Overton to William A. Morrow, 23 January 1934; John Overton to John Collier, 23 January 1934; John Collier to John Overton, 12 February 1934, File 67669-1931-General Service-053, Record Group 75, National Archives.

46. Charles H. Burke, commissioner of Indian affairs, to U.S. Representative J. B. Aswell, 29 December 1925, Record Group 75, 78634-1925-Genl Service File no. 3074.

47. John Collier, commissioner of Indian affairs, to U.S. Senator John Overton, 12 February 1934, File 67669-1931-General Service File no. 53, Record Group 75, National Archives.

48. Senator John Overton to William A. Morrow, 23 January 1934, File 67669-1931-General Service-053, Record Group 75, National Archives.

49. A. C. Hector, superintendent, Choctaw Indian Agency, to W. Carson Ryan, director of education, Bureau of Indian Affairs, 12 September 1934, File 68776-1931-800, part I, National Archives, Record Group 75.

50. A. C. Hector to John Collier, 17 July 1935, File 68776-1931-800, part I, National Archives, Record Group 75.

51. A "half-breed Indian girl" was enrolled in the white school in Columbia, Louisiana, a town about thirty-five miles north of Jena. A. C. Hector to John Collier, 21 March 1936, 27 March 1937, File 68776-1931-800, part I, National Archives, Record Group 75. Similarly, a Chitimacha boy was allowed to attend the white school in nearby Franklin, Louisiana, but his tribal status prevented him from attending white schools in Charenton, only ten miles away. A. C. Hector to C. J. Rhoads, 15 December 1932, File 68776-1931-800, part I, National Archives, Record Group 75.

52. Kelly, "United States Indian Policies, 1900–1980," 73.

53. Barbry, "Tunica-Biloxi Tribalism and Indian Policy Reform, 1922–1947."

54. Representative A. Leonard Allen to Office of Indian Affairs, 17 May 1938; Senator John A. Overton to John Collier, 8 June 1938; William Zimmerman Jr., assistant commissioner, to Allen, 9 June 1938; Zimmerman to Overton, 15 June 1938, file 30322-1938-066, National Archives, Record Group 75.

55. Barbry, "Tunica-Biloxi Tribalism and Indian Policy Reform, 1922–1947," 18; U.S. Office of Federal Acknowledgment, "Anthropological Report on the Tunica-Biloxi Indian Tribe," 20.

56. Fred H. Daiker, assistant to the commissioner, memorandum, 15 September 1938, File 68776-1931-800, part 2, National Archives, Record Group 75.

57. Office of Federal Acknowledgment, "Anthropological Report on the Tunica-Biloxi Indian Tribe," 20.

58. Ernest Downs notes that a copy of the IRA was found in a shoebox full of Eli Barbry's old papers kept by his great-grandson, Mike Barbry, in 1975. Downs, "Documentation of the Tunica-Biloxi-Ofo-Avoyel Community Near Marksville, Louisiana," 208. Ruth Underhill noted that "Eli has been very active in looking up the land rights of the Indians and, for a person who cannot read, has collected an amazing number of documents." Underhill, "Report on a Visit to Indian Groups in Louisiana, Oct. 15–25, 1938."

59. Underhill, "Report on a Visit to Indian Groups in Louisiana."

60. The only Indian-black marriage that I am aware of at that time is that of Herman Pierite Sr. and his wife. According to Inez Sampson, a tribal member and the daughter of Herman Pierite Sr., Percy Pierite fathered children by a black woman around the same time, but never married her. Herman and Percy Pierite were brothers of Joseph Pierite Sr., who married a woman from Biloxi. Marshall Sampson, son of Inez Sampson, says that all current tribal members with African American ancestry are descended from these two men.

61. Willard W. Beatty to "Joe" (not Joe Jennings), 19 January 1939, File 68776-1931-800, part 2, National Archives, Record Group 75.

62. Ranging from folktales about people actually having red bones to the assertion that it came from *red ibo*, a West Indian term applied to any group of mixed ancestry. Pronounced *reddy bone*, it eventually became "red bone," according to J. L. Dillard, an authority on Black English in the United States, cited in Kniffen, Gregory, and

Stokes, *The Historic Tribes of Louisiana from 1542 to the Present*, 92, though the authors do not cite the exact work where Dillard makes this argument. There are similar terms in use to describe various communities around the country of mixed racial heritage, such as Sabines, Yellowhammers, Brass Ankles, Melungeons, Spanish Whites, and Jackson Whites. Older academic literature has often referred to such communities as "tri-racial isolates" or "little races," among other terms, and authors and local communities have often included in these groupings populations that consider themselves Indian, such as the Tunica-Biloxis, the Clifton-Choctaws, and the Houma tribe in Louisiana. While these communities have some members with black ancestry, they are bound together in varying degrees by kinship and Indian identity, not their black, white, or mixed ancestry. Certain members of these mixed Indian communities have downplayed their group's black ancestry to some extent, often in response to attempts by outsiders to inflate it or give it prominence by using terms like "Redbone." It is a convenient argument that they identify as Indians because doing so is "better" than being identified as black, but the fact that some of them could also "choose" to be identified as Creole or black does not mean that they are not an Indian group. A representative sample of the literature on triracial isolates would include the following: Berry, *Almost White*; Ball, "America's Mysterious Race"; Beale, "American Triracial Isolates"; Estabrook and McDougle, *Mongrel Virginians*; Gilbert, "Race, Cultural Groups, Social Differentiation"; Griessman, "The American Isolates" (a short introduction to a section of the journal that includes several relevant articles on the theme); and Parenton and Pellegrin, "The Sabines." A recent article by Dave Davis in *Ethnohistory* makes the assertion that the Houma tribe is "really" a triracial isolate and therefore not "really" a tribe, based solely on OFA proposed findings, with no apparent original research of his own. Davis, "A Case of Identity." Virginia Dominguez makes this assertion in the otherwise respectable *White by Definition*, 204. Forbes also makes the insightful comment that "no one would be so stupid as to ask a Briton how much British ancestry he has (as opposed to Scandinavian, Anglo-Saxon, Norman French, Roman, et cetera) or to ask a Spaniard how much native Iberian ancestry he claims (as opposed to Carthaginian, Roman, Celtic, Germanic or North African, et cetera)." Forbes, "The Manipulation of Race, Caste and Identity," 30–31.

63. Underhill, "Report on a Visit to Indian Groups in Louisiana, Oct. 15–25, 1938," 25.
64. For information on the Bosra claim see U.S. Office of Federal Acknowledgment, "Anthropological Report on the Tunica-Biloxi Indian Tribe," 9–10.
65. Barbry, "Tunica-Biloxi Tribalism and Indian Policy Reform, 1922–1947," 21; U.S. Office of Federal Acknowledgment, "Anthropological Report on the Tunica-Biloxi Indian Tribe," 20.
66. Underhill, "Report on a Visit to Indian Groups in Louisiana, Oct. 15–25, 1938," 27. The striking parallels of this quote to Barbara Bush's quote at the Houston Astrodome after Hurricane Katrina provide the basis for an article on Tunica experiences with Hurricane Katrina. "Almost everyone I've talked to says, 'We're going to move to Houston.' What I'm hearing, which is sort of scary, is they all want to stay

in Texas. Everyone is so overwhelmed by the hospitality. And so many of the people in the arena here, you know, were underprivileged anyway, so this—this is
working very well for them." Klopotek, Lintinger, and Barbry, "Ordinary and
Extraordinary Trauma."

67. Keith Basso's pathbreaking work on the importance of place in Western Apache
culture suggests that scholars need to pay close attention to the connection of
indigenous peoples in particular to their places. Basso, *Wisdom Sits in Places*.

68. In the early 1930s the WPA made a state park out of a mound group near the reservation. It sent a team of archaeologists to investigate the mounds. Chief Eli Barbry
and a couple of other men from the tribe took rifles to the excavation site and
chased them away. One archaeologist finally coaxed their fingers off the trigger by
convincing them that these gravesites were from a prehistoric tribe, not Tunicas.
Later investigations in the 1960s revealed more recent burials, so it is likely that
Tunicas were buried there as well. See American Indian Policy Review Commission, Task Force Ten, Baton Rouge hearings, 56–57; Barbry, "Tunica-Biloxi Tribalism and Indian Policy Reform, 1922–1947," 12–13. The problem continued in the
1970s, with the tribal chairman Joe Pierite Jr. complaining that the state park
authorities let people walk all over the graves of his ancestors. He complained
about this during the AIPRC hearing in Baton Rouge (56–57) and on the ABC News
segment with Vine Deloria. "As a tradition, we . . . pay close attention to our
dead . . . and respect them very highly. So this doesn't look right at all for someone
to be running up and down. Nobody be able to see any tracks across the graveyard." "ABC News: Americans All," 2. According to Joe Pierite Jr., the park put up a
fence around the mounds the day after the broadcast, but there is no fence today.

69. See note 6, above, documenting Tunica presence in Avoyelles Prairie in 1786.

70. Dormon "used her influence to secure aid from the Red Cross and government
loans to grow crops." Barbry, "Tunica-Biloxi Tribalism and Indian Policy Reform,
1922–1947," 9, from correspondence in the Caroline Dormon Collection, Watson
Memorial Library, Northwestern State University, Natchitoches, La. Swanton "disguised a five dollar donation to [Sesostrie Youchigant] as prepayment for language
work they would do in the future." Ibid. On Robert "Stu" Neitzel, Barbry cites
H.F. Gregory: "There was yet another Stu Neitzel that the Tunica and I knew. He
met them in the 1930's and kept up a running correspondence with Frank Speck
about them. The late Joseph Alcide Pierite was his close friend. 'Bob' was their
model friend among non-Indians. He was helpful (especially during the Depression, when it was hardest to do so), one of their closest neighbors for a long time,
but he stayed out of their business, honored their elders and traditions. He shared
their love of the woods and bayous and knew them as the complicated folks they
were, not as stereotypes." Brain and Brown, eds., *Robert S. Neitzel*, 38, cited in Barbry, "Tunica-Biloxi Tribalism and Indian Policy Reform, 1922–1947," 13. Frank
Speck "actively advised tribes of available government aid and contacted the Office
of Education (BIA) and other federal agencies on behalf of the communities. His
efforts encouraged the Tunica-Biloxi and Houmas to actively approach the

bureaucracy in Washington, D.C.—which seemed a world away." Barbry, "Tunica-Biloxi Tribalism and Indian Policy Reform, 1922–1947," 30, cites the following sources in support of this claim: Robert S. Neitzel, Field Notes on the Tunica and Biloxi and Correspondence with Frank Speck, 1938–40, Frank G. Speck Papers, Library of the American Philosophical Society, Philadelphia; Underhill, "Report on a Visit to Indian Groups in Louisiana, Oct. 15–25, 1938," 1; Frank G. Speck, University of Pennsylvania, to W. C. Beatty, Department of the Interior, Bureau of Indian Affairs, 7 February 1939, File 68776-1931-800, Record Group 75, National Archives. Haas worked extensively with Sesostrie Youchigant, documenting the Tunica language and many Tunica stories before they were lost forever. Haas, *Tunica Texts*.

71. Barbry, "Tunica-Biloxi Tribalism and Indian Policy Reform, 1922–1947," 13, 23–24. Barbry cites among others H. F. "Pete" Gregory's homage to Neitzel in Brain and Brown, eds., *Robert S. Neitzel*, 38.

72. Willard W. Beatty to William Zimmerman, 7 February 1939, File 68776-1931-800, part 2, National Archives, Record Group 75.

73. F. H. Daiker, assistant commissioner, to Horace Pierite, 20 February 1939, File 30322-1938-066, Record Group 75, National Archives. Identical letter sent to Eli Barbry, 1 May 1939, same file. This response despite the recent decision of the solicitor to extend recognition to the Mole Lake Chippewas. See chapter 1.

74. Barbry, "Tunica-Biloxi Tribalism and Indian Policy Reform, 1922–1947," 20. Cites Representative A. Leonard Allen to Mr. Wheat, Land Division, Department of the Interior, 7 and 29 October 1940; William Zimmerman Jr. to Eli Barbry, 12 November 1940, File 30322-1938-066, Record Group 75, National Archives. Barbry may have corresponded with Senator Russell Long in 1951. See note 4 to chapter 3.

75. U.S. Office of Federal Acknowledgment, "Anthropological Report on the Tunica-Biloxi Indian Tribe," 20–21.

*Chapter 3: Tunica Activism*

1. A. H. McMullen, superintendent of the Choctaw Indian Agency, to William Zimmerman, 1 March 1949, Records of the Choctaw-Mississippi Agency, Record Group 75, National Archives, cited in U.S. Office of Federal Acknowledgment, "History Report on Tunica-Biloxi Indian Tribe," 14.

2. This according to Rose Pierite White, Joe Pierite Sr.'s youngest daughter and one of the first Tunica-Biloxis admitted to white schools in Marksville. I could find no corroborating record of this event in the Avoyelles Parish School Board minutes, but the correspondence with McMullen is confirmed, as is the integration of Tunica children into white schools around this time.

3. Attorney Francis C. Gremillion, Marksville, to Senator Russell B. Long, 22 July 1951, cited in Native American Rights Fund, *Petition for Recognition of the Tunica-Biloxi Indian Tribe in Compliance with 25 CFR Part 54*, 3. A footnote states that the letter is in possession of "the Pierite family."

4. The Tunica-Biloxi petition cites a letter from Senator Russell Long to Eli Barbry

dated 28 September 1950, informing Barbry that the senator had requested federal services for the tribe. It could be that a recording error was to blame, and that the letter from Long to Barbry was actually written in September 1951, in response to the known letter of Gremillion to Long of 22 July 1951. I have not seen the letters, so I cannot offer any further suggestions. That the letter was addressed to Barbry, who had not been the chief since 1947, suggests that Barbry was still actively pursuing recognition for the tribe, even though he had been deposed as chief. Russell Long began his career in the Senate in 1948, so unless he was responding to a letter to his predecessor, Senator John Overton, who had died in office that year, Barbry appears to have continued his activism even after stepping down from official tribal leadership.

5. U.S. Office of Federal Acknowledgment, "Anthropological Report on the Tunica-Biloxi Indian Tribe," 21.

6. Among the pictures that the tribal member Brenda Lintinger has in a digital collection is one of Rose Pierite White, with a caption indicating her title as princess. Rose Pierite White told me about the duties of the role.

7. I have been told of at least one tribal member who was one-eighth Indian in ancestry who graduated from a high school in East Texas in 1945. Her father insisted that she and the other children never tell anyone they were Indian for fear that they would not be able to enroll in the white schools. There may be other tribal members who graduated from high school elsewhere, but Rose Pierite (White was her married name, added later) was the first to graduate from a local school.

8. Rose Pierite White cited the date of the appearance as 1961 or 1962. Since the Pierite family appeared with Michel Smith, the correct date is likely August 1961, when several local newspapers covered his excavation and finds. "Old Money, Metal Pieces Found in Ancient Grave"; "Archaeologist to Probe Marksville Burial Site"; "Tunicas Find Grave in Marksville."

9. This according to Rose Pierite White. I still lack paper confirmation that they were requesting recognition this early from the state. I know that they were asking by the early 1970s, and that they were told then that they needed to incorporate first, but I do not know whether that was so in the early 1960s. The picture of Joseph Pierite Sr. and his daughters in generic Indian regalia appearing with Michel Smith on a television show is discussed in the note above. KALB, the only station operating in Alexandria at the time, has no records or archives from that era, so the date and content cannot be verified, though it is most likely August 1961. White's statement that state recognition was being sought at that time is bolstered by her having specifically connected the recognition efforts with the TV program. In a chronological recounting of the recognition efforts, she recalled that the tribe began to be involved with CENA (Coalition of Eastern Native Americans) later, around 1970 (the organization was formed in 1972). CENA helped them organize and write a charter by 1974.

10. Louisiana Public Broadcasting, "A Promise from the Sun."

11. Representative Speedy O. Long to Stewart Udall, secretary of the interior, 20 July

1965, copy in possession of the Pierite family. Letter quoted in Native American Rights Fund, *Petition for Recognition of the Tunica-Biloxi Indian Tribe in Compliance with 25 CFR Part 54.*

12. Letter quoted in Native American Rights Fund, *Petition for Recognition of the Tunica-Biloxi Indian Tribe in Compliance with 25 CFR Part 54*, 34. Graham Holmes, assistant comissioner (legislation), to Representative Speedy O. Long, 18 March 1965. Copy kept by the Barbry family.

13. Deloria, *Custer Died for Your Sins*, 245–46.

14. Native American Rights Fund, *Petition for Recognition of the Tunica-Biloxi Indian Tribe in Compliance with 25 CFR Part 54*, 60–62. Petition notes that Chief Joseph Pierite had addressed the convention of the National Congress of American Indians in Albuquerque in 1969 regarding the status of Louisiana Indians, and that the NCAI responded with a resolution to support the "4,000 Indian people living in the State of Louisiana in dire poverty" as much as possible out of its offices in Washington without "any help from the Bureau of Indian Affairs or the State of Louisiana."

15. Cullen, "Tunicas Move toward Organization, Recognition." The CENA date of inception is cited elsewhere as 1971 and 1973, but Cullen's article, published in 1973, and an interview with the CENA figure W.J. Strickland in 1974 reliably cite the date of organization as December 1972. The organization was incorporated in March 1973. "Interview with WJ Strickland."

16. Indian Angels incorporated as a nonprofit organization on 3 December 1969 in Baton Rouge. Transcript of Task Force 5 and Task Force 10 joint hearings in Baton Rouge, Louisiana, March 1976, 11. American Indian Policy Review Commission, Task Force Ten, Baton Rouge hearings. The only available history of the group is Dennis Booker's master's thesis comparing its approach to Indian identity with the Koasati (Coushatta) approach to Indian identity. Booker, "Indian Identity in Louisiana."

17. "Located South of Marksville." In 1968 Chief Pierite requested the state Department of Highways to place a sign in front of the Tunica-Biloxi reservation that would read, "Tunica and Biloxi Trading Post." The department obliged. Native American Rights Fund, *Petition for Recognition of the Tunica-Biloxi Indian Tribe in Compliance with 25 CFR Part 54*, 49.

18. Donna Pierite, Joe Pierite Jr.'s daughter-in-law, recalls that on the many occasions when she and her husband would appear with Joe Pierite Jr. at various public events or meetings, he would always ask her to wear beads or something red. He wanted their appearance to demonstrate to the outside world their pride in themselves and their Indian ancestry.

19. The Indian Angels were never really radical or numerous, but they were very vocal. They initiated the first modern powwows in the state, knowing that the beads, feathers, and dancing would generate public interest, even though they also knew that the Plains regalia and dancing styles of powwows were not native to the area. Powwows provided them with opportunities to politick, in addition to ave-

nues for cultural expression. The Indian Angels positioned themselves as spokes-persons for Indians of Louisiana, and applied political pressure directly and indirectly on various state politicians through their high-profile events. See Booker, "Indian Identity in Louisiana." During interviews in 1998 and 1999 the anthropologist H. F. "Pete" Gregory also provided personal reminiscences about the Indian political scene in the 1970s with reference to Sarah Peralta and the Indian Angels.

20. American Indian Policy Review Commission, Task Force Ten, Baton Rouge hearings, 160. Governor Edwin Edwards, a native of the Marksville area, paid special attention to "minority" issues in his gubernatorial campaign of 1971, and in 1972 instituted the Commission on Indian Affairs, an unfunded entity, as partial fulfillment of his campaign promises. He directed the commission to promote economic development in tribal communities and encourage cultural survival programs. The commission suggested that a funded office be created to permanently coordinate state Indian policy. Based on that recommendation Edwards created the Governor's Office of Indian Affairs in 1973 within the Health and Human Resources Administration. Ernest Sickey, the Coushatta tribal chairman who had previously been vice-commissioner of the Commission on Indian Affairs, was appointed director and given a small salary. It is not clear at this point to what extent the Indian Angels' political maneuvers prompted Edwards to pay attention to Indian affairs in the state. He may have been motivated by their work, his awareness of the Tunica people near his hometown, the political efforts of the Coushattas, or other undetermined factors. A review of Edwards's archives may provide some clues.

21. Booker, "Indian Identity in Louisiana," 42–61. The Indian Angels and the Louisiana Office of Indian Affairs, though seemingly conflicted in the methods they used, both worked hard to improve the lives of Indians in Louisiana, and both worked with tribes to help them organize, achieve recognition, and receive various forms of funding. Two fundamental differences turned out to be key factors in the eventual dominance of the LOIA voice in Louisiana Indian politics. First, the Office of Indian Affairs had an institutionalized position, with the appearance of access to power, that the Indian Angels simply did not have. Louisiana tribes had been eager to work with formal government offices for a number of years, so many enthusiastically embraced the new state program created for them. Second, the Office of Indian Affairs focused much more on developing programs through tribal structures, while the Indian Angels, though they did spend some energy on tribally based initiatives, seemed to think of Indians as a singular interest group. As a primarily urban pan-Indian group, they regarded Indians in some ways as more of a racial group than a set of independent political, cultural, and social entities. They easily molded themselves along the lines of other racial power movements of the period, but the model tended to negate cultural distinctions between tribal communities and the significance of tribal polity, which ran counter to the political strategies of leaders in tribal communities. The Indian Angels' confrontational methods and continual claims to represent Indian voices in Louisiana also began to

grate on tribal leaders. Many of their efforts were geared toward the urban Indian community in Baton Rouge, and sometimes they even raised money to send aid to distant tribes, such as the Northern Cheyennes. Not that tribal communities in Louisiana were unmoved by or unaware of the problems of urban Indians in Baton Rouge or Indians outside the state, but they had pressing needs of their own that they felt were better addressed through their tribes' political standing with the Office of Indian Affairs. Ultimately, Indian tribes in Louisiana believed that their greatest realizable asset was their ability to establish relationships with the state and federal governments, so they maintained a steady focus on activism based on tribal recognition.

22. "ABC News: Americans All"; Grant, "Tunicas, Indian Author Are TV Subject"; Cullen, "Tunicas Move toward Organization, Recognition." On a side note, central Louisiana did not have an ABC affiliate until 1985, when KLAX in Alexandria began broadcasting ABC programs. For Tunicas in Marksville it would have been nearly impossible to tune in to the documentary from a Baton Rouge station.

23. Cullen, "Tunicas Move toward Organization, Recognition."

24. "ABC News: Americans All," 5. Note that Deloria saw no need to have the support of the large black community in the area. His idea of coalition building at the time meant ensuring that local whites in power would not work to block Indian efforts for self-determination. Blacks were irrelevant to the equation because they themselves had little access to power. At the time Deloria did not see much potential in grassroots coalition building between people of color to force access to power. In *Custer Died for Your Sins* he argued that Indians did not belong in the civil rights movement or other movements among people of color, because the relationship between Indian tribes and the United States is one between sovereign nations, which other groups of color failed to understand. The sovereign-to-sovereign relationship by its nature allows Indian tribes to have more access to power than they could achieve through protest, making protest a waste of time and energy and a potential affront to the very politicians with whom Indians needed to cultivate relationships. In later years Deloria became more supportive of coalitions among Indians and other people of color, but he always maintained that tribal sovereignty must remain the central focus of Native American political expression.

25. The Coushattas were administratively recognized as eligible for federal services on 27 June 1973. There was some discussion that they had been terminated, since they were receiving federal services from the mid-1930s to 1953. The BIA withdrew services from the tribe and conveyed trust land in fee to tribal members at that time in anticipation of Congressional termination, but legislation "failed to materialize." Raymond V. Butler, acting director, Office of Indian Services, to secretary of the interior, 13 June 1973; Marvin L. Franklin, assistant to the secretary of the interior, to David Garrison, 27 June 1973. Copies of both letters provided in "A Report on the Landless Tribes of Washington State," box 315, "Unidentified Records," Records of the American Indian Policy Review Commission, 1975–77. See also Johnson, *The Coushatta People*.

26. Booker, "Indian Identity in Louisiana," 48.

27. Replaced by the Job Training Partnership Act (JTPA).

28. State of Louisiana, House Concurrent Resolution 240. See Native American Rights Fund, *Petition for Recognition of the Tunica-Biloxi Indian Tribe in Compliance with 25 CFR Part 54*, 50–51. See also American Indian Policy Review Commission, Task Force Ten, Baton Rouge hearings, 46, testimony of Ernest Downs: "Mr. Sickey helped the Tunicas write this state recognition bill that was presented before the Assembly and insured that the bill got passed." Joe Pierite Jr., the son of Chief Joseph Pierite and also the first elected chairman of the Tunica tribe, during testimony to the American Indian Policy Review Commission in 1976 cited help that the Coushattas gave his tribe in organizing and achieving state recognition, undoubtedly a reference to Sickey. American Indian Policy Review Commission, Task Force Ten, Baton Rouge hearings, 29.

29. Testimony of Helen Gindrat, Houma Tribe, Inc. (one of two predecessors that joined to form the United Houma Nation), American Indian Policy Review Commission, Task Force Ten, Baton Rouge hearings, 104–6.

30. Poe, "Neglect Peaceful Louisiana Indian." The quote in the article is from Ernest Downs, who was working on the Tunica-Biloxi petition at the time. The Poarch Creeks and Ysleta del Sur Tiguas were other key examples.

31. Native American Rights Fund, *Petition for Recognition of the Tunica-Biloxi Indian Tribe in Compliance with 25 CFR Part 54*, 73.

32. American Indian Policy Review Commission, Task Force Ten, Baton Rouge hearings, 49.

33. "Indian Children Grant Awarded." About $250,000 went to LaFourche and Terrebonne Parishes for Houma children, and $41,000 to East Baton Rouge Parish.

34. See note 68 to chapter 2, above.

35. Ernest Downs testified about this in the AIPRC Baton Rouge hearing: "I'd also like to add that that dam lowered the level of water in a place called Trou' Poupone, which in old times and as late as the 1930s served as a sacred spot where ritual diving went on during the corn feast and when people passed away there was a special place that people would dive into the water. And this place is now out of Tunica hands and is ecologically unbalanced because of this Coulee Project." American Indian Policy Review Commission, Task Force Ten, Baton Rouge hearings, 63. Mary Haas's *Tunica Texts*, 153, refers to diving at the place where the Avoyelles tribe is said to have emerged, which is a place the Tunicas regard "with considerable superstition," according to Haas. Tribal members have verified that this was the same place. Haas also documents that the *fête du blé*, the Tunica green corn ceremony, involves wading into water, but she does not name the Trou' Poupone itself. Haas, *Tunica Texts*, 67.

36. The tribe later became involved in a lengthy lawsuit over the rights to the grave goods. More on this in chapter 4.

37. American Indian Policy Review Commission, Task Force Ten, Baton Rouge hearings, 64–66.

38. Transcription is bad all the way through the Louisiana hearings, partly because the Washington transcribers could not understand Louisiana accents, partly because they were just bad transcribers. I have therefore taken minor liberties with the text of the transcript. In this passage, for example, the transcript reads: "and then that was the end of the line as far as containing a wizard." Clearly Pierite did not say "containing a wizard." Since the original tapes are unlocatable at this point, I made an educated guess that he said "continuing with us," though he might have said "continuing a ways, so . . ." or "retaining a lawyer." If the intention is ambiguous, that fact will be noted.

39. The wording here was ambiguous. The transcript reads, "But, however, we tried those ups and downs ourselves." Either reading is possible, though I have used the wording I believe more likely.

40. Lacour, "Indian Tribe's Recognition Expected during Bicentennial."

41. This according to Pete Gregory, who has assisted a number of Louisiana tribes with recognition petitions. I have not found direct written evidence to support the claim, but the claim is supported by the details of the case. Downs had already compiled the tribal history and presented it to the AIPRC in 1976, and the Tunicas submitted a completed petition, which takes years to compile, less than two weeks after publication of the regulations in the *Federal Register* in 1978. Further, with the exception of the Passamaquoddy and Penobscot tribes, which were recognized as a result of a federal court case, no tribes were federally recognized between 1974 and 1978, while there had been a brief flurry of acknowledgments before that.

42. Upon reviewing the draft report of the AIPRC task force on recognition in 1977, Governor Edwin Edwards, who was born and raised in Marksville, sent a letter to Senator James Abourezk, AIPRC chairman, stating his strong support for the "immediate federal recognition of all authentic native American tribes, especially the four nonrecognized groups in Louisiana: the Houma Alliance, the Houma Tribe Incorporated, the Jena Band of Choctaws, and the Tunica-Biloxi Tribe." Governor Edwin Edwards to Senator James S. Abourezk, 19 April 1977, included in Native American Rights Fund, *Petition for Recognition of the Tunica-Biloxi Indian Tribe in Compliance with 25 CFR Part 54*. Similarly, the tribe obtained the support of some of the Louisiana Congressional delegation, as it had in the past. Representatives David C. Treen, Lindy Boggs, and Jerry Huckaby "expressed interest in getting the forgotten Louisiana bands recognized." Poe, "Louisiana's Forgotten Indians." The Houma Alliance and the Houma Tribe later united to form the United Houma Nation because a staff member at the Office of Federal Acknowledgment, Holly Reckort, told them they would have a better chance of being recognized if they all applied together, according to Kirby Verrett, former chairman of the United Houma Nation, in an interview in 1998. When OFA issued an initial finding against recognition of the United Houma Nation, one of the reasons cited was that the group could not prove it had been a single polity except for individual satellite communities. In other words, they should have applied separately.

43. Pitts, "Louisiana Indians on Legal Warpath." Note that this comment was made

less than two weeks after the *Mashpee* decision (8 November 1978), in which the federally nonrecognized Mashpee tribe was denied standing to sue under the Indian Trade and Intercourse Acts. See note 47, below.

44. See Juneau, "The Judicial Extinguishment of the Tunica Indian Tribe," 43–47, esp. n. 12, which details Guste's efforts with the state legislature. Guste wrote in a letter to the legislature that a "federal designation of 'tribe status' greatly enhances the right to assert a claim under the 'Non-Intercourse Act' and entitles the designated 'tribe' to federal intervention to 'recover' lands conveyed in violation of the Non-Intercourse [Act]." Guste then cites the economic stagnation that lands claims cases cause: "They create a cloud on the validity of real estate titles, and the result is a slow-down or cessation of economic activity because property cannot be sold, mortgages cannot be acquired, title insurance becomes unavailable, and bond issues are placed in jeopardy." William Guste Jr. to Members of the Louisiana Legislature, 3 July 1978. Juneau offers more detailed information on the effect of the letter, which the legislature took to heart by removing language from certain Indian recognition bills that could be construed as a determination of Indian tribal status by the state.

45. See chapter 9 for further discussion of this controversy.

46. Thompson, "La. Indians Sue for Land, Money." See also "Tunicas Remain 'Optimistic' on Land Claim." Earl Barbry stated in an interview that the tribe filed the land claims suit before filing for recognition in 1978, but Thompson's article states that the tribe "may" file a land claims suit, according to the LBIA director, Peter Mora. A ruling from 1991 indicates that the tribe waited too long to file the land claim, because of "the six-year statute of limitations prescribed by the Tucker Act, 28 U.S.C. § 2501 (1988), and the limitation on actions inherent in the Indian Claims Commission Act of 1946." Tunica-Biloxi Tribe v. United States.

47. See primarily Campisi, *The Mashpee Indians.* Other items have been written on the case, but this is the most comprehensive. See also James Clifford, "Identity in Mashpee," *The Predicament of Culture,* 277–346; Mashpee Tribe vs. New Seabury.

48. Charrier v. Bell, 496 So.2d 601 (La. App. 1 Cir. 1986); Shelton, "Treasure Case Goes Higher."

49. Chairman Barbry recalled an incident involving the council that inspired him to become involved in tribal government. "Well," he begins, "although I've always had an interest in my people, in particular, I was born and raised here on the reservation, and I guess a love for the land more than anything else is what brought that on. Because one day at work back in the '70s, right before I got on the council, someone informs me that there was going to be a meeting with the tribal members and the mayor of Marksville that a deal had been made to use the reservation for a garbage dump. And so that kind of stirred up my curiosity, and I went straight to the mayor and asked him what it was about.

"The city council and the mayor had proposed to the tribal council at that time to pay us fifty dollars a month and make a gravel road to the back of the reservation where they would start dumping. And at the time we only had 130 acres. And

I couldn't understand why anybody in their right mind would want to turn this beautiful piece of property—and that's all this tribe had—would want to turn that into a garbage dump. And I suppose when you have nothing and you're trying to generate some kind of income for your tribe, you go to extremes to do that, but that's something that I just couldn't understand. So I told the mayor before leaving his office, I said I don't know what kind of deal y'all have, and who is responsible for this, but don't attempt to put a garbage truck on that reservation, because you're going to have to run over me. And the mayor and I are good friends.

"So I went to the next council meeting and when this subject came up, I addressed the tribal council and expressed my concern. And being raised on the reservation, like the ones on the council at the time—which I have a great deal of respect for; they're quite a bit older than I was—I asked them to consider what it was like when we were growing up, them as well as myself, how we would go out there and enjoy the reservation and the land, and I wanted our kids to have that same opportunity. It was one of the only, one of the few pieces of real estate in this area that hasn't been completely destroyed by man. And I wanted my kids to be able to grow up and have the same experience or the same feeling that we had growing up when we were kids. And that's how I became involved in it.

"I told the council, if the tribe needs the money that bad, I won't—I wasn't making that much money at the time—I said, I'll give you fifty dollars a month just to leave it alone. So it was called for a vote and nobody voted for it. I guess it was just a matter of pointing it out to them. I guess the need to do something or to try to do something for the tribe kind of bonded me to that aspect of it. [I asked: You ran for council after that or chairman after that?] I guess I was appointed vice-chairman shortly thereafter. And then in '78, the chairman resigned and [people wanted] me to assume that position, which I didn't really want to. In fact, I went back and talked to the chairman, because I had a great deal of respect for him, and asked him if he'd take back his position because I didn't want it. I was just married, had some young kids, and I wanted to devote my time and energy to raising my family. So when he had made up his mind that he didn't want to be in that position anymore, I went ahead and took it. As a result, I've devoted over twenty years of my life to this."

That the transition was quite as friendly as Barbry describes is doubtful, but his recounting of the transition may have involved some attempt to salve old wounds.

50. Hager, "Tunicas Still Await Recognition."
51. As Tom Biolsi suggests, federal Indian law dominates and structures relations between Indians and states, and such is certainly the case in federal acknowledgment procedures. Biolsi, *Deadliest Enemies*, 6.
52. 25 CFR Part 54.7(e)(4), 43 Fed. Reg. 39363, 5 September 1978.
53. See chapter 9 for further details. Information provided by Herman Pierite's grandson, and a current tribal council member, Marshall Ray Sampson.
54. Hager, "Tunicas Still Await Recognition."

*Chapter 4: Treasures*

1. American Indian Policy Review Commission, Task Force Ten, Baton Rouge hearings, 24.
2. Current tribal landholdings amount to 724 acres of land held in trust and 731 acres of land with fee simple title, up from the 133 acres taken into trust for the tribe at the time of recognition. Tunica-Biloxi Tribe, property inventory.
3. American Indian Policy Review Commission, Task Force Ten, Baton Rouge hearings, 31.
4. Native American Rights Fund, *Petition for Recognition of the Tunica-Biloxi Indian Tribe in Compliance with 25 CFR Part 54*, 60, full statement included in petition. The language of the statement indicates that Claude Medford Jr., a Choctaw anthropologist and friend who attended the convention with Pierite, collaborated in composing it.
5. Though the final determination for federal acknowledgment was published on 27 July 1981, recognition did not become effective for another sixty days, on 25 September 1981.
6. Faine, *The Tunica-Biloxi Indians*, 7.
7. Faine reports that there was a high incidence of medical need in 1984 among tribal members and that tribal members almost always went to the physician whenever needed. This contrasts with Joe Pierite Jr.'s testimony in 1976, before federal health programs were instituted, saying that tribal members essentially went without health care for lack of insurance or funds. American Indian Policy Review Commission, Baton Rouge hearings, 1975–77, entry NC3-220-77-9, box 315, "Unidentified Records," Record Group 220, National Archives II, College Park, Md., 49–50. Earl Barbry reported that the IHS funding was the first federal funding to come through after recognition, but according to Faine the majority of Tunica-Biloxi households had no medical insurance. Faine's questionnaire only asks whether the family had received medical benefits from any private or public health care programs in the past year, failing to specify tribal or IHS benefits, though he specified several other forms of public health aid.
8. Faine, *The Tunica-Biloxi Indians*, 7–8.
9. The Tunica tribal member John Barbry was one of the scholarship recipients. Executive Director's Report, Governor's Commission on Indian Affairs.
10. A survey in 1984 noted that the tribe's educational achievements had in fact surpassed those of residents of Avoyelles Parish in general. By that time it claimed 57 percent of tribal adults over twenty-five had earned a high school diploma, compared with 39 percent parishwide. Such a number seems a little doubtful, since Ernest Downs estimated in 1976 that 75 percent of the population was illiterate. Faine's self-reported diploma rate could be accurate, since the population in 1984 was extremely young, with a median age of 22.4 and only 19 percent of tribal members over forty-five years old. Faine, *The Tunica-Biloxi Indians*, 3, 9. Downs in American Indian Policy Review Commission, Baton Rouge hearings, 1975–77, entry

NC3-220-77-9, box 315, "Unidentified Records," Record Group 220, National Archives II, College Park, Md., 40.

11. The tribe filed suit in 1990 but the statute of limitations had expired. The decision entered by the Court of Appeals seems to rest on a misunderstanding of federal responsibilities to the tribe under the Indian Trade and Intercourse Acts. Its arguments are weakly constructed and willfully ignore trust responsibilities for political reasons. Tunica-Biloxi Tribe v. United States. This is one of many instances in tribal life confirming Tom Biolsi's observation that the law repositions tribal relations with the federal government into relations with individual states in an attempt to deflect attention from the coloniality of the relationship between indigenous peoples and settlers and between Indians and whites. Biolsi, *Deadliest Enemies*.

12. For a complete assessment of the collection, including a retelling of the Peabody's acquisition efforts and the beginnings of the court case, see Brain, *Tunica Treasure*. See also Brain, *Tunica Archaeology*.

13. During my fellowship at the School of American Research I serendipitously had a chance to talk with Stephen Williams, a regular guest at the school's colloquium series. Some of the information provided here about the courses of action taken by the Peabody team is supplemented by Williams's memory and opinions.

14. Brain, *Tunica Treasure*, 1–32.

15. Ibid., 27.

16. Ibid.

17. Charrier v. Bell; Brain, *Tunica Treasure*, 30.

18. Brain, *Tunica Archaeology*, 57, cites H. F. "Pete" Gregory, letter to Herman Viola, Native American Scholars Program, Smithsonian Institution. Department of Anthropology Archives, Smithsonian Institution, Washington, 1979. Here Brain also notes that the first excavation at the present tribal location was done by Stu Neitzel, that the grave goods were divided between Chief Horace Pierite and the Marksville Museum, and that the "skeletal remains were reburied at the site in a small cypress box made by Horace Pierite and Joseph Pierite, Sr." I infer from this description that the tribal leaders who reburied tribal bones conducted a small ceremony with reburial, but this is only a presumption.

19. Brain, *Tunica Archaeology*, 60.

20. Charrier v. Bell, "Written Reasons for Judgment," 13, 15.

21. Trillin, "Louisiana: The Tunica Treasure."

22. Cullen and Wright, "Tunica Treasure," § H, p. 5.

23. Judge C. Lenton Sartain's decision in Charrier v. Bell.

24. Charrier v. Bell.

25. Smith, Original Brief on Behalf of Leonard Charrier, 3. Document available from the National Indian Law Library, a division of the Native American Rights Fund. Plaintiff's argument found without merit in 496 So. 2d 601 (La. App. 1 Cir. 1986).

26. Youchican v. Texas & Pacific Railway. See also the discussion above detailing the case of Fulgence Chiki and the land claims of the tribe that might have been resolved more favorably for the tribe if they had had standing as a federal tribe.

27. Day, "Tunica-Biloxi Today."

28. Vizenor, *Manifest Manners*.

## Chapter 5: Tribal Enterprise and Tribal Life

1. Court decisions ranging from Bryant v. Itasca County (1976) to California v. Cabazon Band of Mission Indians (1987) affirmed the right of tribes to operate high-stakes gaming facilities as long as the games that they operated were otherwise legal in any form in the state in which the reservation was located. *Cabazon* in particular was seen as throwing open the floodgates, since it was the first case to address card games rather than strictly bingo, and state governors vigorously protested the decision. The Indian Gaming Regulatory Act of 1988, rather than enabling tribal gaming, actually put limits on it, forcing tribes to negotiate gaming compacts with states; *Cabazon* set no such terms for Indian gaming. The IGRA was a compromise, endorsed by Ronald Reagan and sponsored by John McCain, intended to both protect tribal gaming as an economic development resource for tribes and give states enough say that they would not press their Congressional delegations to pass legislation abolishing the right entirely under the doctrine of plenary power. See Mason, *Indian Gaming*.

2. See for example National Indian Gaming Association, "Majority of Americans Support Tribal Gaming According to National Poll," which states that 65 percent of American voters support Indian gaming according to a poll conducted by an independent firm with a margin of error of $\pm 3\%$.

3. Per capita distribution of gaming profits must be approved by the National Indian Gaming Commission, a regulatory body created by the IGRA, and the IGRA stipulates that tribal government operations and programs and economic development initiatives take priority over per capita payments. Indian Gaming Regulatory Act of 1988, §2710 (2–3). Jessica Cattelino notes that only 32 percent of gaming tribes even have per capita distribution of gaming revenues, with the remainder devoting funds exclusively to tribal programming needs. Cattelino, *High Stakes*, 103.

4. Wanamaker, "Let the Games Begin."

5. Cattelino, *High Stakes*, esp. chapter 3.

6. In 1998 the state organized a parish-by-parish vote on legalized gambling. Each parish would decide for itself whether it wanted legalized gambling, thereby allowing the strongly anti-gambling, predominantly conservative Protestant parishes of the northeastern part of the state to vote gambling out while the less conservative parishes could still have gambling if they desired. Of Louisiana's sixty-four parishes, thirty-three voted against gambling.

7. See "Taxing Casinos." The State Senate proposed the toll road concept in trying to figure out ways to tax tribal casinos. See Morgan, "Indian Leader Angered," which mentions the attempt to tax casino food and beverage sales. The state had earlier balked at the request of the Tunica-Biloxi Tribe to refund the state sales tax the tribe had paid on the purchase of a tribal police car, in addition to demanding that

state tax be paid on vehicles not used exclusively on the reservation. Tunica Biloxi Tribe v. Louisiana. The case was resolved in favor of the state. See also "Tunica Tax War Wages On."

8. Seminole Tribe of Florida v. Florida. See also Canby, *American Indian Law in a Nutshell*, 283.

9. Cattelino, *High Stakes*, 182, citing Florida v. Seminole Tribe of Florida.

10. California v. Cabazon Band of Mission Indians; Canby, *American Indian Law in a Nutshell*, 284–85.

11. See Mason, Introduction, *Indian Gaming*.

12. Dyer, "Foster Wants Bigger 'Take' from Indian Casinos."

13. Wilkins and Lomawaima suggest that no sovereign entity operates completely independent of others, including the states and even the federal government (which places limits on its own sovereignty in relation to tribal sovereigns within its borders), despite its own claims to plenary power over Indian tribes at times. Rather than simply accept this history, however, they argue that competing sovereigns can "rise above our errors" and practice "mutual respect for the inherent sovereignty of our partners." Wilkins and Lomawaima, *Uneven Ground*, 250.

14. Two illustrative examples: the Mashantucket Pequots tried hydroponic lettuce production and pig farming, both failed ventures, before gambling made them one of the wealthiest tribes in the country. The Ysleta del Sur (Tigua) Pueblo tried to grow spices commercially in a giant glass pyramid greenhouse that sizzled plants in the hot El Paso sun. Wherry, Afterword; Martin, "Development at Ysleta del Sur Pueblo, Texas," 62, 243.

15. The casino was originally named Grand Casino Avoyelles, since the tribe signed a seven-year management contract with Grand Casinos of Minnesota. In 2000 the tribe bought out the rest of the contract but had to rename the casino within a year since Grand Casinos was no longer involved with it. This was an expensive proposition, since the tribe had already spent so much money positioning the Grand Casino Avoyelles in the casino and destination resort industry, according to John Barbry, who works in the casino's marketing department. On an interesting side note, Barbry told me that the tribe had initially wanted to name the operation Grand Casino Tunica-Biloxi, but since Grand Casinos already operated a Grand Casino Biloxi in Biloxi, Mississippi, and was planning a Grand Casino Tunica in Tunica, Mississippi, the tribe decided to go with another name that would not offer any confusion. The Avoyelles tribe makes up part of the Tunica-Biloxi ancestry and is also the namesake of the parish within which the reservation is located, so the name worked for the tribe on two levels.

16. The Burger King near the casino was at one time one of the busiest in the nation, but the tribe sold or leased all its fast-food operations in 2009.

17. Peterson, "Assimilation, Separation, and Out-Migration in an American Indian Group."

18. "Critical mass" is discussed by Bruce Miller as a result of new viability in the Upper Skagit community after federal recognition. Miller, "After the F.A.P.," 94.

19. One of the challenges of tribal economic development is that it still requires hard decisions about what to fund, but it is likely that a newspaper will be funded again at some point in the future since its function is so valuable.

20. Jessica Cattelino notes that many Seminoles were alarmed by the bureaucratization of tribal cultural transmission, as language, history, and cultural education shifted from families to tribal governmental responsibility in the wake of declining Seminole and Mikasuki language fluency. Certainly this makes sense as a cause for concern among the Seminoles, whose language and distinct cultural traditions have remained remarkably vibrant, with eighteen hundred speakers of the tribal languages. The Tunica-Biloxi situation merits an approach suited to the context, however. Cattelino, *High Stakes*, 66–78.

21. "Families Coping with Catastrophic Situations."

22. Lintinger, "Tribal Family Gets New Home for Their Little Angels."

23. See Klopotek, Lintinger, and Barbry, "Ordinary and Extraordinary Trauma."

24. More detailed financial data are available in Tunica-Biloxi Tribe, "1998 Tunica-Biloxi Community Review."

25. See for example "Marksville Mayor Dr. Richard Michel Pleased with Town's and Tribe's Growth, Success & Prosperity"; "Mayor Quebedeaux of Mansura Reports Crime Rate Decreases Since Tribal Casino Opened."

26. For an analogous situation in the Upper Skagit community after federal recognition see Miller, "After the F.A.P.," 92.

27. See for example Henry, "Disenrolled Tribal Members Complain of Unfairness."

28. U.S. Office of Federal Acknowledgment, "List of Petitioners by State as of September 22, 2008," 22.

29. A tribal enrollment committee handles run-of-the-mill enrollments of children of tribal members and other well-documented descendants of known and acknowledged tribal members. Cases where complicated decisions have to be made are referred to the tribal council.

30. For example Strong and Van Winkle, " 'Indian Blood,' " 557; Trigger, *The Children of Aataentsic*, esp. 826–31; and sources too numerous to cite on the many Southeastern confederacies of the contact era.

31. Gonzales, "Gaming and Displacement," 125.

32. Jessica Cattelino notes that the Seminole tribe faced similar concerns at the time of the purchase of the Hard Rock Café in 2007, when the tribal council could not let members know about the enormous acquisition before announcing it to the general public without risking an increase in the purchase price. "As their tribally owned businesses expand, it is unclear how Seminoles will balance a commitment to distributed power and knowledge within the tribal polity against corporate requirements for information control." Cattelino, *High Stakes*, 195.

33. Lintinger, "Anna Mae Juneau."

34. Moreau v. Valentine, discussed in Juneau, "The Judicial Extinguishment of the Tunica Indian Tribe," 60–73.

35. Moreau v. Valentine, quoted in Juneau, "The Judicial Extinguishment of the Tunica Indian Tribe," 61.

36. This could mean that women merely had land ownership rights in the Tunica tribe, but even this indicates that women were not entirely disempowered in the Tunica past. It could also be that Moreau saw the Tunicas as vulnerable because of a lack of male leadership at the time.

37. See Brain, *Tunica Archaeology*, 320–21, for the all-male list of tribal leadership. That the women hid away Zenon La Joie and named him chief may suggest that even they thought men were the proper chiefs, but it may also be that the oral history was adjusted to fit the tribe's present understanding of itself. In either case female leadership in the interim need not be doubted.

38. Pesantubbee, *Choctaw Women in a Chaotic World*, 25–26.

39. "Biloxi Tribe, et al., 1924, Signed copy of statement by Biloxi Indian tribe and members of the Choctaw Indian Tribe residing in different parts of the State of Louisiana. October 9, 1924, Woodworth, Louisiana." The name Dosey should likely be Dorsey. See the notes on Biloxi community membership by James Owen Dorsey (not related). Dorsey, Field notes and unpublished papers.

40. Generally potlatch traditions in the Pacific Northwest, the buffalo and horse cultures of the Plains, and the elaborate mounds of the South and Midwest seem to have emerged from relatively prosperous peoples. Not to suggest that only wealth leads to cultural vibrancy and innovation, but that it can emerge from these conditions as easily as from conditions of poverty. See Paredes, "Paradoxes of Modernism and Indianness in the Southeast," and Cattelino, *High Stakes*, for more in-depth discussions of outsiders' expectations of tribal poverty linked to notions of authenticity and cultural decline, and the resulting political costs of this association for tribes.

41. In a brief history of Marksville written for the local newspaper, Joseph Pilcher suggests that the festival had been a large event to which non-Indians were invited even in the early twentieth century. "Until a score or more of years ago," he wrote in 1929, "the Tunicas continued to hold these war dances [in association with the fête du blé], which were attended by the citizens of Marksville and the surrounding country. But all these things have become history. The Tunicas themselves are fast becoming extinct, and the tribe will soon be no more. The great tale of a passing race is written on the faces of the remaining half-breeds now living near Marksville." Pilcher, "History of Marksville."

42. Lintinger, "Tribal Craftsmen Carry on Cultural Traditions."

43. Barbry is not a veteran, a usual prerequisite to becoming a gourd dancer. However, if invited to be a gourd dancer by someone who is already a gourd dancer, the requirement can be waived, according to Barbry.

44. "Tribal Flag Presented at December General Meeting."

45. Lintinger, "Baskets, Baskets, Everywhere . . ."; Lintinger, "Tribal Members Learn the Art of Pine-Needle Basket Weaving from Cryer Family Members."

46. Lintinger, "Anna Mae Juneau." Compare Hill, *Weaving New Worlds*.

47. It is worth noting that Seminoles in Florida often evoke the idea that living in a chickee is important for cultural survival in their tribe. See for example Cattelino, *High Stakes*, 109, 155; LaDuke, *All Our Relations*, 27–45.

48. See chapter 9; and Klopotek, Lintinger, and Barbry, "Ordinary and Extraordinary Trauma."

49. Spilde, "Rich Indian Racism."

50. The quote is from Spilde, but for more detailed information on American Indian wealth in relation to the general population see Taylor and Kalt, "American Indians on Reservations."

51. Deloria, *Custer Died for Your Sins*, 256. I disagree with Deloria's assertion that an ideological root distinguishes Indian issues from those of other communities of color, but share his view that ideology is a critical terrain that indigenous peoples must contest.

## Chapter 6: Jena Choctaws under Jim Crow

1. Sibley, "A Report from Natchitoches in 1807"; Kinnaird and Kinnaird, "Choctaws West of the Mississippi, 1766–1800." Choctaw territory extended from near present day Memphis south to the Gulf of Mexico, and from present Louisiana east to present Alabama.

2. Kniffen, Gregory, and Stokes, *The Historic Tribes of Louisiana from 1542 to the Present*, 71–105.

3. U.S. Office of Federal Acknowledgment, "Historical Technical Report, Jena Band of Choctaw Indians," 7, citing Sibley, "A Report from Natchitoches in 1807," 24.

4. Mary Jones claims that her mother's family, whose last name was Batise / Baptiste, had been in Louisiana for much longer than other families, and that there were no people with that last name in Mississippi. The OFA report notes that there were Choctaw Baptistes in Mississippi on the 1880 census ("Genealogical Report, Jena Band of Choctaw Indians," 24). It is possible that Jones was referring to another ancestor within the Baptiste line, but the point she makes is that some of the families are said to have a longer tenure in Louisiana than those who came from Mississippi after the Civil War.

5. They had been associated with the plantation of the Whatley family since the 1870 census at least, though the Whatleys had been living in the area since the early 1800s. OFA cites Whatleys on the Catahoula Parish census in 1810. U.S. Office of Federal Acknowledgment, "Genealogical Report, Jena Band of Choctaw Indians," 17–19. Watt claims that the Reverend William Whatley moved to Eden, near present Jena, from Georgia in 1815. Watt, "Federal Indian Policy and Tribal Development in Louisiana," 63.

6. Correlation of Anglo surnames between the Jena Band and the Mississippi Band of Choctaws clearly indicates a link between the groups that postdates heavy interaction with Anglos. Gatschet also indicated that the people he interviewed had

lived in Scott and Newton Counties in Mississippi before the Civil War. Gatschet, Field notes.

7. Watt, "Federal Indian Policy and Tribal Development in Louisiana," 68.

8. Watt contends that the Jena Choctaws may have doctored their testimony before the Dawes Commission to comply with a perceived need to document ties to Mississippi. "From some of the statements in the [Dawes] testimonies, it is assumed that the Catahoula Choctaws were intent on establishing some connection with Mississippi, resulting in contradictory statements. For instance, Sally Ann Allen answered successive questions by saying that she did not know where she was born, that she had not lived in any state other than Louisiana, and that she was born in Mississippi. The contradictions may stem from confusion by the questions or from the inexperience of direct examination, but it is more likely that the Catahoula Choctaws perceived a need to be associated with Mississippi in order to be identified as a Mississippi Choctaw." Watt, "Federal Indian Policy and Tribal Development in Louisiana," 93.

9. The OFA report states that the Dawes Commission and the Choctaw Nation considered nonremoved Choctaws eligible for enrollment as long as they came and occupied an allotment in Western Choctaw lands (Indian Territory), and those who chose to do so were enrolled in the (Western) Choctaw Nation as Mississippi Choctaws. U.S. Office of Federal Acknowledgment, "Historical Technical Report, Jena Band of Choctaw Indians," 20, citing Dawes Commission, Commission and Commissioner to the Five Civilized Tribes, *Annual Report*, 18, 80; and Choctaw Nation, "Memorial to the Congress of the United States." Those who remained in select communities in Mississippi were recognized as a tribe by the federal government in 1920.

10. U.S. Office of Federal Acknowledgment, "Historical Technical Report, Jena Band of Choctaw Indians," 20–23. According to the OFA report, they were identified as full-blood Mississippi Choctaws despite their addresses in Louisiana.

11. Chitto Harjo (Crazy Snake), a Muscogee Creek, led the movement of traditionalist full-bloods who violently opposed allotment and the reduction in Creek land and sovereignty that accompanied it. He and his followers declared a new government and enforced their laws by violence and intimidation against Creeks and other Indians who moved onto their allotments. Watt, "Federal Indian Policy and Tribal Development in Louisiana," 96, notes this possibility, citing Debo, *And Still the Waters Run* for her information on the "Snake Uprising."

12. Bill Lewis chose not to try to enroll himself or his large family since he felt he was doing well in Louisiana. Watt, "Federal Indian Policy and Tribal Development in Louisiana," 85. Ida Umber was the sole member of the group to enroll, having met and married her husband in Indian Territory. Watt, "Federal Indian Policy and Tribal Development in Louisiana," 94.

13. The Dawes Commission invited all full-blooded Choctaws in Mississippi, Louisiana, and Alabama to enroll as Mississippi Choctaw full-bloods.

14. U.S. Office of Federal Acknowledgment, "Historical Technical Report, Jena Band of Choctaw Indians," 26.

15. Watt, "Federal Indian Policy and Tribal Development in Louisiana," 107–8.

16. U.S. Office of Federal Acknowledgment, "Historical Technical Report, Jena Band of Choctaw Indians," 23–28. I have not thoroughly examined the original census records or Dawes Commission files and recompiled these family histories. The report lays all the evidence on the table, whether it is helpful to the tribe or not, so the Jena genealogist's and OFA genealogist's findings in this case seem accurate.

17. Mary Jones said of the Jena Choctaws, "They were homesteading, but back then they didn't know that you had to go put your name down on that land that you claim. They didn't do that, so they lost all that land, but they lived there and do sharecrop for the Whatleys." Their ancestors had moved to the land and cleared enough of it to raise crops to feed themselves before there were any white or black people on it, but they lost their rights to the land through homestead claims of others. It is possible that some of their ancestors, particularly through the Batisse line, held land in the area before the arrival of whites, but since the tribal council signed an agreement with the state of Louisiana in which they conceded that they had no aboriginal land claims against the state in return for a letter of support for federal recognition from the governor, it is unlikely that funds will be expended in the near future to delve further into such a claim. The Jena Band accepts that the bulk of its ancestors came from Mississippi in the mid-nineteenth century, and further research to prove or disprove that is beyond the scope of this project. On occupations, Mattie Penick, a local white woman advocating for the Jena Choctaws to be educated, noted in a letter to the Department of Indian Affairs in 1934 that laundry was "the chief occupation of the women." Mattie Penick to W. Carson Ryan, 1 June 1934, File 25436-1931-150-800, National Archives and Records Administration, Record Group 75. For other information on occupation see Watt, "Federal Indian Policy and Tribal Development in Louisiana; also Kniffen, Gregory, and Stokes, *The Historic Tribes of Louisiana from 1542 to the Present.*

18. Watt concluded from the ledgers that the Jena Choctaws' dinner table probably resembled that of local non-Indians, with purchases of ammunition for hunting, feed for livestock, tobacco, and staple foods such as flour, sugar, lard, coffee, and salt. Other purchases included furniture, washtubs, and kitchen items for the home, and files, axes, and rope for work duties. Luxury purchases were rare. Watt, "Federal Indian Policy and Tribal Development in Louisiana," 117–19.

19. Watt, "Federal Indian Policy and Tribal Development in Louisiana," 130–31. Watt also notes that the Jena Choctaws would not likely have sharecropped if they had been in an area where blacks were the predominant sharecroppers or tenant farmers. LaSalle Parish sharecroppers and tenant farmers were predominantly white, so the Jena Choctaws could enter that line of work without the risk of being identified with blacks. Watt, "Federal Indian Policy and Tribal Development in Louisiana," 122.

20. Gregory, "The Jena Band of Louisiana Choctaw," 6.

21. The current chief, Christine Norris, asserts that the experience of racism affects only those who outwardly appear Indian, who are identified with a tribe and

placed in the Indian social category all their lives. People with Indian ancestry without that experience should not have the right to claim the benefits of tribal status and, conversely, groups of people with that experience certainly deserve to be recognized as tribes. Theresa O'Nell articulately discusses the ways stories about racist experiences bind and elevate Flathead identity on the Flathead reservation. O'Nell, "Telling about Whites, Talking about Indians."

22. Wade, "First School for State Indians Held in LaSalle Parish." The literacy campaign included blacks and whites throughout the state. See "From School Board Office"; "Negroes of Avoyelles Eager to Attend School"; "Night School Being Established." In LaSalle Parish "school officials established schools for both whites and negroes in various parts of the parish. About the time the schools had accomplished their purpose—to a great extent at least, Supt. E. E. Richardson of the LaSalle parish schools found that near Eden several families of Indians resided, none of whom could read nor write. Steps were immediately taken to educate the Indian children insofar as 24 lessons (the number furnished from state funds) would do so." Wade, "First School for State Indians Held in LaSalle Parish."

23. Gregory suggests that the "school" was not permitted to reopen because the all-white church in which the classes were held opposed education of the Choctaws in general, since education might free Choctaws from their subservient status. Gregory, "The Jena Band of Louisiana Choctaw," 6. Mary "Pick" Pipes, the one-hundred-three-year-old widow of J. L. Pipes, confirmed that whites were opposed to holding Indian school in the white Baptist church, and suggested that whites finally stopped the classes from being held in the Methodist church too.

24. Roy Nash, "Indians of Louisiana," 12 June 1931, Bureau of Indian Affairs, Central Correspondence File 25436-31-150, General Services, Record Group 75, National Archives, 9.

25. Ibid., 7.

26. Ibid., 9.

27. Ibid., 12.

28. Handwritten note on "Inspection Report," signed Daiker. Fred Daiker, "Inspection Report 5-358" on Roy Nash's report on Louisiana Indians (12 June 1931), 7 August 1931. Bureau of Indian Affairs, Central Correspondence File 25436-31-150, General Services, Record Group 75, National Archives.

29. Ray Lyman Wilbur, secretary of the interior, to T. H. Harris, Louisiana State Superintendent of Education, 3 March 1932, File 68776-1931-800, part I, Record Group 75, National Archives.

30. Several sources refer to the law prohibiting married women from teaching (for example "Jena Indians Learn What Their Ancestors Forgot"), but other articles in the *Jena Times* contain references to married women teaching in public schools by the 1940s, so I am not clear when, how, or where the rule barring married women from teaching was enforced. Mrs. C. W. Flowers, for example, is noted as a schoolteacher in an article in 1946, "Lasall Parish Teachers Seek $400 Pay Raise."

31. "Jena Indians Learn What Their Ancestors Forgot."

32. Ibid.

33. C. J. Rhoads to Senator Huey Long, 3 March 1932, File 68776-1931-800, part I, Record Group 75, National Archives.

34. Mrs. Charles S. Penick to W. Carson Ryan, 1 June 1934, Bureau of Indian Affairs, Central Correspondence File 25436-31-150, General Services, Record Group 75, National Archives; E. E. Richardson, superintendent, LaSalle Parish School Board, to Senator John Overton, 10 May 1932, File 68776-1931-800, part I, Record Group 75, National Archives; Watt, "Federal Indian Policy and Tribal Development in Louisiana," 142.

35. Helene Sliffe to T. H. Harris, 13 April 1933, Bureau of Indian Affairs, Central Correspondence File 25436-31-150, General Services, Record Group 75, National Archives. Sliffe also reports that older students found the reading material "too juvenile," and that efforts were under way to find more age-appropriate reading materials. Margaret Connell Szasz notes that this was a common enough problem in Indian education because of the large number of "over-age" Indian students who had had no access to education as younger children. Szasz, *Education and the American Indian*, 117.

36. Gregory, "The Jena Band of Louisiana Choctaw," 7; Watt, "Federal Indian Policy and Tribal Development in Louisiana," 136. Malt tax was levied on malt syrup, a legal substance widely used to make home-brewed beer during Prohibition. Halfpenny, "Michigan Home Brewing During Prohibition."

37. E. E. Richardson, superintendent, LaSalle Parish School Board, to Senator John Overton, 10 May 1932, File 68776-1931-800, part I, Record Group 75, National Archives, emphasis mine.

38. See chapter 9. A Louisiana statute made the marriage of an Indian with a person of African blood illegal, recognizing the social distinction between the races. State of Louisiana, Act 220 of 1920. In 1932 the Louisiana attorney general issued an opinion stating that marriage between Indians and whites was not prohibited under the state's antimiscegenation laws, confirming that Indians could be classified with whites for many purposes. State of Louisiana, *Opinions Attorney General*.

39. M. S. Robertson reports that a "half-breed Indian girl completed the seventh grade in 1928 in the public schools of Columbia, Louisiana, where she was living at the time." Columbia is thirty-four miles from Jena. M. S. Robertson, assistant state supervisor of elementary schools, to W. Carson Ryan, 28 March, 1934. Earlier correspondence indicates that a similar situation occurred for a Chitimacha boy, who was allowed to attend the white school in nearby Franklin, Louisiana, but whose tribal status prevented him from attending white schools in Charenton, only ten miles away. A. C. Hector to C. J. Rhoads, 15 December 1932, File 68776-1931-800, part I, National Archives, Record Group 75.

40. The state education official M. S. Robertson stated in an article in the *Times-Picayune* in 1938: "Nobody wanted the Indians when we put up a school for them. The La Salle parish school board refused to let them go to the white schools. They themselves would not go to the negro schools." "Jena Indians Learn What Their

Ancestors Forgot." Oral corroboration came from multiple personal discussions, as well as the statement above, "Indians don't need education—they got work!" in Gregory, "The Jena Band of Louisiana Choctaw," 6. Watt also cites the case of a Jena Choctaw who left the community in 1927, returning for the first time in 1985. He cited exclusion from schools in Jena as the primary reason why he had left. Watt, "Federal Indian Policy and Tribal Development in Louisiana," 132.

41. J.D. Russell, as reported by Harvey K. Meyer, superintendent, Choctaw Indian Agency, to commissioner of Indian affairs, 19 February 1940, 23 February 1940, File 68776-1931-800, part I, National Archives, Record Group 75.

42. E. E. Richardson, superintendent, LaSalle Parish School Board, to Senator John Overton, 10 May 1932, File 68776-1931-800, part I, Record Group 75, National Archives.

43. Harvey K. Meyer, superintendent, Choctaw Indian Agency, to commissioner of Indian affairs, 19 February 1940, 23 February 1940, File 68776-1931-800, part I, National Archives, Record Group 75.

44. See for example "Briefs from the School Board Office," *Jena Times*, 11 September 1947, 1, which after citing enrollment numbers for blacks and whites (but not Indians) states: "an intensive drive is being planned to get all children of school age in school." Similar efforts among both white and black (but not Indian) illiterates are noted in Marksville during the years of the state's literacy campaign. See "From School Board Office."

45. See Watt, "Federal Indian Policy and Tribal Development in Louisiana," 154, and Harvey K. Meyer to commissioner of Indian affairs, 25 January 1940, File 68776-1931-800, part I, National Archives, Record Group 75.

46. Samuel H. Thompson to W. Carson Ryan Jr., 27 March 1933; Helene Sliffe to T. H. Harris, Louisiana superintendent of state education, 13 April 1933, File 25436-1931-150-800, National Archives and Records Administration, Record Group 75, available in Gregory, "The Jena Band of Louisiana Choctaw," 12.

47. Szasz, *Education and the American Indian*, 16–36. Other educational policy and boarding school histories used here include Child, *Boarding School Seasons*; Lomawaima, *They Called It Prairie Light*; LaFlesche, *The Middle Five*; Hoxie, *A Final Promise*; Johnston, *Indian School Days*; Adams, *Education for Extinction*.

48. Szasz, *Education and the American Indian*, 16–36.

49. Ibid., 105.

50. Child, *Boarding School Seasons*.

51. Whether this was a reflection of sentiments held by Ryan and his successor, Willard Beatty, against increasing boarding school enrollments or a federal decision that Indians from federally nonrecognized tribes were not entitled to federal educational support of that type is not clear. Nonfederal Indians have at times been allowed to attend federal Indian schools. According to Karen Blu, several Lumbees may have attended Carlisle. Blu, *The Lumbee Problem*, 82. More than fifty nonfederal Indians from Maine attended Carlisle Indian School, which operated from 1879 to 1918. Abbe Museum web site. The Mashpee tribal member Nelson Simons, among

others, attended Carlisle. Campisi, *The Mashpee Indians*. Ruth Underhill apparently suggested the possibility of attending boarding schools for Tunica young adults aged eighteen to thirty during her visit in 1938, but since the Tunicas declined, federal educational policy for them was never tested during that time, and students under eighteen were not offered any option at all aside from emigrating to Texas to attend public schools there. Underhill, "Report on a Visit to Indian groups in Louisiana, Oct. 15–25, 1938," 26. Cedric Sunray has undertaken a project to document the attendance of nonfederal Indians in federal Indian schools in the 1940s and 1950s. Primary documents can be found at http://www.helphaskell.com/purpose.html, accessed 6 April 2009.

52. Refusals often contained such less-than-soothing admonitions as "there are many other States in the eastern part of the country where there are Indians who are not, however, wards of the Federal Government and toward whom the Government has never assumed responsibility." C. J. Rhoads to L. A. Law, superintendent, St. Mary Parish, 11 April 1932, File 68776-1931-800, part I, National Archives, Record Group 75.

53. Mrs. Charles (Mattie) Penick to Willard Beatty, 8 November 1940, File 68776-1931-800, part I, National Archives, Record Group 75.

54. Wilkins and Lomawaima, *Uneven Ground*, 129–67.

55. U.S. Office of Federal Acknowledgment, "Genealogical Report, Jena Band of Choctaw Indians," 10.

56. Watt, "Federal Indian Policy and Tribal Development in Louisiana," 233–51.

57. The Chitimachas of south central Louisiana had a somewhat limited federal recognition since they had no treaties, but they had 261 acres of land, donated to the tribe by a local benefactor in 1916 to be held in trust by the federal government. The Office of Indian Affairs seems to have forgotten about this relationship over the years. The Chitimachas, through the state superintendent T. H. Harris, had to remind them of this fact in 1932, when they still sought some form of education for their children. Harris wrote to Ray Lyman Wilbur, "By the way, the Indian chief and some of the other older Indians in the Charenton community told me recently that the Indians have a reservation there of several hundred acres. I have been unable to secure locally any definite information on the subject. I wish you would find out the facts and notify me. Heretofore the parish school board has made no attempt to provide a school for the twenty or thirty children living in that community, nor has the Federal Government. I organized a little school there recently, and I shall keep it going long enough to teach the children to read and write, and I am recommending that the school board make no exception of those children by providing a school for them as it does for the other races in the parish." Wilbur put the note in a memorandum to the Indian office, to which he appended, "Will you be kind enough to let me know whether we have any facts to send him?" Ray Lyman Wilbur, "Memorandum for the Indian Office," 25 April 1932. C. J. Rhoads, in response to a similar inquiry from Huey Long initiated by a neighbor of the Chitimachas, Miss Alice Peters, wrote, "It is true, as your correspondent suggests,

that there is in St. Mary's Parish, a tract of land occupied by the Chittimanches, which was deeded to the United States for the use and benefit of these Indians pursuant to the Act of May 18, 1916 (39 Stat. L. 123). This deeded tract contained about 261 acres and its value was formerly reported to be $6000 to $7000. You will realize, of course, that this property would, if it were taxable, yield only a small return to the Parish as a contributing revenue toward the education of the Indian children. It does not seem, therefore, that these facts would afford sufficient ground for the assumption of the responsibility for the Indians by the Government. It is our understanding that the Indians residing thereon are not wards of the Federal Government and, in any case, we have no appropriations available for their benefit. There is, it is true, an annual appropriation for payment of tuition for Indian children in State public schools. It is possible that tuition could be paid in the local schools of the Parish were it not for the fact that the Indians are not admitted to the white schools and will not attend the negro schools. Under the circumstances, we can offer no encouragement for Federal assistance." C. J. Rhoads to Senator Huey Long, 26 April 1932. Alice Peters wrote later, pleading the Chitimacha case. "Are we going to throw them down because their reservation is not very valuable? If the Indians were more prosperous they would not pitifully beg everyone to help them get a school for their children. They could send them away from home, even, though, they would find it very expensive." Alice M. Peters to C. J. Rhoads, 12 August 1932. Rhoads replied, denying federal responsibility. C. J. Rhoads to Alice M. Peters, 21 September 1932, File 68776-1931-800, part I, National Archives, Record Group 75.

58. Samuel H. Thompson to W. Carson Ryan Jr., 27 March 1933, File 25436-1931-150-800, National Archives and Records Administration, Record Group 75; Fred Daiker, handwritten note on "Inspection Report 5-358," Roy Nash's report on Louisiana Indians (12 June 1931), 7 August 1931, Bureau of Indian Affairs, Central Correspondence File 25436-31-150, General Services, Record Group 75, National Archives.

59. M. S. Robertson, assistant state supervisor of Elementary Education, to W. Carson Ryan Jr., director of Indian education, 28 March 1934; W. Carson Ryan, memorandum to Higgins, 5 April 1934, File 68776-1931-800, part I, National Archives, Record Group 75.

60. A. C. Hector, superintendent of Choctaw Indian Agency in Mississippi, to John Collier, commissioner of Indian affairs, 10 August 1934, File 68776-1931-800, part I, National Archives, Record Group 75. The statement that the Jena Band had "for years been separated from any other Indians" is not only wrong but oddly put. First, the Jena Band did have regular contact with other Indians in the state, including the Tunicas, Biloxis, and Coushattas. Second, while Hector describes the group as "six or seven families" of "pure blood" Choctaws living near each other, he sounds as though he is imagining one isolated family cut off from the tribe, not a group of several dozen Choctaw speakers maintaining an insular social entity. Hector would later become a more avid supporter of educational allocations for the Jena Band, after being informed that the money would come separately from the

budget for the Mississippi Choctaws. A. C. Hector to John Collier, 17 July 1935, File 68776-1931-800, part I, National Archives, Record Group 75.

61. A. C. Hector to W. Carson Ryan Jr., 12 September 1934, File 68776-1931-800, part I, National Archives, Record Group 75.

62. Ibid.

63. A. C. Hector to John Collier, 17 July 1935, File 68776-1931-800, part I, National Archives, Record Group 75.

64. As OFA notes in its historical report, although Carson Ryan agreed to fund the school through the Louisiana Department of Education, correspondence with M. S. Robertson and Penick and funding allotment records for the state suggest that funding was never received. Watt, "Federal Indian Policy and Tribal Development in Louisiana," 141, suggests that funding had been disbursed, probably based on the earlier correspondence between Ryan and Robertson, though she cites the correspondence files generally rather than naming a specific document to support the statement. There is some evidence that federal funding may have been disbursed in some other way, however. OFA cites a letter written by Penick 3 March 1935 to the commissioner of Indian affairs, with the file annotation in its bibliography reading "File ?" The letter notes that a building in the town of Jena was being rented that spring to use for the school. It is not clear what became of the earlier schoolhouse in nearby Searcy. M. S. Robertson wrote to A. C. Hector later that spring with the comment that "it is necessary for us to rent a little building in Jena," phrasing that suggests the building was already being rented. Since the only agency to suggest in 1935 that it would fund the school was the BIA rather than the state or parish board of education, it seems likely that funds were allocated to the school for this purpose. U.S. Office of Federal Acknowledgment, "Historical Technical Report, Jena Band of Choctaw Indians," 31, "Source Materials," 18; M. S. Robertson to A. C. Hector, 23 May 1935, CCF File 68776-1931-800, part I, National Archives, Record Group 75.

65. Watt, "Federal Indian Policy and Tribal Development in Louisiana," 142–47, citing various newspaper clippings from the papers of Mattie Penick.

66. Willard W. Beatty, director of education, Bureau of Indian Affairs, memorandum to William Zimmerman, assistant commissioner of Indian affairs, ?16 May 1938, File 68776-1931-800, part I, National Archives, Record Group 75.

67. Willard W. Beatty, director of education, Bureau of Indian Affairs, memorandum to William Zimmerman, assistant commissioner of Indian affairs, 16 May 1938, File 68776-1931-800, part I, National Archives, Record Group 75.

68. L. W. Page, superintendent, Choctaw Indian Agency, to John Collier, commissioner of Indian affairs, 8 September 1938, File 68776-1931-800, part I, National Archives, Record Group 75.

69. Paul L. Fickinger, associate director of education, Bureau of Indian Affairs, to Harvey K. Meyer, superintendent, Choctaw Agency, 17 February 1940; Harvey K. Meyer to commissioner of Indian affairs, 25 January 1940; M. S. Robertson, in his new capacity as director of education for the Works Progress Administration, to

Harvey K. Meyer, 23 January 1940, File 68776-1931-800, part I, National Archives, Record Group 75. The "we" referred to in Fickinger's statement included Fickinger, William Zimmerman, Joe Jennings, Ruth Underhill, and Willard Beatty. See "Memorandum for the Record," Paul L. Fickinger, 5 March 1940, same file.

70. Watt, "Federal Indian Policy and Tribal Development in Louisiana," 154.

71. See chapter 1. Reid P. Chambers, associate solicitor, Indian affairs, "Memorandum: Secretary's Authority to Extend Federal Recognition to Indian Tribes," to solicitor, Department of the Interior, 20 August 1974, copy in American Indian Policy Review Commission, "Unidentified Records," box 315, folder: "A Report on the Landless Tribes of Washington State."

72. Harvey K. Meyer, superintendent, Choctaw Indian Agency, to commissioner of Indian affairs, 19 February 1940, 23 February 1940, File 68776-1931-800, part I, National Archives, Record Group 75.

73. Harvey K. Meyer, superintendent, Choctaw Indian Agency, to commissioner of Indian affairs, 19 February 1940, 23 February 1940, File 68776-1931-800, part I, National Archives, Record Group 75.

74. Paul L. Fickinger to Harvey Meyer, 22 April 1940, File 68776-1931-800, part I, National Archives, Record Group 75. Note the two-month lapse in reply, indicating the priority that Jena Choctaws were given at the time.

75. Paul L. Fickinger to Dr. A. A. Fredericks, president, Louisiana State Normal College, 24 October 1940, File 68776-1931-800, part I, National Archives, Record Group 75.

76. Mattie Penick, frustrated with the federal refusal to provide educational funds for the Jena Choctaws, enlisted the aid of A. A. Fredericks, president of Louisiana State Normal College in Natchitoches, where Penick had received her teaching degree. Fredericks persuaded the Louisiana Congressional committee to make inquiries on behalf of the Jena Choctaws, but to no avail. A. A. Fredericks to Willard Beatty, 4 September 1940; Senator John Overton to John Collier, 7 September 1940; Representative A. Leonard Allen to Willard Beatty, 9 September 1940; Senator Allen J. Ellender to Willard Beatty, 9 September 1940; Paul L. Fickinger to Dr. A. A. Fredericks, 24 October 1940, File 68776-1931-800, part I, National Archives, Record Group 75. Penick wrote to Willard Beatty after the most recent rejection and proposed that the government pay for them to board at the Normal College. She listed several reasons why this situation would be beneficial, even proposing that the tribal chief move to Natchitoches to work as a docent in the "Indian Museum" in the college.

77. See note 38, above.

78. In Louisiana the Tunica-Biloxis, Clifton-Choctaws, Chitimachas, and Houmas also refused to be placed in black schools, though the Houmas were the only group that successfully created an Indian school without federal intervention. The Clifton-Choctaws developed their own school, but it was not designated an Indian school. Lumbee history contains similar experiences with formal education. See Sider, *Lumbee Indian Histories*. See also Williams, "Patterns in the History of the Remaining Southeastern Indians, 1840–1975."

79. "Jena Indians Learn What Their Ancestors Forgot."

80. Penick wrote to Willard Beatty regarding the possibility of placing Choctaw children in a boarding situation at Louisiana State Normal College in Natchitoches and described the Little Indian Club to him. "During their last year of school," she wrote, "the many letters requesting information concerning the Indians, prompted me to organize a State-wide Indian Club. School bus loads of club members from various points in the State came to spend the day with the Indian boys and girls and a beautiful relationship was born among them. The Indian children were in the spotlight and felt that they were 'wanted,' for the first time in their lives. Continuation of this club under the sponsorship of the La. State Normal College will help the children in the training school to accept them and at the same time offer a history of the Louisiana Indians to the children of our state." Penick to Willard Beatty, 8 November 1940, File 68776-1931-800, part I, National Archives, Record Group 75. Despite the likelihood that it did make the Choctaw students feel "wanted" in some way, an element of racial display and colonial curiosity is also present.

81. "Jena Indians Learn What Their Ancestors Forgot."

82. U.S. Office of Federal Acknowledgment, "Historical Technical Report, Jena Band of Choctaw Indians."

83. Ibid., 34; William Zimmerman to J. Fair Hardin, assistant U.S. attorney, 11 March 1936, Bureau of Indian Affairs, Central Correspondence File 25436-31-150, General Services, Record Group 75, National Archives.

84. Notably A. C. Hector to Paul Fickinger, 6 July 1937, Bureau of Indian Affairs, Central Correspondence File 68776-1931-800, General Services, Record Group 75, National Archives.

85. John Collier, letter to Archie C. Hector, superintendent, Choctaw Agency, 28 August 1935, File 40616-35, Central Classified Files, Record Group 75, National Archives. While Zimmerman and others considered the Jena Choctaws eligible for enrollment in Mississippi, they were nonetheless treated as a separate group eligible for separate funding for their school. That apparently did not constitute unambiguous federal recognition in the OFA administrators' minds, because "Paul Fickinger, associate director of education for the Office of Indian Affairs, told the superintendent that after 'considerable study,' the Indian Office had decided that 'there is little responsibility accruing to the Federal government for these [Louisiana] Indian groups.'" See U.S. Office of Federal Acknowledgment, "Historical Technical Report, Jena Band of Choctaw Indians," 36–37.

## Chapter 7: Jena Choctaw Persistence

1. The tribal leader Chris Jackson, for example, refused to move to town. Other family members waited until after his death in 1958 to move to town. U.S. Office of Federal Acknowledgment, "Historical Technical Report, Jena Band of Choctaw Indians," 39, citing interview with Mary Jackson Jones, 11 May 1994. Watt, "Federal

Indian Policy and Tribal Development in Louisiana," 204, discusses the population shift as well.

2. OFA suggests that the date of integration was 1943, based on oral testimony given in 1990 that Choctaw children were enrolled when Choctaw men enlisted to fight in the Second World War. U.S. Office of Federal Acknowledgment, "Historical Technical Report, Jena Band of Choctaw Indians," 39, citing "Governor's Commission, 1990," which matches no document listed in the bibliography. The tribal elder Mary Jackson Jones corroborated this date and the reason for integration in an interview with the author in 2004. Marilyn Watt's research, based on oral testimony as well, vaguely notes that "for some reason, the attitude of the LaSalle Parish School Board changed after World War II, and by 1945 the [Jena] Choctaws were enrolled in the white public schools." She reports that one of the first Jena Choctaws to enroll in white Jena schools remembers only that the decision to enroll Choctaw children was "sudden," so the Choctaws do not seem to have been directly involved in bringing about this change of heart on the school board. Watt, "Federal Indian Policy and Tribal Development in Louisiana," 154. Sarah Sue Goldsmith gives 1946 as the date of integration, presumably based on interview sources. Goldsmith, "The Jena Band."

3. Military participation as a way of claiming inclusion in the nation was a consistent theme for communities of color in the Second World War, from the African American "Double V" campaign for victory in the war and victory over racism on the home front, to the service of Japanese Americans in the much-decorated 442d Regimental Combat Team (despite the imprisonment of some of their relatives in American internment camps), to the high enlistment rates of Mexican Americans and other immigrant communities. Native Americans had the highest per capita enlistment rate of any group in the war.

4. "Look Out, Schickgruber"; "Pagan Indians Favor One White Man's Idea"; "Indians of New Mexico Training for War Jobs"; "Hand Gone, Indian Air Hero Keeps on Firing."

5. "Compulsory Education." Also, "Educate Them All."

6. "Educate Them All."

7. "Compulsory School Attendance Law to Be Enforced." The law in question was Louisiana Act 239, 1944. Louisiana passed its first compulsory attendance law in 1910, and by 1918 every state in the country had enacted compulsory education laws under a similar movement that began in the 1850s, but they were not uniformly enforced. The original movement was intended to transform immigrants "into virtuous, productive American citizens" and thus shared a central spirit with Indian education policy. Katz, A History of Compulsory Education Laws, 17.

8. "LaSalle Parish School Board Elects Officials at Jan. 6th Session."

9. Watt, "Federal Indian Policy and Tribal Development in Louisiana," 154.

10. The former tribal chairman Clyde Jackson, highlighting the educational needs of the tribe, likes to joke that his father was drafted into the Second World War right out of first grade, and only later mentions that his father was twenty when he fin-

ished first grade at the Penick Indian School. He was not allowed to go to school but was drafted to defend the United States. Marilyn Watt discusses these trends in her dissertation. The OFA historical report for the Jena Band repeats much of her information, which was confirmed in my own interviews with tribal members. Watt, "Federal Indian Policy and Tribal Development in Louisiana," 154–57; U.S. Office of Federal Acknowledgment, "Historical Technical Report, Jena Band of Choctaw Indians," 38–40.

11. Watt, "Federal Indian Policy and Tribal Development in Louisiana," 157; U.S. Office of Federal Acknowledgment, "Historical Technical Report, Jena Band of Choctaw Indians," 40; U.S. Office of Federal Acknowledgment, "Anthropological Report, Jena Band of Choctaw Indians," 15–16, 20.

12. While Watt suggests that the mayor of the nearby town of Pollock, M. D. Regions, was involved in recognition from the beginning, Jerry Jackson suggests that Watt was wrong, and that Regions only became involved later. Watt, "Federal Indian Policy and Tribal Development in Louisiana," 171. Mary Jackson Jones recalls that Regions wanted to be involved in the tribal government and that he also "wanted to be the chief." He sensed that the tribe would become more powerful, and he apparently wanted to have access to the opportunities that he foresaw for it. The tribe maintained a relationship with Regions until state recognition, but quickly tired of him and discouraged him from continuing to participate in their affairs. Hiram F. Gregory recounts a conflicting story in an article written in 1977 with the help of Regions and several Jena Choctaws: that Commissioner David Garrison of the Governor's Commission on Indian Affairs, a white man with a connection to the Coushattas, appointed Regions "coordinator" for the tribe in 1973. Gregory, "The Jena Band of Louisiana Choctaw," 16.

13. Correspondence, Jerry Jackson to Ernest Sickey, indicates that Jena tribal bylaws were created in the same way. Jackson sent Sickey a copy of the Jena articles of incorporation and wrote, "If you can send me something to go by, I can have the By Laws to your office by the end of the week." His statements reveal the seat-of-the-pants initiation that unrecognized tribes had into bureaucratic requirements. Louisiana Office of Indian Affairs Archives, accession P1992-207, Indian Affairs: 1981–1984, Loc 19202-7, Louisiana State Archives, Baton Rouge. Louisiana Senate Concurrent Resolution 60, 1974, recognizing the Jena Band of Choctaws, cited in Watt, "Federal Indian Policy and Tribal Development in Louisiana," 174.

14. Watt describes the celebration, which was partly funded by the LaSalle Parish government, as a day of softball and crafts displays that included visitors from the Coushatta, Tunica-Biloxi, and Chitimacha tribes, and the Oklahoma and Mississippi Choctaws.

15. Watt, "Federal Indian Policy and Tribal Development in Louisiana," 176.

16. The document sanctioning the alliance of the Tunica, Choctaw, and Biloxi people of central Louisiana in 1924 does have a female signatory (see "Her Mark" in Tunica section), but that person appears to have been a Biloxi or Choctaw-Biloxi, based on the field notes of James Owen Dorsey. All the Jena Choctaw signatories

are males. "Biloxi Tribe, et al., 1924, Signed copy of statement by Biloxi Indian tribe and members of the Choctaw Indian Tribe residing in different parts of the State of Louisiana. October 9, 1924, Woodworth, Louisiana"; Dorsey, Field notes and unpublished papers, National Anthropological Archives, Smithsonian Institution, no. 4800, Biloxi 3.6.1.2.

17. Pesantubbee, *Choctaw Women in a Chaotic World*.

18. Perdue, *Cherokee Women*, esp. chapters 2, 6; Sturm, *Blood Politics*, 27–51; Saunt, *A New Order of Things*; and Galloway, *Choctaw Genesis*, 338–60, among many others.

19. American Indian Policy Review Commission, Task Force Ten, Baton Rouge hearings, 114.

20. The initial grant was $50,000. A second grant of $90,000 from HUD was used to add a mini-park and improve the office facility. Watt, "Federal Indian Policy and Tribal Development in Louisiana," 177, 184.

21. American Indian Policy Review Commission, Task Force Ten, Baton Rouge hearings, 117.

22. Handwritten note in grant file, possibly by Ernest Sickey, states, "Consensus among Indians: tribal enterprises will be the long range solution to unemployment problems." Surrounding materials indicate that the note was taken at a meeting in Jena in March 1974 or 1975. Louisiana Office of Indian Affairs Archives, Accession P1992-207, Indian Affairs: 1981–1984, Loc 19202-207, Louisiana State Archives, Baton Rouge.

23. See Cattelino, *High Stakes*.

24. See Barsh and Diaz-Knauf, "The Structure of Federal Aid for Indian Programs in the Decade of Prosperity."

25. American Indian Policy Review Commission, Task Force Ten, Baton Rouge hearings, 132.

26. Ibid., 135.

27. Glenn Coulthard, building on the work of Frantz Fanon, suggests that struggle itself "serves as the mediating force through which the colonized come to shed their colonial identities. . . . In contexts where recognition is conferred without struggle or conflict, this fundamental self-transformation . . . cannot occur, thus foreclosing the realization of authentic freedom." Coulthard, "Subjects of Empire." The struggle probably did make eventual recognition more valuable on some level, but most Jena Choctaw tribal leaders would hesitate to suggest that the tribe benefited from being federally nonrecognized for so many years.

28. See chapter 9.

29. See for example "William Lewis, 47, Shoots Military Police, Fishville," which identifies Lewis as a "Choctaw Indian who lives on Charlie Whatley's place."

30. Grabowski, "Coiled Intent," 271.

31. U.S. Office of Federal Acknowledgment, "Summary under the Criteria and Evidence for Proposed Finding for Federal Acknowledgment of the Jena Band of Choctaw Indians," 1–13.

32. Ibid., 21–22.

33. Shapard had even been the one to approve the original regulations and later testified at a Congressional hearing that the regulations do not work, and that the revisions of 1994 that were supposed to make them less subjective had actually made
them more subjective. U.S. Congress, "Hearing before the Subcommittee on
Native American Affairs of the Committee on Natural Resources," 163.

34. Bush, "Memorandum of Disapproval for the Jena Band of Choctaws of Louisiana
Restoration Act."

35. McCulloch and Wilkins speak indirectly to this issue, arguing that the more asser-
tive a tribe is of its sovereignty, the less likely it is to be recognized or receive the
sympathy of local non-Indians. McCulloch and Wilkins, " 'Constructing' Nations
within States."

36. Indeed, when George W. Bush became president in 2001 he overturned several
decisions to acknowledge tribes that had been made in the closing days of the Clinton White House. Moreover, his administration was notably stingy, fickle, and
receptive to state complaints based in anti-gaming sentiments rather than the
merits of each case. Instability characterized the highest post in federal Indian
affairs under his administration, with a succession of quick departures indicating a
discontent with administration policy and a distaste for the duties of the office even
among the largely conservative appointees to the position. Such an environment is
hardly conducive to petitions for federal acknowledgment. Only two of fifteen petitioners for acknowledgment reviewed under Bush were acknowledged.

37. For a brief history of the reversal of OFA's Positive Final Determinations see Toensing, "Eastern Pequots' Appeal of Recognition Reversal Rejected"; and Toensing,
"Judge Denies Schaghticoke Federal Recognition Appeal."

38. U.S. Office of Federal Acknowledgment, "Status Summary of Acknowledgment
Cases as of 22 September 2008. For information on the Abramoff scandal see chapter 8.

## Chapter 8: Jena Choctaw Recognition

1. "Jena Band of Choctaws Receives Federal Recognition as an Indian Tribe."

2. For literature on historical trauma and Native Americans see Duran and Duran,
*Native American Postcolonial Psychology*; and Duran, Duran, and Brave Heart,
"Native Americans and the Trauma of History."

3. In fact at least one Jena Choctaw teenager was sent to Mississippi to live with a
Choctaw family and attend the Choctaw schools.

4. Belvin, "Was It Worth the Gamble?"; Belvin, "Kinder Casino Has Been Positive";
Belvin, "Marksville Storyline Has Not Changed."

5. See Bridges, *Bad Bet on the Bayou*.

6. Goldsmith, "The Jena Band."

7. American Indian Policy Review Commission, *Final Report of the American Indian
Policy Review Commission*, 461–84.

8. Jena Choctaws do not recall ever using the word "halito," for example, a greeting

that is commonly the first word learned in Oklahoma-based Choctaw-language programs.

9. Tri-Millenium Corp. v. Jena Band of Choctaw Indians.

10. See Bridges, *Bad Bet on the Bayou*, esp. 233–375.

11. One of the factors that helped diminish the split between Lewis and Jackson developed while preparing the petition for recognition. The tribe produced a genealogical chart and put it on a wall in the tribal center, with a picture of each tribal member next to the member's name. They made children memorize their genealogy and point out their ancestors. Adults stopped to look at the chart as well: some had not realized that certain tribal members were their cousins; others had not known that a parent had been raised by someone other than a biological parent because of death or some other circumstance. The wall laid out all that family history plainly and made tribal members realize how closely related they all were. The representation of the tribe on the wall as a single entity reinforced the genealogical lessons, creating a lasting vision of tribal unity.

12. Quote reconstructed from memory shortly after a conversation with Christine Norris and Cheryl Smith that was unrecordable because of its location, 22 May 2008.

13. The tribe has not been able to overcome the ruling in Seminole v. Florida that invalidates the provision of the IGRA allowing tribes to sue states for failing to negotiate a gaming compact in good faith.

14. "Natchitoches Jurors Oppose Plan Seen as Prelude to Casino"; "Another Casino in Troubled State"; Turner, "Federal Officials Trap Themselves with Indian Casino Decision"; Sayre, "Proposed Reservation Casino Doesn't Make Sense for the State"; Sayre, "Foster Support for Indian Casino Puzzling"; Gill, "Foster Bluffs on Gambling Again"; Turner, "Analysis: Casino Tribe Searches for Land"; Dyer, "Candidates Oppose Expansion of Gambling"; "No Good Casino Plans in Works"; "Blanco Rejects Bad Casino Bet."

15. Opponents later pressed the issue that DeSoto Parish does not fall within the tribe's historic area, a claim that partly relies on a narrow view of the terms "historic area" and "tribe" and partly returns to the OFA's positivist assessment of tribal history. It is very well known that Choctaws *lived in* (rather than traveled through, as the press has suggested) the northwestern area of the state since at least the early 1800s. No historian will dispute that, since it is so clear from the documentary record. See Sibley, "A Report from Natchitoches in 1807." Whether the group now identified as the Jena Choctaws has any direct ancestors who lived in that area is a different question. Since the tribe conceded in its petition for recognition that its ancestors likely came from Mississippi after the Civil War, it is not claiming that any specific ancestors lived in DeSoto Parish. The answer is, for the most part, unknowable. That the tribe was a part of the greater Choctaw nation, which had numerous people in Louisiana as far west as DeSoto Parish, is clear. Add to this the possibility that the Jena Choctaw ancestors who eventually settled in their present area are descended from families that knew Louisiana well and returned there frequently before settling, and their claim that DeSoto Parish is part of their "aborigi-

nal territory" becomes much sturdier. But the OFA historical assessment states that there is "no evidence to connect any of the Jena Choctaws with the earliest Choctaw inhabitants of Louisiana," and the press and opponents of tribal gaming have seized on that as a statement of fact. See Turner, "Analysis: Casino Tribe Searches for Land." Evidence suggests that the Jena Choctaw ancestors *may have* settled in the area because they knew of it from earlier trips, but here the OFA's historically questionable and entirely positivist assessment comes back to haunt the tribe, even after they have gone through the petitioning process. The Choctaw-Apache Tribe in neighboring Sabine Parish likely welcomed the rejection on some level, since it has a stronger claim to the region and may decide to pursue gaming nearby if it attains federal acknowledgment.

16. "Another Casino in Troubled State." See note 14, above, for other, similar examples.

17. Dyer, "Vitter Opposes New Indian Casino Proposal"; "Jena Choctaws Once Wanted Casino in Caddo Parish"; "No Break for Indian Casino"; Courreges, "Choctaws Defend Deal"; Gill, "Foster Bluffs on Gambling Again"; Turner, "Analysis: Casino Tribe Searches for Land."

18. "Another Casino in Troubled State."

19. Sayre, "Coushatta's Lobbying Costly, Leads to Probe"; Milhollon, "Choctaw Band Sues Governor In LaSalle."

20. Sabludowsky, "Louisiana Election Buzz."

21. For a concise history of gaming and political corruption see Bridges, *Bad Bet on the Bayou*, chapter 1. Roemer himself later oversaw the legalization of video poker in 1991, desperate to generate revenue for a nearly bankrupt state government after the collapse of the petroleum industry in the 1980s.

22. A popular bumper sticker in Louisiana at the time read, "Vote for the crook. It's important."

23. Bridges, *Bad Bet on the Bayou*.

24. John Scott and Paul Nelson identify race, political party, and religion as the most significant factors in determining whether a parish approved the continuation of gaming in 1996, noting that blacks and Democrats were more likely to favor gaming while Southern Baptists were more likely to oppose it. Significantly, Scott and Nelson do not correlate religion with Anglo-American cultural and racial politics (versus those of Acadians, French, and Creoles, who are more likely to be Catholic), but I would suggest that the "Southern Baptist" vote would be the vote of whites who are most likely to cling to a claim of white moral superiority over nonwhites that is so central to the racial discourse on this issue. Scott and Nelson, "Voting with a Hand on the Bible and Not on the Wallet."

25. Dyer, "Candidates Oppose Expansion of Gambling."

26. The *Washington Post* ran a series of articles exposing the scandal, and the story was front-page news in many national newspapers between 2004 and 2006. Rather than list the long litany of articles, I direct readers to one primary source and two secondary sources: U.S. Congress, " 'Gimme Five' "; Stone, *Heist*; Continetti, *The K Street Gang*.

27. As Jerry Jackson notes, the 15 percent voluntary contribution that the tribe would pay for the Logansport site (which includes a 6 percent offset for local civil services that all tribes in the state pay, a 6 percent tribal contribution, and a 3 percent contribution from the casino management company) would not be paid if the tribe developed a site in its service area.

28. While the Chitimacha tribe did operate a high-stakes bingo hall in Charenton before the casino era, the bingo operation was replaced by a class III facility, which proved a more profitable use of the gaming space. Toney, "Tribe's Bingo Parlor to Open in September." See also Sovereign Nation of the Chitimacha, http://www .chitimacha.org / tribal_about_gaming.htm, accessed 2 February 2009. There is a discrepancy in the dates between the article cited and the web site, but it seems more likely that the bingo hall opened in 1988, since the newspaper reported that it had not yet opened at that date, than in 1985, as the web site suggests. The transition away from class II gaming is noted by the web site to have occurred in 1994.

29. Big Noise Tactical Media, "The Jena 6."

*Chapter 9: On the Outside, Looking In*

1. The meeting of the two men in a hospital in Alexandria was reported by several Clifton-Choctaws and corroborated by Rose Pierite White. Only one version of the story included Mobilian Jargon. Another close relative of Thomas confirmed that he spoke "Indian," but whether that meant Mobilian Jargon or Choctaw proper is uncertain. Emmanuel Drechsel, a specialist on the Mobilian Jargon, wrote in 1979 that he saw no evidence for residual use of Mobilian Jargon at Clifton. Drechsel suggests in his more recent work that a few older members of the Clifton community may have remembered either Mobilian Jargon or Choctaw, but apparently only a few undiagnostic words or phrases. He cites Hiram Gregory, who asserts that people at Clifton spoke Mobilian Jargon but called it Choctaw, but this assertion is unconfirmed. Drechsel also states that Joe Pierite Sr., who had died by the time Drechsel began his fieldwork, is reported to have spoken Mobilian Jargon, but Jena Choctaw informants noted that Pierite always spoke Choctaw proper to them, perhaps evidence that Joe Thomas spoke Choctaw as well. Drechsel, "Mobilian Jargon," 157, 162–66; Drechsel, *Mobilian Jargon*, 46, 206, 246–47. Russell Everett recorded an intriguing possibility while doing linguistic fieldwork in Clifton in 1958. One of his consultants, a man born in the 1880s, would "frequently . . . [give] a word unknown to the interviewer. On such occasions he undoubtedly noticed a look of bewilderment upon the face of the interviewer and he hastened to explain that it was a word the folks around there used." Everett was doing dialect research, so it is mind-boggling that he did not try to record the words that "folks around there used." These could have been words in Choctaw or Mobilian Jargon, but Everett chalked up their use to lack of education and chose not to embarrass the informant by pursuing the matter any further. Everett, "The Speech of the Tri-Racial Group Composing the Community of Clifton, Louisiana," 23–24.

2. Gregory, "Pieces and Patches"; more generally in Kniffen, Gregory, and Stokes, *The Historic Tribes of Louisiana from 1542 to the Present*.

3. Drechsel, "Mobilian Jargon." Also Faine, *The Clifton-Choctaw Community*, 11. Faine's study and several Clifton tribal members have indicated that their relationship with Sickey was positive, even though, regarding the Clifton-Choctaws, East Baton Rouge Choctaws, and Choctaw-Apaches, who had all received state recognition by 1980, Sickey stated, "Where are all these other Choctaws coming from? I've lived here all my life and the first time I've heard of them is in the last five years. I think [Pete Mora] was trying to establish his own constituency and justify his existence in a state office." Further, the Inter-Tribal Council of Louisiana at that time had authority to administer CETA funds, which they withheld from these groups. Thompson, "Tribes Have Little Legal Pull."

4. Amos Tyler to Leslie Gay, Bureau of Indian Affairs, 22 March 1978, Clifton-Choctaw Reservation, letter of intent to petition, Branch of Acknowledgment and Research file obtained under FOIA.

5. Articles of incorporation dated 18 September 1977, Norris Tyler papers, in possession of Norris Tyler.

6. Russell I. Everett notes in his master's thesis on Clifton speech that the Clifton community was very concerned at the time of his fieldwork that the lumber companies were just about to move out of the area, taking all the jobs with them. The community was relatively prosperous at the time if one can believe Everett, who wrote that the community grew much of its own food and that "almost every family" had "a car or truck usually about three years old." Everett, "The Speech of the Tri-Racial Group Composing the Community of Clifton, Louisiana," 7, 18, 20.

7. For an analysis based on world-systems theory of Choctaw participation in the timber industry in Oklahoma see Faiman-Silva, *Choctaws at the Crossroads*. See also James Carson's critique of her work, Review of *Choctaws at the Crossroads*. Brian C. Hosmer has examined logging in the Menominee community in Wisconsin. Hosmer, *American Indians in the Marketplace*.

8. Gregory, "Pieces and Patches," 9.

9. Everett, "The Speech of the Tri-Racial Group Composing the Community of Clifton, Louisiana," 18.

10. Faine, *The Clifton-Choctaw Community*, 11.

11. Redman, "Move Afoot to Unify Mixed-Breed Indians."

12. Ibid.

13. Ibid.

14. See Martin, "Development at Ysleta del Sur Pueblo, Texas."

15. They seemed to rotate the title of chairman of the Tribal Council each year. Norris Tyler served the first year, followed by his cousin Amos Tyler the next year, and Amos Tyler's wife, Corine Tyler, the year after that.

16. Tyler to Gay, Bureau of Indian Affairs, 22 March 1978, Clifton-Choctaw Reservation, letter of intent to petition.

17. Even, "Uproar over Tribe Put Down."

18. Ibid.

19. Pitts, "Louisiana Indians on Legal Warpath."

20. Larry Rainwater formed the Louisiana Band of Choctaws by calling for an organizational meeting at his home in local newspapers, inviting all Choctaw descendants to attend. See "Choctaw Tribe Plans Meeting."

21. Juneau, "Judicial Extinguishment of the Tunica Indian Tribe," 47 n. 12, details Guste's efforts to gut tribal recognition bills in the state legislature. Guste wrote in a letter to the legislature that a "federal designation of 'tribe status' greatly enhances the right to assert a claim under the 'Non-Intercourse Act' and entitles the designated 'tribe' to federal intervention to 'recover' lands conveyed in violation of the Non-Intercourse [Act]." William Guste Jr. to Members of the Louisiana Legislature, 3 July 1978.

22. U.S. Office of Federal Acknowledgment, Status of Acknowledgment Cases, date of receipt of Choctaw-Apache letter of intent to petition, 2 July 1978.

23. Thompson, "Tribes Have Little Legal Pull." Jerry Jackson, a Jena Choctaw, voiced a similar opinion in 2000, except that he believed it was Sickey who had begun the trend by urging the Houmas to organize.

24. Thompson, "Louisiana Indian Tribes Fighting for U.S. Recognition."

25. Thompson, "Tribes Have Little Legal Pull."

26. Ibid.

27. Gerald Sider has noted that many of the War on Poverty programs preferred channeling funds through "community action agencies" rather than state, city, or county offices, which were regarded as corrupt, inefficient, and detached from the problems the programs addressed. While Sider's comments reflect experiences from the late 1960s, it is likely that some of that attitude carried over to the present dispute. Sider, *Lumbee Indian Histories*, 261.

28. See for example Kreeger, "Louisiana Indians"; Cooke, "Hundreds Change Race to Qualify for Indian Funds." James Clifton raised important questions about the relationship between funding and Indian identity but resolved them oddly, arguing that people claimed to be Indian and perpetuated Indian identity primarily for money. Asking for assistance, of course, does not mean that people are not Indian or would not call themselves Indian without the availability of resources. Clifton was more inconsistent than he imagined on these issues, but postured himself as the defender of truth against Indians, whom he portrayed as deceitful, money-grubbing opportunists. Clifton, Introduction, *The Inverted Indian*. On the level of funding in the 1970s in general see Barsh and Diaz-Knauf, "The Structure of Federal Aid for Indian Programs in the Decade of Prosperity, 1970–1980." Barsh and Diaz-Knauf also criticize the programs for the amount of funding that never benefited Indian communities. More recently see Coates, "Put the Money Out, and They Will Come."

29. See Forbes, "The Manipulation of Race, Caste and Identity"; Blu, *The Lumbee Problem*; Campisi, *The Mashpee Indians*.

30. James Andrews to Paul Thomas, 11 February 1898, original in possession of Norris

Tyler, reproduced in Miller and Rich, "A History of the Clifton Community," 13. The possibility also remains that Thomas was in fact seeking a pension for some- one other than himself, though it seems most likely that he wrote on his own behalf or on behalf of the community as a whole. There are many records of white people writing to officials on behalf of their Indian neighbors, and this document could have been a reply to one of those letters, though that does not seem likely in view of the oral histories indicating Paul Thomas's Choctaw ancestry.

31. Goldsmith, "Reclaiming the Past." Sarpy repeated this information in interviews with the author.

32. Miller and Rich, "A History of the Clifton Community," 10. Miller and Rich were volunteers with the Mennonite Central Committee (MCC) who lived among the Clifton for two years and helped them to research and document community his- tory in preparation for a petition for federal recognition. The MCC placed volun- teers with the Houmas and the Choctaw-Apaches to do similar work. In support of this theory, Miller and Rich cite personal communication with Robert K. Thomas, noted Cherokee anthropologist and ethnohistorian. Thank you to Shari Miller Wagner for providing me with a copy of selections from that work.

33. Jackson told me so personally in an interview in 1999, but his opinion is also dis- cussed in Calongne, "Jena Tribe."

34. The Jena chief Cheryl Smith describes the articles as "horrible." The article was supposed to say that the Clifton-Choctaws were blacks with only a little Indian ancestry, but ended up being distorted to say that they were not Indian at all, she contends. Calongne, "Genealogist Says Clifton-Choctaws are not Indians"; Calongne, "Jena Tribe"; Calongne, "La. Tribe Fights to Prove Its Heritage."

35. Calongne, "Genealogist Says Clifton-Choctaws are not Indians," 1.

36. Ibid.

37. Interview from 1964–65, cited in Barber, *Above the Falls*. Barber calls their homes a "reservation," which has led to a search for any documents relating to the creation of a state reservation there in the late nineteenth century, but it may be that this is just an idiomatic description picked up by locals to refer to Indian homes. Interest- ingly, Parker describes a murder that may have been the death of Sesostrie You- chigant's father: "In 1895, a group of Indians were returning to their homes out on Sieper. They were drunk and two of them got into a fight and a third one got in between them to stop the fighting. He was stabbed and died right there on the road. Willie Forrest was one of the two eyewitnesses and testified in court in Alex- andria. The one who did the stabbing was sentenced for life. Doc Nichols and I attended the Indian's funeral at night." Barber, *Above the Falls*, 385–86.

38. Drechsel, *Mobilian Jargon*, 264. As Drechsel has argued, the Indian presence in cen- tral Louisiana had to be significant in the early twentieth century to create a situa- tion in which non-Indians would feel a need to learn a trade language such as Mobilian Jargon as late as the 1950s. Drechsel's fieldwork revealed that only older people still remembered any Mobilian by the 1970s, confirming that the younger generations had ceased to find it useful.

39. There is currently a town called Pinewood between Leesville and Rosepine in western Louisiana. The state-recognized Four Winds Tribe Cherokee Confederacy has its headquarters eight miles from Pinewood, in DeRidder, Louisiana, but I am not familiar with its organization or history, and it draws its membership from several parishes in western Louisiana. "Pinewood" could refer to a historic town no longer in existence, or either of these locations.

40. "I went to a Choctaw ball and danced for three nights. We played ball for three days. They danced every night. The people danced in two circles around the fire all night long. They danced in circles far from the fire which lay in the center. Two thousand Indians danced. The Choctaw danced at Pinewood." Haas, *Tunica Texts*, 153. Youchigant says that his father had actually moved to Pinewoods and remarried, though his new wife and little children all died and he was killed in a fight or robbery (151). Youchigant mentions Biloxis in this settlement (145), stating that "they became (mixed with) various races," or, in a literal translation, "They turned into different kinds of people," a possible reference to intermarriage with Clifton families. Because he refers primarily to a Choctaw settlement, this was not likely the Biloxi-Choctaw group at Indian Creek near Lecompte that became part of the Tunica-Biloxi Tribe. It is possible that he is referring to the Glenmora Choctaws, a settlement also in Rapides Parish, but just over twenty miles south and east of Clifton. It is not likely that he is referring to the Coushattas at Kinder since he would clearly have known they were not primarily Choctaws. It is also not likely that he was referring to the Mississippi Choctaws or the St. Tammany Parish Choctaws (see Bushnell, *The Choctaw of Bayou Lacomb, St. Tammany Parish, Louisiana*), who were much farther away than these other Choctaw settlements.

41. Annie Parker, interview quoted in Barber, *Above the Falls*, 386. "Bobbie Shele" was a mistranscription of "bobasheeli," a Choctaw term meaning brother. According to the web site of the Mississippi Choctaw, "In Choctaw it denotes having suckled at the same breast, as in the case of siblings," http://www.choctaw.org/show.asp?durki=18, accessed 27 July 2003.

42. "Biloxi Tribe et al., 1924, Signed copy of statement by Biloxi Indian tribe and members of the Choctaw Indian Tribe residing in different parts of the State of Louisiana."

43. Miller and Rich, "Traditional Medicines."

44. Balthazar, *Cane River and Its Creole Stories*; interview with Anna Lavalais Neal, Clifton, Louisiana, 7 October 1994. The Baptiste that Neal refers to is likely a relative of the Jena Choctaws and perhaps the Coushattas, who have a significant number of Choctaw ancestors, some of whom carry that surname or a variant of it.

45. Miller and Rich, "A History of the Clifton Community," 12.

46. Theodore R. Quasula, acting director, Bureau of Indian Affairs, Office of Tribal Services, to Henry M. Neal Sr., 13 August 1991, 5, Clifton-Choctaw file, Branch of Acknowledgment and Research. It should be noted that even the Jena Choctaws' initial petition failed to link present membership with nineteenth-century predecessors. In the Jena case this failure represented inadequate data rather than a lack of Indian ancestry.

47. U.S. Office of Federal Acknowledgment, "Genealogical Report, Jena Band of Choctaw Indians," 18; U.S. Office of Federal Acknowledgment, "Historical Technical Report, Jena Band of Choctaw Indians," 16.

48. U.S. Office of Federal Acknowledgment, "Historical Technical Report, Jena Band of Choctaw Indians," 20–23.

49. Sturm, *Blood Politics*.

50. The 1910 census for Rapides Parish, Louisiana, lists many Clifton, Tyler, and Smith families as mulatto. This is clearly not a complete and diagnostic genealogical connection, but it is obvious that these are the ancestors of at least some of the modern Clifton families.

51. The 1910 Indian Schedule for Rapides Parish included the surnames Brandy, Saul, Murphy, Jackson, Lee, Thompson, Wash, and Johnson. Murphy and Jackson are surnames found in the Jena community; Jackson and Johnson are found in the Biloxi-Choctaw community.

52. U.S. Bureau of the Census, *Measuring America*, 55.

53. Ibid., 56.

54. Forbes, *Africans and Native Americans*, esp. 84–88, 94–95, 102–3.

55. See also Williams, "Patterns in the History of the Remaining Southeastern Indians, 1840–1975."

56. U.S. Bureau of the Census, *Measuring America*, 56. "Proportions of Indian and other blood.—If the Indian is a full-blood, write 'full' in column 36, and leave columns 37 and 38 blank. If the Indian is of mixed blood, write in column 36, 37, and 38 the fractions which show the proportions of Indian and other blood, as (column 36, Indian) 3 / 4, (column 37, white) 1 / 4, and (column 38, negro) 0. For Indians of mixed blood all three columns should be filled, and the sum, in each case, should equal 1, as 1 / 2, 0, 1 / 2; 3 / 4, 1 / 4, 0; 3 / 4, 1 / 8, 1 / 8; etc. Wherever possible, the statement that an Indian is of full blood should be verified by inquiry of the older men of the tribe, as an Indian is sometimes of mixed blood without knowing it."

57. Jolivette, *Louisiana Creoles*. See also Mills, *The Forgotten People*.

58. Thank you to Susan Dollar for mentioning the significance of this distinction in a conversation in 2003.

59. For an article on this issue see Brian Klopotek, "Of Shadows and Doubts: White Supremacy, Decolonization, and Black-Indian Relations," *Sovereign Acts*, ed. Frances Negron-Muntaner (Boston: South End, 2009).

60. Let it be said that the BIA did not know the parameters of its service population at the time either.

61. Mills, *The Forgotten People*; Forbes, "The Manipulation of Race, Caste and Identity"; Dominguez, *White by Definition*.

62. Dominguez, *White by Definition*, 204.

63. Forbes, "The Manipulation of Race, Caste and Identity," 24, emphasis in original.

64. Jolivette, *Louisiana Creoles*. Indeed one western Louisiana Creole of color who identified as triracial and considered himself African American was shocked when a DNA test suggested he was about 40 percent Indian and 60 percent white, with no

indication of African ancestry. Arihara, "Black like I Thought I Was." While such racial "tests" are notoriously unreliable and misleading in some ways, an indication of such large amounts of Indian ancestry certainly stands as evidence that Indian ancestry is not a "myth" among western Louisiana Creoles of color. As Frank Porter notes, academic decisions about "triracial isolates" are usually based on confused local oral testimonies about the origins of the groups, as in Brewton Berry's study *Almost White*. "Consequently," Porter writes, "an attempt to establish the origins of some Indian communities must contend with an unwieldy body of folk history, local bias, naiveté, and scanty historical evidence." Berry, *Almost White*; Porter, "Nonrecognized American Indian Tribes," 8.

65. See Lovett, " 'African and Cherokee by Choice.' "

66. Merrell, "The Racial Education of the Catawba Indians," 374.

67. Coleman, " 'Tell the Court I Love My [Indian] Wife,' " 75.

68. Any Indian person there with more than one-quarter African "blood" (later one-sixteenth) would be classified as "colored" and thus have access to fewer rights and resources than those classified as Indians, who were those of more than one-quarter Indian blood (later one-sixteenth). Rountree, *Pocahontas's People*, 200, 211.

69. Thompson and Peterson, "Mississippi Choctaw Identity," 180.

70. Blu, *The Lumbee Problem*, 62–65.

71. On Cherokees see Sturm, "Blood Politics, Racial Classification, and Cherokee National Identity"; and Miles, *Ties That Bind*. On Creeks see Saunt, *Black, White, and Indian*. On Seminoles see Mulroy, *The Seminole Freedmen*. Generally see Miles and Holland, eds., *Crossing Waters, Crossing Worlds*; Brooks, ed., *Confounding the Color Line*.

72. Greenbaum, "What's in a Label?"; Campisi, *The Mashpee Indians*, 27–28, 88–91, 94; more generally see parts II and III of Brooks, ed., *Confounding the Color Line*. David Wilkins assesses the way these social and political boundaries reveal themselves in the Lumbee case. "One of the primary reasons the Lumbees have been denied federal recognition is that we are said, very quietly these days, to exhibit too much of an ad-mixture of non-Indian racial characteristics, with an emphasis being placed almost exclusively on our perceived, and real, mixtures with African-Americans. This is interesting, since the documentary and oral evidence of my people points to the Lumbees having intermarried actually more with whites than with African-Americans. But, as Wilma [Mankiller] noted in her comments, Indian white intermarriage or 'hanky-panky,' if you will, has been acceptable historically while Indian black involvement, or 'hanky-panky,' was deemed to dilute or to corrupt the tribe's cultural and genetic identity. This is a perverse form of racism, folks, and I think we can all agree upon that!" Wilkins, Comments in "Exploring the Legacy and Future of Black / Indian Relations."

73. Underhill, "Report on a Visit to Indian Groups in Louisiana, Oct. 15–25, 1938."

74. Barbry went on to say that he unequivocally did *not* support the recognition efforts of a group in the Marksville area claiming to be Tunica that had formed in early 2000.

75. Everett, "The Speech of the Tri-Racial Group Composing the Community of Clifton, Louisiana," 6, 15.

76. It might be argued that Creoles of color maintained similar boundaries between themselves and blacks and whites, but that does not mean that the Clifton-Choctaws are Creoles of color. Though they have intermarried with the Cane River Creoles to some extent, the Cliftons have maintained a distinct identity as Indians. The boundary between the communities is reinforced by the very strong Baptist tradition at Clifton, which is not found in any Creole community (Susan E. Dollar, personal communication, 21 March 2003). While they may share ancestors (even some Indian ancestors), the identities of the communities evolved differently, just as French and English cultures maintained distinctions while exchanging bloodlines and cultural practices.

77. Miller and Rich, "A History of the Clifton Community," 16.

78. B. G. Dyess, Rapides Parish registrar of voters from 1964 to 1988, said in 1987 that he had known the Clifton people since the 1940s, and that "the people outside the Choctaw community have always regarded and accepted the people there as Indians. Those of the tribe, registered to vote, are classified as Indians." Calongne, "Genealogist Says Clifton-Choctaws Are Not Indians," § A, 2.

79. Calongne, "Genealogist Says Clifton-Choctaws Are Not Indians," § A, 2.

80. The web site of Northwood High School, which Clifton students attend, states that the school opened in 1900, http://www.rapides.k12.la.us/northwood/history.htm. An elderly informant, who remembers the people involved but consistently jumbles dates, places the beginning of the school in the early 1900s and suggests that the parish began paying for a teacher in 1915. The superintendent of Rapides schools gave 1924 as the date when Rapides began administering the school. Calongne, "Genealogist Says Clifton-Choctaws Are Not Indians," 1.

81. Jasper Clifton, one of the men of the community, offered half of his own house to be used as the school. His log cabin, of "dog trot" design, in which two large rooms were separated by a covered breezeway to keep the cabin cool in the sweltering Louisiana heat, provided a suitably detached temporary space for instruction. He moved his sizable family into one side of the cabin and let the community use the other side as a school until a new facility was built.

82. Information from community members and Everett, "The Speech of the Tri-Racial Group Composing the Community of Clifton, Louisiana," 18.

83. Faine writes that the school closed in 1969, information likely gathered from Miller and Rich (*The Clifton-Choctaw Community*, 29). The date given in Barber, *Above the Falls*, 388, by the superintendent of Rapides schools (Calongne, "Genealogist Says Clifton-Choctaws Are Not Indians," 1), and on the Northwood High School web site (http://www.rapides.k12.la.us/northwood/history.htm) is 1971. Myrtlene Shackleford, former tribal chair, recalls the date as 1970, when she was in the fifth grade. I have not seen any indisputable historical records of the exact year.

84. Officially, black and white schools were desegregated earlier, but a lawsuit initiated in 1965 concluded that a de facto system of segregation based on gerrymandered

neighborhood boundaries remained in place at that time. More than 90 percent of black students continued to attend almost exclusively black schools. The courts continued to oversee the desegregation of Rapides Parish schools at least into the 1980s. Valley v. Rapides Parish School Board. Before integration Clifton students moving out of the community school would have been forced to attend Wetter-mark school, a predominantly black school targeted for integration by the appeal in 1970 of the lawsuit filed in 1965, but they were sent instead to the predominantly white Boyce school. Myrtlene Shackleford reports that she attended Boyce for three years before any blacks were integrated into the school.

85. Faine, *The Clifton-Choctaw Community*, 7.

86. Adelle v. Beauregard. Contrary to Dominguez, *White by Definition*, 34, see Mills, *The Forgotten People*, for evidence that the antimiscegenation laws in French Louisiana and elsewhere in the South were not as strictly enforced as legislators had hoped. Mills argues that these laws were designed primarily to prevent property from passing from whites to blacks and part-blacks through the laws of marriage and inheritance, rather than to prevent liaisons between whites and people of color. Further, while according to Dominguez Adelle v. Beauregard states *explicitly* that Indians are "persons of color," the passage from the decision is more ambiguous. The central question of the case was whether the plaintiff could be considered a slave without proof of ownership, and the court found that only "negroes" can be generally assumed to be slaves by their race. "Persons of colour," on the other hand, "maye have descended from Indians on both sides, from a white parent, or mulatto parents in possession of their freedom. Considering how much probability there is in favor of the liberty of those persons, they ought not to be deprived of it on presumption." It is not clear that the judge meant that people descended *exclusively* from Indians on both sides (thus, full-blooded Indians) *must* be designated "persons of colour" or meant rather that a person with visible African ancestry could be descended from Indian (read: free) grandmothers and still be free because he or she was not born a slave. The judge drew a distinction between a "free person of color" and a slave, without specifying whether an Indian must always be classified as a person of color. Moreover, the judgment does not address the issue of descent from Indians on one side. Finally, as has become increasingly common knowledge, many thousands of Indians were enslaved in the Southeast, and though many were shipped to Carribean islands, a good many contributed to the gene pool of slave descendants in the United States too, so that even a person listed as "negro" might be as much Indian as African.

87. Act 220 of 1920.

88. James O'Connor, assistant attorney general, "Marriage between White Persons and Indians Is Not Prohibited in Louisiana," *Opinions and Reports of the Attorney General of the State of Louisiana (1932–1934)*, 587; Pascal, *Readings in Louisiana Family Law*, 28.

89. An implication made clear in the aforementioned opinion from the Louisiana attorney general's office, which stated that the phrase "persons of color" in Loui-

siana's marriage code had "reference to negroes only," though "negroes" seemed to mean anyone with known African ancestry.

90. Neil Foley draws heavily on Toni Morrison's ideas about southern European immigrants becoming white in the United States by demonstrating their hatred of blacks as he grapples with similar issues of racial formation in Mexican-American integration activism in Texas of the 1930s. Foley, "Becoming Hispanic."

91. Andrew Jolivette suggests that there is a movement among Creoles of color to have Creole added as a new category on the census, because Creoles are constrained to identify as either white or black or mixed rather than as a distinct ethnic group with black, white, *and* indigenous roots. Jolivette, *Louisiana Creoles.*

92. While typically the term "white supremacy" conjures images of Klan robes and neo-Nazi skinheads, the term as it is used in contemporary ethnic studies also refers to the everyday ideology of white racial superiority and domination carried even by people who do not consider themselves racist, carried even by people of color.

93. Saunt, *Black, White, and Indian*, 2005; Saunt, *A New Order of Things*; Miles, *Ties That Bind*; Perdue, *Slavery and the Evolution of Cherokee Society*; Perdue, *Cherokee Women*; and Littlefield, *Africans and Seminoles.*

94. George Lipsitz suggests the value of this formulation in his work. Lipsitz, *American Studies in a Moment of Danger*, 138. My thinking here draws heavily on Phil Deloria's work, as explained in chapter 10.

95. Following Omi's and Winant's definition of racial formation as "the sociohistorical process by which racial categories are created, inhabited, transformed, and destroyed," and a racial project as "simultaneously an interpretation, representation, or explanation of racial dynamics, and an effort to reorganize and redistribute resources along particular racial lines." Omi and Winant, *Racial Formation in the United States from the 1960s to the 1990s*, 55–56.

96. The Clifton families have no apparent concern for—or terminology for—the distinction between cross-cousins and parallel cousins.

97. Since clan was the determining factor and the Choctaws were matrilineal, the father's brother's children, for example, could be acceptable marriage partners. This was also true in the days before kin were recognized bilaterally among the Cherokee. Sturm, *Blood Politics*, 160.

98. While first-cousin marriage invokes a strong emotional response from most Americans, it was a fairly common practice historically in the United States and remains so in the rest of the world. One community member was instructed by her doctor to examine her own genealogy for close marriages in the family tree after two of her children were born with birth defects. The doctor's instructions were based on modern America's exaggerated perception that first-cousin marriages are likely to cause various genetic defects among the offspring. The community member began investigating the close marriages in her family tree, but first-cousin marriages alone are not a cause for genetic defects. What may have put her at risk was the relatively small founding population of the Clifton community, which created a higher-than-

normal rate of occurrence for certain recessive alleles. While this characteristic of the community is connected to consanguinal marriages, it is not a direct result of any specific close marriage. See Ottenheimer, *Forbidden Relatives*, esp. chapter 6 ("Biogenetics and First Cousin Marriage").

99. U.S. Office of Federal Acknowledgment, "Historical Report on the United Houma Nation, Inc." and "Summary under the Criteria and Evidence for Proposed Finding against Federal Acknowledgment of the United Houma Nation, Inc." More recently, U.S. Office of Federal Acknowledgment, "Summary under the Criteria and Amended Proposed Finding against Federal Acknowledgment of the Biloxi, Chitimachi Confederation of Muskogees, Inc." and "Summary under the Criteria and Amended Proposed Finding against Federal Acknowledgment of the Pointe-Au-Chien Indian Tribe." Each report was accepted by the assistant secretary for Indian affairs on 22 May 2008.

100. Strong and Van Winkle, " 'Indian Blood,' " 557. Only later did the federal government intervene and begin tracking not just *Indian* blood quanta but, almost farcically, *tribal* blood quanta, as though a social identity were created solely by a genetically inherited code. On the other hand, Strong and Van Winkle note, Indian blood is also used as a "resource" that legitimates claims to aboriginal rights under federal law and tribal membership in the local setting. Patricia Albers writes: "it was only after the imposition of US and Canadian sovereignty that [Plains Assiniboin, Cree, and Ojibwa] ethnic names took on any real importance, and then it was only because these were invested with the legal power of treaties written by nation-states." Before that time "ethnicity in the generic and highly abstract sense of a 'tribal' name did not always function as [a] marker of geopolitical boundaries. Given a pluralistic pattern of land use and alliance making, most of their ethnic categories did not have a high level of salience or any a priori power to organize and distribute people across geographic space." Kinship and sodalities were much more important organizational factors. Albers, "Changing Patterns of Ethnicity in the Northeastern Plains, 1780–1870." Similarly, while there were linguistic and cultural differences in tradition between one "tribe" and the next in Louisiana, these differences rarely amounted to boundaries that prevented relationships from forming between communities or individuals.

101. Duthu, "The Houma Indians of Louisiana," 418.

102. Abu-Lughod, "Writing against Culture," 146.

103. The classic study of these processes in the southeastern United States is Merrell, *The Indians' New World*. Alexandra Harmon discusses the extremely porous tribal boundaries that existed before federal intervention in the Puget Sound region. Harmon, *Indians in the Making*. Perdue, *Cherokee Women*, esp. chapters 2 and 6; Sturm, *Blood Politics*, 27–51; Saunt, *A New Order of Things*; and Galloway, *Choctaw Genesis*, 338–60, among many others, discuss this history.

104. Paredes, "Federal Recognition and the Poarch Creek Indians," 133–36.

105. Once people left, those who were so inclined had a hard time moving back, because there was no longer any land available in the community for their homes.

"And that's why it's not more of us back than it is," Corine Tyler explains, "because during the Depression and all, a lot of the land was lost—was sold to the timber companies in order to try to survive. Land wasn't precious back then, but it is now. And especially in our area, because the land was lost to the lumber companies, and they won't sell you any back at all." Federal status would make it more likely that they could gain control of a portion of land suitable to the community's housing needs. Tyler further explains an inadequate and now discontinued land leasing program available from the timber companies: "Here sometime back, I don't know what era it would have been, they were letting people lease land to live on from the company, and they let the people that had the little leases, they let them buy the little spot they were on, but that's all. Just where your house is. I think it was a limit of two acres." While these small plots may have been adequate for one family's housing needs, such temporary concessions are hardly adequate as a land base for a tribal community trying to develop its economy. Further, the tribe wanted to start a housing project to alleviate the substandard housing conditions of the people who did have homes in the community, a need that fell outside the scope of the lumber company program.

106. See Gregory, "Pieces and Patches," 9–11.

107. Gregory suggests that asymmetrical quilting patterns typical of Clifton, while generally ascribed to African American roots, were also typically practiced by other Southern Indian communities. He cites no source. Gregory, "Pieces and Patches."

108. On the Southern embrace of things Indian see Martin, " 'My Grandmother Was a Cherokee Princess.' "

109. Silva, *Toward a Global Idea of Race*, xxxiii.

110. Elizabeth Povinelli notes that the declining practice of traditional culture has similarly been used in Australian courts to undermine aboriginal Australian political and territorial claims. "Perhaps only this context would have motivated local indigenous people to speculate that the failure of [a particular land claim] was the result of their failure to have and hold onto their 'traditional culture' after 120 years of often brutal colonization." Povinelli, *The Cunning of Recognition*, 7–8.

111. Paredes, "Paradoxes of Modernism and Indianness in the Southeast," 345.

112. Ibid.

113. William W. Quinn, former OFA staff member, comments on this phenomenon of Southern Indians adopting generic "Indian" crafts and regalia. "For those unacknowledged groups petitioning for federal acknowledgment which otherwise meet the criteria in 25 CFR 83, the adoption or lack of adoption of such explicit pan-Indian forms of Indian identity is irrelevant. The petitioners with socially and politically distinct communities which have maintained tribal cohesion since historic times will be successful, regardless of these trappings. Conversely, the recently formed groups with all the pan-Indian cultural fanfare will not." Quinn, "Southeastern Indians," 270–71.

114. Barbara Kirshenblatt-Gimblett notes that people who study and display folklife and folk crafts (including but certainly not limited to anthropologists) are overly con-

cerned with a reified notion of authenticity. That is, they only value folkways that are passed down from one generation to the next in an uninterrupted, uninterrogated string of "tradition." Revivalists or outsiders skilled in another group's ethnic craft do not meet their standards of authenticity, nor do hybrid productions that are conscious of expectations for marketing displays of Indianness. Regarding the Clifton-Choctaw, this means that Clifton pine-needle basketmakers could be considered inauthentic, since the craft was introduced into the community in the 1970s, and hybrid productions such as the asymmetrical quilt with a nonlocal "thunderbird" design, however original and aesthetically pleasing the presentation, would not be considered authentically "Indian." Kirshenblatt-Gimblett, *Destination Culture*.

115. See the web site for the joint project of the tribe, the U.S. Forest Service, and the Louisiana Regional Folklife Program and Northwestern State University of Louisiana, http://www.nsula.edu/regionalfolklife/CurrentResearch/splitbasket/cscb .htm. Marilyn Watt notes that in the 1980s George Allen learned to make baskets from a non-Indian who had learned from a Bayou Lacombe Choctaw. One of Allen's baskets was acquired by the Smithsonian Institution for its collections. Watt, "Federal Indian Policy and Tribal Development in Louisiana," 217.

116. While the Indian Arts and Crafts Act of 1990 allows members of state-recognized Indian tribes such as the Clifton-Choctaws to legitimately claim status as Indians for the purposes of marketing Indian arts and crafts, there remains a sentiment, often enforced in practice, that only federal Indians should be allowed to market their arts and crafts as authentic.

117. Faine, *The Clifton-Choctaw Community*, though it borrowed heavily from work done by Miriam and Rich.

118. Theresa O'Nell articulately discusses the ways storytelling similarly bounds and elevates Flathead identity on the Flathead reservation. O'Nell, "Telling about Whites, Talking about Indians."

119. U.S. Department of Energy, Smart Communities Network, "Success Stories."

120. North Central Regional Center for Rural Development at Iowa State University, "Measuring Community Success and Sustainability."

121. U.S. Office of Federal Acknowledgment, "The Official Guidelines for the Federal Acknowledgment Regulations." While this statement is misleading, since federal recognition is so central to many people's definitions of who qualifies as an Indian or as an Indian tribe, the point that the tribe is not barred from continuing to exist is pertinent.

122. Paredes, "Paradoxes of Modernism and Indianness in the Southeast," 357.

*Chapter 10: Conclusions and Implications*

1. See McCulloch and Wilkins, " 'Constructing' Nations within States," 36, for a discussion of the important "moral value of the perceived rewards or punishments" associated with recognition.

2. Moreover, if the decision by the U.S. Supreme Court in Carcieri v. Salazar (2009) is

left unaddressed by Congress, the trust status of the land of tribes recognized since 1934 will be jeopardized, throwing every form of economic development in Indian country into a tailspin.

3. Seminole Tribe of Florida v. Butterworth.

4. See note 28 to chapter 8, above.

5. Land claims cases fueled a similar backlash against federal recognition in the 1970s and 1980s.

6. American Indian Policy Review Commission, *Report on Terminated and Nonfederally Recognized Indians*, 1695.

7. Martin discusses the value of appropriate political and economic institutions in her dissertation, "Development at Ysleta del Sur Pueblo, Texas," 70.

8. For more detailed information on American Indian wealth in relation to the general United States population see Taylor and Kalt, "American Indians on Reservations"; and Lindsay, "Study."

9. I adapt this phrase from what Jacquelyn Dowd Hall has called the "long civil rights movement"; in her view the movement was both longer and broader than is traditionally believed. Hall, "The Long Civil Rights Movement and the Political Uses of the Past." Rather than beginning with the Montgomery bus boycott in 1955 and ending with the assassination of Martin Luther King Jr. in Memphis in 1968, the "long civil rights movement" encompasses an unbroken string of African American activism from earlier generations to the continued activism for racial equality in the present day. Similarly, the Indian renaissance went beyond literature and the arts, began before the publication of *House Made of Dawn*, and continues into the present. See note 48 to chapter 1, above.

10. See Louisiana Regional Folklife Program, region 2, Red River Valley and the Neutral Strip, "Choctaw Split Cane Basketry."

11. The Choctaw anthropologist Claude Medford introduced pine-needle basketmaking into the community in the late 1970s: http://www.louisianavoices.org/Unit8/edu_unit8_biography_kthomas.html.

12. Rhinehart, "Miami Indian Language Shift and Recovery"; Leonard, "Miami Language Reclamation in the Home"; Miami Nation of Indians of Indiana v. Department of Interior.

13. Cattelino, *High Stakes*, 66–78.

14. See Duran and Duran, *Native American Postcolonial Psychology*; Gone, "Mental Health, Wellness, and the Quest for an Authentic American Indian Identity," 55–80; O'Nell, *Disciplined Hearts*.

15. For a more detailed view of federal services available to Indian tribes through the federal government see http://www.firstgov.gov/Government/Tribal.shtml #land. The Indian Child Welfare Act of 1978, not noted on this web page, limits protections to federally recognized tribes.

16. Omi and Winant use the term "racial project" to describe efforts to interpret, represent, or explain racial dynamics and at the same time "reorganize and redistribute resources along particular racial lines. Racial projects connect what race *means*

in a particular discursive practice and the ways in which both social structures and everyday experiences are racially *organized*, based upon that meaning." Omi and Winant, *Racial Transformation in the United States from the 1960s to the 1990s*, 56.

17. Beaulieu, "Curly Hair and Big Feet," 305.

18. Quinn, "Southeastern Indians," 260.

19. Pascoe, *What Comes Naturally*, 123.

20. Greenbaum, "In Search of Lost Tribes," 362.

21. Clifford, *The Predicament of Culture*, 337.

22. Ibid., 289.

23. Sider, *Lumbee Indian Histories*, 283.

24. Letter cited by Jack Campisi in "The New England Tribes and Their Quest for Justice," *Tribes and Tribulations: Misconceptions about American Indians and Their Histories*, by Laurence M. Hauptman (Albuquerque: University of New Mexico Press, 1995), 188.

25. Noonan, *Persons and Masks of the Law*, cited in Wilkins, *American Indian Sovereignty and the U.S. Supreme Court*, 8.

26. Abu-Lughod, "Writing against Culture," 142, citing James Clifford, "Introduction: Partial Truths," *Writing Culture: The Poetics and Politics of Ethnography*, ed. James Clifford and George Marcus, 6.

27. George Roth, an anthropologist with OFA, goes so far as to accuse an OFA critic of "present[ing] a particular view," implying that he, as a representative of OFA, does *not* present a particular view in his rebuttal. The critic certainly did present a particular view, one that was largely accurate if occasionally misleading, but so did Roth. Roth, "Comment in Reply [to Russel Barsh]," 21.

28. Barsh, "Dialogue on Federal Acknowledgment of Indian Tribes," 20.

29. See Starna, " 'Public Ethnohistory' and Native-American Communities."

30. Greenbaum, "In Search of Lost Tribes," 364; McCulloch and Wilkins, " 'Constructing' Nations within States," 365; Campisi, *The Mashpee Indians*, 42.

31. For Southeastern examples that discuss the primacy of the local and the contextuality of anything approaching a national government or even tribal identity in early contact years, see Galloway, *Choctaw Genesis*; Perdue, *Cherokee Women*; and Saunt, *A New Order of Things*. For examples elsewhere see Binnema, *Common and Contested Ground*; Harmon, *Indians in the Making*, esp. 131–59; Dowd, *A Spirited Resistance*; Strong and Van Winkle, " 'Indian Blood' "; Albers, "Changing Patterns of Ethnicity in the Northeastern Plains, 1780–1870"; and Tanner, *The Falcon*.

32. U.S. Office of Federal Acknowledgment, "Procedures for Establishing that an American Indian Group Exists as a Tribe," section II ("Review of Public Comments"), 9288.

33. Harmon, *Indians in the Making*, 144.

34. Ibid., 142.

35. Blu, "Region and Recognition."

36. Ibid., 81, citing Karen I. Blu, letter to Senator Daniel Inouye, chairman, Select Committee on Indian Affairs, regarding Carleton and Lumbee, 27 April 1992.

37. Several scholars have adeptly critiqued how popular notions of Indianness are tied to constructions of authenticity that require Indians to practice the same traditions as their ancestors to be considered "real" or "authentic" Indians. See for example Raibmon, *Authentic Indians*; Garroutte, *Real Indians*; Povinelli, *The Cunning of Recognition*.

38. Indians have criticized expectations that they will look, talk, and act like their ancestors as a unique aspect of their racialization, as nationwide efforts from the federal government down to the local schoolhouse have placed enormous pressure on them to abandon their language and culture and integrate into American society, even as they are forced to display certain expected cultural markers, such as wearing feathers and retaining their tribal languages, to be accepted as "real" Indians by outsiders. See Deloria, *Custer Died for Your Sins*, esp. 1–27, 92–93; Gerald Vizenor, "Socioacupuncture: Mythic Reversals and the Striptease in Four Scenes," *Crossbloods*, 83–97; O'Nell, "The Making and Unmaking of the 'Real' Indians," *Disciplined Hearts*, 45–73.

39. Paschal, "The Imprimature of Recognition," 226.

40. The second GAO report followed up on issues identified in the first. U.S. Government Accountability Office, "Timeliness of the Tribal Recognition Process Has Improved, but It Will Take Years to Clear the Existing Backlog of Petitioners."

41. The Lumbee, having been recognized as Indians and simultaneously denied services and protections as an Indian tribe by Congress in 1956 (H.R. 4656), are currently only eligible for Congressional recognition, which they have been actively seeking for a number of years, most recently through the Lumbee Recognition Act of 2009. H.R. 4656 became 70 Stat. 254 (1956), "An Act Relating to the Lumbee Indians of North Carolina." A bill to recognize six tribes in Virginia has received support from the state Congressional delegation, but it requires that the tribes give up their right to operate casinos. The tribes included in this legislation are the Chickahominy, Eastern Chickahominy, Upper Mattaponi, Rappahannock, Monacan, and Nansemond. Thomasina E. Jordan Indian Tribes of Virginia Federal Recognition Act of 2009. Two other Virginia tribes, the Pamunkey and the Mattaponi, which each have reservation land dating to colonial Virginia, feel that they have strong enough cases to make it through OFA without those restrictions, and have not sought inclusion in the bill. Native Hawaiians' recognition has been considered by Congress annually since Rice v. Cayetano (2000) declared that restricting the vote in elections for the Office of Hawaiian Affairs to Native Hawaiians amounted to racial discrimination, whereas if Hawaiians were recognized as a sovereign indigenous nation, they would have more legal support for programming exclusive of non-Hawaiians. The so-called Akaka Bill would give Hawaiians something analogous to the "domestic dependent nations" status applied to Indian tribes, and therefore has been opposed by a number of people in the Hawaiian sovereignty movement, who argue that since Hawaiians never formally ceded *any* of their sovereignty, they would rather negotiate a different, preferably independent relationship with the United States and other nations—a relationship that recognizes their

sovereignty as complete. Its most recent incarnation is the Native Hawaiian Government Reorganization Act of 2009, S. 1011, 111th Cong., 1st sess. My understanding of opposition to the bill comes from conversations with Noenoe Silva, Hoku Aikau, Kehaulani Kauanui, and Keala Kelly, among others. For a published critique of the logics and potential impacts of the bill see Kauanui, *Hawaiian Blood*, esp. chapter 6. On the limits of Congressional recognition see Adams, "Special Report."

42. According to Jerry Jackson, OFA recommended that he not sign the bill, because OFA researchers were not yet convinced that they had the necessary political cohesion to be recognized as a tribe. Bush, "Memorandum of Disapproval for the Jena Band of Choctaws of Louisiana Restoration Act."

43. U.S. Congress, *Work of the Department of the Interior's Branch of Acknowledgment and Research within the Bureau of Indian Affairs*.

44. Benjamin, "Bureau of Indian Affairs Getting Out of Recognition Business"; "Native American Agency Wants to Give Up Key Role"; Barry, "Agency Willing to Relinquish Power to Recognize Tribes."

45. Interview with R. Lee Fleming, 27 June 2000. Changes in OFA internal regulations required OFA staff to stop doing original research for the petitioners to fill in possible gaps, shifting even more of the research burden to the tribes. U.S. Office of Federal Acknowledgment, "Changes in the Internal Processing of Federal Acknowledgment Petitions."

46. Information on FAIR available in U.S. Congress, *Work of the Department of the Interior's Branch of Acknowledgment and Research within the Bureau of Indian Affairs*.

47. Press briefing by Bruce Babbitt, secretary of the interior, and Ada Deer, assistant secretary of the interior for Indian affairs, 29 April 1994. According to Lee Fleming, OFA began with seven staff members. In June 2000 there were eleven staff members, six of whom were enrolled in federally recognized tribes, and one of whom claims Cherokee ancestry but has not yet been able to document that heritage in the historical records. Fleming himself is very white in appearance, with light brown hair, blue eyes, and western European facial features, which means he is at least aware that someone can be a tribal member without looking like a nickel Indian.

48. Fleming, "Testimony of R. Lee Fleming, Director, Office of Federal Acknowledgement for the Hearing Before the Committee on Indian Affairs, United States Senate, on the Federal Acknowledgement Process."

49. U.S. Office of Federal Acknowledgment, "Letters of Intent Received as of September 22, 2008."

50. McCaleb's official title is assistant secretary of the interior, Indian affairs. Adams, "Department of Interior Official Floats Reform Plan for Tribal Recognition."

51. Fleming, "Testimony of R. Lee Fleming, Director, Office of Federal Acknowledgement for the Hearing Before the Committee on Indian Affairs, United States Senate, on the Federal Acknowledgement Process," 3.

52. In the hearings on S. 611, the Indian Federal Recognition and Administrative Procedures Act of 1999, Eastern Cherokee leaders dismissed criticisms of OFA's

promptness as an exaggeration based on the number of cases yet to be reviewed versus the number of cases decided. While it is true that most of the petitioners had not yet submitted complete documentation, as they note, the long delays in justice created by OFA procedures themselves should not be discounted as a factor contributing to the length of the petitioning process. Jones and McCoy, "Testimony of Leon Jones, Principal Chief and Dan McCoy, Tribal Council Chairman, Eastern Band of Cherokee Indians, Cherokee, North Carolina, on S. 611, the Indian Federal Recognition and Administrative Procedures Act of 1999," 5.

53. See Campisi, *The Mashpee Indians*; Clifford, *The Predicament of Culture*, 277–346; Gordon and Newfield, "White Philosophy."

54. See Adams, "Gover Says 'Bring It On' to Yet Another BIA Probe"; Melmer, "Gover and Anderson Strike Back at Critics."

55. U.S. Office of Federal Acknowledgment, "Procedures for Establishing that an American Indian Group Exists as a Tribe," 9283.

56. 25 CFR §§ 83.9–11.

57. Weatherhead, "What Is an 'Indian Tribe'?"

58. Cohen, *Handbook of Federal Indian Law*, § 2.02[1], 119, cited by Stevens, J., dissenting opinion in Carcieri v. Salazar.

59. U.S. Office of Federal Acknowledgment, "Status Summary of Acknowledgment Cases as of 22 September 2008."

60. Lee Fleming reports that petitioners frequently submit incredibly inadequate materials. OFA will not spend time trying to make sense of unanalyzed material anymore, such as photographs of unidentified people, lists of names that do not discuss their connections to each other, how certain the connection is, and according to whom. It is vital that tribes find researchers to work with them on their petitions to help ensure their adequacy in this process before they submit them.

61. On the other hand, it is possible that having black ancestry would make it more likely for whites to continue to distinguish the group, since Indian ancestry has not always prevented families from having white status.

62. Much of my thinking on national identities is derived from Connor, *Ethnonationalism*, and on this point in particular the essay "Beyond Reason: The Nature of the Ethnonational Bond," 196–209.

63. Quinn, "Southeastern Indians," 265.

64. Greenbaum, "What's in a Label?," 107–26. There are records that identify slaves by race, but in cases where race was identified not in the records but only in oral history, OFA will not consider the ancestor to have been Indian. Of course, because of the ways the "one-drop rule" racialized all people of any African ancestry as "black," African Americans are overwhelmingly mixed-race people, despite popular white misconceptions about blackness. A PBS documentary in 2006 used DNA testing to track African American ancestry, and while the margin of error on such tests is enormous, they confirmed Native American ancestry in Chris Tucker, whose mother was certain she was part Native, and Oprah Winfrey, who was cer-

tain she was 100 percent "black." Judd, director, "African-American Lives." Jack Forbes, cited above, has done extensive research on such practices. Forbes, *Africans and Native Americans*. Alan Gallay has documented the extent of the Indian slave trade in the seventeenth and eighteenth centuries. Though many Indian slaves were sold to plantations in the Caribbean islands, their descendants were likely sold back to southern whites as "Africans." Gallay, *The Indian Slave Trade*. Gary Mills documents Native American lines in the Cane River Creole community, in particular how the racial classification of one person could change from free person of color to Indian to white to mulatto depending on the context. Mills, *The Forgotten People*, esp. 84–88, 94–95, 102–3.

65. Quinn, "Southeastern Indians," 264–65 (8–9 using Quinn's pagination within the volume). Greenbaum analyzes the same passage in "What's in a Label?," 118. Quinn's repeated and egregious exposures of his uninterrogated biases, his willingness to claim authority to represent what he imagines is a singular "real" Indian point of view, and his shortcomings as a social scientist certainly make him an easy target, but there are very serious repercussions for petitioning tribes of his uncontested decisions. The one benefit of his desire to present and publish papers on a topic on which he considered himself an expert is that it helpfully exposed his ideas to review. Staff members at OFA, working behind mirrored glass and immune from being seen or reviewed, make decisions that permanently label groups as Indian or non-Indian. Quinn's publicly stated ideas make it easier to "see" and critique OFA decision makers as individuals with specific and reviewable prejudices.

66. Most recently Davis, "A Case of Identity: Ethnogenesis of the New Houma Indians," in a poorly informed rehash of the OFA recommendation in 1994 against recognition for the Houmas, revives the tradition of calling mixed-race Indians poseurs. Older examples include Berry, *Almost White*; Edgar Thompson, "The Little Races," *American Anthropologist*, new series 74, no. 5 (October 1972), 1295–1306; Gilbert, "Race, Cultural Groups, Social Differentiation." For a discussion of the literature see Porter, "Nonrecognized American Indian Tribes."

67. See note 90 to chapter 9, above.

68. Deloria, *Indians in Unexpected Places*, 8–9.

69. Coulthard, "Subjects of Empire," citing Povinelli, *The Cunning of Recognition*.

70. Sturm, *Blood Politics*, 203.

71. Thomas Biolsi's insights on the role of law in constituting social relations and regulating the direction of politics and struggle in Indian country are key to this issue. "There are two connected ways in which federal Indian law has shaped (and constrained) political space for Native Americans, their allies and their opponents," Biolsi argues. "One way is by defining what particular social relations are most immediately experienced as actionable injustice and therefore receive political attention and serve as the focus of struggle. . . . The other, closely linked way in which law shapes political space is by siting struggle between particular (legally constituted) classes of interested parties in particular and determinate places within

the social formation. . . . Both of these linked subpolitical processes are responsible for producing and reproducing particular political fronts." Biolsi, "Bringing the Law Back In," 552.

72. See note 66, above.

73. While the cases here provide instructive examples of revitalization before or even without recognition, the case of the Miami Tribe of Indiana provides another pronounced illustration of tribal revitalization despite nonrecognition. Having lost federal recognition in 1897, the portion of the band that did not remove to Indian Territory in 1846 has maintained community ties regardless of the loss of federal status. The tribe petitioned for recognition through OFA but was denied recognition in 1992. OFA stated that while the Miami Tribe maintained a community until just after the Second World War, it has not constituted a distinct community since that time. Several appeal efforts have failed, making it unlikely that the Miami Tribe will be federally recognized in the near future. Miami Nation of Indians of Indiana v. Department of Interior. Nonetheless, the tribe is carrying forth revitalization efforts on an impressive scale that rivals—and in some ways exceeds—the efforts of its federally recognized relatives in Oklahoma.

74. Paredes, "Federal Recognition and the Poarch Creek Indians"; Bruce G. Miller, "After the F.A.P."; Starna, " 'We'll All Be Together Again.' "

75. See Asch, "Comments."

# Bibliography

Abbe Museum website, http://www.abbemuseum.org/pages/wabanaki/timeline/
hard-times.html, accessed 18 November 2008.

"ABC News: Americans All: Vine Deloria." Transcript. Howard Enders, producer and
director; Melba Tolliver, reporter. Broadcast 7 January 1974.

Abu-Lughod, Lila. "Writing against Culture." *Recapturing Anthropology: Working in the
Present*, ed. Richard G. Fox, 137–62. Santa Fe: School of American Research, 1991.

Adams, David Wallace. *Education for Extinction: American Indians and the Boarding School
Experience, 1875–1928.* Lawrence: University Press of Kansas, 1995.

Adams, Jim. "Gover Says 'Bring It On' to Yet Another BIA Probe." *Indian Country Today*,
1 August 2001, http://IndianCountry.com/?323.

———. "Department of Interior Official Floats Reform Plan for Tribal Recognition."
*Indian Country Today*, 7 October 2002.

———. "Special Report: Settlements of Early '80s Continue to Haunt Tribes: New
England Courts Show Contempt for Tribal Governments." *Indian Country Today*,
19 March 2004, http://www.indiancountry.com/?1079710270.

Adelle v. Beauregard, 1 Mart. 183, 1810 La. LEXIS 24 (La. 1810).

Albers, Patricia C. "Changing Patterns of Ethnicity in the Northeastern Plains, 1780–
1870." *History, Power, and Identity: Ethnogenesis in the Americas, 1492–1992*, ed.
Jonathan D. Hill. Iowa City: University of Iowa Press, 1996.

Allen, Chadwick. *Blood Narrative: Indigenous Identity in American Indian and Maori
Literary and Activist Texts.* Durham: Duke University Press, 2002.

American Indian Chicago Conference. "The Voice of the American Indian: Declaration
of Indian Purpose." American Indian Chicago Conference, University of Chicago,
13–20 June 1961.

American Indian Policy Review Commission (AIPRC), Task Force Ten. Baton Rouge
hearings, 1975–77, entry NC3-220-77-9, box 315, "Unidentified Records," Record
Group 220, National Archives II, College Park, Md.

———. Records of Temporary Committees, Commissions, and Boards: Records of the
American Indian Policy Review Commission, NARA, RG 220.

——. *Report on Terminated and Nonfederally Recognized Indians: Final Report to the American Indian Policy Review Commission.* Washington: U.S. Government Printing Office, 1976.

——. *Final Report of the American Indian Policy Review Commission.* Washington: U.S. Government Printing Office, 17 May 1977.

*American State Papers: Public Lands*, vol. 2. Washington: U.S. Government Printing Office, 1832.

"Another Casino in Troubled State." *Advocate* (Baton Rouge), 26 February 2002, § B, p. 6 [editorial].

"Archaeologist to Probe Marksville Burial Site." *Baton Rouge State Times*, 4 August 1961.

Arihara, Shino. "Black like I Thought I Was: Race, DNA, and a Man Who Knows Too Much." *LA Weekly*, 9 October 2003, http://www.laweekly.com/2003-10-09/calendar/black-like-i-thought-i-was, accessed 10 April 2009.

Asch, Michael. "Comments," following Biolsi, "Bringing the Law Back In." *Current Anthropology* 36 no. 4 (August–October 1995), 559.

Baca, Lawrence. "The Legal Status of American Indians." *Handbook of North American Indians*, vol. 4, *History of Indian-White Relations*, ed. Wilcomb E. Washburn, 230–37. Washington: Smithsonian Institution, 1988.

Ball, Bonnie. "America's Mysterious Race." *Read*, May 1964, 64–67.

Balthazar, Kathleen. *Cane River and Its Creole Stories.* Southfield, Mich.: Cane River Media, 2001.

Barber, Patsy K. *Above the Falls: And Historic Cotile.* Lecompte, La.: Bayou Boeuf, 1994.

Barbry, John. "Tunica-Biloxi Tribalism and Indian Policy Reform, 1922–1947." Unpublished MS completed in partial fulfillment of the requirements for the MA in history at the University of New Orleans. Copy in possession of the author.

Barry, Ellen. "Agency Willing to Relinquish Power to Recognize Tribes." *Boston Globe*, 26 May 2000, § B, p. 1.

Barsh, Russel Lawrence. "Dialogue on Federal Acknowledgment of Indian Tribes: A Challenge for Anthropologists." *Practicing Anthropology* 10, no. 2 (1988), 2, 20–22.

Barsh, Russel Lawrence, and K. Diaz-Knauf. "The Structure of Federal Aid for Indian Programs in the Decade of Prosperity, 1970–1980." *American Indian Quarterly* 8, no. 1 (winter 1984), 1–36.

Basso, Keith. *Wisdom Sits in Places: Landscape and Language among the Western Apache.* Albuquerque: University of New Mexico Press, 1996.

Beale, Calvin L. "American Triracial Isolates." *Eugenics Quarterly* 4 (December 1957), 187–96.

Beaulieu, David. "Curly Hair and Big Feet: Physical Anthropology and the Implementation of Land Allotment on the White Earth Chippewa Reservation." *American Indian Quarterly* 8, no. 4 (fall 1984), 281–314.

Belvin, Kari. "Kinder Casino Has Been Positive"; "Marksville Storyline Has Not Changed"; "Was It Worth the Gamble? Marksville Casino Has Not Changed Much in a Year." *Daily Town Talk* (Alexandria, La.), 4 June 1995, § A, pp. 11–12.

Benedict, Jeff. *Without Reservation: The Making of America's Most Powerful Indian Tribe and Foxwoods, the World's Largest Casino.* New York: Harper Collins, 2000.

Benjamin, Caren. "Bureau of Indian Affairs Getting Out of Recognition Business." Associated Press State and Local Wire, 24 May 2000, BC cycle.

Berry, Brewton. *Almost White: A Study of Certain Racial Hybrids in the Eastern United States.* New York: Macmillan, 1963.

Big Noise Tactical Media. "The Jena 6." Documentary video, narrated by Mumia Abu-Jamal, 2008.

"Biloxi Tribe et al., 1924, Signed copy of statement by Biloxi Indian tribe and members of the Choctaw Indian Tribe residing in different parts of the State of Louisiana, October 9, 1924, Woodworth, Louisiana."

Binnema, Theodore. *Common and Contested Ground.* Norman: University of Oklahoma Press, 2001.

Biolsi, Thomas. "Bringing the Law Back In." *Current Anthropology* 36, no. 4 (August–October 1995), 543–71.

———. *Deadliest Enemies: Law and the Making of Race Relations on and off Rosebud Reservation.* Berkeley: University of California Press, 2001.

Bishop, Kathleen L., and Kenneth C. Hansen. "A Report on the Landless Tribes of Washington State." NARA, RG 220, AIPRC.

"Blanco Rejects Bad Casino Bet." *Advocate* (Baton Rouge), 14 April 2005, § B, p. 8 [editorial].

Blu, Karen I. *The Lumbee Problem: The Making of an American Indian People.* Lincoln: University of Nebraska Press, 1980, 2001.

———. "Region and Recognition: Southern Indians, Anthropologists, and Presumed Biology." *Anthropologists and Indians in the New South,* ed. Rachel A. Bonney and J. Anthony Paredes, 71–85. Tuscaloosa: University of Alabama Press, 2001.

Blumenthal, Richard. Statement of Attorney General Richard Blumenthal before the Senate Indian Affairs Committee, "Federal Recognition for American Indian Tribes" (17 September 2002), Federal Document Clearing House, Congressional Testimony.

Bonney, Rachel A., and J. Anthony Paredes, eds. *Anthropologists and Indians in the New South.* Tuscaloosa: University of Alabama, 2001.

Booker, Dennis. "Indian Identity in Louisiana: Two Contrasting Approaches to Ethnic Identity." Master's thesis in geography and anthropology, Louisiana State University, 1973.

Bordewich, Fergus. *Killing the White Man's Indian: Reinventing Native Americans at the End of the Twentieth Century.* New York: Doubleday, 1996.

Borrows, John. *Recovering Canada: The Resurgence of Indigenous Law.* Toronto: University of Toronto Press, 2002.

Brain, Jeffrey P. *Tunica Treasure.* Cambridge: Peabody Museum of Archaeology, Harvard University, 1979.

——. *Tunica Archaeology*, vol. 78 of *Papers of the Peabody Museum of Archaeology and Ethnology*. Cambridge: Harvard University, 1988.

Brain, Jeffrey P., and Ian W. Brown, eds. *Robert S. Neitzel: The Great Sun*. Lower Mississippi Survey, Peabody Museum, Bulletin no. 9. Cambridge: Harvard University, 1982.

Bridges, Tyler. *Bad Bet on the Bayou: The Rise of Gambling in Louisiana and the Fall of Governor Edwin Edwards*. New York: Farrar, Straus and Giroux, 2001.

Brookings Institution, Institute for Government Research. *The Problem of Indian Administration*. Baltimore: Johns Hopkins University Press, 1928.

Brooks, James, ed. *Confounding the Color Line: The Indian-Black Experience in North America*. Lincoln: University of Nebraska Press, 2002.

Bryan v. Itasca County, 426 U.S. 373 (1976).

Bureau of Indian Affairs. Central Correspondence Files, 68776-1931-800, General Service File 67669-1931-053, General Service File 78634-1925-307.4, File 30322-1938-066, File 40616-35, General Service File 25436-31-150. Record Group 75, National Archives II, College Park, Md.

Bush, George H. W. "Memorandum of Disapproval for the Jena Band of Choctaws of Louisiana Restoration Act," 21 October 1992, www.csdl.tamu.edu / bushlib / 1992 / 92102105.html.

Bushnell, David I., Jr. *The Choctaw of Bayou Lacomb, St. Tammany Parish, Louisiana*. Bureau of American Ethnology, Bulletin 48. Washington: U.S. Government Printing Office, 1909.

California v. Cabazon Band of Mission Indians, 480 U.S. 202 (1987).

Calongne, Kathy. "Genealogist Says Clifton-Choctaws Are Not Indians." *Daily Town Talk* (Alexandria, La.), 7 August 1988, § A, pp. 1–2.

——. "Jena Tribe: Cliftons Should Prove Ancestry to Get Grant." *Daily Town Talk* (Alexandria, La.), 7 August 1988, § A, p. 2.

——. "La. Tribe Fights to Prove Its Heritage." *Times-Picayune*, 14 August 1988, § C, p. 8.

Campisi, Jack. "New England Tribes and Their Quest for Justice." *The Pequots in Southern New England: The Rise and Fall of an American Indian Nation*, ed. Laurence M. Hauptman and James D. Wherry. Norman: University of Oklahoma Press, 1990.

——. *The Mashpee Indians: Tribe on Trial*. Syracuse, N.Y.: Syracuse University Press, 1991.

Canby, William C., Jr. *American Indian Law in a Nutshell*. 3rd edn. St. Paul: West Group, 1998.

Carcieri v. Salazar, 555 U.S. 129 (2009).

Carson, James. Review of *Choctaws at the Crossroads*. *Journal of American History* 88, no. 1 (June 2001), www.historycooperative.org / journals / jah / 88.1 / br_19.html.

Cattelino, Jessica. *High Stakes: Florida Seminole Gaming and Sovereignty*. Durham: Duke University Press, 2008.

Chang, David A. *The Color of the Land: Race, Nation, and the Politics of Landownership in Oklahoma, 1832–1929*. Chapel Hill: University of North Carolina Press, 2010.

Charrier v. Bell, 380 So. 2d 155 (La. App. 1 Cir. 12 / 17 / 1979).

Charrier v. Bell, 496 So. 2d 601 (La. App. 1 Cir. 10 / 15 / 1986).

Child, Brenda. *Boarding School Seasons: American Indian Families, 1900–1940*. Lincoln: University of Nebraska Press, 1998; 2nd edn forthcoming.

Choctaw Nation. "Memorial to the Congress of the United States." H. Rept. 3080, 54th Cong., 2d sess.

"Choctaw Tribe Plans Meeting." *Times-Picayune*, 3 December 1973, § 1, p. 3.

Clifford, James. *The Predicament of Culture: Twentieth-Century Ethnography, Literature, and Art*. Cambridge: Harvard University Press, 1988.

Clifford, James, and George Marcus, eds. *Writing Culture: The Poetics and Politics of Ethnography*. Berkeley: University of California Press, 1986.

Clifton, James A. "Factional Conflict and the Indian Community: The Prairie Potawatomi Case." *The American Indian Today*, ed. Stuart Levine and Nancy O. Lurie, 184–211. Baltimore: Penguin, 1972.

——. Introduction, *Being and Becoming Indian: Biographical Studies of North American Frontiers*, ed. James A. Clifton. Chicago: Dorsey, 1989.

——. Introduction, *The Invented Indian: Cultural Fictions and Government Policies*, ed. James Clifton. New Brunswick, N.J.: Transaction, 1990.

Clifton-Choctaw Reservation. Articles of Incorporation, 18 September 1977. Norris Tyler Papers (in possession of Norris Tyler).

Coates, Guy. "Put the Money Out, and They Will Come." *Daily Town Talk* (Alexandria, La.), 14 May 1997, § A, p. 5.

Cohen, Felix. "The Erosion of Indian Rights, 1950–53." *Yale Law Journal* 62 (1952–53).

——. *Handbook of Federal Indian Law*. Albuquerque: University of New Mexico Press, 1971.

Coleman, Arica L. " 'Tell the Court I Love My [Indian] Wife': Interrogating Race and Self-Identity in *Loving v. Virginia*." *Souls* 8, no. 1 (2006), 67–80.

Commissioner of Indian Affairs. Annual Report of the Commissioner of Indian Affairs to the Secretary of the Interior for the Fiscal year Ended June 30, 1911. Washington: U.S. Government Printing Office, 1912.

"Compulsory Education." *Jena Times*, 18 May 1944, 8.

"Compulsory School Attendance Law to Be Enforced." *Jena Times*, 5 October 1944, 1.

Connor, Walker. *Ethnonationalism: The Quest for Understanding*. Princeton: Princeton University Press, 1994.

Continetti, Matthew. *The K Street Gang: The Rise and Fall of the Republican Machine*. New York: Doubleday, 2006.

Cooke, Lori. "Hundreds Change Race to Qualify for Indian Funds." *Times-Picayune*, 11 March 1979, § 2, p. 5.

Coulthard, Glenn S. "Subjects of Empire: Indigenous Peoples and the 'Politics of Recognition' in Canada." *Contemporary Political Theory* 6 (2007), 437–60.

Courreges, Patrick. "Choctaws Defend Deal: Tribe's Chief Calls Criticism Political." *Advocate* (Baton Rouge), 2 March 2002, § A, p. 1.

Coushatta Tribe. "Red Shoes People: A History of the Sovereign Nation of the Coushatta Tribe of Louisiana," http://www.coushattatribela.org/history.html.

Cramer, Renée Ann. *Cash, Color, and Colonialism: The Politics of Tribal Acknowledgment*. Norman: University of Oklahoma Press, 2005.

Cullen, Ed. "Tunicas Move toward Organization, Recognition." *Sunday Advocate* (Baton Rouge), 12 August 1973, § A, p. 16.

Cullen, Ed, and Dick Wright. "Tunica Treasure: The Tale Goes On." *Sunday Advocate* (Baton Rouge), 30 August 1981, § H, pp. 1–5.

Curry, Jan. "A History of the Houma Indians and Their Story of Federal Nonrecognition." *American Indian Journal* 5, no. 2 (February 1979), 8–28.

Darby, W. *Immigrants Guide to Western and Southwestern States and Territories*. New York: Kirk and Mercein, 1818.

Davis, Dave D. "A Case of Identity: Ethnogenesis of the New Houma Indians." *Ethnohistory* 48, no. 3 (summer 2001), 473–94.

Dawes Commission, Commission and Commissioner to the Five Civilized Tribes. *Annual Report*. Washington: U.S. Government Printing Office, 1899.

Day, Bill. "Tunica-Biloxi Today." *On the Tunica Trail*. 3rd edn, 17–21. Baton Rouge: Louisiana Archaeological and Antiquities Commission, Department of Culture, Recreation, and Tourism, Anthropological Study Series no. 1, 1994.

Debo, Angie. *And Still the Waters Run*. New York: Gordian, 1966.

Deloria, Philip J. *Indians in Unexpected Places*. Lawrence: University Press of Kansas, 2004.

Deloria, Vine, Jr. *Custer Died for Your Sins: An Indian Manifesto*. New York: Macmillan, 1969; repr. Norman: University of Oklahoma Press, 1988.

Deloria, Vine, Jr., and Clifford M. Lytle. *American Indians, American Justice*. Austin: University of Texas Press, 1983, 1997.

Deloria, Vine, Jr., and David E. Wilkins. *Tribes, Treaties, and Constitutional Tribulations*. Austin: University of Texas Press, 1999.

Dempsey, E. S. "Senate Indian Affairs Committee Considers Lumbee Recognition." *Indian Country Today*, 30 September 2003, www.indiancountry.com / ?1064942679.

Dominguez, Virginia. *White by Definition: Social Classification in Creole Louisiana*. New Brunswick: Rutgers University Press, 1986.

D'Oney, J. Daniel. *A Kingdom of Water: A History of the Houma Nation*. Lincoln: University of Nebraska Press, forthcoming.

Dormon, Caroline. Caroline Dormon Collection, Watson Memorial Library, Northwestern State University, Natchitoches, La.

Dorsey, James Owen. Field notes and unpublished papers. National Anthropological Archives, Smithsonian Institution, no. 4800, Biloxi 3.6.1.2.

Dowd, Gregory. *A Spirited Resistance*. Baltimore: Johns Hopkins University Press, 1992.

Downs, Ernest C. "Documentation of the Tunica-Biloxi-Ofo-Avoyel Community near Marksville, Louisiana." American Indian Policy Review Commission, Task Force 10, *Report on Terminated and Nonfederally Recognized Indians: Final Report to the American Indian Policy Review Commission*. Washington: U.S. Government Printing Office, 1976.

——. "A National Conference on Tribal Recognition." *American Indian Journal* 4, no 5 (May 1978), 2–3.

——. "The Struggle of the Louisiana Tunica Indians for Recognition." *Southeastern*

*Indians since the Removal Era*, ed. Walter L. Williams, 72–89. Athens: University of
Georgia Press, 1979.

Drechsel, Emanuel J. "Mobilian Jargon: Linguistic, Sociocultural, and Historical
Aspects of an American Indian Lingua Franca." Ph.D. diss., Department of
Anthropology, University of Wisconsin, 1979.

———. *Mobilian Jargon: Linguistic and Sociohistorical Aspects of a Native American Pidgin.*
Oxford: Clarendon, 1997.

Duran, Bonnie, Eduardo Duran, and Maria Yellow Horse Brave Heart. "Native
Americans and the Trauma of History." *Studying Native America: Problems and
Prospects*, ed. Russell Thornton. Madison: University of Wisconsin Press, 1998.

Duran, Eduardo, and Bonnie Duran. *Native American Postcolonial Psychology.* Albany:
State University of New York Press, 1995.

Duthu, N. Bruce. "The Houma Indians of Louisiana: The Intersection of Law and
History in the Federal Acknowledgment Process." *Louisiana History* 38 (fall 1997),
409–36.

Duthu, Bruce, and Hilde Ojibway. "Future Light or Feu-Follet?" *Southern Exposure* 13,
no. 6, 24–32 [special issue: *We Are Here Forever: Indians of the South*].

Dyer, Scott. "Foster Wants Bigger 'Take' from Indian Casinos." *Advocate* (Baton
Rouge), 27 December 1998.

———. "Vitter Opposes New Indian Casino Proposal: Jena Choctaws Seek Gambling
Hall Near Logansport." *Advocate* (Baton Rouge), 23 January 2003, § B, pp. 1–2.

———. "Candidates Oppose Expansion of Gambling." *Advocate* (Baton Rouge), 15
September 2003, § A, p. 1.

"Educate Them All." *Jena Times*, 18 May 1944, 4.

Estabrook, Arthur H., and I. E. McDougle. *Mongrel Virginians: The Win Tribe.*
Baltimore: Williams and Wilkins, 1926.

Even, Dan. "Uproar over Tribe Put Down." *Times-Picayune*, 26 April 1978, § 1, p. 8.

Everett, Russell I. "The Speech of the Tri-Racial Group Composing the Community of
Clifton, Louisiana." Master's thesis, Louisiana State University, Department of
Speech, 1958.

Executive Director's Report, Governor's Commission on Indian Affairs, 7 December
1983. Accession p1992-92, Indian Affairs: 1981–84, loc 19202-207. Louisiana State
Archives, Baton Rouge.

Faiman-Silva, Sandra. *Choctaws at the Crossroads: The Political Economy of Class and
Culture in the Oklahoma Timber Region.* Lincoln: University of Nebraska Press, 1997.

Faine, John R. *The Clifton-Choctaw Community: An Assessment of the Status of a Louisiana
Indian Tribe.* Baton Rouge: Institute for Indian Development, 1986.

———. *The Tunica-Biloxi Indians: An Assessment of the Status of a Louisiana Indian Tribe*, 7.
Baton Rouge: Institute for Indian Development, 1986.

"Families Coping with Catastrophic Situations." *Tunica-Biloxi Tribe of Louisiana*
(newsletter), January 2000, 7–9.

Fisher, Dexter. Introduction, *Cogewea: The Half-Blood*, by Mourning Dove. Lincoln:
University of Nebraska Press, 1981.

Fixico, Donald. *Termination and Relocation: Federal Indian Policy, 1945–1960.* Albuquerque: University of New Mexico Press, 1986.

Fleming, Lee. "Testimony of R. Lee Fleming, Director, Office of Federal Acknowledgement for the Hearing before the Committee on Indian Affairs, United States Senate, on the Federal Acknowledgment Process," 11 May 2005, http://www.doi.gov/ocl/2005/FedAcknowledgement.htm, accessed 2 September 2008.

Florida v. Seminole Tribe of Florida, 181 F.3d 1237 (1999).

Fogelson, Raymond D. Review of *Indians of the Southeastern United States in the Late 20th Century*, ed. J. Anthony Paredes. *American Anthropologist*, new series 95, no. 2 (June 1993), 500–501.

Foley, Neil. *The White Scourge: Mexicans, Blacks, and Poor Whites in Texas Cotton Culture.* Berkeley: University of California Press, 1997.

——. "Becoming Hispanic: Mexican Americans and Whiteness." *White Privilege: Essential Readings on the Other Side of Racism*, ed. P. S. Rothenberg, 49–59. New York: Worth, 2002.

Forbes, Jack D. *Africans and Native Americans: The Language of Race and the Evolution of Red-Black Peoples.* 2nd edn. Urbana: University of Illinois Press, 1993.

——. "The Manipulation of Race, Caste and Identity: Classifying Afroamericans, Native Americans and Red-Black People." *Journal of Ethnic Studies* 17, no. 4, 1–51.

"From School Board Office." *Weekly News* (Marksville, La.), 16 February 1929, 4.

Gallay, Alan. *The Indian Slave Trade: The Rise of the English Empire in the American South, 1670–1717.* New Haven: Yale University Press, 2002.

Galloway, Patricia. " 'So Many Little Republics': British Negotiations with the Choctaw Confederacy, 1765." *Ethnohistory* 41, no. 4 (fall 1994), 513–37.

——. *Choctaw Genesis: 1500–1700.* Lincoln: University of Nebraska Press, 1995.

Garroutte, Eva Marie. *Real Indians: Identity and the Survival of Native America.* Berkeley: University of California Press, 2003.

Gatschet, Albert. Field Notes, 16 October 1886, 24 October 1886. National Anthropological Archives, Smithsonian Institution.

Gilbert, William Harlen, Jr. "Race, Cultural Groups, Social Differentiation: Memorandum concerning the Characteristics of the Larger Mixed-Blood Racial Islands of the Eastern United States." *Social Forces* 24, no. 4 (May 1946), 438–47.

Gill, James. "Foster Bluffs on Gambling Again." *Times-Picayune*, 26 January 2003 [editorial].

Goldsmith, Sarah Sue. "The Jena Band: Choctaw Traditions Keep Tribe Together." *Advocate Magazine* (Baton Rouge), 2 June 1996.

——. "Reclaiming the Past: Louisiana Native Americans Seeking Federal Recognition." *Advocate Sunday Magazine* (Baton Rouge), 16 June 1996, 21.

Gone, Joseph P. "Mental Health, Wellness, and the Quest for an Authentic American Indian Identity." *Mental Health Care for Urban Indians: Clinical Insights from Native Practicioners*, ed. Tawa Witko. Washington: American Psychological Association, 2006.

Gonzales, Angela. "Gaming and Displacement: Winners and Losers in American Indian Casino Development." *International Social Science Journal* 175 (2003), 123–33.

Gordon, Avery, and Christopher Newfield. "White Philosophy." *Critical Inquiry* 20 (summer 1994), 737–57.

Grabowski, Christine. "Coiled Intent: Federal Acknowledgment Policy and the Gay Head Wampanoags." Ph.D. diss., City University of New York, 1994.

Grant, Ron. "Tunicas, Indian Author Are TV Subject." *Daily Town Talk* (Alexandria, La.), 4 December 1973, § B, p. 1.

Green, Rick. "Dodd Drops Tribal Recognition Reform Plan." *Hartford Courant*, 31 October 2002, § B, p. 9.

Green, Sara Jean. "Chief Seattle's Tribe Clings to Its Identity." *Seattle Times*, 18 June 2001.

Greenbaum, Susan. "In Search of Lost Tribes: Anthropology and the Federal Acknowledgment Process." *Human Organization* 44, no. 4 (winter 1985), 361–67.

———. "What's in a Label? Identity Problems of Southern Indian Tribes." *Journal of Ethnic Studies* 19, no. 2 (summer 1991), 107–26.

Gregory, Hiram F. "The Jena Band of Louisiana Choctaw." *American Indian Journal* 3, no. 2 (February 1977).

———. "Pieces and Patches: A Whole from Many Traditions." *Splittin' on the Grain: Louisiana Folklife* 8, no. 1 (March 1983), 9–11.

Griessman, B. Eugene. "The American Isolates." *American Anthropologist* 74 (June 1972), 693–94.

Haas, Mary. *Tunica Texts*. Berkeley: University of California Press, 1948.

———. *Tunica Dictionary*. Berkeley: University of California Press, 1953.

Hagan, William T. "United States Indian Policies, 1860–1900." *Handbook of North American Indians*, vol. 4, *History of Indian-White Relations*, ed. Wilcomb E. Washburn, 51–65. Washington: Smithsonian Institution, 1988.

Hager, George. "Tunicas Still Await Recognition." *Times-Picayune*, 19 November 1978, § 1, p. 8.

Halfpenny, Rex. "Michigan Home Brewing during Prohibition," http://www.michigan beerguide.com/news.asp?articleid=24, accessed 2 August 2003.

Haliwa-Saponi Tribe. Haliwa-Saponi Petition for Federal Acknowledgment. National Anthropological Archives, National Museum of Natural History, Smithsonian Institution, 1989.

Hall, Jacquelyn Dowd. "The Long Civil Rights Movement and the Political Uses of the Past." *Journal of American History* 91, no. 4 (March 2005), 1233–63.

"Hand Gone, Indian Air Hero Keeps on Firing." *Jena Times*, 1 October 1942, 9.

Hargroder, Charles M. "Treen's Indian Pick 'Just Isn't Qualified.'" *Times-Picayune*, 25 December 1980, § 1, p. 20.

Harmon, Alexandra. *Indians in the Making: Ethnic Relations and Indian Identities around Puget Sound*. Berkeley: University of California Press, 1998.

Harring, Sidney L. *Crow Dog's Case: American Indian Sovereignty, Tribal Law, and United States Law in the Nineteenth Century*. Cambridge: Cambridge University Press, 1994.

Harris, Cheryl. "Whiteness as Property." *Harvard Law Review* 106, no. 8 (1993), 1707.

Hauptman, Laurence M., and Jack Campisi. "There Are No Indians East of the

Mississippi." *Tribes and Tribulations: Misconceptions about American Indians and Their Histories*, by Laurence M. Hauptman, 93–108 (Albuquerque: University of New Mexico Press, 1995).

Henry, Ray. "Disenrolled Tribal Members Complain of Unfairness." *Indian Country Today*, 7 November 2007, http://www.indiancountrytoday.com/archive/28143214.html, accessed 23 March 2009.

Hill, Sarah H. *Weaving New Worlds: Southeastern Cherokee Women and Their Basketry*. Chapel Hill: University of North Carolina Press, 1997.

Hosmer, Brian C. *American Indians in the Marketplace: Persistence and Innovation among the Menominees and Metlakatlans, 1870–1920*. Lawrence: University Press of Kansas, 1999.

Hoxie, Frederick. *A Final Promise: The Campaign to Assimilate the Indians, 1880–1920*. Lincoln: University of Nebraska Press, 1984; repr. Cambridge: Cambridge University Press, 1989.

"Indian Children Grant Awarded: HEW to Give $306,507 for 8 Parishes." *Times-Picayune*, 11 July 1974, § 6, p. 5.

"Indians of New Mexico Training for War Jobs." *Jena Times*, 2 July 1942, 6.

"Interview with WJ Strickland," 1, 4 November 1974, Samuel Proctor Oral History Program, Department of History, University of Florida, http://www.uflib.ufl.edu/ufdc/?b=UF00006827&v=00001, accessed 7 October 2008.

"Jena Band of Choctaws Receives Federal Recognition as an Indian Tribe." *Advocate* (Baton Rouge), 19 May 1995, § B, p. 6.

"Jena Choctaws Once Wanted Casino in Caddo Parish." AP State and Local Wire, 26 February 2002.

"Jena Indians Learn What Their Ancestors Forgot." *Times-Picayune*, 3 April 1938, § 2, p. 5.

Johnson, Bobby. *The Coushatta People*. Phoenix: Indian Tribal Series, 1976.

Johnson, Troy R. "The Roots of Contemporary Indian Activism." *American Indian Culture and Research Journal* 20, no. 2 (1996), 127–54.

Johnson v. M'Intosh, 21 U.S. 543, 8 Wheat. 543 (1823).

Johnston, Basil. *Indian School Days*. Norman: University of Oklahoma Press, 1988.

Joint Tribal Council of the Passamaquoddy Tribe v. Morton, 528 F.2d 370 (1st Cir. 1975).

Jojola, Ted. Foreword, *Irredeemable America: The Indians' Estate and Land Claims*, ed. Imre Sutton. Albuquerque: University of New Mexico Press, 1985.

Jolivette, Andrew. *Louisiana Creoles: Cultural Recovery and Mixed-Race Native American Identity*. Lanham, Md.: Lexington, 2007.

Jones, Leon, and Dan McCoy. "Testimony of Leon Jones, Principal Chief and Dan McCoy, Tribal Council Chairman, Eastern Band of Cherokee Indians, Cherokee, North Carolina, on S. 611, the Indian Federal Recognition and Administrative Procedures Act of 1999, Presented to the Committee on Indian Affairs of the United States Senate, Washington, D.C., May 24, 2000."

Judd, Graham, director. "African-American Lives." PBS Paramount, 2006.

Juneau, Donald. "The Judicial Extinguishment of the Tunica Indian Tribe." *Southern University Law Review* 7 (1980), 43–99.

Katz, Michael S. *A History of Compulsory Education Laws.* Bloomington, Ind.: Phi Delta Kappa Educational Foundation, 1976.

Kauanui, J. Kehaulani. *Hawaiian Blood: Colonialism and the Politics of Sovereignty and Indigeneity.* Durham: Duke University Press, 2008.

Kelly, Lawrence C. "United States Indian Policies, 1900–1980." *Handbook of North American Indians,* vol. 4, *History of Indian-White Relations,* ed. Wilcomb E. Washburn, 67–80. Washington: Smithsonian Institution, 1988.

Kinnaird, Lawrence, and Lucia B. Kinnaird. "Choctaws West of the Mississippi, 1766–1800." *Southwestern Historical Quarterly* 83 (April 1980), 349–70.

Kirshenblatt-Gimblett, Barbara. *Destination Culture: Tourism, Museums, and Heritage.* Berkeley: University of California Press, 1998.

Klopotek, Brian. "Dangerous Decolonizing: Indigenous Methodologies, White Supremacy, and Black-Indian Relations." *Narrating Native Histories in the Americas,* ed. Florencia Mallon. Durham: Duke University Press, forthcoming.

Klopotek, Brian, Brenda Lintinger, and John Barbry. "Ordinary and Extraordinary Trauma: Race, Indigeneity, and Hurricane Katrina in Tunica-Biloxi History." *American Indian Culture and Research Journal* 32, no. 2 (August 2008), 55–77.

Kniffen, Fred B., Hiram F. Gregory, and George A. Stokes. *The Historic Tribes of Louisiana from 1542 to the Present.* Baton Rouge: Louisiana State University Press, 1987, 1994.

Kreeger, M. M. "Louisiana Indians." *Times-Picayune,* 10 March 1978, § 1, p. 18 [letter to the editor].

Lacour, Barbara B. "Indian Tribe's Recognition Expected during Bicentennial." *Times-Picayune,* 18 January 1976, § 2, p. 2.

LaDuke, Winona. *All Our Relations: Native Struggle for Land and Life.* Boston: South End, 1999.

LaFlesche, Francis. *The Middle Five: Indian Schoolboys of the Omaha Tribe.* Lincoln: University of Nebraska Press, 1978 [orig. pubd 1900].

"LaSalle Parish School Board Elects Officials at Jan. 6th Session." *Jena Times,* 11 January 1945, 1.

"Lasall Parish Teachers Seek $400 Pay Raise; Refuse $250." *Jena Times,* 22 August 1946, 1.

Lawrence, Charles R., III. "The Id, the Ego, and Equal Protection: Reckoning with Unconscious Racism." *Stanford Law Review* 39 (1986–87), 317.

Leonard, Wesley. "Miami Language Reclamation in the Home: A Case Study." Ph.D. diss., University of California, 2007.

Levine, Stuart, and Nancy O. Lurie, eds. *The American Indian Today.* Baltimore: Penguin, 1969.

Lewis, David. "Termination of the Confederated Tribes of the Grande Ronde Community of Oregon: Politics, Community, and Identity." Ph.D. diss., University of Oregon, 2009.

Lincoln, Kenneth. *Native American Renaissance.* Berkeley: University of California Press, 1982.

Lindsay, Jay. "Study: American Indians Making Significant Income Gains, but Still Trail Overall Population." Associated Press State and Local Wire, 5 January 2005.

Lintinger, Brenda. "Anna Mae Juneau: Basket Weaver." *Tunica-Biloxi Tribe of Louisiana* (newsletter), July–August 1998, 8.

——. "Baskets, Baskets, Everywhere . . ." *Tunica-Biloxi Tribe of Louisiana* (newsletter), July–August 1998, 9.

——. "Tribal Craftsmen Carry on Cultural Traditions." *Tunica-Biloxi Tribe of Louisiana* (newsletter), July–August 1998, 8.

——. "Tribal Family Gets New Home for Their Little Angels." *Tunica-Biloxi Tribe of Louisiana* (newsletter), November 2001, 1, 4–5.

——. "Tribal Members Learn the Art of Pine-Needle Basket Weaving from Cryer Family Members." *Tunica-Biloxi Tribe of Louisiana* (newsletter), August 2002, 1, 16.

Lipsitz, George. *The Possessive Investment in Whiteness: How White People Profit from Identity Politics*. Philadelphia: Temple University Press, 1998; rev. and enlarged, 2006.

——. *American Studies in a Moment of Danger*. Minneapolis: University of Minnesota Press, 2001.

Littlefield, Alice, and Martha C. Knack, eds. *Native Americans and Wage Labor: Ethnohistorical Perspectives*. Norman: University of Oklahoma Press, 1996.

Littlefield, Daniel F. *Africans and Seminoles: From Removal to Emancipation*. Westport: Greenwood, 1977.

"Located South of Marksville: Indians Open Trading Post on Reservation." *Daily Town Talk* (Alexandria, La.), 1 November 1968, § D, p. 9.

Lomawaima, Tsianina. *They Called It Prairie Light: The Story of the Chilocco Indian School*. Lincoln: University of Nebraska Press, 1994.

"Look Out, Schickgruber Catawbas on Warpath." *Jena Times*, 7 May 1942, 7.

Louisiana, State of. Act 220 of 1920. Louisiana Revised Statutes 9:201.

——. House Concurrent Resolution 240, Legislature of the State of Louisiana. Official Journal Louisiana Senate, 14 July 1975, p. 79; 11 July 1975, p. 56.

——. *Opinions Attorney General* (1932–34), 587.

Louisiana Folklife Project. "Folkllife in Education Project," http://www.louisiana voices.org/Unit8/edu_unit8_biography_kthomas.html.

Louisiana Public Broadcasting. "A Promise from the Sun." Video documentary of the Tunica-Biloxi Tribe, Louisiana Public Broadcasting, completed 1999. Not yet released.

Louisiana Purchase Treaty, 30 April 1803. General Records of the U.S. Government, Record Group 11, National Archives.

Louisiana Regional Folklife Program, Northwestern State University of Louisiana, http://www.nsula.edu/regionalfolklife/CurrentResearch/splitbasket/cscb.htm.

Louisiana Regional Folklife Program, region 2, Red River Valley and the Neutral Strip, "Choctaw Split Cane Basketry," http://www.nsula.edu/regionalfolklife/Current ResearchProjects/splitbasket/cscb.htm.

Louisana State Archives, Baton Rouge. Indian Affairs, 1981–84.

Louisiana State Land Office, Baton Rouge. *Pintado Papers*, vol. 20.

"La. Tribe Fights to Prove Its Heritage." *Times-Picayune*, 14 August 1988, § C, p. 8.

Lovett, Laura. " 'African and Cherokee by Choice': Race and Resistance under

Legalized Segregation." *American Indian Quarterly* 22, nos. 1–2 (winter–spring 1998), 203–29.

Lurie, Nancy Oestreich. "The Voice of the American Indian: Report on the American Indian Chicago Conference." *Current Anthropology* 2, no. 5 (December 1961), 478–500.

———. "Sol Tax and Tribal Sovereignty." *Human Organization* 58, no. 1 (spring 1999), 108–17.

Mankiller, Wilma, and Michael Wallis. *Mankiller: A Chief and Her People*. New York: St. Martin's, 1993.

"Marksville Mayor Dr. Richard Michel Pleased with Town's and Tribe's Growth, Success and Prosperity." *Tunica-Biloxi Tribe of Louisiana* (newsletter), December 1999, 1, 3, 8.

Martin, Deborah Lee. "Development at Ysleta del Sur Pueblo, Texas: The Influence of Culture on the Development Process within an American Indian Community." Ph.D. diss., University of Wisconsin, 1994.

Martin, Joel W. " 'My Grandmother Was a Cherokee Princess': Representations of Indians in Southern History." *Dressing in Feathers: The Construction of the Indian in American Popular Culture*, ed. S. Elizabeth Bird. Boulder: Westview, 1996.

Mashpee Tribe v. New Seabury Corp., 592 F.2d 575 (1st Cir. 1979).

Mason, W. Dale. *Indian Gaming: Tribal Sovereignty and American Politics*. Norman: University of Oklahoma Press, 1997.

"Mayor Quebedeaux of Mansura Reports Crime Rate Decreases since Tribal Casino Opened." *Tunica-Biloxi Tribe of Louisiana* (newsletter), January 2000, 1, 3–4.

McCulloch, Anne Merline, and David E. Wilkins. " 'Constructing' Nations within States: The Quest for Federal Recognition by the Catawba and Lumbee Tribes." *American Indian Quarterly* 19, no. 3 (summer 1995), 361–88.

McNickle, D'Arcy. *Native American Tribalism: Indian Survivals and Renewals*. New York: Oxford University Press, 1973.

Melmer, David. "Gover and Anderson Strike Back at Critics." *Indian Country Today*, 2 May 2001, http://www.indiancountry.com/?397.

Merrell, James. "The Racial Education of the Catawba Indians." *Journal of Southern History* 50, no. 3 (August 1984), 363–84.

———. *The Indians' New World: Catawbas and Their Neighbors from European Contact through the Era of Removal*. New York: W. W. Norton, 1989.

Meyer, Melissa. *The White Earth Tragedy: Ethnicity and Dispossession at a Minnesota Anishinaabe Reservation, 1889–1920*. Lincoln: University of Nebraska Press, 1994.

Meyers, Mark D. "Federal Recognition of Indian Tribes in the United States." *Stanford Law and Policy Review* 12, no. 2 (2000), 271–300.

Miami Nation of Indians of Indiana v. Department of Interior, 255 F.3d 342 (7th Cir. 2001).

Mihesuah, Devon A., ed. *Repatriation Reader: Who Owns American Indian Remains?* Lincoln: University of Nebraska Press, 2000.

Miles, Tiya. *Ties That Bind: The Story of an Afro-Cherokee Family in Slavery and Freedom*. Berkeley: University of California Press, 2005.

Miles, Tiya, and Sharon P. Holland, eds. *Crossing Waters, Crossing Worlds: The African Diaspora in Indian Country*. Durham: Duke University Press, 2006.

Milhollon, Michelle. "Choctaw Band Sues Governor in LaSalle; Group Wants Money for Denied Casino." *Advocate* (Baton Rouge), 2 June 2005.

Miller, Bruce G. "After the F.A.P.: Tribal Reorganization after Federal Recognition." *Journal of Ethnic Studies* 17, no. 2 (summer 1989), 89–100.

——. *Invisible Indigenes: The Politics of Nonrecognition*. Lincoln: University of Nebraska Press, 2003.

Miller, Mark. "Ambiguous Tribalism: Unacknowledged Indians and the Federal Acknowledgment Process." Ph.D. diss., University of Arizona, 2001.

——. *Forgotten Tribes: Unacknowledged Indians and the Federal Acknowledgment Process*. Lincoln: University of Nebraska Press, 2004.

Miller, Shari, and Miriam Rich. "A History of the Clifton Community." MS prepared for the Clifton-Choctaw community. Copy in possession of the author.

——. "Traditional Medicines." *Splittin' on the Grain: Louisiana Folklife* 8, no. 1 (March 1983), 14.

Mills, Gary B. *The Forgotten People: Cane River's Creoles of Color*. Baton Rouge: Louisiana State University Press, 1977.

Mississippi Band of Choctaws web site, http://www.choctaw.org, accessed 27 July 2003.

Momaday, N. Scott. *House Made of Dawn*. New York: Harper and Row, 1968, 1989.

Moreau v. Valentine, Civ. no. 1599 (La. 6th Dist. Ct. Avoyelles Ph., filed 12 April 1842).

Morgan, Robert. "Indian Leader Angered: Barbry Feels Question about Gaming Devices Out of Line." *Daily Town Talk* (Alexandria, La.), 16 March 1995, § D, p. 1.

Morton v. Maynor, 510 F.2d 1254 (D.C. Cir. 1975).

Mulroy, Kevin. *The Seminole Freedmen: A History*. Norman: University of Oklahoma Press, 2007.

Nagel, Joane, and C. Matthew Snipp. "Ethnic Reorganization: American Indian Social, Economic, Political, and Cultural Strategies for Survival." *Ethnic and Racial Studies* 16, no. 2 (April 1993), 203–35.

"Natchitoches Jurors Oppose Plan Seen as Prelude to Casino." *Advocate* (Baton Rouge), 23 October 1998, § B, p. 7.

National Congress of American Indians. "Indian Recognition," 1978, published on the internet by the Fourth World Documentation Project Archives of the Center for World Indigenous Studies, http://www.cwis.org/fwdp/Americas/recogniz.txt.

——. "The National Congress of American Indians Declaration of Principles on Tribal Recognition by the US Government." *American Indian Journal* 4, no 5 (May 1978), 4.

——. "Testimony of the National Congress of American Indians on the Supreme Court Decision in *Carcieri v. Salazar* and Executive Branch Authority to Acquire Trust Land for Indian Tribes." U.S. Senate, Committee on Indian Affairs, 21 May 2009.

National Indian Gaming Association. "Majority of Americans Support Tribal Gaming According to National Poll." Press release, 12 July 2006, http://216.109.157.86/press_release/Majority%20Of%20Americans%20Support%20Indian%20Gaming%20According%20To%20National%20Poll.htm, accessed 22 October 2009.

"Native American Agency Wants to Give Up Key Role." *Record* (Bergen County, N.J.), 25 May 2000, § A, p. 13.

Native American Rights Fund. *Petition for Recognition of the Tunica-Biloxi Indian Tribe in Compliance with 25 CFR Part 54*, submitted to Cecil D. Andrus, secretary of the interior, 17 September 1978.

"Negroes of Avoyelles Eager to Attend School." *Weekly News* (Marksville, La.), 16 May 1929, 1.

Neitzel, Robert S. Field notes on the Tunica and Biloxi and correspondence with Frank Speck, 1938–40, Frank G. Speck Papers, Library of the American Philosophical Society, Philadelphia.

"Night School Being Established." *Weekly News* (Marksville, La.), 10 May 1929, 1.

"No Break for Indian Casino." *Advocate* (Baton Rouge), 26 January 2003, § B, p. 8 [staff editorial].

"No Good Casino Plans in Works." *Advocate* (Baton Rouge), 20 January 2004, § B, p. 6 [editorial].

Noonan, John T. *Persons and Masks of the Law*. New York: Farrar, Straus and Giroux, 1976.

Norris Tyler papers. Collection of Clifton-Choctaw government–related documents in possession of Norris Tyler.

North Central Regional Center for Rural Development at Iowa State University. "Measuring Community Success and Sustainability," http://www.ag.iastate .edu/centers/rdev/Community_Success/casestudy1.html.

Northwood High School, Boyce, Rapides Parish, Louisiana, web site, http://www .rapides.k12.la.us/northwood/history.htm.

O'Brien, Jean. *Dispossession by Degrees: Indian Land and Identity in Natick, Massachusetts*. New York: Cambridge University Press, 1997.

"Old Money, Metal Pieces Found in Ancient Grave." *Times-Picayune*, 4 August 1961.

Omi, Michael, and Howard Winant. *Racial Formation in the United States from the 1960s to the 1990s*. 2nd edn. New York: Routledge, 1994.

O'Nell, Theresa Deleane. "Telling about Whites, Talking about Indians: Oppression, Resistance, and Contemporary American Indian Identity." *Cultural Anthropology* 9, no. 1 (February 1994), 94–126.

——. *Disciplined Hearts: History, Identity, and Depression in an American Indian Community*. Berkeley: University of California Press, 1996.

*On the Tunica Trail*. 3rd edn. Baton Rouge: Louisiana Archaeological and Antiquities Commission, Department of Culture, Recreation, and Tourism, 1994. Anthropological Study Series no. 1.

Ottenheimer, Martin. *Forbidden Relatives: The American Myth of Cousin Marriage*. Urbana: University of Illinois Press, 1996.

"Pagan Indians Favor One White Man's Idea: War." *Jena Times*, 11 June 1942, 9.

Paredes, J. Anthony. "Federal Recognition and the Poarch Creek Indians." *Indians of the Southeastern United States in the Late 20th Century*, ed. J. Anthony Paredes, 120–39. Tuscaloosa: University of Alabama Press, 1992.

——. "Paradoxes of Modernism and Indianness in the Southeast." *American Indian Quarterly* 19, no. 3 (summer 1995).

——. "In Defense of the BIA and the N.P.S.: Federal Acknowledgment, Native American Consultation, and Some Issues in the Implementation of the Native American Graves Protection and Repatriation Act." *St. Thomas Law Review* 10, no. 35 (fall 1997), 35–44.

——, ed. *Indians of the Southeastern United States in the Late 20th Century*. Tuscaloosa: University of Alabama Press, 1992.

Parenton, Vernon J., and Roland J. Pellegrin. "The Sabines: A Study of Racial Hybrids in a Louisiana Coastal Parish." *Social Forces* 29 (December 1950), 148–54.

Parker, Dorothy. *Singing an Indian Song: A Biography of D'Arcy McNickle*. Lincoln: University of Nebraska Press, 1994.

Pascal, Robert. *Readings in Louisiana Family Law*. Baton Rouge: Louisiana State University Press, 1962.

Paschal, Rachael. "The Imprimatur of Recognition: American Indian Tribes and the Federal Acknowledgment Process." *Washington Law Review* 66 (1991), 209–28.

Pascoe, Peggy. *What Comes Naturally: Miscegenation and the Making of Race Law in America*. New York: Oxford University Press, 2009.

Perdue, Theda. *Slavery and the Evolution of Cherokee Society, 1540–1866*. Knoxville: University of Tennessee Press, 1979.

——. *Cherokee Women: Gender and Culture Change, 1700–1835*. Lincoln: University of Nebraska Press, 1999.

Pesantubbee, Michelene. *Choctaw Women in a Chaotic World: The Clash of Cultures in the Colonial Southeast*. Albuquerque: University of New Mexico Press, 2005.

Peterson, John H., Jr. "Assimilation, Separation, and Out-Migration in an American Indian Group." *American Anthropologist* 74 (1972), 1286–95.

Philp, Kenneth R. *Termination Revisited: American Indians on the Trail to Self-Determination*. Lincoln: University of Nebraska Press, 1999.

Pilcher, Joseph Mitchell. "History of Marksville." *Weekly News* (Marksville, La.), 9 November 1929, 11.

Pitts, Stella. "Louisiana Indians on Legal Warpath." *Times-Picayune*, 19 November 1978, § 1, p. 1.

Poe, Edgar. "Neglect Peaceful Louisiana Indian." *Times-Picayune*, 16 November 1975, § 1, p. 15.

——. "Louisiana's Forgotten Indians." *Times-Picayune*, 1 May 1977, § 1, p. 42.

Porter, Frank W., III. "Nonrecognized American Indian Tribes: An Historical and Legal Perspective." Newberry Library Center for the History of the American Indian, Occasional Paper Series no. 7 (1983).

Povinelli, Elizabeth. *The Cunning of Recognition: Indigenous Alterity and the Making of Australian Multiculturalism*. Durham: Duke University Press, 2002.

Prashad, Vijay. *Everybody Was Kung Fu Fighting: Afro-Asian Connections and the Myth of Cultural Purity*. Boston: Beacon, 2001.

Quasula, Theodore R., acting director, BIA Office of Tribal Services, to Henry M. Neal
Sr., 13 August 1991, 5. Clifton-Choctaw file, Branch of Acknowledgment and
Research.

Quinn, William W., Jr. "Southeastern Indians: The Quest for Federal Acknowledgment
and a New Legal Status." *From Big Game to Bingo: Native Peoples of the Southeastern
United States: A Retrospective Occasioned by the Sesquicentennial of the Great Removal*,
ed. J. Anthony Paredes and J. Leitch Wright Jr., 255–74. Proceedings of a conference
conducted at Florida State University, 5–7 March 1987.

——. "The Southeast Syndrome: Notes on Indian Descendant Recruitment
Organizations and Their Perceptions of Native American Culture." *American Indian
Quarterly* 14, no. 2 (spring 1990), 147–54.

——. "Federal Acknowledgment of American Indian Tribes: The Historical
Development of a Legal Concept." *American Journal of Legal History* 34, no. 4
(October 1990), 331–64.

Raibmon, Paige. *Authentic Indians: Episodes of Encounter from the Late Nineteenth-Century
Northwest Coast*. Durham: Duke University Press, 2005.

Redman, Carl. "Move Afoot to Unify Mixed-Breed Indians." *Daily Town Talk*
(Alexandria, La.), 16 September 1978.

Red Shirt, Delphine. "These Are Not Indians." *Hartford Courant*, 8 December 2002.

"Republican Tied to Abramoff Pushes Anti-gaming Bill," http://www.indianz.com/
News/2005/008825.asp, accessed 20 April 2008.

Rhinehart, Melissa A. "Miami Indian Language Shift and Recovery." Ph.D. diss.,
Michigan State University, 2006.

Rice v. Cayetano, 528 U.S. 495 (2000).

Robinson, Melissa B. "Senate Committee Hears Criticisms of Indian Recognition
Process." Associated Press State and Local Wire, 18 September 2002.

Roediger, David. *The Wages of Whiteness: Race and the Making of the American Working
Class*. New York: Verso, 1991.

Roth, George. "Comment in Reply [to Russel Barsh]." *Practicing Anthropology* 10, no. 2
(1988), 21–22.

——. "Federal Tribal Recognition and the South." *Anthropologists and Indians in the New
South*, ed. Rachel A. Bonney and J. Anthony Paredes, 49–70. Tuscaloosa: University
of Alabama Press, 2001.

Rothenberg, P. S., ed. *White Privilege: Essential Readings on the Other Side of Racism*. New
York: Worth, 2002.

Rountree, Helen C. *Pocahontas's People: The Powhatan Indians of Virginia through Four
Centuries*. Norman: University of Oklahoma Press, 1990.

Rubinstein, Robert A. "A Conversation with Sol Tax." *Current Anthropology* 32, no. 2,
(April 1991), 175–82.

Ruby, Robert H., and John A. Brown. *Esther Ross: Stillaguamish Champion*. Norman:
University of Oklahoma Press, 2001.

Sabludowsky, Stephen. "Louisiana Election Buzz: Jindal, GOP Make Gambling
Campaign Issue." 16 October 2007, http://www.bayoubuzz.com/News/

Louisiana / Politics / Elections / Louisiana_Election_Buzz__Jindal_GOP_Make_ Gambling_Campaign_Issue__4907.asp, accessed 4 April 2008.

Saunt, Claudio. *A New Order of Things: Property, Power, and the Transformation of the Creek Indians, 1733–1816*. Cambridge: Cambridge University Press, 1999.

———. *Black, White, and Indian: Race and the Unmaking of an American Family*. Oxford: Oxford University Press, 2005.

Sayre, Alan. "Proposed Reservation Casino Doesn't Make Sense for the State." Associated Press State and Local Wire, 17 January 2003.

———. "Foster Support for Indian Casino Puzzling." *Advocate* (Baton Rouge), 20 January 2003, § B, p. 7.

———. "Coushatta's Lobbying Costly, Leads to Probe." *Advocate* (Baton Rouge), 15 November 2004, § B, p. 11.

Scott, John L., and Paul S. Nelson. "Voting with a Hand on the Bible and Not on the Wallet: The 1996 Video Poker Referendum in Louisiana." *American Journal of Economics and Sociology* 66, no. 3 (July 2007), 571–91.

Seminole Tribe of Florida v. Butterworth, 658 F.2d 310 (5th Cir. 1981).

Seminole Tribe of Florida v. Florida, 517 U.S. 44 (1996).

Shelton, Melinda. "Treasure Case Goes Higher." *Sunday Advocate* (Baton Rouge), § B, p. 1.

Sibley, John. "Historical Sketches of the Several Indian Tribes in Louisiana, South of the Arkansas and between the Mississippi and River Grande." *American State Papers*, Indian Affairs, vol. 1. Washington, 1832.

———. "A Report from Natchitoches in 1807," ed. Annie Abel. New York: Museum of the American Indian, 1922.

Sider, Gerald. *Lumbee Indian Histories: Race, Ethnicity, and Indian Identity in the Southern United States*. Cambridge: Cambridge University Press, 1993.

Sifuentes, Edward. "San Pasqual Casino Backers Face Problems." *North County Times*, 26 January 2002.

Silva, Denise Ferreira da. *Toward a Global Idea of Race*. Minneapolis: University of Minnesota Press, 2007.

Smith, J. Arthur, III. Original Brief on Behalf of Leonard Charrier, Plaintiff-Appellant, Court of Appeal, 1st Circuit, State of Louisiana, Docket no. CA 350867, Charrier v. Bell, 30 August 1985. Documents relating to the case available from the National Indian Law Library, Boulder, Colo.

Snipp, C. Matthew. *American Indians: The First of This Land*. New York: Russell Sage Foundation, 1989.

Spilde, Katherine A. "Rich Indian Racism: The Uses of Indian Imagery in the Political Process." Paper presented to the 11th International Conference on Gambling and Risk Taking, Las Vegas, 20 June 2000, http://www.indiangaming.org/library/articles/rich-indian-racism.shtml, accessed 12 November 2007.

Starna, William. "The Southeast Syndrome: The Prior Restraint of a Non-Event." *American Indian Quarterly* 15 (fall 1991), 493–502.

——. " 'Public Ethnohistory' and Native-American Communities: History or Administrative Genocide?" *Radical History Review* 53 (1992), 126–39.

——. " 'We'll All Be Together Again': The Federal Acknowledgment of the Wampanoag Tribe of Gay Head." *Northeast Anthropology* 51 (1996), 3–12.

State v. Chiqui, 49 La. Ann. 131, 21 So. 513 (1897).

Stillaguamish v. Kleppe, 1976 U.S. Dist. LEXIS 17381.

Stone, Peter H. *Heist: Superlobbyist Jack Abramoff, His Republican Allies, and the Buying of Washington.* New York: Farrar, Straus and Giroux, 2006.

Straus, Terry, Ron Bowman, and Michael Chapman. "Anthropology, Ethics, and the American Indian Chicago Conference." *American Ethnologist* 13, no. 4 (November 1986), 802–4.

Strong, Pauline Turner, and Barrik Van Winkle. " 'Indian Blood': Reflections on the Reckoning and Refiguring of Native North American Identity." *Cultural Anthropology* 11, no. 4 (1996), 547–76.

Sturm, Circe. "Blood Politics, Racial Classification, and Cherokee National Identity: The Trials and Tribulations of the Cherokee Freedmen." *American Indian Quarterly* 22, nos. 1–2 (winter–spring 1998), 230–58.

——. *Blood Politics: Race, Culture, and Identity in the Cherokee Nation of Oklahoma.* Lincoln: University of Nebraska Press, 2002.

Sunray, Cedric. "Haskell Endangered Legacy Project," http://www.helphaskell.com/purpose.html, accessed 6 April 2009.

Szasz, Margaret Connell. *Education and the American Indian: The Road to Self-Determination since 1928.* Albuquerque: University of New Mexico Press, 1974, 1999.

Talton v. Mayes, 163 U.S. 376 (1898).

Tanner, John. *The Falcon.* New York: Penguin, 1994 [orig. pubd 1830].

"Taxing Casinos: Tribal Official Complains about State Effort." *Daily Town Talk* (Alexandria, La.), 19 March 1997, § A, p. 1.

Taylor, Jonathan B., and Joseph P. Kalt. "American Indians on Reservations: A Databook of Socioeconomic Change Between the 1990 and 2000 Censuses." Harvard Project on American Indian Economic Development, January 2005, http://www.ksg.harvard.edu/hpaied/pubs/cabazon.htm, accessed 12 November 2007.

Thiong'o, Ngugi Wa. *Decolonising the Mind: The Politics of Language in African Literature.* Portsmouth, N.H.: Heinemann, 1986.

Thompson, Bobby, and John H. Peterson Jr. "Mississippi Choctaw Identity: Genesis and Change." *The New Ethnicity: Perspectives From Ethnology*, ed. John W. Bennett. St. Paul: West, 1975.

Thompson, Duane. "Louisiana Indian Tribes Fighting for U.S. Recognition: 'Being a Tribe Is a Business.' " *Times-Picayune*, 6 January 1980, § 1, pp. 1, 5.

——. "Tribes Have Little Legal Pull." *Times-Picayune*, 7 January 1980, § 1, p. 12.

——. "La. Indians Sue for Land, Money." *Times-Picayune*, 8 January 1980, § 1, p. 2.

Thompson, Mark. "Nurturing the Forked Tree: Conception and Formation of the American Indian Policy Review Commission." *New Directions in Federal Indian*

Policy: A Review of the American Indian Policy Review Commission. Contemporary
American Indian Issues Series, no. 1 (1979), 5–18. Los Angeles: American Indian
Studies Center, UCLA.

Thwaites, Reuben Gold, ed. *The Jesuit Relations and Allied Documents: Travels and
Explorations of the Jesuit Missionaries in New France, 1610–1791.* New York: Pageant,
1959.

Toensing, Gale Courey. "Eastern Pequots' Appeal of Recognition Reversal Rejected."
*Indian Country Today*, 23 January 2006, http://www.indiancountrytoday.com/
archive/28169114.html, accessed 30 March 2009.

———. "Judge Denies Schaghticoke Federal Recognition Appeal." *Indian Country Today*,
4 September 2008, http://www.indiancountrytoday.com/home/content/
27907904.html, accessed 30 March 2009.

———. "Schagticoke Files 2nd Circuit Appeal for Acknowledgment Restoration." *Indian
Country Today*, 19 March 2009, http://www.indiancountrytoday.com/national/
41530002.html, accessed 22 March 2009.

Tolley, Sara-Larus. *Quest for Tribal Acknowledgment: California's Honey Lake Maidus.*
Norman: University of Oklahoma Press, 2006.

Toney, Ellyn. "Tribe's Bingo Parlor to Open in September." *Advocate* (Baton Rouge),
14 August 1988, § B, p. 3.

Trask, Haunani-Kay. "Settlers of Color and 'Immigrant' Hegemony: 'Locals' in
Hawaii." *Amerasia Journal* 26 no 2 (2000), 1–24.

"Tribal Flag Presented at December General Meeting." *Tunica-Biloxi Tribe of Louisiana*
(newsletter), November–December 1998, 18–20.

Trigger, Bruce G. *The Children of Aataentsic: A History of the Huron People to 1660.*
Kingston: McGill-Queen's University Press, 1976; 2nd edn 1987.

Trillin, Calvin. "Louisiana: The Tunica Treasure." *New Yorker*, 27 July 1981, 41.

Tri-Millennium Corp. v. Jena Band of Choctaw Indians, 725 So. 2d 533 (La. App. 1998).

Tunica-Biloxi Tribe. "1998 Tunica-Biloxi Community Review." Marksville, La.: Tunica-
Biloxi Tribe, March 1999.

———. Property inventory, 11 July 2006.

Tunica-Biloxi Tribe v. Louisiana, 964 F.2d 1536 (5th Cir. 1992).

Tunica-Biloxi Tribe v. United States, 1991 U.S. App. LEXIS 10716 (Fed. Cir. May 17, 1991).

"Tunicas Find Grave in Marksville." *Opelousas Daily World Magazine*, 13 August 1961,
§ A, p. 10.

"Tunicas Remain 'Optimistic' on Land Claim." *Advocate* (Baton Rouge), 1 July 1982.

"Tunica Tax War Wages On." *Daily Town Talk* (Alexandria, La.), 15 April 1994.

Turner, Dan. "Federal Officials Trap Themselves with Indian Casino Decision." *Times*
(Shreveport, La.), 26 September 2002.

———. "Analysis: Casino Tribe Searches for Land." *Shreveport Times*, 2 March 2003,
www.nwlouisiana.com/html/09F9BAA5-3DEA-42BD-B14D-B53BA9CE83D2.shtml,
accessed 23 July 2003.

Underhill, Ruth M. "Report on a Visit to Indian Groups in Louisiana, Oct. 15–25, 1938,"
p. 20. File 68776-1931-800, part 2, National Archives, Record Group 75.

U.S. Bureau of the Census. 1910 Census, Rapides Parish, La.

———. *Measuring America: The Decennial Censuses from 1790 to 2000*. Washington: U.S. Bureau of the Census, September 2002.

U.S. Congress. An Act Relating to the Lumbee Indians of North Carolina. H.R. 4656, 84th Cong., 70 Stat. 254 (1956).

———. *Federal Recognition Administrative Procedures Act: Hearing before the Committee on Indian Affairs, United States Senate, One Hundred Fourth Congress, First Session, on S. 479 to Provide for Administrative Procedures to Extend Federal Recognition to Certain Indian Groups, July 13, 1995*. Washington: U.S. Government Printing Office, 1995.

———. " 'Gimme Five': Investigation of Tribal Lobbying Matters." Final Report before the 109th Cong., 2d sess., 22 June 2006, http://indian.senate.gov/public/_files/Report.pdf, accessed 30 November 2008.

———. "Hearing before the Subcommittee on Native American Affairs of the Committee on Natural Resources, House of Representatives, 103rd Congress, 2nd Session, on HR 2549, HR 4462, HR 4709, 'Federal Recognition of Indian Tribes,' July 22, 1994." Washington: U.S. Government Printing Office, 1995.

———. Indian Arts and Crafts Act of 1990. Public Law 101-644. Regulations at 61 Fed. Reg. 54551–56 (21 October 1996) (to be codified at 25 CFR Part 309).

———. Indian Child Welfare Act of 1978, 25 USC § 1901 et seq.

———. Indian Federal Recognition Administrative Procedures Act of 1998. H.R. 361, 106th Cong. (1999).

———. Indian Federal Recognition and Administrative Procedures Act of 1999. S. 611, 106th Cong.

———. Indian Gaming Regulatory Act of 1988, 25 USC § 2701 et seq.

———. Indian General Allotment Act of 1887 (Dawes Act), ch. 119, 24 Stat. 388 (25 U.S.C. 331 et seq.).

———. Indian Trade and Intercourse Act of 1834, 25 U.S.C. § 177.

———. Joint Resolution to Provide for the Establishment of the American Indian Policy Review Commission. S.J. Res. 133, 93d Cong., Public Law 93-580 (1975).

———. Lumbee Acknowledgment Act of 2003. S. 420, 108th Cong.

———. [Lumbee Recognition Act.] H.R. 5042 [Senate companion S. 2672], 100th Cong. (1987).

———. [Lumbee Recognition Act.] H.R. 2335, 101st Cong. (1990).

———. Lumbee Recognition Act. H.R. 1426, 102d Cong. (1991).

———. Lumbee Recognition Act. S. 1036, 102d Cong. (1993).

———. Lumbee Recognition Act. H.R. 898, 108th Cong. (2003).

———. Lumbee Recognition Act. H.R. 31, 111th Cong. (2009).

———. Major Crimes Act, 18 USC § 1153.

———. Native Hawaiian Government Reorganization Act of 2009. S. 1011, 111th Cong.

———. Thomasina E. Jordan Indian Tribes of Virginia Federal Recognition Act of 2009. H.R. 1385, 111th Congress (2009).

———. *Work of the Department of the Interior's Branch of Acknowledgment and Research within the Bureau of Indian Affairs: Hearing before the Committee on Indian Affairs,*

United States Senate, One Hundred Seventh Congress, Second Session, to Receive
Testimony from the Bureau of Indian Affairs on the Process Established by the Branch of
Acknowledgment and Research for the Review of Petitions of Tribal Groups That Are
Seeking Federal Recognition, June 11, 2002. Washington: U.S. Government Printing
Office, 2002.

U.S. Department of Energy, Smart Communities Network. "Success Stories:
Community Projects That Work." www.sustainable.doe.gov / success /
champion.shtml.

U.S. government. "Tribal Governments and Native Americans," official web portal,
http://www.firstgov.gov / Government / Tribal.shtml#land.

U.S. Government Accountability Office. "Indian Issues: Improvements Needed in
Tribal Recognition Process." November 2001, http://www.gao.gov / new.items /
d0249.pdf.

——. "Timeliness of the Tribal Recognition Process Has Improved, but It Will Take
Years to Clear the Existing Backlog of Petitioners." Statement of Robin M. Nazzaro,
director, Natural Resources and Environment, Testimony before the Committee on
Resources, House of Representatives, 10 February 2005, http://www.doi.gov / bia /
docs / ofa / admin_docs / GAO_Report_d05347t.pdf, accessed 3 December 2008.

U.S. Office of Federal Acknowledgment. "Anthropological Report, Jena Band of
Choctaw Indians." Fed. Reg., 21 October 1994.

——. "Anthropological Report on the Tunica-Biloxi Indian Tribe."

——. "Changes in the Internal Processing of Federal Acknowledgment Petitions," 65
Fed. Reg. 7052–53, 11 February 2000.

——. "Genealogical Report, Jena Band of Choctaw Indians."

——. "Genealogical Report, Tunica-Biloxi Indian Tribe."

——. "Historical Report on the United Houma Nation, Inc."; "Summary under the
Criteria and Evidence for Proposed Finding against Federal Acknowledgment of
the United Houma Nation, Inc." Fed. Reg., 22 December 1994.

——. "Historical Technical Report, Jena Band of Choctaw Indians." Fed. Reg.,
31 October 1994.

——. "History Report on Tunica-Biloxi Indian Tribe."

——. "Letters of Intent Received as of September 22, 2008," http://www.doi.gov /
bia / docs / ofa / admin_docs / num_letter_intent_092208.pdf. accessed 27 February
2009.

——. "List of Petitioners by State as of September 22, 2008," http://www.doi.gov / bia /
docs / ofa / admin_docs / Petitioners_by_State_092208.pdf, accessed 26 September
2009.

——. "The Official Guidelines for the Federal Acknowledgment Regulations."

——. "Procedures for Establishing That an American Indian Group Exists as a Tribe."
25 CFR § 83.

——. Proposed acknowledgment regulations, 16 June 1977, 42 Fed. Reg. 30647.

——. "Recommendation and Summary of Evidence for Proposed Finding for Federal
Acknowledgment of the Tunica-Biloxi Indian Tribe of Louisiana Pursuant to 25 CFR

54," Memorandum from commissioner of Indian affairs to acting deputy assistant secretary, Indian affairs, 4 December 1980.

——. "Status of Acknowledgment Cases."

——. "Status Summary of Acknowledgment Cases as of 22 September 2008," http://www.doi.gov/bia/docs/ofa/admin_docs/Status_Summary_092208.pdf, accessed 7 March 2009.

——. "Summary under the Criteria and Amended Proposed Finding against Federal Acknowledgment of the Biloxi, Chitimachi Confederation of Muskogees, Inc.," http://www.doi.gov/bia/docs/ofa/adc/056a_BCCM/056a_apf.pdf, accessed 30 January 2009.

——. "Summary under the Criteria and Evidence for Proposed Finding for Federal Acknowledgment of the Jena Band of Choctaw Indians." Fed. Reg., 21 October 1994.

——. "Summary under the Criteria and Amended Proposed Finding against Federal Acknowledgment of the Pointe-Au-Chien Indian Tribe," http://www.doi.gov/bia/docs/ofa/adc/056b_PACIT/056b_apf.pdf, accessed 30 January 2009.

——. Amos Tyler to Leslie Gay. "Letter of Intent to Petition," 22 March 1978, Clifton-Choctaw Reservation.

United States v. Holliday, 70 U.S. 407 (1865).

United States v. Sandoval, 231 U.S. 28 (1913).

United States v. Washington, 520 F.2d 676 (9th Cir. 1975).

Valley v. Rapides Parish School Board, 646 F.2d 925 (5th Cir. 1981).

Vizenor, Gerald. *Crossbloods: Bone Courts, Bingo, and Other Reports.* Minneapolis: University of Minnesota Press, 1976, 1990.

——. *Manifest Manners: Notes on Postindian Survivance.* Lincoln: University of Nebraska Press, 1999.

Wade, J. P. "First School for State Indians Held in LaSalle Parish; History of Tribe near Jena Is Related." *Shreveport Times*, 31 October 1929.

Wah, Lee Mun. *The Color of Fear.* Berkeley: Stir Fry, 1994.

Walker, Deward E., Jr. "Some Limitations of the Renascence Concept in Acculturation: The Nez Perce Case." *The American Indian Today*, ed. Stuart Levine and Nancy O. Lurie, 236–56. Baltimore: Penguin, 1969.

Wanamaker, Tom. "Let the Games Begin: Fiscal Responsibility in Indian Country." *Indian Country Today*, 4 November 2003, http://www.indiancountry.com/?1067959760.

Warrior, Robert. "A Room of One's Own at the ASA: An Indigenous Provocation." *American Quarterly* 55, no. 4 (December 2003), 681–87.

Watt, Marilyn. "Federal Indian Policy and Tribal Development in Louisiana: The Jena Band of Choctaw." Ph.D. diss., Pennsylvania State University, 1986.

Weatherhead, L. R. "What Is an 'Indian Tribe'? The Question of Tribal Existence." *American Indian Law Review* 8 (1980), 1–47.

Wheeler-Howard Act (Indian Reorganization Act), 25 U.S.C. § 461 et seq., 48 Stat. 984 (1934).

Wherry, James D. Afterword, *The Pequots in Southern New England: The Fall and Rise of an American Indian Nation*, ed. Laurence M. Hauptman and James D. Wherry. Norman: University of Oklahoma Press, 1990.

Wilkins, David. "Breaking into the Intergovernmental Matrix: The Lumbee Tribe's Efforts to Secure Federal Acknowledgment." *Publius: The Journal of Federalism* 23 (fall 1993), 123–42.

——. *American Indian Sovereignty and the U.S. Supreme Court: The Masking of Justice*. Austin: University of Texas Press, 1997.

——. Comments in "Exploring the Legacy and Future of Black / Indian Relations," moderated by Wilma Mankiller with Willard R. Johnson, Daniel F. Littlefield Jr., Patrick Minges, Deborah Tucker, and David Wilkins, 57th Annual Session, National Congress of American Indians, Afternoon Concurrent Breakout Session, St. Paul, 14 November 2000. Kansas City, Kans.: Kansas Institute of African American and Native American Family History, 2001, http://web.mit.edu/wjohnson/www/kiaanafh/KIAANAFH_PORTAL_PAGE. html.

Wilkins, David E., and K. Tsianina Lomawaima. *Uneven Ground: American Indian Sovereignty and Federal Law*. Norman: University of Oklahoma Press, 2001.

"William Lewis, 47, Shoots Military Police, Fishville." *Jena Times*, vol. 38, no 14, 1.

Williams, Walter L. "Patterns in the History of the Remaining Southeastern Indians, 1840–1975." *Southeastern Indians Since the Removal Era*, ed. Walter L. Williams, 193–210. Athens: University of Georgia Press, 1979.

——, ed. *Southeastern Indians since the Removal Era*. Athens: University of Georgia Press, 1979.

Wollock, Jeffrey. "On the Wings of History: American Indians in the 20th Century." *Native Americas: Hemispheric Journal of Indigenous Issues* 20, no. 1 (spring 2003), 14–31.

Works Progress Administration. *Survey of Federal Archives in Louisiana*. Indian Land Claims, and Other Documents, 74–75. Baton Rouge: Louisiana State University, 1940.

Youchican v. Texas & Pacific Railway, 147 La. 1080, 86 So. 551 (Lexis 1654).

# Index

Page numbers in *italics* refer to illustrations.

*Carcieri v. Salazar*, 279 n. 1, 343 n. 2

casino gambling. *See* gaming

Catahoula Choctaws, 128, 315 n. 8

Cattelino, Jessica, 98, 99–100, 246–47, 310 n. 3, 312 n. 20, 312 n. 32

CENA (Coalition of Eastern Native Americans), 64–68, 301 n. 9, 301 n. 15

CETA (Comprehensive Employment and Training Act), 67, 69, 156, 203, 332 n. 3

Charrier, Leonard, 89–93

Child, Brenda, 137, 292 n. 12

Chitimachas: anti-black racism and, 323 n. 78; coalition of Louisiana Indians and, 48, 294 nn. 34–35; education and, 295 n. 42, 318 n. 39, 320 n. 57, 323 n. 78; educational funding and, 49, 52, 295 n. 45, 296 n. 51, 320 n. 57; federal funding and, 145–46, 203; gaming and, 242, 331 n. 28; recognition and, 318 n. 39, 320 n. 57, 321 n. 57; recognition date of, 242, 293 n. 27, 321 n. 57; school integration and, 318 n. 39; statistics on, 295 n. 42; trust status and, 141–42, 320 n. 57

Choctaw-Apaches, 202–3, 329 n. 15, 332 n. 3, 334 n. 32

class stratification, 106–7, 240

Clifford, James, 38, 197–99, 253, 255, 331 n. 1, 334 n. 38

Clifton, James, 333 n. 28

Clifton-Choctaws, 11; advantages of recognition procedure and, 15–16, 226–33, 242–43; African American ancestry and, 15, 205, 212–13, 216–17, 218, 264–65, 266, 338 n. 78; anthropologists and, 227, 231, 252, 255, 257; anti-black racism and, 14, 218, 219, 221, 264–65, 323 n. 78; blackness and, 214, 217, 219, 297 n. 62; coalition of Louisiana Indians and, 47–48; community center and, 201, *228*, *230*, 232–33, 251; community schools and, 14, 217, 338 nn. 80–81, 338 n. 83; crafts, material culture, and, 227–32, 246, 342 n. 107, 344 n. 11; Creoles of color and, 211–13, 214,

217, 219, 338 n. 76; cultural vitality and, 15–16, 226–33, 237–38, 245, 271–72, 342 n. 107; economic development and, 15, 200, 226, 233–34, 243, 244, 332 n. 6, 342 n. 105; education and, 14, 15, 200, 217, 218–19, 323 n. 78; enrollment and, 204, 210; family relationships and, 204, 205, 208–11, 219, 243–44, 256–57; federal funding and, 200–201, 243; funding for recognition and, 243–44; gaming corporate partnerships and, 234–37, 242–43; genealogies and, 204–7, 208–9, 211–12, 232, 334 n. 31, 334 n. 32, 334 n. 34, 335 n. 44, 336 n. 50; generational differences and, 236–37; goals and, 205, 233, 237–38; historical records and, 204, 205, 207–8, 209–13, 225, 232, 334 n. 32, 335 nn. 37–40, 335 n. 41, 336 n. 50; Indian identity and, 15, 197, 204, 205–6, 209, 212, 217, 231, 257, 338 n. 78, 343 n. 116; intermarriage and, 208, 219, 297 n. 62; intermingling and, 224–25; intertribal relationships and, 198–99, 202–3, 205–6, 216, 332 n. 3; land and, 204, 342–43 n. 105; language and, 209, 257, 335 n. 41; Mobilian Jargon and, 197–99, 331 n. 1, 334 n. 38; as nonfederal tribe, 15–16, 231–32, 344 n. 113; organization of tribal government and, 199–200, 201, 204, 248, 256–57, 332 n. 5, 332 n. 15; poverty and, 199–201, 204; practices and, 222, 341 nn. 96–98; recognition procedures and, 15–16, 197–99, 201–2, 204–5, 226–33, 232, 242–43, 331 n. 1; recognition status and, 1; removal and, 209–10; service area and, 212, 336 n. 60; social health and, 200–201, 226–27, 233, 251, 332 n. 6, 342 n. 105; state recognition and, 202, 227, 237–38, 243; tribal identity and, 14–16, 204–6, 222–23, 225–29, 232, 237–38, 271–72; whiteness and, 217–19

Clifton family, 224

Coalition of Eastern Native Americans (CENA), 64–68, 301 n. 9, 301 n. 15

coalition of Louisiana Indians, 23, 47–48, 116, 294 n. 32, 294 nn. 34–35

Cohen, Felix, 24–25, 141

Collier, John, 19–21, 25, 50–52

colonialism: acknowledgment policy and, 18, 21, 31, 36, 39, 59, 253, 262, 269–70; anti-black racism and, 219–21; BIA and, 9; decolonization and, 15, 18, 158–59, 327 n. 27; federal-tribal relationships and, 190–91; gaming and, 13; gender roles and, 116; ideology and, 125, 314 n. 51; nonfederal tribes and, 22, 31; recognition and, 2–3, 5, 36, 124–25, 138; sovereignty and, 7; white supremacist ideology and, 44, 268

Commission on Indian Affairs, 67, 302 n. 20, 326 n. 12

Congressional bills, 162–64, 258–59, 262, 346 n. 41

Connecticut gaming backlash, 4, 99, 164, 262, 276 n. 6, 276 n. 8, 289 n. 61

Coulthard, Glenn, 269, 327 n. 27

Coushattas: coalition of Louisiana Indians and, 48, 294 n. 34; colonialism and, 190–91, 192; community schools and, 132; economic development and, 171; educational funding and, 52, 132; federal funding and, 52, 131–32, 145–46; federal-tribal relationships and, 65; gambling and, 171; intermarriage and, 51–52; LOIA and, 66; organization of tribal government and, 150, 326 n. 12; racial politics and, 190–91; recognition and, 23–24, 67, 282 n. 20, 303 n. 25; school integration and, 13; termination and, 303 n. 25; trust status and, 141–42, 295 n. 41

crafts and material culture, 95, 231–32, 245, 342 n. 110, 342 nn. 113–14

Creoles of color: African American ancestry and, 213, 265, 336 n. 64; identity and, 219, 222, 297 n. 62, 330 n. 24, 338 n. 76, 340 n. 91; Indian identity and, 211–13, 214, 217, 219, 265, 297 n. 62, 336 n. 64, 349

n. 64; whiteness and, 340 n. 91. *See also* African Americans; mulattos

Cryer, Lula, 120

cultural vitality: gaming and, 12, 97–98, 101–4, 117–18, 240, 310 n. 3, 312 nn. 19–20, 313 n. 40; Indian renaissance and, 31, 228, 229, 245, 287 n. 48, 344 n. 9; language revitalization and, 246–47; Louisiana Indians and, 149–50; nonfederal tribes and, 5, 10, 15, 150, 245, 271, 350 n. 73; recognition and, 5, 10–11, 16, 125, 246–47, 271–72; recognition procedures and, 245, 271

culture: assumptions about, 224, 277 n. 32, 341 n. 103; ethnonational groups and, 6, 255, 265, 277 n. 12, 277 n. 14; loss of, 18, 292 n. 12, 346 n. 38; material, 95, 231–32, 245, 342 n. 110, 342 nn. 113–14

Dawes Commission, 128–30, 159, 204, 208, 210, 315 n. 8, 315 nn. 8–9, 316 n. 16

decolonization, 15, 18, 158–59, 327 n. 27

Deloria, Phil, 268

Deloria, Vine, Jr.: on acknowledgment policy, 24, 27, 285 n. 32; on ideological struggles for Indians, 125, 314 n. 51; on Indian connection to place, 298 n. 68; Institute for the Development of Indian Law and, 68, 290 n. 1; NCAI and, 63–64; on racial minority status, 303 n. 24; on recognition, 24, 283 n. 21; on recognition movement, 66, 303 n. 24; on sovereignty, 125, 303 n. 24; on tribal identity, 24, 38

Department of Interior, 25, 26, 30, 48–49, 74, 285 n. 29, 286 n. 40. *See also* BIA; OFA

dispossession and removal, 3, 23, 41, 208, 247, 281 n. 11, 293 n. 29

Dominguez, Virginia, 213, 214, 297 n. 62, 339 n. 86

Downs, Ernest, 11, 71, 83, 290 n. 1, 305 n. 41

Drechsel, Emmanuel, 199, 332 n. 1, 334 n. 38

Duthu, N. Bruce, 224

economic development: enrollment conflicts and, 112–13; enterprises and, 100, 311 n. 14; gaming and, 12, 100–101, 105–7, 240, 242, 310 n. 1; gender roles and, 115; LOIA and, 66–67; returnees and, 12, 105–7; tribal identity and, 113; white supremacist ideology and, 240–41

education: assimilationism and, 136–38, 144, 270, 277 n. 14, 292 n. 15, 319 n. 51; boarding schools and, 136–38, 247, 270, 277 n. 14, 292 n. 15, 319 n. 51; community schools and, 14, 132, 217, 338 nn. 80–81, 338 n. 83; compulsory, 148, 325 n. 7; curriculum for, 133, 140, 318 n. 35; educational attainment and, 20–21, 88, 144–45, 147, 173–74, 200, 252, 309 nn. 9–10; literacy campaigns and, 131, 133, 148–49, 169, 317 n. 22, 318 n. 36, 319 n. 44; married women as teachers and, 132–33, 317 n. 30; Meriam Report reforms and, 136, 294 n. 36; scholarship funds and, 88, 309 n. 9; State Department of Education, 48, 50, 131–33, 135, 139, 145, 148, 320 n. 57, 322 n. 64; Title VII programs in, 173; white supremacist ideology and, 136–38, 144–45, 270, 277 n. 14, 292 n. 15, 319 n. 51

educational funding, 48–50, 131–33, 135–42, 146, 295 nn. 40–42, 322 n. 64

educational integration, 136–37, 143, 267–68, 269

educational segregation: African Americans and, 135, 141, 143; anti-black racism and, 8, 13, 15, 18, 134, 141–44, 267–68. *See also* white supremacist ideology

Edwards, Edwin, 65, 176, 188–89, 302 n. 20, 331 n. 22

enrollment, 109–13, 214, 312 n. 29. *See also* allotments

ethnic studies, 6–9, 269

ethnonational groups, 6, 255, 265, 277 n. 12, 277 n. 14

eugenics, 20–21, 38, 280 n. 6

Everett, Russell, 216–17, 332 n. 1, 332 n. 6

exclusive vs. inclusive ideologies, 121, 225–26, 234, 267

executive branch, 3, 25, 258, 279 n. 1, 284 n. 24

family relationships: organization of tribal governments and, 147, 151, 154–55, 179–81, 182–83, 248; tribal identity vs., 152, 154, 179, 255

FAP (Federal Acknowledgment Project), 78, 80–81, 275 n. 1. *See also* OFA

federal acknowledgment policy, 16, 20, 22–23, 24, 254, 273, 283 n. 24; African American ancestry and, 4, 15, 36, 51, 210; colonialism and, 18, 21, 31, 36, 39, 59, 253, 262, 269–70; contradictions and, 5, 49–50, 145–46; Department of the Interior and, 25, 26; discursive aspects of, 1, 31, 239, 270, 344 n. 16; inconsistencies and, 10, 79–80, 127, 145, 325 n. 85; Indian identity and, 270–72, 349 n. 71; informed parties and, 263; Institute for the Development of Indian Law and, 68, 71–73, 290 n. 1; interested parties and, 263, 264; IRA and, 19, 25, 141, 279 n. 1; nationhood and, 2, 4, 5, 168, 253; oral histories and, 4, 349 n. 64; power and, 1, 3, 5, 253, 270; race production and, 5, 37, 253; reforms and, 27–29, 257, 285 n. 32, 286 n. 38, 328 n. 33, 346 n. 40; removal and, 247; statistics, 15; termination and, 3, 25, 61, 63, 276 n. 4, 283 n. 23, 303 n. 25; white supremacist ideology and, 5, 6, 18, 59. *See also* OFA

Federal Acknowledgment Project (FAP), 78, 80–81, 275 n. 1

federal funding, 157, 203–4, 225–26, 333 n. 28

federal government, 22–23, 25, 98, 258, 279 n. 1, 284 n. 24; Abramoff scandal and, 190–91, 193, 262; assimilationism and, 44, 136; Congressional bills and, 162–64, 258–59, 262, 346 n. 41; intermingling

federal government (*cont.*)
and, 341 n. 100; nationhood and, 3, 53, 77, 194; obligations of, 27, 30, 51–52, 145–46, 252–53, 285 nn. 30–31, 286 n. 40, 294 n. 39, 325 n. 85; racial projects and, 8–9, 144; tribal size redress and, 86–87. *See also* service areas

federal-Indian trusts, 22, 30, 49, 263, 279 n. 1, 343 n. 2

federal recognition, 239; advantages and disadvantages of, 5, 10, 16, 18, 117, 122–23, 240–47, 270; alternatives to, 162–64, 258–59, 262, 346 n. 41; assimilationism and, 138, 245, 247, 266; BIA and, 24–25; colonialism and, 2–3, 5, 124–25, 138; cultural vitality and, 5, 10–11, 16, 125, 246–47, 271–72; decolonization and, 15, 18, 158–59, 327 n. 27; discursive aspects of, 270; economic aspects of, 10, 16; expectations of, 171–72; funding for, 5, 13–14, 15, 29, 157–59, 199, 243–44, 250, 261; gaming and, 14; Indian identity and, 9, 249, 252; Initial Reservation Plan and, 176–77, 181, 185, 190–91; language revitalization and, 246–47; moral arguments and, 41, 49, 78, 192, 241, 254, 255; nonrecognition vs., 23, 34, 78, 81, 83, 195, 237, 238, 243; organization of tribal governments and, 3, 275 n. 2; politics of, 162–64, 262–64, 328 n. 36; racial politics and, 5, 16, 30–31, 35–39, 154, 249, 269–70, 289 n. 61; racial projects and, 5, 18, 251–53, 267, 269; research by tribes and, 29, 157, 199, 250, 260, 261, 264, 348 n. 60; social health and, 5, 10, 16, 249–51; sovereignty and, 3, 21, 37, 125, 248–49, 269, 280 n. 9, 289 n. 65; transition protocol and, 172, 244, 286 n. 38; tribal identity and, 10, 13, 30–34, 36–37, 113, 247, 252, 286 n. 40, 288 n. 55, 288 n. 59; white supremacist ideology and, 264–70

federal recognition movement, 303 n. 24; AICC and, 23, 24, 31, 282 n. 15, 282 n. 16;

civil rights movement and, 281 n. 12, 303 n. 24, 344 n. 9; history of, 31, 287 n. 48; intertribal alliances and, 23–24, 66, 281 n. 13; Louisiana Indians and, 281 n. 13; nonfederal-federal tribal relationships and, 23, 282 n. 15; nonfederal tribes and, 23, 31–34, 281 n. 13; racial projects and, 269; Task Force 10 and, 29–30; termination and, 24, 31, 281 n. 12

federal-tribal relationships, 2–3; colonialism and, 190–91; gaming and, 13; Indian identity and, 7; organization of tribal governments and, 248; racial politics and, 190–91; sovereignty and, 21–22, 194, 239, 269, 271, 311 n. 13

federal-tribal-state relationships, 77–78, 89, 100, 125, 242, 244, 308 n. 51, 309 n. 11, 311 n. 13

federal tribes: African American ancestry and, 51, 215; colonialism and, 22, 35; federal funding and, 157; Indian identity and, 10, 38, 254–55, 265–66; Title VII programs in education and, 173; tribal identity and, 154; trust status and, 30; white supremacist ideology and, 22, 35

Five Civilized Tribes of Oklahoma, 128–30, 159, 204, 208, 210, 214, 293 n. 20, 315 nn. 8–9, 316 n. 16

Flemming, Lee, 259, 260, 347 n. 47, 348 n. 60

Forbes, Jack, 211, 213, 297 n. 62

Foster, Mike, 100, 175, 177, 185–89

Freedom of Information Act (FOIA), 259, 260

free people of color, 212–13, 265. *See also* African American ancestry; African Americans

gaming, 100, 239; achievements of tribes and, 94; backlash against, 4, 99, 134, 164, 241, 242, 262, 276 n. 6, 276 n. 8, 289 n. 61; colonialism and, 13; corporate partnerships and, 13–14, 163–64, 175–77, 234–

IGRA (cont.)

Institute for the Development of Indian Law, 68, 71–73, 290 n. 1

integration, 136–37, 143, 267–68, 269

intermarriage, 51–52, 134, 218, 297 n. 62, 318 n. 38, 339 n. 86, 339 n. 89

intermingling, 222–24, 341 n. 100, 341 n. 103

intertribal relationships, 202, 225; African American ancestry and, 206, 215; alliances and, 23–24, 65–66, 208, 281 n. 13, 326 n. 16, 327 n. 22; coalition of Louisiana Indians and, 47–48, 116, 294 n. 32, 294 nn. 34–35; gaming and, 190–91, 193, 194, 262; ITC and, 65–66, 156, 157, 203, 206, 216, 332 n. 3. *See also* nonfederal-federal tribe relationships

IRA (Indian Reorganization Act), 19, 25, 141, 279 n. 1

ITC (Inter-Tribal Council), 65–66, 156, 157, 203, 206, 216, 332 n. 3

Jackson, Clyde, 83, 146, 149–50, 155–58, 161, 178, 272, 325 n. 10

Jackson, Jerry: on coalition of Louisiana Indians, 333 n. 23; economics and, 242–43; on federal funding, 173; gaming and, 175–78, 331 n. 27; intertribal relationships and, 194, 206, 237, 326 n. 12; on Jena Choctaws, 160; organization of tribal government and, 150, 152, 155–56, 161, 178–79, 182–83; photograph of, 193; on politics, 164; post-recognition and, 171–72; on recognition, 166, 181–82, 195–96; recognition lobbying and, 162, 164, 347 n. 42

Jackson family, 130, 151, 179–80, 329 n. 11

Jena Choctaws, 315 nn. 5–6, 316 n. 18; Abramoff scandal and, 190–91, 193; advantages of recognition and, 12, 149, 150, 155, 156–57, 181–82, 195–96; allotments and, 129, 162, 179; anthropologists and, 128, 160–62, 198, 308 n. 4, 344 n. 11; anti-black racism and, 134, 141–44,

147, 219; assimilation and, 147, 324 n. 1; blackness and, 130, 132, 142, 143, 316 n. 19; boarding schools and, 137–38, 247; class distinctions and, 130; colonialism and, 144, 169, 170, 185–86, 194, 324 n. 80, 329 n. 13, 329 n. 15; community racial politics and, 130–31, 169–71, 194, 317 n. 23, 324; Congressional bills and, 162–64, 258, 347 n. 42; crafts, material culture, and, 231, 246, 343 n. 115; cultural vitality and, 14, 166–67, 183–84, 245–46, 271–72; Dawes Commission and, 12, 128–30, 159, 210, 315 n. 8; disadvantages of recognition and, 155–56, 157, 194–95; economic development and, 14, 130, 157, 163, 175, 178, 181–82, 241–42, 244; educational attainment and, 147, 173–74; educational curriculum and, 133, 140, 318 n. 35; educational funding and, 52, 127, 131–33, 135–41, 145–46, 322 n. 64; enrollment and, 129, 160, 168, 315 n. 12; expectations of recognition and, 171–72; family relationships and, 147, 151, 154–55, 179–81, 182–83, 246, 248, 256; federal funding and, 156–57, 181–82, 244, 327 n. 20; federal-tribal-state relationships and, 242, 244; funding for recognition and, 13–14, 158–59; gaming and, 13–14, 163–64, 175–77, 181, 184–87, 191–92, 235, 241, 242, 247, 331 n. 27; gender roles and, 147, 151–52, 248; genealogies and, 130, 159–60, 161–62, 180, 209, 316 n. 16, 329 n. 11, 335 n. 46, 336 n. 51; generational differences and, 147, 151–52, 155–56; health care and, 172–73, 250–51; historical records and, 159–60, 161–62, 185, 210, 329 n. 15, 336 n. 51; Indian identity and, 129, 158, 159; Initial Reservation Plan and, 176–77, 181, 185, 190–91; insularity and, 130, 137–38, 139, 321 n. 60; intermarriage and, 51–52, 134, 168, 318 n. 38, 329 n. 3; landlessness and, 130, 162–63, 171–72, 196, 316 n. 17; language

Jena Choctaws (*cont.*)

and, 130, 138, 147, 160, 174, 246, 247, 257, 320 n. 11; literacy campaigns and, 131, 133, 148–49, 169, 317 n. 22, 318 n. 36; military service and, 147–48, 325 n. 10; as nonfederal tribe, 13, 133, 138; OFA and, 128, 145, 314 n. 4, 316 n. 16; Oklahoma Choctaws and, 13–14, 129, 162–64, 179, 256; organization of tribal government and, 147, 149–52, 154–56, 161, 172, 178–83, 248, 251, 256, 326 n. 12; per capita payments and, 178, 182, 184, 185; postrecognition, 181–84, 193–96; poverty and, 137, 156, 167, 184; racial politics and, 14, 130–31, 154–55, 169–71, 194, 249, 264, 317 n. 23, 324; recognition and, 1, 12–13, 113, 122, 127, 139–40, 141–42, 145–46, 150, 157–63, 162, 165–69, 195, 283 n. 20; removal and, 44, 130, 144; school integration and, 13, 134–35, 143, 147–48, 318 n. 39, 325 n. 2; school segregation and, 12, 13, 131–45, 296 n. 51, 318 n. 35, 319 nn. 39–40, 319 n. 44, 322 n. 64, 323 n. 76, 325 n. 10; Second World War and, 147–48, 325 n. 3, 325 n. 10; service area and, 173, 177, 182, 184–85, 187, 191, 244, 247, 250, 331 n. 27; services for members and, 160–61, 173, 175, 181, 183, 187; social health and, 14, 173, 183–84, 196, 246, 250–51; sovereignty and, 152, 167, 182–83, 185–90, 249–50, 328 n. 36; state recognition and, 149, 150, 326 n. 14; state's rights to block gaming and, 184–87, 329 n. 13, 329 n. 15; state support for recognition and, 163, 305 n. 42; tribal identity and, 13, 130–31, 134, 141, 147, 154, 158, 168, 180–81, 246, 247, 256, 271–72, 329 n. 11; trust status and, 176–77; wage labor and, 130, 316 n. 19; whiteness and, 130–31, 134–35, 139, 142, 143, 316 n. 19, 316 n. 21, 319 nn. 39–40. *See also* Mississippi Choctaws; Oklahoma Choctaws

Jena six, 192–94

Jennings, Joe, 254

Johnson, Steve, 107

Johnson-O'Malley Act, 139, 146, 226, 295 n. 40

Jolivette, Andrew, 213, 340 n. 91

Jones, Mary Jackson, 150–52, 154, 165–68, 170–71, 178, 206, 314 n. 4, 316 n. 17, 325 n. 2, 326 n. 12

JTPA (Job Training Partnership Act), 156. *See also* CETA

Juneau, Anna Mae, 115, 120

Juneau, Donald, 42–43, 44, 202, 292 n. 7, 306 n. 44

Kickingbird, Kirke, 27, 68, 285 n. 32

Kirshenblatt-Gimblett, Barbara, 343 n. 14

La Joie, Zenon, 115–16, 313 n. 37

land claims: African Americans and, 55; backlash against recognition and, 344 n. 5; landlessness and, 130, 162–63, 171–72, 196, 316 n. 17; Tunicas and, 50–51, 55–56, 58, 59, 76, 84, 88–89, 298 nn. 67–68, 306 n. 46, 308 n. 2

language: English proficiency, 130, 147; Mobilian Jargon, 197–99, 331 n. 1, 334 n. 38; revitalization of, 246–47

law: acknowledgment policy and, 2, 16, 26–27, 31, 36, 253, 254; antimiscegenation, 218, 318 n. 38, 339 n. 86, 339 n. 89; *Carcieri v. Salazar*, 279 n. 1, 343 n. 2; gaming and, 100, 310 n. 1; inheritance, 46, 53, 90–91, 339 n. 86; Jena six case, 192–94; *Passamaquoddy v. Morton*, 27–28, 30, 74–75, 252, 279 n. 1, 281 n. 9, 285 nn. 30–31, 305 n. 41

Lewis, Victor, 277 n. 13

Lewis family, 130, 131, 151, 179–80, 315 n. 12, 328 n. 29, 329 n. 11

Lintinger, Brenda, 98, 99, 107, 280 n. 1

literacy campaigns, 131, 133, 148–49, 169, 317 n. 22, 318 n. 36, 319 n. 44

Lomawaima, Tsianina, 137, 311 n. 13

Lopez family, 120

Louisiana (Baton Rouge) Band of Choctaws, 202, 332 n. 3, 333 n. 20

Louisiana Department of Education, 48, 50, 131–33, 135, 139, 145, 148, 320 n. 57, 322 n. 64

Louisiana Indians: anti-black racism and, 214, 221–22, 267–68; antimiscegenation laws and, 218, 318 n. 38, 339 n. 86, 339 n. 89; assimilationism and, 47, 49, 57–58, 132, 313 n. 41; coalition of, 23, 47–48, 116, 294 n. 32, 294 nn. 34–35; cultural vitality and, 149–50; educational funding and, 295 nn. 40–42; family vs. tribal identity and, 152, 154, 179, 255; genealogies and, 205–6; historical records and, 210–11, 336 nn. 50–51; Indian Angels and, 64–66, 301 n. 16, 302 nn. 19–21; insularity and, 52, 130, 137–38, 139, 321 n. 60; intermingling and, 222–24; Little Indian Clubs and, 144, 324 n. 80; NCAI and, 64, 84, 301 n. 14; obligations of federal government and, 51–52, 145–46, 325 n. 85; recognition movement and, 281 n. 13; school integration and, 136–37; state recognition and, 2, 202, 206, 333 n. 21; white supremacist ideology and, 5–6, 220–22, 267–68. *See also* Native Americans

Louisiana Office of Indian Affairs (LOIA), 65, 67–68, 199, 202–3, 302 nn. 20–21

Louisiana Purchase Treaty, 41, 42, 50, 278 n. 24, 291 n. 7

Lumbees: African American ancestry and, 214–15, 265–66, 337 n. 72; anti-black racism and, 214–15, 337 n. 72; boarding schools and, 319 n. 51; Congressional bills and, 346 n. 41; education and, 323 n. 78; Indian identity and, 257, 346 n. 41; intermarriage and, 337 n. 72; recognition applications and, 20, 280 n. 3; recognition movement and, 31–33, 281 n. 13; school segregation and, 214; tribal identity and, 38

Major Crimes Act, 45, 293 n. 20

marriage, 132–33, 317 n. 30. *See also* intermarriage

Mashantucket Pequots, 39, 258, 276 n. 8, 311 n. 14

Mashpees, 38, 76, 307 n. 43

material culture and crafts, 95, 231–32, 245, 342 n. 110, 342 nn. 113–14

McCulloch, Anne Merline, 325 n. 35

Melacon, Chief, 43–44, 53, 83–84, 115–16

mental health, 14, 38–39, 84, 143, 166–67, 187, 205, 237, 249–50, 271

Meriam Report, 136, 294 n. 36

methods, research, 16–18, 278 nn. 28–29, 279 nn. 30–32

Meyer, Harvey, 141, 142

Miami Tribe of Indiana, 246, 259, 350 n. 73

Miller, Mark, 9

Miller, Shari, 317, 334 n. 32, 338 n. 83

Mississippi Choctaws, 291 n. 4; Abramoff scandal and, 190–91; anti-black racism and, 214; coalition of Louisiana Indians and, 116, 294 n. 32; colonialism and, 190, 192; economic development and, 88; enrollment and, 129, 160, 208, 315 n. 13; federal funding and, 139–40; history of recognition and, 23–24; intermarriage and, 51–52; Jena Choctaws and, 13, 127, 159–60, 256; language and, 174; removal and, 129, 315 n. 9. *See also* Clifton-Choctaws; Jena Choctaws

Mohegans, 241, 258

Mora, Pete, 198, 199, 202–3, 305 n. 41, 332 n. 3

moral arguments: gaming and, 178, 188, 189, 190, 236; Indian identity and, 43, 124, 135, 220, 268, 292 n. 10; recognition and, 41, 49, 78, 192, 241, 254, 255

Moreau, Celestin, 43–44, 83

Moreau, Celestin, Jr., 55, 115, 313 n. 36

mulattos, 159, 210–11, 214, 219, 336 n. 50, 336 n. 56, 339 n. 86, 340 n. 86, 348 n. 64

Murphy, Christy, 173, 174

NAGPRA (Native American Graves Protection and Repatriation Act), 93, 249

Nash, Roy, 131–32

National Congress of American Indians (NCAI), 24, 32–33, 35, 63–64, 84, 279 n. 1, 301 n. 14

nationhood: acknowledgment policy and, 2, 4, 5, 168, 253; federal government and, 3, 53, 77, 194. *See also* Indian identity; sovereignty; tribal identity

Native Americans, 278 n. 17; ideological struggles and, 125, 314 n. 51; Indian identity and, 7, 8; intermingling and, 222–24, 341 n. 100, 341 n. 103; military service and, 147–48, 325 n. 3, 325 n. 10; racial minority status and, 7–8, 194, 277 n. 12, 303 n. 24; racial politics and, 7–8; services for members and, 160–61, 173, 175, 181, 183, 187; sovereignty and, 7–8; tribal programs and, 97–98, 185, 310 n. 3; wage labor and, 130, 316 n. 19; white supremacist ideology and, 5–6, 220–22, 267–68. *See also* Indian identity; Louisiana Indians; nationhood; people of color; tribal identity

Native Hawaiians, 8, 278 n. 17, 346 n. 41

NCAI (National Congress of American Indians), 24, 32–33, 35, 63–64, 84, 279 n. 1, 301 n. 14

Neal, Anna, 206, 209, 335 n. 44

Neal, Henry, 209

Neal family, 209, 224–25, 335 n. 44

Nietzel, Robert "Stu," 52, 58, 90, 298 n. 70, 309 n. 18

nonfederal-federal tribe relationships: Indian identity and, 38–39, 225, 249, 267, 272, 290 n. 70; recognition movement and, 23, 282 n. 15; tribal identity and, 30, 37, 38–39, 215, 249, 290 n. 70. *See also* intertribal relationships

nonfederal tribes, 239; acknowledgment policy and, 9–10, 38; advantages of recognition and, 243; African American ancestry and, 51, 215; AIPRC Task Force 10 recommendations and, 28, 74; BIA and, 225–26; boarding schools and, 137, 247, 320 nn. 51–52; colonialism and, 22, 31; cultural vitality and, 5, 10, 15, 150, 245, 271, 350 n. 73; education and, 173; federal funding and, 157, 225–26; Indian identity and, 10, 38, 254–55, 265–66; intertribal organizations and, 225; obligations of federal government and, 27, 30, 252–53, 285 nn. 30–31, 286 n. 40, 294 n. 39; power relationships between government and, 22–23; racial politics and, 22–23, 154, 249; recognition movement and, 23, 31–34, 281 n. 13; recognition vs. nonrecognition and, 23, 34, 78, 81, 83, 195, 237, 238, 243; research by, 29, 78–80, 157, 199, 250, 260, 261, 264, 348 n. 60; social health and, 10, 22, 38–39, 40, 250–51; tribal identity and, 30–31, 33–39, 154, 249, 290 n. 70; trust status and, 30; white supremacist ideology and, 22, 35, 36, 39

non-Indian community: community politicking for state recognition and, 62–66, 300 n. 9, 301 n. 18, 302 n. 21, 303 n. 22; gaming by, 13, 97, 98–99, 184, 234–35, 242, 310 n. 6; gaming partnerships with, 13–14, 163–64, 175–77, 234–37, 242–43; Indian gaming viewed by, 103–4, 209–10; Indian identity views and, 56, 105, 118, 121–22, 209–10, 253, 298 n. 68, 338 n. 74; racial projects and, 144. *See also* white supremacist ideology

nonrecognition: OFA and, 145, 164, 215, 254–55; recognition vs., 23, 34, 78, 81, 83, 195, 237, 238, 243; state, 75

Noonan, John T., 254

Norris, Christine: Clifton-Choctaws and, 205; on education, 172; health care programs and, 172; Indian identity and, 219; organization of tribal government and, 152, 180–81; on per capita payments, 184; photograph of, *153*; racial politics

and, 316 n. 21; on recognition procedures, 195; on sovereignty, 182; tribal
identity and, 17
nurturing indigeneity, 121, 225–26, 234, 267

OFA (Office of Federal Acknowledgment):
academic assessments and, 21, 80, 252,
255, 260, 294 n. 39, 345 n. 27; African
American ancestry and, 265–67, 348
n. 64, 349 nn. 65–66; backlash against
gaming and, 4, 134; Branch of Acknowledgment and Research and, 261, 275
n. 1; conflicts of interest and, 77–78, 254,
286 n. 38; criticism and support of, 1, 4,
15, 146, 257, 258, 259–60, 276 nn. 5–6, 276
n. 8, 346 n. 40; decision making and,
253–57; Federal Acknowledgment Project and, 78, 81, 275 n. 1; nonrecognition
and, 145, 164, 215, 254–55; power and, 1,
3, 253; racial politics and, 262–63; recognition and, 3–4, 9, 273; reforms and,
259–61, 347 n. 47, 347 n. 52; research and,
77, 80, 260, 261, 264, 275 n. 1; state department of education and, 145, 322
n. 64; tribal identity and, 1, 49–50, 129,
230–31, 252; whiteness and, 267. *See also*
BIA
Office of Native American Programs, 29.
*See also* Administration for Native
Americans
OIA (Office of Indian Affairs). *See* BIA (Bureau of Indian Affairs)
Oklahoma Choctaws: anti-black racism
and, 214; Clifton-Choctaw allotments
and, 204, 206–10; Congressional bills
and, 162–64; enrollment and, 129, 208,
210; federal funding and, 156; intermingling and, 222; Jena Choctaws and, 13–
14, 129, 162–64, 179, 256; language and,
174, 320 n. 11, 328 n. 8, 332 n. 1; removal
and, 129, 315 n. 9. *See also* Five Civilized
Tribes of Oklahoma
Omi, Michael, 5–6, 340 n. 95, 344 n. 16

O'Nell, Theresa, 316 n. 21, 343 n. 118
oral histories, 4, 336 n. 64, 337 n. 72, 348
n. 64
organization of tribal governments: acknowledgment policy and, 22, 281 n. 10;
family relationships and, 147, 151, 154–
55, 179–81, 182–83, 248; federal-tribal relationships and, 248; gender roles and,
115–17, 147, 151–52, 248, 313 nn. 36–37,
326 n. 16; history of, 255–56; Louisiana
Indians and, 2, 333 n. 23; OFA and, 255–
56; oral tradition and, 22, 248, 281 n. 10;
recognition and, 3, 275 n. 2

Paredes, J. Anthony, 223, 226, 237
Parker, Annie, 207, 208, 334 n. 37
Pascoe, Peggy, 253
*Passamaquoddy v. Morton*, 27–28, 30, 74–75,
252, 279 n. 1, 281 n. 9, 285 nn. 30–31, 305
n. 41
Pauckatuck / Eastern Pequots, 164, 264
Paugussets, 164, 254
Penick, Mattie, 132–33, 135–36, 137, 139–41,
144, 316 n. 17, 322 n. 64, 323 n. 76, 324
n. 80, 325 n. 10
people of color: free, 212–13, 265; Great
Depression and, 50, 295 n. 43; ideology
and, 125, 314 n. 51; inclusion claims and,
147–48, 325 n. 3; Indian identity and, 143,
339 n. 86. *See also* African Americans;
Native Americans
per capita payments, 97–98, 108, 111–12,
124, 178, 182, 184–85, 240, 310 n. 3
Pesantubbee, Michelene, 116, 152
Pierite, Donna, 102, 104, 108, *119*, 120, 123–
24, 301 n. 18
Pierite, Elisabeth, 102, 288 n. 55
Pierite, Ernest, 44–45, 47–48, 294 n. 35
Pierite, Herman, Sr., 79, 221, 296 n. 60
Pierite, Horace, Jr., 68, 91–92, 309 n. 18
Pierite, Horace, Sr., 53, 59, 61–64, 309 n. 18
Pierite, Jean-Luc, 103, *119*
Pierite, Joseph, Jr., 65, 68–69, 71–74, 80, 84,

tribal identity (*cont.*)

252; family relationships vs., 152, 154, 179, 255; federal funding debates and, 203–4, 333 n. 28; federal tribes and, 154; gaming and, 105–6, 107, 247; insularity and, 130, 137–38, 139, 321 n. 60; nonfederal-federal tribal relationships and, 30, 37, 38–39, 215, 249, 290 n. 70; nonfederal tribes and, 30–31, 33–39, 154, 249, 290 n. 70; OFA and, 1, 49–50, 129, 230–31, 252; recognition and, 10, 13, 30–34, 36–37, 113, 247, 252, 286 n. 40, 288 n. 55, 288 n. 59; whiteness and, 6, 348 n. 61; white supremacist ideology and, 125, 314 n. 51. *See also* Indian identity; nationhood

trust status, 22, 30, 49, 263, 279 n. 1, 343 n. 2

Tulalips, 34–36, 288 n. 59

Tunica-Biloxi (Tunicas), 291 n. 6, 294 n. 30; activism and, 44–48, 50, 52–56, 59, 61–66, 72–81, 281 n. 13, 294 nn. 34–35, 296 n. 58, 298 n. 68, 299 n. 4, 305 nn. 41–42, 306 n. 46, 306 n. 49; advantages of recognition and, 12, 76, 86–89, 117, 122, 124–25, 240, 241; African American ancestry and, 15, 54–55, 61, 79, 84, 111, 215, 221, 265–66; AIPRC hearings and, 71–73, 83, 305 nn. 38–39; anthropologists and, 47, 52–54, 58, 63, 298 n. 70; anti-black racism and, 79, 216, 221, 323 n. 78; archaeology and, 56, 62, 89–94, 247, 291 n. 5, 298 n. 68, 309 n. 18; assimilationism and, 47, 57–58, 313 n. 41; BIA and, 47; boarding schools and, 319 n. 51; coalition of Louisiana Indians and, 47–48, 116, 294 n. 32; colonialism and, 12, 56, 100, 123, 298 n. 68; community politicking for state recognition and, 62–66, 300 n. 9, 301 n. 18, 302 n. 21, 303 n. 22; crafts, material culture, and, 90, 95, 120–21; cultural vitality and, 56, 70–71, 88, 94–95, 118–21, 245, 247, 271–72, 304 n. 35, 313 n. 41; disadvantages of recognition and, 117, 122–23, 240; economic development and, 12, 70, 85, 88, 100, 240, 244; educa-

tion and, 48–50, 61–62, 84, 88, 132, 300 n. 7, 309 nn. 9–10, 319 n. 51, 321 n. 57, 323 n. 78; family relationships and, 216, 240; federal funding and, 48–50, 86–87, 88, 132, 309 n. 9, 321 n. 57; federal-tribal relationships and, 11; federal-tribal-state relationships and, 89, 309 n. 11; fête du blé, 56, 88, 103, 118–20, 304 n. 35, 313 n. 41; gender roles and, 115–17, 152, 313 nn. 36–37, 326 n. 16; gourds and, 120, 121, 313 n. 43; Great Depression and, 50, 295 nn. 43–44; health care and, 70, 86, 87, 308 n. 7; illiteracy and, 71–75, 296 n. 58; Indian identity and, 53, 54, 55, 111; inheritance laws and, 46, 53, 90–91; intermarriage and, 51–52, 54–55, 215, 221, 296 n. 60, 297 n. 62; intermingling and, 223; intertribal relationships and, 216, 338 n. 74; land claims and, 50–51, 55–56, 58, 59, 76, 84, 88–89, 298 nn. 67–68, 306 n. 46, 308 n. 2; language and, 207, 246; local dispossession and, 41–44, 292 n. 10; NCAI and, 63–64, 301 n. 14; non-Indian community and, 56, 103–4, 105, 118, 121–22, 298 n. 68; organization of tribal government and, 67, 68–69, 98, 102–4, 108–9, 114, 248, 256; poverty and, 50, 85–86, 107–8, 117, 122; powwow and, 103, 118–22, 288 n. 55; racial politics and, 78–79, 112–13, 123–25, 264, 288 n. 55; reactions to recognition and, 85–86; recognition dates, 1, 41, 78, 80, 85, 122, 308 n. 5; recognition history and, 11, 23–24, 41, 47, 52–56, 215, 296 n. 58; recognition procedures and, 71, 74, 77–81, 305 n. 41; removal and, 11, 41–43, 44, 56, 57, 59, 100, 117, 292 n. 10, 297 n. 66; research and, 78–80; reservation and, 44–45, 47, 49–50, 56–57, 70–72, 86–88, 102–3, 240, 306 n. 49, 308 n. 2; returnees and, 121; school integration and, 61–62, 84, 300 n. 7; school segregation and, 323 n. 78; service area and, 87–88; social health and, 12, 70, 84, 86, 87, 240, 247, 250, 251;

Brian Klopotek is an associate professor in the Department
of Ethnic Studies at the University of Oregon.

Library of Congress Cataloging-in-Publication Data
Klopotek, Brian, 1972–
Recognition odysseys : indigeneity, race, and federal tribal recognition
policy in three Louisiana Indian communities / Brian Klopotek.
p. cm. — (Narrating native histories)
Includes bibliographical references and index.
ISBN 978-0-8223-4969-3 (cloth : alk. paper)
ISBN 978-0-8223-4984-6 (pbk. : alk. paper)
1. Federally recognized Indian tribes—Louisiana. 2. Indians of North
America—Legal status, laws, etc.—Louisiana. 3. Indians of North
America—Louisiana—Government relations—1934– I. Title. II. Series:
Narrating native histories.
KFL505.K567 2011
323.1197′0763—dc22      2010038149